BEYOND LEVIATHAN

BEYOND LEVIATHAN

Critique of the State

―――――――

by ISTVÁN MÉSZÁROS

Edited, with an Introduction and Notes, by
JOHN BELLAMY FOSTER

MONTHLY REVIEW PRESS
New York

Copyright © 2022 by George Mészáros
All Rights Reserved

Library of Congress Cataloging-in-Publication Data
available from the publisher.

ISBN paper: 978-1-58367-949-4
ISBN cloth: 978-1-58367-950-0

Typeset in Bulmer MT Std

MONTHLY REVIEW PRESS, NEW YORK
monthlyreview.org

5 4 3 2 1

Contents

Introduction by John Bellamy Foster | 7

Preface | 41

PART ONE
FROM RELATIVE TO ABSOLUTE LIMITS:
HISTORICAL ANACHRONISM OF THE STATE | 55

1. The Historic Anachronism and Necessary Suppression of the State | 57
2. Freedom Is Parasitic on Equality | 86
3. From Primitive to Substantive Equality—via Slavery | 95
4. Capital's Deepening Structural Crisis and the State | 124
5. The Historic Circle Is Closing | 141

PART TWO
THE MOUNTAIN WE *MUST* CONQUER:
REFLECTIONS ON THE STATE | 165

6. The Mountainous State | 167
7. The End of Liberal-Democratic Politics | 182
8. The "Withering Away" of the State? | 189
9. The Wishful Limitations of State Power | 195
10. The Assertion of Might-as-Right | 200
11. Eternalizing Assumptions of Liberal State Theory | 212
12. Hegel's Unintended Swan Song and the Nation-State | 223
13. Capital's Social Metabolic Order and the Failing State | 238
14. Himalayan Obstacle: Conclusion to Part Two | 259

PART THREE
ANCIENT AND MODERN UTOPIAS | 261

15 From Plato's Cave to the Sombre Light of *The Laws* | 263
16 Equality in the Broken Mirror of Justice:
    The Meaning of Aristotelian *Politea* | 298
17 Primitive Accumulation of Capital and the
    World of More's *Utopia* | 317
18 Machiavelli and Campanella on the Road
    to Giambattista Vico | 334
19 From Bacon and Harrington to Thomas Paine
    and Robert Owen | 349
20 Thomasius and Bloch's Principle of Hope | 361

APPENDICES | 369
1. Original Plan for *Beyond Leviathan* | 371
2. Historical Boundaries of the Legal and
   Political Superstructure | 373
3. Substantive Equality and Substantive Democracy | 386
4. How Could the State "Wither Away"? | 392

Notes | 438
Index | 476

Introduction

ON SEPTEMBER 19, 2012, ISTVÁN MÉSZÁROS WROTE TO ME, "There is one more book I would very much like to write, and I am working on it as much as my strength permits. This is, as you know, my long-standing project on the state of which some partial results have been incorporated into my books, including *Beyond Capital* and *Social Structure and Forms of Consciousness*. Probably six to nine months will be still dedicated to the strictly preparatory stage, but I hope that in July next year when you come to England I can show you something."[1] Three years later, on October 10, 2015, he indicated: "I have the complete framework of the entire large book on the state worked out, after ten years of preparatory writing. (Some of it you saw in my big volume of files.)" It consisted at this point of "almost 200 little 'articles,'" running from several hundred to a few thousand words in length.[2] This book-length, handwritten manuscript, or what he called the "second version" of his work on the state, provided an extraordinarily detailed theoretical analysis of the problem of the state, stretching over the entire history of political theory from Plato and Aristotle to the present. This second-version draft was to be succeeded, in his plan, by a "third version," which was to be the final draft of his book, *Beyond Leviathan: Critique of the State*.[3]

Beyond Leviathan was originally projected as a work of 600 to 700 pages.[4] The first outline for the book, drawn up in the form of a preliminary Table of Contents in December 2015, indicated that it was to be divided into three parts: *The Historic Challenge*, *The Harsh Reality*, and *The Necessary Alternative*, with a total of twelve chapters.[5] In the next year or so, however, the scale of *Beyond Leviathan* was to expand, with each of the envisioned three parts now being seen as occupying a separate volume, with chapters expanding to the size of parts, and the chapter sections to the size of chapters. The first volume, *Beyond Leviathan: Critique of the State*, Part One, *The Historic Challenge*, was nearly completed when Mészáros died, following a stroke, on October 1, 2017. It is this volume that is being published here under the title of the entire work. The earlier second-version draft manuscript, mainly consisting of materials that were originally to be the basis for the second and third volumes of *Beyond Leviathan*, is to be published subsequently, in a single volume, to be entitled *Critique of Leviathan: Reflections on the State*. Together, these works, along with relevant sections of his previous books, constitute his entire systematic critique of the state, one of the great contributions in the history of political theory.

Mészáros's plan to write a major work on the state had its origins several decades prior to the last five years of his life, in which he was primarily concerned with that project. In 1970, with the completion of *Marx's Theory of Alienation*, which won the Isaac Deutscher Memorial Prize, he began to focus on what he called "the structural crisis of capital," articulated in his Deutscher Lecture, "The Necessity of Social Control," in January 1971, and in the preface to the third edition of *Marx's Theory of Alienation* that year.[6] His original plan in the years that immediately followed—during which he wrote his books on *Lukács's Concept of Dialectic* (1972) and *The Work of Sartre* (1979), as well as *The Power of Ideology* (1989)—was to concentrate on completing his great theoretical work *Social Structure and Forms of Consciousness*, eventually published in two volumes, *The Social Determination of Method* and *The Dialectic of Structure of History*, in 2010 and 2011.[7] Yet, he was compelled to set aside his crucial work on *Social Structure and Forms of Consciousness* for many years, in order to address the question of the structural crisis of capital and the conditions of the transition to socialism in *Beyond Capital: Toward a Theory of Transition* (1995), his immense, nearly 1,000-page work, for which he is today chiefly known.[8]

Beyond Capital was, as its title and subtitle indicated, a theory of the necessity of transcending the capital relation, a critique directed at both contemporary capitalist and at post-revolutionary societies of the Soviet type. Yet, transcending capital necessarily involved, in Mészáros's perspective, transcending the threefold modalities of capital, labor, and the state. His overall project was thus necessarily extended even at that stage to the critique of the state and to the question, integral to Marx's perspective, of "How Could the State Wither Away?" In addition, *Beyond Capital* explored the questions of "The Historical Actuality of the Socialist Offensive" and "The Communal System," both of which concerned the state.[9] It was precisely these discussions that were to form the chief influences on Hugo Chávez in charting the strategic course of Venezuela's Bolivarian Revolution, leading to Chávez calling Mészáros the "pathfinder" of twenty-first-century socialism.[10] In *The Dialectic of Structure and History* Mészáros devoted a chapter to "Key Concepts in the Dialectic of Base and Superstructure," in which the third section was devoted to "Customs, Tradition and Explicit Law: Historical Boundaries of the Legal and Political Superstructure," describing the evolution of law and the state.[11]

Once *Beyond Capital* was completed, Mészáros was able to return to the task of finishing *Social Structure and Forms of Consciousness,* which he accomplished while completing a number of smaller works evolving out of his economic and political commitments, including *Socialism or Barbarism* in 2001, *The Challenge and Burden of Historical Time* in 2008 with its analysis of "The Alternative to Parliamentarianism," and *The Structural Crisis of Capital* in 2010.[12] The second volume of *Social Structure and Forms of Consciousness*, *The Dialectic of Structure and History,* was completed in 2011. Even then, there was a further delay in turning to his long-contemplated work on the state, as he devoted time to producing an expanded edition of his *The Work of Sartre*.[13] Hence, it was only in 2012 that he began his great work on the critique of the state in earnest.

TOWARD A HISTORICAL THEORY OF THE STATE

In the preface to *Beyond Leviathan* Mészáros points out that "All of the major theories of the state have been produced in historical periods of great turmoil, from Plato, Aristotle and Augustine through Machiavelli and Hobbes, all the way to Jean-Jacques Rousseau and G. W. F. Hegel, as well as, of course, to Marx, V. I. Lenin, and their comrades like Rosa Luxemburg and Antonio Gramsci" (44). In all the important theories of the state, prior to historical materialism, however, the modern forms of which were written in the ascending phases of bourgeois development, the goal was some kind of corrective adjustment—no matter how radical-seeming in their particular historical contexts—of the existing "command structure [superimposed] on societal decision-making." This applied also to the great utopian theories of the state. In contrast, the "Marxian-inspired" approach to the state represented a sharp break with all that had come before, in its insistence on the necessity for "the 'withering away of the state'—or the total eradication of the state—from the modality of social reproduction." This is because it was impossible to go "beyond capital" (and beyond its basis in alienated labor and class) without also going beyond the state, as a form of "expropriation of humanity's overall decision-making process" (45).[14] Merely overthrowing the capitalist state was never enough because it could be restored; what was needed was its *eradication* (144). It was this challenge of developing a full-fledged *Critique of the State*, exploring the entire history of state theory, in order to delineate the origins, development, and eventual demise of the state as a *form* of society's inescapable need for an overall command structure, that forms the structure of *Beyond Leviathan*.

It is crucial to understand how radically Mészáros's critique of the state, viewed in this way, differs from liberal theories of the state, as well as from more critical/social-democratic approaches struggling to operate within the parameters established by the hegemonic liberal-democratic theory. In this respect, it is significant that Mészáros's second-version draft manuscript commenced with a response to his close friend the Italian philosopher and "liberal socialist" Norberto Bobbio's "Is There a Marxist Theory of the State?"[15] Bobbio's answer to the question raised in his article was that there was no fully worked out theory of the state in Karl Marx or in subsequent Marxian theory, however insightful it might be in some respects. Hence, he referred to "the non-existence or inadequacy of a Marxist political science" from the standpoint of the treatment of the socialist state. Whereas "Marx may have wanted to write a critique of politics alongside the critique of economics, he never wrote it," nor did subsequent Marxist theorists. In Bobbio's view, Marx and subsequent Marxian theorists, such as Lenin, Luxemburg, and Gramsci, had developed criticisms of the capitalist state from the standpoint of the human "subject," but their analysis displayed a lack of consideration of concrete "institutions" and the nature of the state under socialism. Further, the Marxian argument on the "withering away" of the state was seen by Bobbio as lacking any contemporary significance.[16] Bobbio punctuated this argument on the paucity of Marxian reflections on the state with a quotation from the Italian Marxist Lucio Colletti, decrying the "lack of a theory of the socialist state or socialist democracy as an alternative to the theory, or theories of the bourgeois state and bourgeois democracy." This was accompanied with a criticism of an article by Louis Althusser that, according to Bobbio, pointed to the fact that Marx's work had been turned into "a shield between reality and researchers and thus not an aid but an obstacle."[17]

Mészáros had great respect for Bobbio and considered him a close friend and a critical thinker (195).[18] Nevertheless, insofar as the latter argued that a Marxian theory of the state was not even possible in principle, since downplaying the rule of law and of institutions was inherently authoritarian, Bobbio, according to Mészáros, simply betrayed his own deep-seated view that the state as a modern entity was exclusively a liberal-democratic phenomenon (196–97).[19] Nevertheless, such a political standpoint, particularly in the descending phase of capitalism, found itself without firm foundations, insofar as it avoided any historical/genetic account of the state and its evolution. Liberal-democratic approaches to the state, associating it with the rule of law (and right), failed to acknowledge the state's own lawlessness, that is, the frequent transgressions of its own rules, in a situation in which there was no higher authority. The liberal approach focused on a "*Theory of Law*, represented as the *Theory (or Philosophy) of the State*." This was manifested in idealized form in so-called representative democracy backed by legal rights—albeit rights that were constantly transgressed insofar as they contravened the modalities of capital (198). This hegemonic liberal view normally avoided the whole question of "might is right" as practiced by capitalist society, including its political command system in the state. Or else it sought, in contradictory fashion, to attempt to legitimate the existing state and its frequent "emergency" transgressions of its own rules, as in Max Weber's claim that the state is the entity with a "*monopoly of the legitimate use of physical force* within a given territory" (9:3/10:1).[20] At all times liberal theories of the state, in the period of the descending phase of capital, sought to disguise or downplay the reality of class, thereby putting any realistic approach to the state permanently out of reach.

Indeed, Mészáros contended that behind the endless disquisitions on the various rights, laws, and institutions of the hegemonic state form was the poverty of the contemporary liberal-democratic conception of the state itself, which was incapable of answering, except in the most circular, ahistorical, contradictory, and self-legitimating ways, the question "What Is the State?" (202–04).[21] In this respect, the great theories of the bourgeois state, developed during the ascending phase of capitalism, most importantly Hobbes's *Leviathan* and Hegel's *The Philosophy of Right*, stood far above all other liberal theories of the state, in their power and profundity (187).

This critique of contemporary liberal approaches to the state was also evident in Mészáros's response to the work of the distinguished English political theorist Ernest Barker, who, beginning in 1928, occupied the chair in political science (endowed by the Rockefeller Foundation) at the University of Cambridge.[22] Here Mészáros focused on Barker's introduction to his translation of Otto Gierke's *Natural Law and the Theory of Society*, in which Barker, reaching back into the natural law tradition, provided a particularly clear presentation of the typical modern liberal conception of the contemporary state as the consummation of law.

For Barker, "The state is essentially law, and law is the essence of the state," defined by their mutual relation. The state is simply a group or association, like any other, generated by society through voluntary association, but with the specific, higher purpose of promoting law based on the higher authority or sovereignty conferred on the state.[23] Thus, in Barker's words, the state is "*constituted* by and under this *constitution* [the legal act or acts establishing its sovereign authority], and thus . . . the State exists to perform the legal or juridical purpose for which it was *constituted*."[24] Such "circular" definitions, Mészáros objected, exclude all questions of power, class, and the actual concrete distinctions between state and society, along with all questions of production (204–205). The "materiality of the state" is denied in favor of an idealized conception that removes from consideration all historical-based analyses, including those of the great bourgeois theories of the state that emerged in the sixteenth to nineteenth centuries.[25]

Nevertheless, a "liberal socialist" like Bobbio, who sought to construct a social democratic political theory grounded in the principles of liberalism, continually raised crucial questions about what was necessary to control capital. He sought to construct a system of universal rights to be irreversibly introduced to constrain the rule of capital through the state, law, and right. In this respect he went so far as seeking to establish the rights of future generations against capital's trend toward environmental destruction.[26] Yet, though Bobbio was correct in insisting in this way on the need for substantive equality, he was wrong, Mészáros insisted, in thinking that capital was controllable. "Capital— by its very nature and innermost determinations—is *uncontrollable*. Therefore, to invest the energies of a social movement into trying to *reform* a substantively *uncontrollable* system, is a much more futile venture than the labour of Sisyphus."[27]

Although highlighting the weaknesses of contemporary liberal theories of the state in this way, Mészáros did not turn for answers either to the Old Left or the New Left, with the result that he "had to follow a lonely road."[28] In the case of the Old Left, his critique of the continuing role of capital in post-revolutionary societies exercised in and through the state, placed him frequently in conflict with official Marxism, as in the case of the Italian Communist Party. At the same time, he rejected the irrational swings between voluntaristic idealism and pessimistic structuralism (later followed by post-structuralism and postmodernism) of the British New Left. Although closest to the so-called instrumentalist view of the state associated with a figure like Ralph Miliband, Mészáros found such analysis hopelessly inadequate since it did not even begin to approach the question of capital's order of social metabolic reproduction in which the whole question of the state had to be viewed. Consequently, no treatment can be found in Mészáros's work of the Marxian debates on the capitalist state of the 1960s–1980s, revolving around the question of the relative autonomy of the state, associated with the work of Nicos Poulantzas and Ralph Miliband, or concerned with Gramsci's theory of hegemony. In this respect, Mészáros preferred to point to the harsh lessons represented by such political leaders as François Mitterrand and Tony Blair, not to mention Margaret Thatcher and Ronald Reagan.

The real challenge of a theory of Leviathan had to be seen in terms of the existence of capital as an organic system, in which the various parts reinforced the whole, and thus could only be transcended through the long uphill struggle to create an alternative system of social metabolic reproduction. As Mészáros wrote in an early proposal for *Beyond Capital* directed to a British publisher, "Perhaps more than anything else, the lack of a comprehensive analysis of postwar developments—social, economic, political and ideological—handicapped the 'new left' in its attempts at offering a viable alternative to the traditional forms of political action. Theoretical discussions tended to be fragmentary, partial, and affected by ephemeral fashions."[29] Refusing the later tendency toward theoretical disarmament on the left in favor of a popular indeterminism, Mészáros rejected all attempts to set aside Marx's metaphor of base and superstructure. Rather, he adopted a position, akin to that of Raymond Williams, that this relation had to be perceived in a *historical and non-deterministic* fashion, which recognized nonetheless the materiality of the state.[30]

Since Mészáros was primarily concerned with the problem of the eradication of the state form as crucial to the socialist struggle, he took his inspiration not from the literature of the post–Second World War period, in which the analysis was overwhelmingly about how to carry out struggles within the parameters of the capitalist state, but from the theories aimed at the eventual "withering away" of the state associated with Marx's *Critique of the Gotha Programme* and Lenin's *State and Revolution*.[31] Unlike most of the Western left, he was concerned with the conception of the "historical actuality of the socialist offensive" aimed at going beyond capital, beyond Leviathan, and beyond alienated labor.

What was called in socialist discussions "the withering away of the state" was, for Mészáros, "not a 'romantic faithfulness to Marx's unrealisable dream,' as some people try to discredit and dismiss it." Rather,

> In truth the "withering away of the state" refers to nothing mysterious or remote but to a perfectly tangible process which must be initiated right in our own historical time. It means, in plain language, the progressive reacquisition of the alienated powers of political decision-making by the individuals in their enterprise of moving toward a genuine socialist society. Without the requisition of these powers—to which not only the capitalist state but also the paralysing inertia of the structurally well-entrenched material reproductive practices are fundamentally opposed—neither the new mode of political control of society as a whole by its individuals is conceivable, nor indeed the *nonadversarial* and thereby *cohesive and plannable* everyday operation of the particular productive and distributive units by the self-managing freely associated producers.[32]

Judged from this standpoint, which denied the permanence of the state—conceived as a form of hierarchical decision-making or command structure imposed through various alienations on the underlying population—a whole new theory of the state in Marxist terms was needed, one that would encompass the origins, development, and eventual eradication of the state. Hence, Mészáros to a considerable extent accepted the claims of Bobbio and others that no fully developed Marxist theory of the state had yet emerged. Such a theory could only be developed in a meaningful way in historical terms, addressing the major state theories and their underlying material relations from ancient times to the present. The theoretical structure of *Beyond Leviathan* was therefore concerned with the historic evolution and critique of the state and law, focusing on such key thinkers as Plato, Aristotle, Cicero, Augustine, Niccoló Machiavelli, Thomas More, Francis Bacon, Tommaso Campanella, Giambattista Vico, James Harrington, Thomas Hobbes, Christian Thomasius, Adam Smith, Immanuel Kant, Jean-Jacques Rousseau, François-Noël Babeuf, Thomas Paine, Robert Owen, Johann Gottlieb Fichte, Hegel, Henry Maine, Ernst Troeltsch, Otto Gierke, Weber, Barker, Bobbio, and Robert Nozick; together with Marx, Engels, Lenin, Luxemburg, Gramsci, Max Horkheimer, Ernst Bloch, Jean-Paul Sartre, Ernesto Cardenal, Chávez, and others.[33] Only in this way was it possible to account for the manner in which the state, civil society, the law, sovereignty, class domination, and power had arisen, along with the forces of resistance that pointed toward (or anticipated) the state's revolutionary transcendence. No approach that simply began with the contemporary state, or even with the early modern state, was sufficient, since the Leviathan state contained features that transcended particular social formations and were inherited in part from previous historical formations. The path to the critique of the state thus passed through Plato's hydra laws and nocturnal guardians, Aristotle's treatment of equality, Machiavelli's *Prince*, More's *Utopia*, Hobbes's *Leviathan*, Thomasius's communal property, Rousseau's general will, Kant's perpetual peace, and Hegel's *Recht* philosophy.

All of this, though, was an attempt to clarify the historical problem of the state. In contrast to all previous comprehensive theories of the state, Mészáros's theory was aimed at the withering away of the state as the command center of capital along with the eradication of capital viewed as an absolute necessity, since the question was ultimately one, as Marx had said, of "ruin or revolution."[34] The environmental and military cataclysms brought on by today's Leviathan states are "bound to destroy humanity" eventually if an alternative mode of social metabolic reproduction is not developed (54). There is no choice for

INTRODUCTION

humanity, therefore, but to pursue a critique of the state aimed at a revolutionary praxis of going beyond Leviathan.

MÉSZÁROS'S LIFE

Mészáros was born on December 19, 1930, in Hungary during the Miklós Horthy dictatorship.[35] He was raised alone by his mother, with the help of his maternal grandmother. His mother worked in an airplane factory building engines. Falsifying his date of birth, he began working at age twelve in the same factory, making threads for bolts for wooden planes. Supposedly sixteen, he was classified as an adult male worker, and thus was paid much more than his mother, who had long worked as a factory operative, the injustice of which induced in him a strong, lifelong dedication to the cause of gender equality. The factory conditions were brutal. On one occasion he was not paid his wages but was compensated instead with a piece of brawn (jellied pig's head) that was full of hair, which he then vomited out onto the snow. He decided at that point to devote his life to fighting inequality and injustice.

Mészáros's early life included an audition with the Hungarian National Opera, with none other than Otto Klemperer advising him to persist as a singer, and a period playing football (soccer) with the celebrated Ferenc Puskás, often seen as one of the greatest football players of all time.

Mészáros was attracted to socialism from an early age, which he learned about from books he picked up in second-hand bookshops. He was particularly attracted to the work of Georg Lukács. In 1949, with the emergence of a Soviet-type state in Hungary, he won a scholarship to the prestigious Eötvös Loránd University in Budapest, where Lukács was a professor of aesthetics. A few months later he was almost expelled for publicly defending Lukács, who had fallen into official disgrace in the extreme Stalinist atmosphere of the time and was then under heavy attack from Mátyás Rákosi, the Hungarian Communist Party Secretary. But the director's motion of expulsion was rejected by the college council. In 1950, Mészáros wrote a critique of the government's banning of the National Theater's staging of Mihály

Vörösmarty's classic 1830 Hungarian play, *Csongor és Tünde*, which was denounced by the authorities as a "pessimistic aberration."[36] Mészáros's meticulous defense of the play was published in two consecutive issues of the literary review *Csillag*. The essay received the prestigious 1951 Attila József Prize, leading to the reincorporation of Vörösmarty's work into the National Theatre repertoire and prompting Lukács to nominate Mészáros as his assistant at the Institute of Aesthetics at the University of Budapest.

From 1950 to 1956 Mészáros participated actively in the country's cultural and literary debates as a member of the Hungarian Writers' Association. His 1956 essay "The National Character of Art and Literature" was chosen as the central focus for the plenary meeting, presided over by the composer Zoltán Kodály, of the Petőfi Circle, a group credited with laying the intellectual-political foundations for the Hungarian uprising of October–November of that year. He also edited the magazine *Eszmélet* (Consciousness) cofounded by Kodály, Lukács, and other leading cultural figures.

In 1955, Mészáros met Donatella Morisi, an Italian, in Paris. They were married on February 14, 1956, with Lukács attending the ceremony. István and Donatella went on to have three children: Laura, born 1956; Susie, born 1960; and Giorgio (George), born 1962. Mészáros received his doctoral degree in philosophy in 1955. His dissertation, supervised by Lukács, was titled *Satire and Reality*. Lukács designated Mészáros as his successor at the Institute of Aesthetics and asked him to deliver the inaugural lectures on aesthetics, as an associate professor of philosophy. But in late 1956, Mészáros was forced to depart Hungary with his family, following the Soviet invasion. They left hastily, with few belongings, including only two books, his own volume on aesthetics and Goethe's *Faust*. Mészáros and Lukács remained close and were often in touch until the latter's death in 1971.[37]

After leaving Hungary, the family resided in Italy, where Mészáros taught at the University of Turin (1956–59), during which time he published (in Italian) *The Revolt of the Intellectuals in Hungary* (1958). This was followed by a series of positions in the United Kingdom, at Bedford College in London (1959–61), the University of St. Andrews in Scotland (1961–66), and the University of Sussex (1966–72; 1976–95), where he held the chair in philosophy.[38] In 1971, he received the Isaac Deutscher Memorial Prize for *Marx's Theory of Alienation*. In the following year he took a position as a senior professor of philosophy at York University in Toronto, where he remained for three years before returning to Sussex. In Canada, he was to become a cause célèbre after the authorities refused to grant him a visa on the grounds that he posed a "security risk." Numerous influential figures across the political spectrum, in both Canada and the United Kingdom, protested on his behalf. Eventually a visa was granted, and the Canadian foreign minister resigned.[39]

In 1995, four years after retiring from the University of Sussex, Mészáros published his great work, *Beyond Capital*, with its powerful message that, in the words of Daniel Singer, "what must be abolished is not only classical capitalist society but the reign of capital as such," requiring more radical and fundamental societal transformations.[40] This was followed by a string of works that further developed his analysis, including *The Challenge and Burden of Historical Time*, which won the coveted Libertador Award for Critical Thinking (also known as the Bolívar Prize), which was decided by an international jury and presented to him by Hugo Chávez on September 14, 2009, who referred to Mészáros on the occasion as "one of the most brilliant thinkers on this planet."[41]

In 2007, Donatella Mészáros (Morisi), with whom István Mészáros had shared a "close union" for fifty-two years, and to whom he had dedicated most of his books, died of cancer. The next year he too was diagnosed with an aggressive "grade 3" bladder cancer.[42] His struggles with cancer continued off and on for the rest of his life but did not prevent him from producing an extraordinary outpouring of creative, critical work, culminating in his unfinished *Beyond Leviathan* on which he was at work at the time of his death. He put great store on Dylan Thomas's poem, "Do not go gentle into that good night," with its insistent line "Rage, rage against the dying of the light."[43] For Mészáros, this took on a *social* import.

In a letter written on July 25, 2017, just two months prior to his death, he presented the good news of the appearance of an Italian translation of *Beyond Capital*, writing: "We have a proverb in Hungary which says: 'One swallow does not bring the Summer.' I hope that many swallows will follow my Italian *Beyond Capital*."[44]

MÉSZÁROS AND CHÁVEZ

Mészáros was strongly committed to anti-imperialist struggles. In this respect he allied himself with those fighting for socialist transformation in the Philippines, Nicaragua, Venezuela, Brazil, and elsewhere. He argued that in the descending phase of capitalism there was a "downward equalization of the rate of exploitation," by which he meant a race to the bottom in wages and working conditions, enforced by a global system of monopolistic competition.[45] In 1978 he edited and introduced a book consisting of thirteen essays by the great Filipino historian and political theorist Renato Constantino, titled *Neo-Colonial Identity and Counter-Consciousness: Essays in Cultural Decolonisation*, in which Constantino developed the concept of counter-consciousness into a powerful philosophy of cultural liberation.[46] He also took great interest as well in Brazilian developments and struggles over the state, supporting various socialist movements there. But his most singular contribution to struggles in the Global South was the role he was to play in his strong strategic support of Venezuela's Bolivarian Revolution.

In completing the final version of *Beyond Capital*, Mészáros commented extensively in his chapter "The Historical Actuality of the Socialist Offensive" on the 1993 pamphlet by Chávez titled *Pueblo, Sufragio y Democracia*.[47] Chávez was then in prison after leading an unsuccessful coup in response to the events of the 1989 Caracazo in Venezuela, in which the government killed thousands of protesters. In a remarkable political analysis, Chávez wrote: "The sovereign people must transform itself into the object *and the subject* of power. This option is not negotiable for revolutionaries." He argued that electoral power could be used in a revolutionary way, backed up by powerful social movements, to ensure the forceful presence of the "popular sovereignty whose exercise will really remain in the hands of the people." This, however, would require a "polycentric distribution of power, displacing power from the center toward the periphery." Emphasis needed to be placed on transferring decision-making so as to establish "the autonomy of particular communities and municipalities," bringing to life all the major means of direct democracy, so that "popular sovereignty constitutes itself as the *protagonist* of power. It is precisely at such borders that we must draw the limits of advance of Bolivarian democracy. Then we shall be very near to the territory of *utopia*." Mészáros immediately recognized the revolutionary Rousseauian nature of Chávez's critique of the state which, in Mészáros's words, pointed to the "type of radical transformation [of the political sphere] which foreshadows from the outset the 'withering away of the state' " and thus pointed toward the "sovereignty of labour."[48]

The pages of Mészáros's *Beyond Capital* referring to Chávez were translated for the latter while he was in prison. Chávez was astonished that anyone in England could write so perceptively about his political views. The relationship that developed is best expressed in Mészáros's own words, in a letter to me from February 16, 2015:

> I had no personal contact with him [Chávez] until 2001, other than the Bolivarian Christmas card message he sent me in 1995, by which time he was free. By a strange coincidence this card is dated in his handwriting "19 Dec 1995" which happened to be my 65th birthday. At that time, he had of course no Spanish copy of *Beyond Capital*, but he may have known about its English publication [that is, he may have had some familiarity with parts of the English edition]. For a group of professors at Caracas University—sympathetic to his movement—regularly (at irregular intervals) met and discussed it, finding also a small left publisher (Vadell Hermanos) willing to publish it, who—of course—had no money for a translator. So they started to translate it themselves as the best they could. I was told that their translation was "well-meaning but not very good," except for one member [Eduardo Gasca] who was Professor of Literary Studies and also a very good poet, a master of both languages. In 1997 this

Professor (whose old militant socialist father had just died) told the others: "This book has restored my faith in the future of socialism; I am going to translate it completely—also for my father—by myself for nothing," and he did.[49] In 1999, when this wonderful translation was finished, they asked me to write a special Introduction for the Latin American edition in Spanish and I completed this special translation—nearly 10,000 words, not published in English—in January 2000.[50] That is how it was published by Vadell Hermanos in 2001, and also the Brazilian Portuguese translation [with Boitempo] in 2002.

With immense electoral success Chávez was installed into the Presidency in 2000. I still had no personal contact with him. I never looked for such things with politically powerful people. However, in 2001 the Minister of Culture of his government—at that time the great painter [Manuel Espinoza] whose words about my comments on Attila József's lines concerning us, the "faithful listeners to the laws" (on our relationship to nature) I recently quoted to you in an email—invited me to a Conference, which I accepted. The Conference was taking place in Caracas, at the "Cultural Forum of the Latin American Parliament's Summit on the Social Debt and Latin American Integration," July 10–13, 2001. I delivered my lecture on "The Challenge of Sustainable Development and the Culture of Substantive Equality," contained also on pages 121–29 of *The Necessity of Social Control*, as you know. He learned that I was there and sent a car three times to the Hall where I was lecturing and taking part in the discussions. I could only go on the third occasion, by which time my share at the Conference was over. That is when I first met him in the Miraflores Palace, and that is how our close personal friendship started.

In September of the same year a distinguished academic body invited me to give a lecture at their international conference in Caracas. I gave a lecture on the world economic crisis, published also in my volume *The Challenge and Burden of Historical Time*. On that occasion Chávez and I spent much more time together (hours and hours). By that time, he not only had a Spanish copy of *Beyond*

Capital but also [had] read most of it, with lots of marginal comments and underlining everywhere. That was the time when he gave me the collected writings of Bólivar's teacher Simón Rodríguez. You have the picture of it. After that we met quite a few times, not only in Caracas but on one occasion also in London, when on a state visit—after the day-long negotiations—we had a long evening together in a posh London hotel where he and his team stayed, talking several hours and even consuming a rather awful (and no doubt very expensive) luxury hotel dinner. At the door of his hotel room, when I was leaving, he embraced me and said: "István, take good care of your health: we need you." On most of such occasions Donatella was with me, and she was also very fond of him coupled with great admiration for his great integrity and total dedication to his people. When Donatella died, in June 2007, by coincidence in the same days as Raul Castro's wife, Chávez in a most moving public speech spoke about the two of them, as great revolutionary wives and life Comrades to their husbands.

On every visit in Venezuela also after Donatella's death we spent time talking hours and hours together, usually combined with a dinner in his apartment in Miraflores. On the last occasion he even said that "next time you come we will go away for two weeks." But even a few days would have been wonderful. As you know, January 2013 he asked me to go and see him, and I promised I would do so in November 2013, combining it with my already existing commitment in Brazil, as I have done it on some earlier occasions. In response he sent me the message that he was happy about that. But, as you also know, his health badly deteriorated and in March 2013 he died, a great tragedy for us all. His death affected me more deeply than anything else since the death of Donatella.

This is, very briefly how I can sum up the wonderful relationship of friendship and solidarity I was fortunate to have with him in this critical time of human history.[51]

Two strategic elements of Mészáros's work were to prove essential for Chávez and for the course of the Bolivarian Revolution.[52] The first of these was the conception, drawn from Marx, of capital as a system of social metabolic reproduction, a self-reinforcing, integrated system of complex reproductive relations, which could not be simply abolished, or else changed piecemeal, but had to be replaced with an alternative organic metabolism based in communal relations.[53] The second was the core framework of "The Communal System and the Law of Value" as depicted in chapter 19 of *Beyond Capital*, in which Mészáros provided the strategic foundation for the revolutionary institutionalization of a system of "communal social relations," whereby the population reabsorbed sovereign rule into itself: a new kind of communal state or system, key to the transition to socialism. Such shifting of power to the people was at the same time a way of making the revolution, in Mészáros's terms, "irreversible," since the people would defend with their lives what was their own.[54] In the Organic Law of the Commune, passed in Venezuela in 2010, those elected by the communal assemblies would not be representatives, as in bourgeois representative government, but delegates or spokespeople, *voceros*.[55] In his treatment of communal exchange Mészáros emphasized the creation of exchange directed to use values and basic needs as opposed to commodity exchange, as a way of building inter-communal relations, an idea that was to be expanded on an international scale through the Bolivarian Alliance for the Peoples of Our America (ALBA).

In 2005, in a key moment in the struggle to build twenty-first-century socialism in Venezuela, Chávez, rooting his analysis in Mészáros's work, began to call for the immediate building of a communal economy and state. "The Point of Archimedes, this expression taken from the wonderful book of István Mészáros, a communal system of production and of consumption—that is what we are creating, we know we are building this. We have to create a communal system of production and consumption—a new system. . . . Let us remember that Archimedes said: 'You give me an intervention point [a place on which to stand] and I will move the world.' This is the point from which to move the world today."[56] For Mészáros and Chávez, such a permanent social revolution was the means to the creation of new creative, associated human beings able to make their own culture, their own economy, their own history, and their own collective and individual needs. As Mészáros put it in 2007, in his article "Bolívar and Chávez: The Spirit of Radical Determination," "it remains true today as it was in Bolívar's time that one cannot envisage the sustainable function of humanity's social *macrocosm* without overcoming the internal antagonisms of its *microcosms*: the adversarial and conflictual constituent cells of our society under capital's mode of social metabolic control. For a cohesive and socially viable macrocosm is conceivable only on the basis of the corresponding and humanly rewarding constitutive cells of interpersonal relations."[57] This demanded substantive equality in the cell structure of society: the family, community, and communal structures.[58]

In January 2007, Chávez presented the general strategy of socialism for the twenty-first century in the context of Venezuela's Bolivarian Revolution by introducing the concept of "'the elementary triangle of socialism'—the organic unification of social property, social production, and satisfaction of social [communal] needs." As Michael Lebowitz indicated:

> Once again, Chávez's theoretical step can be traced back to Mészáros's *Beyond Capital*. Drawing upon Marx, Mészáros had argued the necessity to understand capitalism as an organic system, a specific combination of production-distribution-consumption, in which all the elements coexist simultaneously and support one another. The failure of the socialist experiments of the twentieth century, he proposed, occurred because of the failure to go beyond "the vicious circle of the capital relation," the combination of circuits "all intertwined and mutually reinforcing one another" that thereby reinforced "the perverse dialectic of the incurably wasteful capital system." In short, the lack of success (or effort) in superseding all parts of "the totality of existing reproductive relations" meant the failure to go "beyond capital."[59]

In Mészáros's conception, the initial successes of the political revolutions in Venezuela and Bolivia were the product of their break with the Leviathan state through their initiation of constitutional conventions that rewrote the constitutions of their countries to increase the power of the population. Even before encountering Mészáros's work, Chávez had reached back into the Bolivarian tradition and, via Bolívar's teacher Simón Rodríguez to Rousseau, challenged the dominant form of representative government.[60] This critique was deepened through Mészáros's reading of Rousseau's argument, emphasizing that aspects of executive power could be delegated while the legislative power must remain entirely with the sovereign people. As Chávez put it: "By socialism we mean unlimited democracy. . . . From this comes our firm conviction that the best and most radically democratic options for defeating bureaucracy and corruption is the construction of a communal state which is able to test an alternative institutional structure at the same time as it permanently reinvents itself."[61] This took the form of the "Organic Law of the Commune" in 2010, followed by Chávez's urgent calls in his last speech, "Strike at the Helm," on October 20, 2012, to expand the communes as the essence of the revolution and its irreversibility.[62]

In 2010 Chávez and Mészáros had a long discussion on the need for a New International as an absolute necessity for the development of socialism globally in the face of the ongoing attempts by the United States and its European allies to "recolonize the world." They agreed that this new organization would be called a "New International" and not a "Fifth International" in order to break with the sequence of a series of Internationals that had emphasized doctrinal unity in ways that undermined the socialist cause. Chávez asked Mészáros to draft a paper along the lines of their discussions, which Mészáros did that year, titled "Reflections on the New International."[63] Chávez intended to carry out a global initiative along these lines after his next election. However, his illness in the following year and death in 2013 prevented any action. Mészáros was to publish the "Reflections on the New International" in *The Necessity of Social Control* in 2015. In addition to laying out the whole dialectic of an alternative system of social metabolic reproduction that would go beyond capital and socialism it outlined the New International as an organization "with the *broad general principle and the fundamental emancipatory objective of a socialist transformation of society*" while rejecting any "*doctrinal prescription* as to the sustainable particular ways of instituting the *practical measures and modes of action*." The object was to maximize vernacular revolutionary traditions responding to particular historical conditions and to "create a mode of operation" that would be "*cooperatively additive and cohesive*, instead of fragmenting."[64]

It was in this context of revolutionary struggles with respect to the state in Venezuela and elsewhere that Mészáros began in September 2012 to devote his energies full time to his massive work, *Beyond Leviathan: Critique of the State*.

CATEGORIES OF THE CRITIQUE OF LEVIATHAN

Beyond Leviathan necessarily relies on a set of categories that allow Mészáros to engage with the fundamentally different problems associated with a critique of the state aimed at its historical transcendence. Some of these were developed primarily in *Beyond Capital*, such as: (1) his emphasis on the *capital system* as a wider category extending beyond the capitalist system as such, in which the capital relation (including the fundamental exploitation of labor) retains its dominance through the state, even in post-revolutionary societies; (2) his concept of *social metabolic reproduction*, which sees relatively stable social systems as organic (even if alienated) orders in which all the elements reinforce each other; and (3) his notion of *second-order mediations*, which explains how alienated systems of *social metabolic reproduction* are structured, albeit in contradictory and destructive fashion, to create a makeshift social whole. These have all been explained elsewhere.[65]

Central to all of Mészáros's work is the concept of *substantive equality*, contrasted to formal equality, and any (inherently contradictory) notion of partial equality. It is substantive equality, which constitutes, for Mészáros, the defining characteristic of socialism as a system of social metabolic reproduction, and which requires, for its realization, a social order beyond capital, beyond Leviathan, and beyond (alienated) labor. The issue of substantive equality thus pervades his entire analysis and is especially evident in *Beyond Leviathan* in his discussions of Aristotle, Hobbes, Babeuf, Kant, and Marx. In *Beyond Leviathan* the concept of substantive equality is directly addressed in Appendix 3 on "Substantive Equality and Substantive Democracy." However, it is developed conceptually most fully, extending to questions of labor, women's oppression, and international inequality/conflict, in chapter 5 of *Beyond Capital* on "The Activation of Capital's Absolute Limits."[66] The state is a hierarchal and repressive form of the necessary *overall political command structure* which all class societies must have in some form (98, 237). In the case of the state, which stands above and is alienated from society, a hierarchical political command structure is necessitated by the lack of cohesion in the *constitutive cells* of class societies, where human beings are alienated from one another in and through production and by virtue of class relations, extending to all social forms. In contrast, a socialist society of substantive equality requires a different *microcosm* or set of constitutive cells organically connected to a different *macrocosm* or overall political command structure, based on communal relations rooted in associated producers, constituent power, and forms of communal exchange (42).

Throughout his analysis Mészáros adopts the perspective of the *materiality of the state*, recognizing that the state has to be seen as historically situated in relation to production and social metabolic reproduction as a whole.[67] As a product of class society, the state is necessarily a top-down system of class power. Yet, what Marx called the "legal and political superstructure" is not to be identified merely with the state, but encompasses elements of civil society, that is, the polity as a whole.[68] No society can do without a political command structure of some kind, though in a socialist society based on substantive equality the necessary bases of the alternative political command structure, beyond Leviathan, would emanate from the bottom of society, or from communal/collective constitutive cells within the microcosm, forming the basis of social control of the macrocosm.

In the case of the capital system, the constitutive cells of society consist of individual capitals, in the form of corporations and wealthy owners, dominating over the working class (and other subaltern classes and groups) while engaged in incessant intercapitalist competition.

This gives rise to capitalism's insurmountable *centrifugal tendencies* making it *uncontrollable* (113–15). Although the state constitutes the force meant to give stability to the capitalist order, capital remains the primary extra-state force within society as a whole, often subsuming the state with its own power dynamics. The growth of monopolistic capitals and global production only deepens these conditions of *uncontrollability* in capital's descending phase, leading to the structural crisis of capital (115, 139).

While the state in particular nation-states manages temporarily to bridge capital's centrifugal tendencies and uncontrollability within certain parameters of coordinated class rule, the globalization of production brings capital's uncontrollability to the fore. Further, there is no possibility of the creation of a transnational capitalist state transcending the competition between states themselves—a fact recognized above all by Hegel—with the result that capitalism points to ever more destructive wars. The contradictions between political and economic forces internally and between global political power relations leads to both internal and external conflicts within the capitalist state and repeated reassertions of "might is right," despite the state's pretensions to the rule of law.

In the ascending period of the capital system, these contradictions were capable of correction, that is, the system had the quality of *correctiveness* or a capacity for *corrective adjustment,* even if in the form of alienated second-order mediations. In the descending phase of capital, the state's ability to impose corrective adjustments has receded, producing a tendency toward increasingly catastrophic antagonisms (148, 252).[69]

Throughout the history of the state in various class formations, vain attempts were made to establish the state on *irreversible* foundations, whether by way of Plato's laws (which continually reproduced themselves as so many uncontrollable hydra heads), Aristotle's median, Machiavelli's republicanism, Hobbes's absolute sovereignty, Kant's universal peace, or Hegel's universal class (45). In every case, however, the class structure of society, constituting the very basis for the state, contradicted all such notions of irreversibility and pointed to continual class struggle and war. Mészáros wrote: "People often ignore that the fundamental condition of the State's sovereignty (its falsely claimed democratic aspect) is the necessary class oppression of the worker."[70] Under capitalism the modern state has as its objective "the vital qualifying determination already at this stage: its *historical irreversibility*."[71] But given the antagonistic nature of the capital system, the kind of "irreversibility" achieved within the limits of capital only meant that its hierarchical, repressive structure (legitimated by its hydra-headed laws) would continually reinforce itself, despite growing contradictions, short of epochal change unleashed from below. Nowhere was this more evident than in the concept of justice, since "from Ancient Greece onward" the question of justice was "treated (even by the great philosophers) as the *justification* of the *unjustifiable*. Hence, the shift (immediately) from [considerations of] *equality* to '*justice*.'"[72]

Only an alternative social metabolic order, beyond capital, beyond class, beyond (alienated) labor, and beyond Leviathan could achieve what the various state constructions failed to attain, namely a system of social metabolic reproduction based on genuine *irreversibility*, rooted in the drive to substantive equality.[73] In this case, the constitutive cells did not need a state to guarantee a limited period of historical irreversibility, but rather the people themselves, organized on a collective basis, were guarantors of the polity. In such a society the great mass of the people would defend what they had at last won, an associated mode of production, based on the eradication of capital and its Leviathan state. Needless to say, this could not be achieved all at once. There would be many mountains to climb and defeats to endure along the way. Yet, unless the struggle for substantive equality was at the core of the movement at every stage humanity could not go forward at all.

It is here that Mészáros raised the issue of *temporality*. In Hegel's *Philosophy of Right*—the "unintended swan song" that brought his dialectical system to an end—temporality or historical change, was assigned strictly to the past, in conformity with the requirements of liberal political economy (228, 232). Yet, in Mészáros, as in Marx, there was no possibility of superseding the "challenge and burden of historical time."[74] Temporality could move in entirely contradictory fashions

INTRODUCTION   31

in a given historical moment, representing very different historical time scales: cosmic time and human time, the opposition of revolutionary and non-revolutionary time, the variation between short-run and long-run imperatives, and the different rhythms imposed by social relations and productive forces.⁷⁵ The state of the capital system sought to prevail at all times against revolutionary time, in line with a system that, in Marx's words, constantly sought to reduce humanity to "time's carcase."⁷⁶ The struggle against the capital system was thus, in Mészáros's view, a struggle over its restricted temporality at every level, ultimately resting on its control of disposable time. This required an "epochal break."⁷⁷ Without a society of associated producers, that is, socialism, there could be no genuine fulfillment of the necessary planning of qualitative change on behalf of the chain of human generations, transcending "capital's necessary abuse of time at all cost and in all domains."⁷⁸

The "withering away of the state," as it had come to be known within Marxist theory, or the complete eradication of the state as a hierarchical command structure above society was for Mészáros, a negative way of expressing the complete revolution against the alienated capital system, and the coming power of the associated human community.⁷⁹

SOME EDITORIAL NOTES ON THE TEXT

Mészáros did not live to complete *Beyond Leviathan*. This text is from his unfinished Volume 1 of what was to be a three-volume work. The last three chapters and the conclusion of Volume 1 were never written (other than the latter part of his originally planned chapter "From Kant and Lessing to Thomasius and Bloch's Principle of Hope," which has been reconstructed here from his handwritten second-version draft). Most of Parts One and Two of this volume have been published previously, while the finished manuscripts of Part Three were in good shape (apart from the citations). Nevertheless, there were a number of places where significant editorial issues developed in putting the book together.

Chapter 4 in the present text, "Capital's Deepening Crisis and the State," was nowhere to be found. Since Mészáros had indicated that this part of the work was done, I concluded after an inspection of the contents that it was to be based on the talk "Structural Crisis Needs Structural Change" that he delivered in Brazil in June 2011 and London in July 2011, and which was first published in *Monthly Review* in March 2012. I was further convinced of this since he had himself included it in his 2015 book collection *The Necessity of Social Control*, placing it immediately before what was to form Part Two of *Beyond Leviathan*, also included in that book. I therefore adapted it (merely changing it from the form of a talk to a chapter), giving it the title intended for the book. Although Mészáros would undoubtedly have made a few further changes directed at the issue of the state in his final version of this chapter, I refrained from making any substantive changes here (or elsewhere in the book). In its present form, chapter 4 represents a crucial link in his logical chain.

Part Two of the present text, "The Mountain We *Must* Conquer," was expressly written as Part Two of Volume 1 of *Beyond Leviathan* but was published in 2015 as the concluding section of *The Necessity of Social Control*. This followed the pattern adopted by Mészáros in his last few years. Knowing he did not have long to live, he requested that *Monthly Review* and Monthly Review Press publish most of the first two parts of *Beyond Leviathan* as they were completed. The introduction to "The Mountain We *Must* Conquer," written specifically for *The Necessity of Social Control*, was not part of the original plan for *Beyond Leviathan*. I have, however, added that introduction as a separate chapter (chapter 6: "The Mountainous State") in the present text.

With respect to the last three chapters in Mészáros's original plan for this volume, there was no sign of the chapter on "Search for the Truth in the Scottish Enlightenment" besides scattered notes on Adam Smith, whom he referred to as "one the greatest representatives of the Scottish Enlightenment," and saw as emerging out of the natural law tradition.[80] It is quite possible that he intended to combine reflections on Smith in this respect together with Adam Ferguson's treatment of civil society and the state, but there was nothing in the notes he left behind that actually suggested this.[81] There was also no indication of what he intended to address in his unwritten final chapter on "Pessimistic Utopias of Capital's Inescapable Order." In the case of the penultimate chapter planned for *Beyond Leviathan*, "Kant and Lessing and Thomasius and Bloch's Principle of Hope," no Kant-Lessing treatment could be found in Mészáros's notes and drafts or in his published work, although there was a great deal on Kant himself. The treatment of Thomasius and Bloch, however, was found in his second version draft, from which it was excavated. It is provided here as the concluding chapter of the book, titled simply "Thomasius and Bloch's Principle of Hope."

Mészáros's chapter on Thomasius and Bloch, which focuses on Bloch's interpretation of Thomasius, is significant in a number of key respects, making it a fitting conclusion to *Beyond Leviathan*. Most important here is Thomasius's commitment, going beyond the limitations imposed by his time, to a society based on a principle of the "*honestum* of ethicality" grounded in a conception of "reasonable love," which Thomasius derived from Epicurean morality. Internal peace, based on reasonable love, could only be joined with external peace, Thomasius argued, when rooted in substantive justice emanating from *communal property* (364–365).[82] For Mészáros, like Bloch, Thomasius stood for the revolutionary form of natural law tradition and of the seventeenth-century Enlightenment, including a strong "*communal* advocacy" and a radical morality, manifested in the leading role he played in opposing torture and witch trials in the Germany of his day (367).[83] In Thomasius it was possible to perceive an Enlightenment revolt against the alienated powers of Church and state that prefigured the later emergence of the socialist approach to human rights based on substantive equality and communal property (365). Indeed, Thomasius's emphasis on communal property (and implicitly on class) allowed him partially to transcend what Mészáros in his notes referred to as the idealist "'Enlightenment illusion' [of] reclaiming 'sovereignty for the people' and its necessary failure on *class-antagonistic*, material grounds."[84]

Mészáros's analysis here is based squarely on Bloch, on whose scholarship in this respect he had complete faith, and not on knowledge of Thomasius directly or of Epicurus—from whom Thomasius drew his radical conception of morality and natural law.[85] It seems likely that in preparing the final version of his treatment of Thomasius via Bloch, Mészáros would have himself delved more deeply into Thomasius's work. Yet, in many ways this argument was as much about Bloch's principle of hope as it was about Thomasius. It was Bloch's extraordinarily radical reinterpretation of the Enlightenment tradition that was fundamental here, allowing the transcendence of more reified forms of bourgeois thought as this emerged in its ascending phase and lingered on in its descending phase.[86]

Nothing was dearer to Mészáros's heart than Bloch's statement in his *The Principle of Hope* that "just because knowledge destroys rotten optimism, it does not also destroy urgent hope for a good end. For this hope is too indestructibly grounded in the human drive for happiness, and it has always been too clearly a motor of history. . . . The most dogged enemy of socialism is not only, as is understandable, great capital, but equally the load of indifference, hopelessness; otherwise great capital would stand alone."[87]

In his analysis of Bloch and Thomasius in chapter 20, Mészáros made it clear that he was strongly opposed to what he thought of as the reactionary and debilitating aspects of Max Horkheimer and Theodor Adorno's generalized attack on Enlightenment thought and their version of critical theory. In the conflict between Adorno/Horkheimer and Bloch, Mészáros was strongly on Bloch's side, believing that Bloch's work had shown how to build on the revolutionary elements of the Enlightenment and the principle of hope these engendered, refuting Adorno and Horkheimer's blanket criticism of the Enlightenment. For Bloch the Enlightenment, with all of its weaknesses, contributed to establishing a revolutionary dialectic of continuity and change without which forward movement was impossible. In this sense, as Mészáros stated, Bloch, through his incomparable scholarship on the Enlightenment tradition, "naturally . . . sweeps the floor with them [Horkheimer and Adorno]."[88]

Here it is important to understand the very deep divisions that emerged within the broad Frankfurt School tradition and Western Marxism between, on the one hand, those who returned from exile after the Second World War to reside in West Germany under the

American occupational authority (which provided funds for the revival of the Institute for Social Research), notably Adorno and Horkheimer, and those, on the other hand, who chose to return to East Germany, such as Bloch and Bertolt Brecht, or chose to reside in Hungary, in the case of Lukács.[89] Moreover, some of the representatives of the broad Frankfurt School tradition who remained in the United States after the Second World War, like Herbert Marcuse and Paul Baran, were also highly critical of what they saw as the backward turn of Horkheimer and Adorno.[90] Nor were the issues minor ones. They related to the question of whether the revolutionary dialectic emerging out of the critical Enlightenment and reaching maturity in Marxism was viable.

Mészáros voiced his opposition to Horkheimer and Adorno in *The Power of Ideology* and elsewhere, where he sharply criticized Adorno for his scornful, polemical, Cold War–style attacks on Lukács in the later 1950s in *Die Monat* (a publication created by the U.S. Army in West Germany and financed by the Central Intelligence Agency) at a time when Lukács was under house arrest for defying the repressive regime in the East.[91] As Lukács later charged: "A considerable part of the leading German intelligentsia, including Adorno, have taken up residence in the 'Grand Hotel Abyss,' which I described in connection with my critique of Schopenhauer as 'a beautiful hotel, equipped with every comfort, on the edge of an abyss, of nothingness, of absurdity. And the daily contemplation of the abyss between excellent meals or artistic entertainments, can only heighten the enjoyment of the subtle comforts offered.'"[92]

Further nuances Mészáros might have added to his criticism of Horkheimer and Adorno in the final draft of "Thomasius and Bloch's Principle of Hope" are unclear. Nevertheless, chapter 20 points to a sharp divergence within Marxist thought (and critical theory), separating an approach that systematically challenged classical Marxism by rejecting its critical Enlightenment roots in the name of a questionable negative dialectics, from one that sought to bring along all of history in its train in forging the necessary bases of revolutionary praxis for the twenty-first century.

In addition to these issues related to chapters that had to be adapted in the editing of *Beyond Leviathan*, a number of technical problems arose in preparing the final publication of his book. In his original plan for the book, Mészáros divided each volume into what were called "chapters," which were divided into sections with titles. These were, in turn, divided into numbered subsections. This reflected a method of presentation he used in *Beyond Capital* and other works. In the case of what was to be Volume 1 of the *Beyond Leviathan*, or the current text, there were to be three "chapters" each as long as a whole part in most books, while the sections were often the length of chapters in most books. Recognizing the problem that this created, Mészáros indicated to me that we could possibly deviate from this format and call the chapters parts, and the sections chapters, while giving titles to the subsections. Indeed, he encouraged me to give titles to the numbered subsections when publishing chapters in the book in *Monthly Review*, which I did on a number of occasions, with his approval.[93] For the sake of readability, I have therefore changed the chapters to parts, and the chapter sections to chapters, and given titles to the previous numbered chapter subsections now converted into chapter sections. Other than chapters 6 and 14, all part and chapter titles in the text are by Mészáros himself, while the chapter section titles are invariably by me (in Part One, chapters 2 to 5 have section titles that were used with Mészáros's approval).

Appendices 2–4 were all listed by Mészáros as intended appendices for the book. Appendices 2 and 3 were so listed in the general plan for the book, and Appendix 4 was singled out to be added as an addendum to the book in his second-version draft notes.

Only the most minor editing has been applied to the text, primarily to the chapters in Part Three that were not previously published. Throughout the book, but especially in Part Three, there were inconsistencies in the use of citations, sometimes with sources only incompletely cited in the draft text and quotations that needed checking. This was accomplished in almost all cases by going back to the original editions that Mészáros had used and ensuring accuracy and consistency. Many of the details in the citations had to be filled-in in the process.

As indicated, I have left the text as it came from his pen without substantive alterations or extensive notes. Where necessary, although rarely, I have inserted square brackets to indicate an insert into the text by myself, required for sense or clarity. Mészáros's notes and citations are all provided in the endnotes. When an editorial note was needed, these were inserted as footnotes at the bottom of the page.

Some items in the book have appeared in earlier publications. The following pieces in Part One were previously published in issues of *Monthly Review*: Preface (February 2018); chapter 3 (September 2016); chapter 4 (March 2012); chapter 5 (December 2017). Chapter 1 was posted online as a *Monthly Review* Essay (November 2018). Part Two was previously published in István Mészáros, *The Necessity of Social Control* (New York: Monthly Review Press, 2015), 231–98. Appendix 2 is taken from section 3.3 of István Mészáros, *Social Structure and Forms of Consciousness*, vol. 2: *The Dialectic of Structure and History* (New York: Monthly Review Press, 2011), 115-29. Appendix 4 is taken from chapter 13 of István Mészáros, *Beyond Capital* (New York: Monthly Review Press, 1995), 460–95.

A FINAL NOTE

István Mészáros was a very close and dear friend, and we had a long working relationship. It was understood by the two of us that I would take responsibility for editing, introducing, and publishing *Beyond Leviathan* if he did not live to complete it. In his last hours, a letter from me was read to him in which I reiterated this, promising to bring out his entire critique of the state through Monthly Review Press. This included both the volume that lies before you and also his handwritten second-version draft manuscript containing parts of what were originally intended to be volumes 2 and 3 of a three-volume work. The latter draft manuscript will be published separately within a few years as *Critique of Leviathan: Reflections on the State*.

—JOHN BELLAMY FOSTER

BEYOND LEVIATHAN

for Donatella

Preface

Why Leviathan? The readers of this book may well ask the question.

The answer is both very simple and painfully difficult. Very simple in the sense that the state—despite the great variety of its forms, as constituted in history, from the time of so-called Oriental despotism and the early empires to the modern liberal state—cannot be other than Leviathan in imposing its structurally entrenched power on overall societal decision-making. Obviously, that kind of separate, state-imposed resolution of the vital issues of societal reproduction means in reality expropriating and usurping the vital decision-making powers from the social body as a whole.

The answer is also painfully difficult because this alienated form of long-established overall decision-making represents a fundamental challenge for the future, in unavoidable opposition to its perennial domination. That is the case because in our time, in view of the objectively accomplished changes that in the course of history produced the now readily available powers of total destruction, a way must be found to extricate humanity from the ever more dangerous—potentially, in a literal sense, self-annihilating—decision-making practices of the Leviathan state. There can be no hope for the survival of humanity without that.

To be sure, a challenge of this kind and magnitude has never been confronted in all of history. For in order to bring the destructive antagonistic developments not only to a halt but to reverse them in a positive way, in the interest of a historically sustainable mode of existence in the future, human beings must, in the words of Karl Marx, change "from top to bottom the conditions of their industrial and political existence, and consequently their whole manner of being," and that change is inconceivable without an appropriate period of consciously regulated transition from the existing order to a qualitatively different one.[1]

This is a task that cannot be realized within the paralyzing confines of the hierarchical and antagonistic framework of the political/military domain, as is often wrongly projected. For in order to make feasible a historically and, in the long run, viable accomplishment of this kind, a radical transformation is required in our social metabolism. That is to say, a radical social transformation that would deeply affect our modality of decision-making as much in the elementary constitutive cells or microcosms of our societal reproductive order as it would at the most comprehensive level of the global interdependencies.

It is the inseparability of this interrelationship between the elementary constitutive cells of societal reproduction and the broadest globally relevant determinations that is the reason why it is impossible to go *Beyond Leviathan* in the political/military domain without radically overcoming the social metabolic power of capital as such at its material ground. The same determination prevails the other way around. And that means it is impossible to go *Beyond Capital* in the material reproductive order of our society without overcoming the vital challenge of Leviathan's structurally entrenched and superimposed decision-making powers as constituted in history in a great variety of its state formations, asserting themselves more than ever today. In other words, the structural imperatives of going *Beyond Capital* as the material reproductive force of society and going *Beyond Leviathan* as the political/military overall decision-maker are inseparable.

People like to quote from *Leviathan* written by Thomas Hobbes the shocking words that are said to describe what is supposed to be humanity's original "state of nature" in general, to which the political/

military state was meant to provide the corresponding all-embracing answer. Closely connected to the words of *bellum omnium contra omnes*—the war of each against all—they sound like this: "The life of man, [was] solitary, poore, nasty, brutish, and short."[2]

However, as Hobbes made very clear, "It may peradventure be thought, there was never such a time, nor condition of warre as this; and I believe it was never generally so, over all the world: but there are many places, where they live so now."[3] Moreover, "Though there had never been any time, wherein particular men were in a condition of warre one against another; yet in all times, Kings, and Persons of Soveraigne authority, because of their Independency, are in continuall jealousies, and in the state and posture of Gladiators; having their weapons pointing, and their eyes fixed on one another; that is, their Forts, Garrisons, and Guns upon the Frontiers of their Kingdomes; and continuall Spyes upon their neighbours; which is a posture of war."[4]

Naturally, Hobbes offered his own vision of an all-powerful Leviathan state formation as the only legitimate counterforce to all of its predecessors and potential rivals. In due course, we shall examine in proper detail the merits as well as the problematic aspects of his great work.* What is directly relevant at this point is his forceful condemnation of the perennial warfare known in history and aggravated through the civil war in his own time, to which he was hoping to find an alternative. Thus, in the interest of peace he wrote: "The Lawes of Nature are Immutable and Eternall; for Injustice, Ingratitude, Arrogance, Pride, Iniquity, Acception of persons, and the rest, can never be made lawfull. For it can never be that Warre shall preserve life, and Peace destroy it."[5] And for even greater emphasis he added a little later that "all men agree on this, that Peace is Good, and therefore also the way, or means of Peace, which (as I have shewed before) are Justice, Gratitude, Modesty, Equity, Mercy, & the rest of the Lawes of Nature, are good; that is to

---

* Much of the discussion of Hobbes was to have appeared in the second volume of *Beyond Leviathan*, which exists only in preliminary draft form and is not included in the present work.—Ed.

say, Morall Vertues; and their contrarie Vices, Evill. Now the science of Vertue and Vice, is Morall Philosophie; and therefore the true doctrine of the Lawes of Nature, is the true Morall Philosophie."[6]

In this way, the radical theory of the state published by Hobbes in 1651 was proclaimed to be grounded by its author in the most secure philosophical foundation, in terms of the highest morally justified opposition to war. And indeed, war was by him decreed to be categorically contrary to the laws of nature. The fact that nearly three hundred and seventy years after the publication of *Leviathan* by Hobbes humanity is constantly compelled to confront the danger of war in its potentially overwhelming all-destructive form underlines the gravity of these problems.

UNIVERSAL LAW

As a matter of chronological record, all of the major theories of the state have been produced in historical periods of great turmoil, from Plato, Aristotle, and Augustine through Machiavelli and Hobbes, all the way to Jean-Jacques Rousseau and G. W. F. Hegel, as well as, of course, to Marx, V. I. Lenin, and their comrades Rosa Luxemburg and Antonio Gramsci.

This is well understandable. For all of the important theories of the state, including those that fully accepted the retention of its contradictorily self-legitimating overall commanding role, wanted to improve the state's ability to cope with its problems in those periods of severe historic crises to which they responded.[7] Thus, at least in the ascending phase of their society's development, even the state theories written from the standpoint of the ruling order were critical theories in this limited but clearly identifiable historically specific sense, despite their problematic siding with the overall decision-making processes of their own class-exploitative reproductive order. The same goes for the various utopian theories of politics and society which—in their own way, even if often obliquely—offered on the whole the critically modified retention of some superimposed command structure on societal decision-making. By contrast, the Marxian-inspired approach followed a radically different critical attitude, envisaging the "withering away of the state"—or the total eradication of the state—from the modality of social metabolic reproduction, in place of the continued expropriation of humanity's overall decision-making processes.

One of the crucial problems in this respect concerned the unavoidable periodic upheavals and the ensuing reversals in the continued exercise of the established state's laws. Obviously, such upheavals and reversals badly needed to be addressed in all state theory. For without securing in some way the continuity of overall political decision-making, the maintenance of societal reproduction would be rendered impossible under the conditions of antagonistic material and cultural interchanges that prevailed in history and indeed still prevail in our own time.

It was one of Plato's great insights thousands of years ago to focus on the requirement of securing the necessary continuity in question. He realized before anyone else that the law cannot be considered law proper unless its character is universal in the sense of its fully legitimate unassailability. He undertook the establishment of this fundamental requirement in one of his most important and by far the most extensive dialogues on the state, *The Laws*.

Toward the end of this work, which describes in minute detail the utopian state project of Magnesia, the principal interlocutor makes the self-critical point according to which "the service we have still not done for the laws is to discover how to build into them a resistance to being reversed."[8] As a requirement, this is absolutely vital in past state theory, quite irrespective of how successfully it can be accomplished by the particular thinkers under their given historical circumstances. Plato is by no means alone in his forceful advocacy of some kind of irreversibility. Many centuries later, Machiavelli emphasized much the same requirement when he insisted that what truly qualifies a Prince for greatness is not how powerful he is in his lifetime but how enduring his creation as the overall political framework proves to be.[9]

Plato proposes in *The Laws* as his own solution in Magnesia the institution of what he calls the "Nocturnal Council" of guardians in order to secure the stipulated permanency of his ideal state and its laws. He argues about the existing and by him rejected states that "where there are no efficient and articulate guardians, with an adequate understanding of virtue, it will be hardly surprising if the state, precisely because it is unguarded, meets the fate of so many [failing] states nowadays."[10] At the same time, as the necessary condition of success, Plato advocates that the members of the Nocturnal Council—projected by him as some kind of constitutional safeguard—should be "rigorously selected, properly educated, and after the completion of their studies lodged in the citadel of the country and made into guardians whose powers of protection we have never seen excelled in our lives before."[11] He also stipulates the need for finding "the single central concept" (in the multifaceted domain of virtue) through which it becomes possible "to put the various details in their proper place in the overall picture."[12]

However, the great irony is that Plato's stipulation remains only a stipulation. We are never told by Plato, and—given the elusive character of the requirement of the law's irreversibility itself as its own guarantee—we can never be told, what that "single central concept" might be. We get only procedural details—a constantly recurring rather problematical feature of state theories that claim much more by such devices after Plato, to our own days—about how the members of the Council should be selected, educated, lodged, what time of day they should meet, etc. But we never receive even a remote hint at a "single central concept" that could serve as the practical guiding principle of a sustainable state regulation "built into the laws and guaranteeing their irreversibility."

Naturally, we should not be surprised at all by such historic failure, despite Plato's awareness of the great importance of the principle laid down by him. For in any antagonistic societal reproductive order, not to mention a slave-owning society like ancient Greece, there cannot be anything built into the laws that could in any sense guarantee by itself their irreversibility. Not only the predicament of ancient Greece but also countless constitutions thereafter, alternating with their reversals sooner or later, amply proved that plain truth in the course of history. Accordingly, we had to wait a very long time before the conditions required for making the law truly universal in character could objectively arise in actually unfolding history. We have been condemned to wait for it for such a long time because its conditions of realization could become feasible only through the actions of self-determining human beings who would autonomously make their laws for themselves by themselves, beyond the antagonistic determinations of their long-established social metabolic order and its corresponding state formations.

HYDRA'S HEADS

In the course of actual history, one of the most problematical aspects of the law was—and more than ever remains—the endless multiplication of its statutes and regulatory determinations. As a result, we could witness up to the present time the creation of an ever-denser legal jungle in state theory, fully in tune with the existing antagonistic societal order and its political institutions. The law itself can offer no obstacle to that. For the disheartening fact is that for every one of its instances a whole range of "counter-instances" can be devised, so as to be "countered" again, potentially ad infinitum, in the law's institutionally secured and sanctioned pseudo-legitimacy.

This way of conceptualizing the required state practices in the form of an ever-denser legal jungle helped render the modality of societal reproduction in political terms ever more complicated, often in the name of producing greater transparency. Invariably, such practice was pursued in the interest of preserving the substantive inequality established in society for thousands of years, instead of facilitating its meaningful critical evaluation and ultimate consignment to the past. Today this trend continues to drive unmistakably in the direction of making the legal jungle so dense that it should be penetrable only by those practitioners in the field whose professionally pursued and sanctified job is to make that jungle even denser. The parliaments we know all over the world are obvious proof of that.

The apparently insurmountable difficulty regarding this problem is that it cannot be solved in terms of the law itself, in its own terms of reference. For the cause of the failure in this respect is that the institutionalized law as such had been constituted—and constitutionally/circularly/self-servingly legitimated and entrenched—by the exclusion of the subordinate class of society from law-making from the very beginning, and reproduced as well as strengthened in the same way ever since.

The only exception seems to be when in situations of great emergency or a major revolutionary crisis, some forms of "constitutional assemblies" are temporarily established. However, despite their achievements in improving the material conditions of the poorest section of the population in some countries, constitutional assemblies show limited lasting success so far, if any, in changing the structural determination of class-society. Understandably, the inherited "constitutionality requirement"—to which the constitutional assemblies in question dutifully conform, despite that in their primary self-legitimating circularity the traditional constitutions always sustained the established social metabolic order—represents the most easily exploitable danger on this score. To give only one important contemporary example, the cynical exploitation of pretended legality is made evident by the utterly lawless and often even violent activities of the subversive "constitutional opposition" inside Venezuela since the death of its revolutionary president Hugo Chávez. Most revealingly, such subversive forces are sustained in every way by the Leviathan state of North America—very far from constitutionally behaving, ubiquitously interventionist—as the history of several Latin American countries, prophetically anticipated by Simon Bolívar and José Martí, bears eloquent witness.

The contradictorily self-legitimating endless multiplication of legal statutes and regulatory measures in history is all the more problematic and revealing because it had been identified and criticized thousands of years ago, in ancient Greece, to absolutely no avail. It was Plato, again, who raised his critical voice against the intrusion of Hydra—the mythical creature that managed to grow several heads when any one of them had been cut off—into the law, through the perversely devised multiplication and amendment of useless laws and regulatory measures. Plato forcefully condemned that practice by comparing it to disease in this way: "By all their remedies they achieve nothing except engendering and multiplying greater diseases, while always hoping that someone will advise a drug to make them better.... Equally charming are those, who make laws on matters like those already mentioned and constantly amend them in the belief that they will reach finality—unaware that they are just cutting off a Hydra's head."[13]

In the thousands of years since Plato's time, countless numbers of Hydra-heads have been cut off, and continue to be cut off today, multiplying every time, as had occurred already in ancient Greece. Not surprisingly, therefore, in the immensely bureaucratized states of our own time the law is getting ever more cumbersome and impenetrable. That serves, of course, most successfully the continued disenfranchising of the subordinate class of the people in the authoritarian decision-making framework of the Leviathan state, where all such practices are in the material domain hierarchically entrenched and in the political field arbitrarily self-legitimated.

This form of determination represents a very great problem for the future. For, as mentioned above, the realization of humanity's emancipation is inconceivable without an appropriate period of consciously regulated transition from the existing order to a qualitatively different one. And that has necessary implications for the move from our present social system, with its Leviathan state and its laws, sustained by their apologetic jurisprudential underpinning, to a fundamentally different one envisaged by Marx and his comrades.

The state existed and dominated societal reproduction for thousands of years. It would be, therefore, naive to project its abolition or disappearance in a short period of time, let alone immediately. The task is not to project the timescale of its withering away or eradication but to indicate the conditions that must be fulfilled in order to achieve the required change through the qualitative restructuring of the social metabolism in accordance with the historic reality of our time.

To make that task realizable, the elaboration of critical jurisprudence, in sharp contrast to its state-apologetic variety in existence, is bound to play an important role. For the Marxian idea envisioning the state's withering away was feasible not as some kind of spontaneously self-realizing event but as a most active and coherently pursued strategic intervention that identifies from the start the existing state, with its laws in the service of perpetuating substantive inequality, as the urgently necessary critical target of radical change. That also means the necessity to transfer to the social body the totality of the powers expropriated by the Leviathan state in the course of history. To this crucial task critical jurisprudence can contribute in its own meaningful way in the unavoidable period of transition, but by no means in a dominant way, as traditional law always asserted itself in the past. For the task of qualitative restructuring just mentioned is conceivable only through the activation of the great masses of the people—that is, all of society's given and potential producers—for taking full control over the reproductive determinations of their society, from the elementary constitutive cells of the thereby constituted socialist system to the most comprehensive feasible global interdependencies of the highest complexity. In that sense, critical jurisprudence is objectively mandated to sustain in its own ways the much-needed radical social metabolic transformation. In other words, the fundamental meaning of the consciously regulated strategic intervention in critical jurisprudential terms can only be to facilitate the progressive eradication of the state, in all of its dimensions and institutional embodiments, from the societal reproduction process.

THE UTOPIA OF A GLOBAL LEVIATHAN

"Globalization" is a contradictorily unfolding, yet in any case inexorably unfolding, reality on the material plane. But it is totally devoid of sustainability on the political plane. For capital's historically constituted nation-states continue to fight one another even when apologetic ideologists idealize globalization, as if such globalization could be carried forward to its harmonious all-embracing conclusion within the antagonistic framework of the capital system. However, the undeniable reality is that the nation-states fight each other either directly or in their proxy wars. They adopt the modality of proxy wars in openly pursued direct confrontations of the world's dominant powers, for example, the United States and Russia, in which the danger would be the total destruction of the warring countries as well as the rest of humanity. And for the time being, the most powerful nation-state, China, is relatively little involved in such antagonistic interchanges. But what happens when the confrontations over our planet's limited strategic material resources become more acute? Who can guarantee that also under such, far from hypothetical, conditions the proxy wars are not turned into an all-destructive direct global war? For the unpalatable truth is that there cannot be a state of the capital system as a whole, because the state can only be the structurally entrenched and hierarchically dominant Leviathan state in confrontation not only with its own subordinate social class, but also with some other Leviathan state. Despite all attempts to project the contrary, the idea of harmonious globalization on the ground of capital's antagonisms is a self-contradictory fiction. No wonder that at times it is coupled with the nightmare-fantasy of the seriously advocated "global coercive state," as we shall see in the course of the present study.

I must add here the problem of antagonistically colliding ethnicity, combined at times with the revival of historically long persisting religious antagonisms. But even without this religiously antagonistic dimension the contradictions of ethnic confrontations are insoluble by capital's Leviathan state formations in global terms, as we witness their recurrent explosions in our contemporary world. The traditional way of dealing with ethnic confrontations—through the repressive violence imposed by the more powerful nation-state—is unthinkable as a historically sustainable global remedy in the future. For in the past even a fairly big nation-state could be subdued as a subordinate "ethnic entity" when the winning power was powerful enough to make its position prevail on a continuing basis. However, under the conditions of warfare with weapons of "Mutually Assured Destruction," the maintenance of that kind of domination—quite common in the imperialist past—becomes prohibitively dangerous in a politically and militarily globalizing world.

Compared to the ongoing devastating conflagrations in the Middle East on a vast scale, with their undeniable dimension of proxy war, the ethnic and religious conflicts between Armenian Christians and

Azeri Muslims in Nagorno Karabakh are minor. This conflict concerns a relatively small part of the land of Azerbaijan, populated, however, by overwhelmingly Christian Armenians who now claim independence—unrecognized by Azerbaijan. The grave problem is that in some of the armed confrontations of these two hostile ethnic communities, tens of thousands of people have lost their lives and the conflicts are renewed again and again.

In the aftermath of one of these particularly violent conflicts, a television crew went to the disputed hilly region of Nagorno Karabakh and interviewed an old Armenian shepherd asking him: "To whom does the land belong in the area where he was tending his flock?" The old shepherd answered the question with great wisdom: "The land belongs to the sheep."

However, the much more difficult question is: When will Leviathan begin to understand such an answer?

Alas, the answer can only be: never. For understanding the elementary truth and wisdom expressed in that answer is incompatible with Leviathan's nature.

Yet, this kind of question requires a rationally sustainable answer sometime in the not too distant future. But a rationally tenable answer is feasible only Beyond Leviathan! For Leviathan lived with, and exploited for its own purposes, the recurrence of such conflicts. It was always part of its normal *modus vivendi*.

THE DANGER OF GLOBAL CONFLAGRATION

The Leviathan state is failing in more ways than one. Let us consider, in conclusion, only the most dangerous aspect of the unresolved global confrontations. The controversy about it regularly enters the news headlines on account of the opponents of war questioning the legitimacy and safety of the existing nuclear weapons of mass destruction. In recent American presidential debates this controversy took the form of asking: "Whose finger is the safer finger for the delivery of the nuclear bombs on the adversary?" What a gruesome irony to talk about a "safe finger" meant to initiate the total extermination of humanity!

The same question was raised in Britain, when the newly appointed prime minister, Theresa May, was asked whether she would be willing to push the nuclear button. And she answered by saying that she can proudly give the answer: Yes, she would unhesitatingly push that button whenever she was expected to do so as the prime minister of the country. In contrast, the opposition leader was pilloried for saying no at an earlier occasion to the same question.

Obviously, with regard to this crucial matter, Leviathan in charge of the dominant states is playing with fire. And the fire being played with is all-destructive nuclear fire!

To be sure, playing with fire is by no means incompatible with Leviathan's nature. On the contrary, it was always inseparable from that nature in the modality of pursuing some kind of adventurism. For no inherent limits could be set to Leviathan in its determination for gaining overall control in its envisaged political/military domain. The particular Leviathan state could resort in the past to extreme adventurism until some more powerful Leviathan state prevailed over it. Destructive violence had to decide these matters in the end even in the confrontations of the most powerful Empires.

Today the situation is very different in the most relevant sense. To be sure, in view of the persistent social antagonisms of the capital system, the traditional way of settling disputes by war cannot be given up. Leviathan, as historically constituted, knows no other way of solving problems. However, finding self-assurance in the "security" of Mutually Assured Destruction, as it is advocated by capital's "strategic thinkers" in the political/military domain, is the conceivably most dangerous form of adventurism. But in contrast to the violent confrontations of the past, including even the two global wars of the twentieth century, in a future global war there can be no longer any victor in the end. There can be only the end itself.

Thus, in terms of all these problems we must bear in mind, the great dilemma is that humanity either succeeds in the foreseeable future in creating the conditions under which societal reproduction becomes sustainable within the rationally planned and managed decision-making framework of our planetary household, or the endemic violence inseparable from the historically constituted Leviathan states is bound to destroy humanity.

The radical critique of the state in its Marxian spirit is necessary above all for this reason. It must be pursued in the interest of going irreversibly Beyond Leviathan.

— ISTVÁN MÉSZÁROS
MARCH 18, 2017

PART ONE

From Relative to Absolute Limits: Historical Anachronism of the State

CHAPTER ONE

The Historic Anachronism and Necessary Supersession of the State

The state, as we know it, has been constituted across many centuries. In its present-day reality it confronts us with the historically specific determinations of the capital system as a structurally articulated and embedded mode of overall decision-making, with its own fundamental powers as well as their necessary limitations.

Despite all attempts—and corresponding vested interests—bent on the *eternalization* of this mode of overall societal decision-making, establishing conditions in which, as they say, "there can be no alternative," the state is *inherently historical*. This is true not only with respect to the *past*, its ground of objective determination and articulation, but also with regard to the *future* that circumscribes its historical viabilities (or their absence) in terms of the unfolding necessities and developments.

When addressing the grave issues of the state formations of our time, it is vital to keep everything in its proper historical perspective, contrary to the temptation to confine attention simply to the vicissitudes of the capitalist state. As Marx clearly underlined it, capital did not invent the production and exploitation of surplus labor.[1] Likewise, capital did not invent the state, nor did it invent the inescapable need for finding some modality of overall decision-making in all forms of society in tune with the prevailing requirements of the social metabolism.

The need to find and secure a *sustainable mode* of overall decision-making is much more fundamental than the *form* in which that mode can be articulated even on the broadest scale through the state. The need to have a sustainable mode of overall decision-making is an *insurmountable* requirement for humanity, compared to the historically limited form in which such mode can be institutionalized and enforced through the state. Inevitably, reversing the order of priorities deeply affects our understanding of the nature of the whole complex of related issues. Worse still, to confine our approach to the historically specific present-day dimension of the state would be hopelessly distorting.

What must be strongly underlined in the present context is that our primary concern is the nature and manifold transformations of the state in general in its epochal determinations. For the state in some of its forms of existence originated *thousands of years* before capitalism. This fact has weighty implications for grasping the inherent characteristics and the necessary limitations of the state. In this respect it must be recalled that capitalism, to use Marx's expression, *"dates historically speaking only from yesterday."*[2] Accordingly, in our critical assessment of the acute problems of the contemporary state we must evaluate not only the now clearly identifiable political contradictions but also a set of deep-seated and multidimensional historical relationships. This is because the complex relationships in question are characterized by a *materially grounded dialectical interaction* in which *changes* and actually feasible prospects of development cannot be made intelligible at all without fully taking into account the underlying *continuities*.

In this sense, bearing in mind also the significant continuities, the fundamental structural determinations of *the state as such* are of seminal importance. It is in virtue of the fundamental *structural* determinations of the complex of dialectical reciprocities and dynamic interchanges among the various factors of social continuity and discontinuity, inseparable from the historically shaped material ground, that the state can fulfill its decision-making role *transhistorically*, within well defined limits. This is so no matter how weighty might be the inexorably arising historical specificities that must be brought into play under the changing circumstances.

Thus, to take a crucial example, under the conditions of the capitalist mode of societal reproduction the *directly economic* compulsion of the producers in effectively determining the continuing class-oppressive relationship between capital and labor plays a paramount importance, as a *qualitatively novel*, historically specific social characteristic in overall decision-making compared to the slave-owning and feudal past. Indeed, paradoxically, in the *political* domain this *economically* dominant novelty helps create the false appearance of a—ideologically rationalized and idealized—*"democratic system."*

Yet the truth of the matter highlighted by the revealingly persistent epochal continuities inseparable from all forms of antagonistic political formations is that the capitalist state, despite all "democratic" self-mythology, could *never* in its history abandon the *authoritarian* and unceremoniously enforced exploitative *hierarchical* assertion of its rule. It always forcefully protected—and had to protect with all might at its disposal—the *decision-making power of the ruling class*. In our time, such power is vested in the "personifications of capital" (in Marx's words) on account of their *politically*—and even *militarily—secured proprietorship* of the means of production that controls the reproduction of the social metabolism in its entirety. By no means surprisingly, all this must be represented as being fully in consonance with "constitutionality" and unobjectionable "sovereignty," in the best interest of all.

However, the circumstance that the state as such can fulfill its role and assert its power across a variety of ages all the way to the present, even in terms of its most problematic, necessarily authoritarian, determinations, does not mean that it is bound to be able to do that indefinitely, as the apologists of the established order proclaim. Far from it. The state as such—and of course all of the particular state formations—are *inherently historical* within their structurally articulated overall limits, and *fatefully counter-historical* (that is, manifesting the most contradictory form of historicity) beyond such limits.

More concretely, the state is historical in its materially grounded objective constitution and structural determination. Like all human institutions, the state is itself historically produced and maintained across the ages. But by the same token, the state is also inevitably *subject* to the conditions required for making itself *historically viable and sustainable* (or not, when it tends to move toward failure). The overall decision-making power must engage with the *necessarily changing* conditions of historically shaped nature (including ecological ones related in a truly literal sense to a vital nature) so as to ensure the ongoing determinations of the societal reproduction process.

This means, in other words, that the state as the historically constituted "Sovereign" is not simply in a position of forcefully imposing on societal reproduction some *historical necessities* in tune with the prevailing material and structural determinations of their time. The state can certainly do that, as *one side* of the equation, according to the objectively identifiable conditions and institutional forces that happen to prevail under the given historical circumstances. At the same time, and inescapably, the state is also *necessarily subject* in a contrary sense to the newly unfolding *historical necessities*. This is evident not only when it becomes *out of tune* with the emerging, materially constituted needs and conditions of its limited historical specificity—as in the immediate crisis of some *particular* state formation. It is evident even more so in the *epochally defined* challenges to its innermost characteristics and objective structural determinations, whereby it has asserted its power across the ages, namely in the challenges posed to its overarching capacity as *the state as such*.[3]

It is in this sense that the state as constituted in history becomes *in our time* an overpowering *historic anachronism,* under the circumstances of its *epochally descending phase* of development. This elemental change represents not a passing trend but an *irreversibly* descending phase of development, when, as a matter of course, the state's normally enforced mode of operation not only loses its historical legitimacy but becomes *counter-historical* on account of the overall constitution of the *state as such*—and not simply as this or that particular state formation—*necessarily failing* to fulfill its customary overall decision-making and corrective functions in a historically viable form.

THE HISTORIC ANACHRONISM OF THE STATE 61

The *epochally changing* and in the longer run *necessarily prevailing* conditions characteristic of this descending phase of capital are not simply *historical contingencies* that could be more or less easily overcome through the adoption of some suitable *state measures*, as—for instance— the shift from traditional liberal democratic state practices to some dictatorial form of rule, like Benito Mussolini's fascist takeover in Italy experienced in the relatively recent past of European history.[4] They are qualitatively novel *historical necessities* precisely in view of their *epochally defined* character, underlining the grave *structural crisis of politics in general* and the crisis of the traditional mode of overall decision-making in terms of ultimately always authoritarian state-determinations.

The burdensome historical necessities in question, as manifest in the political domain, are not intelligible at all in and by themselves, contrary to the way in which they are as a rule assessed in the interest of retaining the state-legitimating framework of evaluation and social practice. For in actuality, the structural crisis of politics in our time matches in its own way the *structural crisis of capital's social metabolic order* as a whole. Consequently, the inherently *epochal determinations* of this combined structural crisis raise the need for appropriate *epochal solutions*, to be consciously adopted in due course in tune with the challenging *historical necessities*.

1. ANTAGONISTIC POLITICAL FORMATIONS

The materially grounded common denominator of *all* antagonistic political formations, from the most ancient empire-building attempts to the present-day "democratic systems," is the class-exploitative production and extraction of surplus labor. All antagonistic political systems are structurally embedded in some kind of social monopoly of property that can effectively control the given mode of material production and societal reproduction. Without that form of material grounding, the political systems in question would be totally incapable of sustaining themselves.

Understandably, antagonistic political formations are not constituted for eliminating or superseding class antagonism. Since they are materially based on the class-antagonistic modalities of controlling the societal reproduction process and the corresponding exploitative extraction of surplus labor, they must *preserve* it as their own *substantive ground*. And they can do that by sustaining in their own way the production-securing monopoly of property itself—under the historically, at any time feasible, form of its viability—in its given structural prevalence. That must be done no matter how antagonistically the class exploitative dominance of the existing order might be contested by the people who perform the necessary productive tasks. The *primary* role of antagonistic domination must therefore be directed at the social forces that might contest the production-securing monopoly of the historically, under the given conditions, sustainable means of societal reproduction.

To be sure, politically controlling a social metabolic order that is materially structured in an antagonistic way cannot be itself other than antagonistic by its innermost determination. Of course, the particular forms of antagonistic political control can and indeed must vary, from extreme dictatorial to formal democratic varieties, according to the historically changing circumstances. Likewise, as historical records demonstrate, even the particular class configurations of domination and structural subordination vary, in tune with the unfolding historical changes, from the slave-owning and feudal forms to the bourgeois. But the *substance* of the class-exploitative production and extraction of surplus-labor must remain, together with the class-interested usurpation of the overall power of decision-making.

Moreover, the impact of the antagonistically embedded and secured mode of overall decision-making by its very nature cannot be confined to the *internal* dimension of domination, as exercised over the structurally subordinated class of the given particular society. This modality of self-imposing decision-making with its *sovereign unlimitability* must also by necessity project its aspirations for domination *outward*. And, as a matter of principle, absolutely no outside forces are admissible as legitimately limiting the self-asserting power of the established antagonistic political formations without being perceived as violating this claimed "sovereignty" and being properly punished for it as a result.[5]

The sophisticated political and legal theories and justifications devised to this self-serving effect are, of course, elaborated at a relatively late stage of historical development. However, the antagonistic and destructive social practice of securing territorial expansion—from limited tribal conquests to the establishment of vast empires—at the cost of some adversary or enemy goes back to time immemorial.

In this sense, we are confronted by a *twofold antagonism:* the *internal* and the *external.* The latter is oriented to outward domination which would be inconceivable without securing through the *primary internal* class-domination the required stability capable of yielding outward conquests. Thus, the internal and external dimensions of self-assertion of all antagonistic political formations are inseparable. Accordingly, not only the *internal repression* of the structurally subordinated class but also *war,* on ultimately *unlimitable* scale, must be endemic to this usurpatory mode of antagonistic overall decision-making from which the overwhelming majority of society must be *substantively* excluded.

This is so even if, under the *formally "legitimated"* pretenses of nonexistent "consensuality," some incalculably destructive wars—like the relatively recent *Vietnam War,* or even more recently, the *Iraq War,* with their cynical justifications—are "lawfully" imposed on society, as demonstrated by the subsequent state-apologetic legal contortions. At the same time, given the dominance of the ruling ideology, historical consciousness in general is negatively affected in *every country* under the impact of state apologetics. In part, this is because war itself can and often does act in a mystifying way on historical memory. For this reason, so much remains to be both *clarified* and *rectified* in humanity's historical consciousness even when in *epochal terms* the antagonistic modality of overall decision-making power through the known political formations becomes a *historic anachronism,* at the irreversibly descending phase of humanity's class-oppressive systemic development.

2. THE EPOCHAL CRISIS OF THE STATE

It was Marx who, for the first time in history, conceptualized the fundamental *epochal dimension* of these untenable antagonistic structural determinations of the societal reproduction process. This became possible under the conditions of the renewed revolutionary uspheavals all over Europe in the 1840s, following the relative stability after the Napoleonic Wars. At that time, Marx fully realized that thousands of years of materially embedded and politically buttressed class antagonism cannot be overcome without the radical supersession of the state itself. This is why Marx advocated the withering away of the state until the end of his life, despite all disappointments in the development of the working-class movement itself that came to light in a most disheartening way at the time of the debates over the Gotha Program.

Those who deny his unending conviction regarding the necessary withering away of the state as such, from the time of his early critique of the state, are, knowingly or not, in complete disagreement not only with this one aspect of his conception but with the whole of it. For the Marxian view that capital had entered its *epochally irreversible* descending phase of development applied and continues to apply not only to the increasingly destructive economy in its direct relationship to nature, of which Marx was fully aware far ahead of anyone else in his time, but to the capital system in its entirety.[6] In his view, capital's descending phase of development in its entirety was irreversible in a truly epochal sense, irrespective of how difficult and contradictory the full consummation of the overall historical process, in all of its dimensions, might have to be.

Accordingly, it would make no sense at all to exempt the antagonistic political formations from such consideration. For, inseparably from capital's directly material reproductive order, the political dimension had also entered the epochally irreversible descending phase of its historical course of operation. In fact, one side of the two could *never* sustain itself on its own without the supporting power of the other. Moreover, under the emerging circumstances, the increasing material antagonisms could not be mastered by the ruling order without the corresponding transformation of the attempted state-imposed corrective measures through the articulation of the globally belligerent modern imperialism, as indeed we witnessed in the last three decades

THE HISTORIC ANACHRONISM OF THE STATE 65

of the nineteenth century. "Iron Chancellor" Count Otto von Bismarck was one of the most dominant figures of those dramatic decades. And he did not hesitate to enlist even some working-class support in his country for asserting German imperialist aspirations, with the treacherous secret collaboration by Ferdinand von Lassalle who played an infamous role in splitting the German working-class movement.

Thus, the withering away of the state as a contradictorily unfolding prospect appeared on the historical horizon not as the need to overthrow the capitalist state, a naively superficial idea held by many, which was already criticized by Marx., but in response to the fateful destructiveness and growing intensity of the capital system in its entirety. Thus, the historic challenge presented itself as the absolutely vital necessity to radically supersede all conceivable forms of the alienated, antagonistic modality of state-imposed political decision-making. Capital's clearly identifiable destructive power in the material domain could not be defeated in its own limited terms of reference in the materially productive sphere alone. The epochal sustainability of the state's decision-making power and the material preponderance of capital's mode of social metabolic control stood and could only fall together. This is what had set the fundamental emancipatory task—and continues to set it for the future as well—until it is successfully accomplished.

As I stressed in my Isaac Deutscher Memorial lecture, "The Necessity of Social Control," the critique of capital's epochally irreversible *destructiveness* was farsightedly confronted in Marx's writing at a very early stage.[7] At the time of sarcastically criticizing Ludwig Feuerbach for his vacuous characterization and idealization of "nature," Marx highlighted the unavoidable ecological damage produced by capitalistic industry in really existent nature. And in the same early work, on *The German Ideology*, he forcefully underlined that the fundamental structural change of the societal reproductive order that he was advocating concerned the vital historic stake of humanity's survival. This is how he developed that idea already there in different contexts, with growing intensity:

> In the development of the productive forces there comes a stage

when productive forces and means of intercourse are brought into being which, under the existing relations, only cause mischief, and are no longer productive but *destructive forces*....[8] These productive forces receive under the system of private property a one-sided development only and for the *majority* they become *destructive forces*....[9] Thus things have now come to such a pass that the individuals must appropriate the existing totality of productive forces, not only to achieve self-activity, but, also, merely to *safeguard their very existence*.[10]

Capitalism experienced a profound economic crisis throughout the 1850s and the early 1860s. So much so that even the editorial articles of the leading bourgeois theoretical organ, *The Economist*, were written with alarm and even gloom.[11] Nevertheless, while noticing this alarm and even tempted for rejoicing over it for some time, a note of caution was well in order on the socialist side of the fence. Thus, Marx wrote in a letter to Engels:

> There is no denying that bourgeois society for the second time is experiencing its 16th century, a 16th century which, I hope, will sound its death knell just as the first ushered it into the world. The proper task of bourgeois society is the creation of the world market, at least in outline, and of production based on that market. Since the world is round, the colonisation of California and Australia and the opening up of China and Japan would seem to have completed this process. For us, however, the difficult **question** is this: on the [European] Continent revolution is imminent and will, moreover, instantly assume a socialist character. Will it not necessarily be **crushed** in this *little corner of the earth*, since the **movement** of bourgeois society is still in the **ascendant** over a far greater terrain?[12]

This qualification was, of course, absolutely necessary. However, the crucial issue was and always remains that the potentially emerging, and for determinate historical circumstances actually prevailing, political and economic reversals do not eliminate the fundamental historic trend of the capital system's epochally descending phase, although they significantly modify its conditions of unfolding and ultimate assertion. The unavoidable, materially grounded difficulty in this respect is that in really existing history we find not only *tendencies* but inevitably *counter-tendencies*. And, of course, they necessarily interact with one another.

What ultimately decides the issue is the *inherent nature* of the objective historical tendencies and counter-tendencies themselves and the far from arbitrary or wishfully definable *character and modality* of their inevitable interactions. Since we are talking about the materially grounded reality of such interactions, their *reciprocity* is characterized by *objective determinations,* inseparable from their *structurally relevant* historical considerations. In other words, the historical tendencies and counter-tendencies cannot simply be presented in a one-to-one relationship to each other, irrespective of both their structurally and historically determined relative *weight*, equivalent to their *inherent nature*. In their reciprocity, these tendencies and counter-tendencies also have a *differential impact* on one another. And that is indeed what makes some of them historically more sustainable than the others, or even renders some of them with regard to their required historical viability absolutely unsustainable, no matter how much they might be able to dominate the given order—with their state-repressively imposed *counter-historical* preponderance—under the prevailing circumstances.

Grasping these difficult historical relationships in accordance with their true theoretical and practical importance is feasible only within the conceptual framework of a materially grounded *objective dialectic*. For, ignoring such vital material grounding and sweeping aside dialectics altogether can yield in theoretical terms only empty tautologies, and, in the domain of strategically relevant social practice, nothing but hopeless disorientation. Thus it was by no means accidental that the fateful disarming of the German Social Democratic movement that culminated in its disastrous capitulation to imperialism at the outbreak of the First World War was theoretically prepared by the neo-Kantian assault on dialectical thought, carried out by Friedrich Lange, Eugen

Dühring, and others in the last decades of the nineteenth century, in full affinity with the subsequent promotion of Bernsteinian revisionism.[13] This operation was conducted with great cynicism and hypocrisy. The proponents of the neo-Kantian wisdom were on the face of it thundering against Hegel, but their real target was Marx's revolutionary dialectic, which demonstrated the untenable contradictions of the established order and was generating a major impact on the working-class movement. This is what had to be rejected by the supporters of the established order, whose actions were so duplicitous that they had to be carried out in their pretended pro-workers' disguise. That line was followed because the Marxian dialectical exposure of the *systemic contradictions* of capital was concerned with a *materially vital* critique of the established societal reproductive order and its state formation. This is why dialectic had to be ruled out altogether by Marx's adversaries, in order to give some semblance of credibility to their own position.

To quote a letter by Marx:

> What Lange says about the Hegelian method and my application of it is really childish. First of all, he understands nothing about Hegel's method and secondly, as a consequence, far less even about my critical application of it. . . . Herr Lange wonders that Engels, I, etc., take the dead dog Hegel seriously when Büchner, Lange, Dr. Dühring, Fechner, etc., are agreed that they—poor dear—have buried him long ago.[14]

In this sense, it was the materialist, radically critical application of the dialectic to the antagonisms of the existing societal order that had to be eliminated by the neo-Kantian apologetics of society. Eduard Bernstein, too, glorified the same approach. He dismissed the fundamental tenets of Marx's theory (including in a prominent place the idea of any *social or political revolution*) with the pretext that such ideas were only "planks" of a *"dialectical scaffolding"* and in "modern society" they could not have any meaning. In his book of appallingly low theoretical standards, in the same spirit of insulting insolence with which he dismissed Marx's revolutionary theory as nothing more than "dialectical scaffolding,"

Bernstein rejected Marx as a "dualist thinker" and a "slave to a doctrine" while hypocritically paying lip-service to his "great scientific spirit" without indicating in any way what that "scientific spirit" by a "plank-peddler slave of a doctrine" might really amount to in the idealized "modern society." Moreover, with arrogant paternalistic attitude toward the workers, Bernstein also pretended to assume the *moral high ground*—by saying: "Just because I expect much of the working classes, I censure much more everything that tends to corrupt their moral judgement"—and doing that in the midst of his own cynically pursued moral betrayal of the cause of socialism.[15]

These were most revealing *responses* to the social and political crisis inseparable from the epochally descending phase of the capital system's development. For the historical antagonist and *hegemonic alternative* to capital, *labor*, had to be prevented by its own claimed "political arm" from taking a radical stand against the system. This was the primary function of "evolutionary socialism" propagandized without any ground of reality by Bernstein and his followers. In the end, their approach succeeded not in bringing the falsely postulated "evolutionary socialism" by the slightest degree nearer to its realization but, on the contrary, destroying German Social Democracy altogether.

The both theoretically and practically important point to stress is that the nefarious Bernsteinian etc. accommodatory response itself and the object of its disarming action—namely the forces that were beginning to engage in the period that we are talking about in confronting the historic anachronism of capital's rule and its repressive state—cannot be properly understood as standing in a one-to-one relationship. In truth, there is a very good reason why all talk simply about *"reciprocity"*—and of course as a rule conceived in a wishful sense as "mutually balancing reciprocity"—in relation to historical tendencies and counter-tendencies must produce empty tautologies in theory, combined with more or less veiled social apologetics. That reason is because the adoption of such an approach willfully ignores in the relationship concerned—despite its objectively given determinations—the moment or factor of *"overriding importance,"* called by Marx the *"übergreifendes Moment."*

In the real world, the response adopted against its adversary cannot arbitrarily reshape the inherent nature of the historical tendency to which it must respond. The response is a *response* and not some wholly self-constituting and materially, as well as politically, self-grounding entity or complex. As a time-bound counter-tendency arising under determinate historical circumstances, it must confront the problems or dangers represented by what it is called upon to counter with its own resources and modes of feasible action. But the counter-tendency is in the first place necessarily *dependent* on the objective determinations of the tendency to which it must respond. It cannot wipe out at will the given historical necessities and establish its own unchallengeable necessity on some absolute ground.

To be sure, *some* countermoves can always be devised by the ruling order even in a situation of extremely grave revolutionary crisis that threatens it. The ruling order has on its side both the immense material resources of societal reproduction—usable in many different ways against its opponents—and the violent repressive power of the state. But all that is very far from conclusive. For in the case of the capital system's epochally descending phase of development the real issue is and necessarily remains: whether or not the *countermeasures* of the response adopted under the given conditions are *sustainable* not just for the moment but for a *historically viable* future.

As we know from the historical chronicle, the *response* of late nineteenth-century capitalism to its intensifying crisis was the establishment of *monopolistic imperialism*. That is to say, the institution of a form of imperialism that had to be very different from its historical antecedents in the past in a crucial sense. For the new imperialism had to reconstitute itself on increasingly *monopolistic material productive foundations*. At the same time—piling up explosive dangers on the military plane on a totally unforeseeable scale—the monopolistic imperialist capital system was utterly incapable of overcoming its customary military collisions among the handful of dominant state powers that inevitably had to contest one another, as is inherent in the nature of the established national state formations.

The question that remains to be answered: Is this response to capital's epochally descending phase of development—both in the material field and in the state-legitimated political domain—historically viable? As we had to learn from bitter historical experience, the fundamental objective determinations of monopolistic imperialism in the material domain, coupled with the systemic failure to overcome the necessary antagonisms of the national state formations on the political plane, carried with it in due course the necessary eruption of *two world wars*, with their devastating consequences, including the extermination of hundreds of millions of people. This is the undeniable historical record.

Thus, the *response* of the capital system to its epochally descending phase of historical development—characterized by ever-increasing *destructiveness*—was *fatefully self-contradictory*. For the untenable systemic *destructiveness* that perilously signaled the arrival of the epochally descending phase of development itself and brought to the historic stage the *necessary hegemonic alternative* to capital's rule was "countered" by capital through a formerly even unimaginable *escalation of destructiveness* both in the domain of material reproduction, with its uncontrollable impact on nature, and on the state-repressive and military plane, foreshadowing the very real danger of humanity's total self-destruction in the event of another global war. Obviously, *nothing* could be historically less viable than that.

3. A GLOBAL COERCIVE STATE?

In our time, inescapably, the requirement of long-term *historical viability* includes in its concept the necessity of *global sustainability*. In the more remote past this constraint did not assert itself, of course. Imperial conquests and state repressive actions could be pursued without any consideration of their global implications. And even at the outset of the epochally descending phase of the capital system's development, vast areas of planet Earth, with immense populations, were still left behind in a materially productive sense. This offered for some time ample opportunity for monopolistic imperialism to assert its counter-tendency and prolong the capital system's life span.

To be sure, on the military plane the *prohibitive* dimension of humanity's antagonistic interchanges appeared with nuclear weapons soon after the Second World War. But even then *material destructiveness* in the industrially productive domain, also affecting nature on a potentially irreversible scale, was still far less than what it has become as a result of the eruption of the capital system's *structural crisis* through the activation of its *absolute limits*.[16] Thus, in our time, the refusal to abandon the prospect of military destruction on a potentially global scale, as the ultimate arbiter over the necessarily persistent and even intensifying global antagonisms, have become *absolutely prohibitive*. Accordingly, no solution to humanity's antagonistic contradictions can be considered *rational* unless the necessary requirement of its *historical viability* is simultaneously combined with its *global sustainability*.

However, notwithstanding the absolutely prohibitive character of ongoing destruction, the promoters of vested interests defy even the elementary demand for rationality. Instead of *attending to the causes* of global antagonisms in order to overcome them in substantive terms at their social metabolic ground, they advocate the escalation of *state repression* as the enforced "remedy" of their *consequences*. All of this is in the spirit of the fairy tale of "putting the genie back in the bottle," and doing that even in global terms. Thus, the pernicious notion of *"Liberal imperialism"*—on the pretext of acting against "failed states"—was championed most irresponsibly in this sense quite recently. In the same sense, a prominent writer in the field of bourgeois political economy, Martin Wolf, arbitrarily used the self-justificatory notion of "the global community"—in the name of which the most brutal violations of elementary human rights are in fact committed by U.S. imperialism and its "willing allies"—insisting that "the global community also needs the *capacity* and *will to intervene* where states have failed altogether."[17]

In this way, violent state intervention and repression is advocated, despite its potentially catastrophic consequences. And no one can say how far its aggressive endorsement can go. For even the nightmare conception of a *"global coercive state"* is advocated in the name of— wait for it— "rationality" as such. Thus, we read in G. C. A. Gaskin's introduction to the Oxford University Press edition of *Leviathan* by

Hobbes that "it would be *rational* to form a World State, or, one might add, at the very least a United Nations with *sovereign coercive powers.*"[18] Gaskin's notion of such "rationality," which is a complete absurdity, was based on Howard Warrender's article on Hobbes published in *Encyclopedia Americana*. Naturally, at the original roots of such pernicious "rationality" we find the belligerent wishful thinking that global state repression, exercised by the United States, would be permanently capable of fulfilling the role of a "sovereign coercive power." Of course, no one should doubt that there are many believers in that disastrous notion in very powerful state decision-making circles today, especially in the United States. Toward the end of the last millennium, the aggressive propagandists of boundless U.S. power were saying that the twentieth century was the *"American Century,"* and from now on the entire new millennium will be the *"American Millennium."* One is reminded of Sir Winston Churchill's projections that the *British Empire*—over which he was presiding at the time—will be maintained in its glory "over the next thousand years."

But there are some sobering questions that must be faced in terms of the projected "global coercive state."

1. How could the mind-boggling amount of material resources required be provided on a *globally* extended scale, as well as on a *continuing* basis, for such a "global coercive state," at a time when we are experiencing the unacknowledged *state bankruptcy* of the most powerful capitalist states. In the case of the United States, that bankruptcy is approaching the astronomic figure of *twenty trillion* dollars;
2. Would not the *cost* of U.S. destructively coercive action, of which relatively small samples have become evident—in their already prohibitive magnitude—in Vietnam, Afghanistan, and Iraq, have to be *absolutely prohibitive*? Well before the humiliating defeat in the Vietnam War, General Dwight Eisenhower voiced his critique of the catastrophically wasteful and inexorably rising military expenditure. He did that at a time when the *"economic black hole"* in the United States was still very far from the now undeniable astronomic figure;

3. Above all, when will the aggressive state-repression theorists begin to *admit* that the *primary meaning of Sovereignty*—based on the *objective ground* of its necessary determination—is the necessary *internal dominance* over the structurally subordinate members of the given nation-state? Any projection of Sovereignty *outward*, for the purpose of subduing the encountered *interstate* antagonism represented by some other state, must have that *internal domination secured* as the *precondition* of its potentially successful action. Moreover, it must have such internal domination not simply in accordance with the *"Political Theory of Possessive Individualism."*[19] All "possessive *individualism*" in the domain of sovereignty must be constituted as *class-repressive* dominance over those structurally deprived of production-controlling property. Without that it cannot have any meaning at all.

Thus the presumption that the *politically* devised "global coercive state"—situated in the United Nations, or wherever else—could exercise its projected coercive functions without attending to, and eliminating, the *internal antagonisms* that are bound to be generated at the material reproductive level of the particular countries, is totally devoid of meaning. For the elementary requirement in this respect is the radical overcoming of *class-repressive internal antagonism* substantively embedded and hierarchically entrenched in the established social metabolic order.

4. THE STRUCTURAL BARRIERS TO EQUALITY

For a very long time in history it seemed to be workable to dismiss opposition to social antagonism, provided that the authoritarian imposition of order could prevail. In France, for instance, the commoners of the Third Estate, made up at the early stage of capitalistic developments predominantly by the bourgeois forces—who were for some time welcome alongside the other two Estates in the National Consultative Assembly, the Clergy, and the Nobility—could be readily ignored in this way by authoritarian royal power by not summoning that assembly after 1614, until the explosion of the French Revolution itself in 1789.[20] Ironically, however, by the time of the Revolution large masses of workers had greatly swollen the ranks of the Third Estate, creating thereby immense problems for the future. In fact, those great masses played a seminal role at the initial phase of the French Revolution.

Some of the great intellectual figures of eighteenth-century Enlightenment tried to offer a solution to the growing social and political problems without the advocacy of major societal change. They were able to do this thanks to their paradoxical view that the advancement of reason was wedded to a natural system of equality and justice mediated by capital's material-productive power. Thus Adam Smith, for instance, forcefully argued for this Enlightenment vision:

> As every individual ... endeavours as much as he can both to employ his capital in the support of *domestic* industry, and so to direct that industry that its produce may be of the greatest value; every individual necessarily labours to render the annual revenue of the society as great as he can. He generally, indeed, neither intends to promote the public interest, nor knows how much he is promoting it. By preferring the support of domestic to that of foreign industry, he intends only his own security.... By pursuing his own interest he frequently promotes that of the society more effectually than when he really intends to promote it.[21]

Thanks to this firmly held belief about the harmony between individual self-serving interest and nature itself in terms of the public good in general, Smith did not hesitate for a moment to *exclude* not only individual politicians but even the given political institutions from the all-round beneficial management of the productive system which in his view should not be interfered with. This is how he stressed that issue:

> The statesman, who should attempt to direct private people in what manner they ought to employ their capitals, would not only load himself with a most unnecessary attention, but assume an authority

which could safely be trusted, not only to no single person, but to *no council or senate* whatever, and which would nowhere be so dangerous as in the hands of a man who had the folly and presumption enough to fancy himself fit to exercise it.[22]

However, with the eruption of the American and the French Revolutions it became very clear that it was not enough to marginalize the old political order. Something very different had to be put in its place also in the political domain, in view of the intensification of the class antagonisms. For in the French Revolution the great masses of workers—constituting the large majority of society—were beginning to assert their own class interests in their unavoidable conflicts with the bourgeoisie.

In this sense, with the unfolding of the French Revolution, the traditional way of addressing these problems at times of major crises in history—that is, by replacing one type of *ruling personnel* by another, for example, the slave-owning type by its feudal variant, without radically changing the structurally entrenched modality of class oppression itself—had become extremely problematical, to say the least. And that fundamental social dimension of the necessity of societal change that could positively involve the great masses of the working people *never* disappeared again from the social antagonisms. On the contrary, major revolutions in the nineteenth and twentieth century continued to reactivate it, ever closer to a truly global scale, despite temporary reversals and defeats.

Before the French Revolution the most radical of French intellectuals, Jean-Jacques Rousseau, tried to highlight the irrepressible social structural dimension of the antagonism in question. He characterized in a powerful, sarcastic way the existing state of affairs between the ruling order and those who suffered by it:

> The terms of the social contract between these two estates of man may be summed up in a few words: "You have need of me, because I am rich and you are poor. We will therefore come to an agreement. I will permit you to have the honor of serving me, on condition that

you bestow on me the little you have left, in return for the pains I shall take to command you."[23]

The most important part of Rousseau's proposed solution was the adoption of the *General Will* as the way to regulate fundamental decision-making in accordance with the advancement of reason that could counter antagonistic destructiveness. That idea of his advocacy remained by far the most seriously discussed and defended part of his vision to our own days, despite all misrepresentation. Rousseau made it absolutely clear that the idea of *Liberty* could not be sustained on its own, against those who were ignoring the demand for social equality. Indeed, he even categorically asserted that *"liberty cannot exist without [equality]."*[24] The great *Libertador* of South America from Spanish rule, Simón Bolívar, forcefully asserted in his actions the belief in equality in Rousseau's spirit, despite fierce opposition by vested social interests even on his own side.

As we know, Rousseau was no longer alive at the outbreak of the French Revolution but predicted its coming by warning that "I regard [it] as inevitable. Indeed, all the kings of Europe are working in concert to hasten its coming."[25] However, the grave problem remained in Rousseau's theory that the fundamental social antagonism in question was inseparable from production-controlling private property, which *excluded* the overwhelming majority of the people. This was what required a *structurally* different answer from what could be provided even in Rousseau's radical theoretical framework.

The fundamental premises of Rousseau's system were the assumption of *private property* as the sacred foundation of civil society and the *"middle condition"*—his way of introducing social equality—as the only valid form of *distribution* adequate to sacred private property in his view. This is how Rousseau argued his case: "It is certain that the *right of property* is the most sacred of all the rights of citizenship, and even *more important* in some respects than *liberty itself* . . . property is the true foundation of civil society, and the real guarantee of the undertakings of citizens: for if property were not answerable for personal actions, nothing would be easier than to evade duties and laugh at the laws."[26]

Regarding the "middle condition," according to Rousseau its necessity was inherent in the requirements of social life itself. This is how he had put that point: "Under bad governments equality is only apparent and illusory; it serves only to keep the pauper in his poverty and the rich man in the position he has usurped. In fact, laws are always of use to those who possess and harmful to those who have nothing: from which it follows that the social state is advantageous to men only when *all have something and none too much.*"[27]

What was missing from Rousseau's noble vision was a tenable insight into the uncontrollable *self-expansionary dynamism* of capital (which happened to be much better understood by Smith and other bourgeois political economists) and the necessary *material power relations* that had to go with capital's preponderant self-expansion. Consequently, all talk about the naively equitable "middle condition" could only be swept aside sooner or later by actual historical development as utopian wishful thinking. For it was never enough—nor could it ever be even remotely enough in the future—to advocate, no matter with how genuinely held the intentions are, a more equitable *distribution* of wealth without clearly defining the modality of its *production*. In such matters the question of *production* always plays the role of the earlier discussed "moment or factor of overriding importance" (the Marxian *übergreifendes Moment*). This is because critically unquestioned production easily prejudges admissible distribution in favor of its own perpetuation.

5. FORMAL VERSUS SUBSTANTIVE EQUALITY

By the time the great German Enlightenment philosopher Immanuel Kant struggled with these problems, well after the outbreak of the French Revolution, social explosion and military violence engulfed not only France but a significant part of Europe, with a fearful tendency to engulf all of it. Thus, the philosopher offered his alternative to the ongoing bloodletting in these terms:

> The narrower or wider community of all nations on earth has in

fact progressed so far that a violation of law and right in one place is felt in all others. Hence the idea of a *cosmopolitan or world law* is not a fantastic and *utopian* way of looking at law, but a necessary completion of the unwritten code of constitutional and international law to make it a public law of mankind. Only under this condition can we flatter ourselves that we are continually approaching *eternal peace*. No one less than the great artist of nature (*natura daedala rerum*) offers such a guarantee. Nature's mechanical course evidently reveals a *teleology:* to produce *harmony from the disharmony of men even against their will*. . . . The relation and integration of these factors into the end (the moral one) whi*ch reason directly prescribes* is very sublime in theory, but is *axiomatic* and well founded in practice, e.g. in regard to the concept of a *duty toward eternal peace* which that *mechanism* promotes.[28]

In this way, Kant was keen to underline that his own solution to the apparently intractable contradictions was nothing like wishful thinking or the approval of an unrealizable world of utopia on his part. He insisted that what we were witnessing, in his view in a paradoxically violent form, was in fact *nature's teleology* (a kind of Providence) for the *moral end* prescribed by reason itself against—but in a strange way precisely *through—*the selfish ends pursued by the individuals against each other. Thus, he extended reason—in that way qualified— to the moral domain and he did that with reference not only to the idea of nature's sublime teleology but to the projected *mechanism* of nature to promote the *duty of eternal peace*. To a very limited extent, in Rousseau's spirit, Kant even tried to embrace the idea of the General Will, provided that what he called its "practically ineffectual" character could be remedied. This is how he tried to achieve that transformation with his own completion of reason's demand:

> *Nature* comes to the aid of this revered, but *practically ineffectual general will* which is founded in reason. It does this by the *selfish propensities* themselves, so that it is only necessary to *organize the state well* (which is indeed within the ability of man), and to direct these

forces *against each other* in such wise that one *balances the other* in its devastating effect, or even suspends it. Consequently, the result for reason is *as if* both selfish forces were *nonexistent*. Thus man, though not a morally good man, is compelled to be a *good citizen*.[29]

Naturally, actual historical developments refused to adapt themselves to Kant's noble but totally utopian scheme of things, despite the alleged "natural mechanism" that was supposed to turn the forces directed *against* each other into an outcome effectually *balancing* them for the purpose of universally prevailing *good citizenship* in harmony with the moral end. War and military destruction continued for decades even in the post-revolutionary French and European context, between 1795 when Kant wrote his article on *Eternal Peace* and the end of the Napoleonic Wars twenty years later, and it *never* looked like ending its ever more perilous hold over human affairs to our own days. For some years after the First World War, people continued to talk about it in a genuine, but very naïve critical sense, as *"the war to end all wars."* But as a matter of brutally sobering reality, *two decades* later the antagonistically divided forces of humanity were fighting each other in another *global war*. And in our time, in place of securing "Eternal Peace," only the certainty of humanity's total self-destruction has been added—with the weapons of nuclear, chemical, and biological mass destruction—to the explosive dangers of our antagonistic social metabolic order, under the ultimate command structure of our historically anachronistic state, in the event of yet another global war.

In Kant's own scheme of things everything remained within the *political domain*, notwithstanding the German philosopher's moral exhortations and his postulated teleological mechanism of nature. What made all such schemes utterly hopeless was that the *material structural determinations* of the established social reproductive order could not be subjected to any *substantive critique* in the interest of a sustainable qualitative change.

That was the reason the projected "cosmopolitan or world law"— reanimated in the twentieth century even in some institutional variety, like the League of Nations—remained precisely "a fantastic and *utopian* way of looking at law," despite its eloquent denial of such a view by Kant himself. For in reality even the most solemnly decreed laws can be—and as a rule are indeed—twisted and turned with the greatest ease, in the service of diametrically opposed interests, whenever the underlying *material determinations* so require.

The insuperable contradiction in this respect was—and still remains—the wishfully envisaged removal of the *material* dimension of the social antagonisms and their attempted transformation into merely *formal* determinations and differences, under the presumed authority of the stipulated law.

Kant very clearly spelled out this line of approach, with a perversely presumed analogy with some kind of "natural" order of appalling inequality. These were the words of his attempted justification of the unjustifiable:

> The welfare of one man may depend to a very great extent on the will of another man, just as the poor are dependent on the rich and the one who is dependent must obey the other as a child obeys his parents or the wife her husband or again, just as one man has command over another, as one man serves and another pays, etc. Nevertheless, all *subjects* are *equal* to each other *before the law* which, as a pronouncement of the *general will*, can only be one. This law concerns *the form and not the matter of the object* regarding which I may possess a right.[30]

To be sure, no one in their right mind would today ask women to obey their husbands in the way Kant presumed to be right; nor indeed order the members of the structurally subordinate class to "obey the rich who pay them" in the spirit of the Kantian upside-down vision of the material reproductive order. But can we talk today about the *substantive reality* of the legally proclaimed equality of men and women in our society? Or could we consider even for a moment right and proper the monstrous substantive inequalities in our society in all domains just because the law puts its blessing on them?

Tragically, Kant was proved to be right in that the system of law enforced by the state prevailed—and continues to prevail—in the sense that the "equality of the citizens as subjects" acknowledges only the *"form and not the matter"* of the vital issues over which a radically different solution is absolutely imperative. This is why the "citizens' equality" still boils down to the "equal right" to put periodically a piece of paper into the ballot box whereby they *abdicate* their power of decision-making to the ruling order.

Thus, Kant succeeded in "remedying" the "practically ineffectual character of Rousseau's General Will" by emptying it of its material content and turning it into a merely formal device of the pretendedly equitable law. In that way we were also supposed to forget that according to Rousseau, "Laws are always of use to those who possess and harmful to those who have nothing."[31] Thus, Kant had no difficulty whatsoever in decreeing that "the *general equality* of men as subjects in a state coexists quite readily with the *greatest inequality* in the degrees of the *possessions* men have."[32]

6. THE SUBSTANTIVE POWER OF DECISION-MAKING

But here we have arrived at an absolutely fundamental question for our own time. Phrasing that seminally important question in terms of iniquitously distributed material possessions, as it is customarily done in a self-justifying way even among some of the greatest thinkers of the Enlightenment, as we have just seen it done by Kant, is like *"putting the cart before the horse,"* so that it cannot—and rightfully should not—move forward at all. For the way in which material possessions are shared among the individuals, as well as by the social classes, is necessarily *dependent* on a much more fundamental concept of *possession*. And that overarching possession asserts itself as the power capable of allocating the great variety of material possessions among the people.

It is this fundamental concept of possession that has primacy over these issues, directly cutting into the heart of the matter of meaningful equality, in contrast to the reduction of both substantive possession and substantive equality by the social individuals into tendentiously class-exploitative *formal* determinations. To name that absolutely fundamental concept: it is none other than the *possession of the power of decision-making* by the social individuals in a *substantive* and not merely formal sense over all matters of their life.

In the course of history, as we have known it prevailing in its antagonistic modality of social metabolic reproduction, that fundamental *substantive* power of decision-making has been alienated from the social body and exercised by the ultimate command structure of the state in a necessarily *usurpatory* way. As the unavoidably hierarchical superimposed overall command structure—in perpetuation of the established antagonistic social metabolic order—the state *could not* and *cannot* function in any other way, no matter how destructive the consequences might be, even in the form of *global wars*. And the tragic truth remains that the *substantive possession of the power of decision-making* has *never* been returned to the social individuals, not even when the proclaimed *"new type of the state"* promised to found its radically different social legitimacy on that basis.

Significantly, Kant spoke of *"degrees* of the possessions men have," claiming at the same time the full compatibility of their *"greatest inequality"* with Rousseau's General Will emptied of its material content. However, the qualification of *degrees* is applicable only to the kind of iniquitous material possessions defended by Kant and others. The real problem, which happens to be quite insurmountable by the Kantian—or indeed by any other—formal-reductionist device, including the most promoted fiction of the "equitable democratic state" and its ballot box, is that there can be *no degrees of the most vital possession* in question. For that absolutely fundamental type of possession is equivalent to *the substantive power of decision-making* by the social individuals over all matters of their life. That is what had been alienated from the social body ever since the constitution of *separate organs of overall decision-making* across history in the great variety of state formations.

In truth, we either have that *substantive*—that is, not vacuously formal and in reality nullified—decision-making power *or not*. Talking about only *degrees* of it is *self-contradictory,* as it would be if we tried to do the same in the case of "degrees of substantive equality." For if we have only some *degree* of substantive decision-making, the question inevitably arises: Who has the rest of it? And the meaning of that question in the form of a self-evident answer is that, whoever might have it, *we do not have it!* Indeed, in actuality we do not have it because—as a matter of the structurally entrenched *systemic* determination of our *antagonistic* social metabolic order—the *state itself usurps that power of decision-making,* in its superimposed modality of functioning as the *overall command structure* of societal decision-making. Moreover, what makes matters even more difficult in this respect is the historically determined necessity whereby usurping the power of overall decision-making by the state is not an arbitrary process of *"state excesses,"* corrigible by some enlightened intervention in the *political domain* itself, as even the best liberal political theorists diagnosed it in vain. For the duration of its historical necessity—defined by the unfolding historical development itself as a *"vanishing"* necessity—the state is *mandated* to be the usurper of overall decision-making by the *structurally entrenched antagonistic determinations* of our historically constituted social metabolic order.[33] This is what needs to be radically altered at its *causal foundations* if we want to envisage a historically viable solution to our potentially all-destructive antagonisms.

All state formations in history asserted that power of decision-making over *substantive* matters, in a correspondingly *substantive way,* no matter what might be the "formally equitable" ideological rationalization and legitimation of their actions. It is also characteristic of all state formations in history that the violent antagonistic confrontations over their rival borders were endemic to their mode of ultimate decision-making. Capital did not invent wars, just as it did not invent the exploitation of surplus labor. But it certainly created the conditions of *absolutely prohibitive global wars* not only in the form of its now readily available all-destructive weaponry but primarily through the *materially invasive globalization* of its reproductive structures that cannot be matched by some global state formation. The historic anachronism of the state itself on the persistent antagonistic material ground of the capital system is the necessary concomitant of such developments.

Between the two global wars in the twentieth century, one could still dream about the efficacy of some kind of Kantian League of Nations in the service of "Eternal Peace," but not for long. Now the "realists of power" can only project the nightmare solution of a *global coercive state*.

Is there another way of radically overcoming this antagonistic destructiveness when its perpetuation under superimposed state legitimacy becomes suicidal to humanity? That is the absolutely vital question that in our time needs an urgent answer.

CHAPTER TWO

Freedom Is Parasitic on Equality

The ultimate *explanatory ground* of separate/alienated *political decision-making* across history—in other words, its transhistorically recurrent and reimposed *causal foundation*—is the *expropriation of surplus-labor in class society*. That must be the structurally entrenched, at all cost enforced, and in every possible way secured, *precondition* for the ongoing reproduction of all such society. The same determination also happens to be the principal reason why at times of major *periodic crises* and even the *"overthrow"* of any one of the forms of such society, only the *"change in personnel"* prevails. This is the case even when the given *form* (for instance the feudal) is *transmuted* into another *form* (namely the bourgeois), while retaining their shared *class-exploitative*—that is, surplus-labor expropriating—*substance*.

In this way we see transformations from *slavery* to *feudal* and from *feudal* to *capitalist* forms. Also, *within* capitalist formations we are confronted by changes from a variety of *dictatorial* to politically *democratic* forms or, revealingly, the other way around. What is highly revealing in the latter respect is the periodic *"come-and-go"* type of change between *democracy* and more or less enduring *dictatorships*. For nothing can be allowed significantly to interfere with the substantively class exploitative societal reproduction process. In the course of historical development, it at times becomes necessary to adopt some promising political contingencies that point in the direction of potentially substantive change. However, as a rule they must be clawed back if they threaten the dominance of the class-determined antagonistic modality of surplus-labor expropriation.

Aristotle's philosophical genius can offer a broad range of classificatory descriptions of "*Politeia*" (modes of politically exercised rule or "constitution" in the modern sense) but no *causal explanation* whatsoever as to *why* and *how* they are generated and *why* they differ or change. Obviously, in his time in Ancient Greece he could not have a concept of surplus-labor-exploiting class formations that had to prevail also in the political domain.

Similarly, *Hegel*'s philosophical genius can identify historical development in terms of the advancement/unfolding of *Freedom* (definitionally linked in his philosophy to the unfolding and advancement of *Reason)*, but no explanation whatsoever of its *WHY?*, other than the declamatory assumption of "the ways of God," the *Weltgeist*'s (World Spirit's) *Thaeodicaea*. In both cases we notice the class-determined total absence of any sympathy for *substantive equality*.

The substantive relationship between equality and freedom is one of the greatest problems in history itself as well as in its conceptualizations in philosophy. Not surprisingly, in idealist philosophy this vital relationship is presented in a most problematical way. Yet, the key to understanding the idealistically projected "advancement of freedom" itself is the *objectively unfolding* attainment of the historically emerging *type and degree of equality*. For "freedom" in any one of its historically identifiable forms is necessarily *parasitic* on the actually given form and margin of *equality*. In other words, the attainable nature and degree of freedom itself is *feasible*—and in that way also really meaningful—on the more or less limited *margin* of the attained (or indeed *attainable*) form and degree of substantive, materially feasible and historically sustainable equality. This is an absolutely vital consideration both in relation to the assessment of the historical past and in terms of our future.

It is most relevant to recall in this sense the address of *Cyrus the Great* to the "Commoners," as chronicled by Xenophon. These were the most remarkable words of the young warrior and future King of Persia:

> Fellow-citizens of Persia, you were born and bred upon the same soil as we [Peers]; the bodies you have are no whit inferior to ours, and it is not likely you have hearts in the least less brave than our own. In spite of this, in our own country you did not enjoy equal privileges with us, not because you were excluded from them by us, but because you were obliged to earn your own livelihood. Now, however, with the help of the gods, I shall see to it that you are provided with the necessaries of life; and you are permitted, if you wish, to receive arms like ours, to face the same danger as we, and, if any fair success crowns our enterprise, to be counted worthy of an equal share with us.[1]

It goes without saying, the objective historical circumstances had to have the last word, not Cyrus the Great. For in his society, like in all class societies, the crucial question remained: what happens to the socially/economically subordinate position of the people in question when the "Commoners," decreed to be equal by the future King, as they were indeed in their substantive humanity properly acknowledged by Cyrus, had to return home from the war? The "freedom" and privilege conceded to them earlier, matching those of their Peers, was both required—for the sake of military success—and conditioned by the objectively available substantive equality of the given conditions themselves. But they could not be generalized as the historically feasible normality of their society as a whole. On the contrary. The returning "Commoners" had to be inserted again into the dominant class-exploitative structure of their society and carry on producing not only their own "daily provisions" but also those of their "Peers," as required by the prevailing modality of surplus-labor extraction.

1. A RADICALLY DIFFERENT SOCIAL LOGIC AS AN OBJECTIVE NECESSITY

Another vital aspect of this question of the objectively prevailing modality of surplus-labor expropriation and appropriation concerns the historical issue of *primitive egalitarian communality* mentioned by Marx in his *Grundrisse*. To quote Marx's words:

> History shows *common property* (e.g. in India, among the Slavs, the early Celts, etc.) to be the more original form, a form which long continues to play a role in the shape of communal property.... It is simply wrong to place exchange at the centre of communal property as the original constituent element.[2]

Understandably, it is relatively easy to envisage egalitarian communality at the level of directly nature-imposed necessity as *equitable distribution/sharing* when the *imperative of survival* prevails and conditions human behavior. Once, however, an *increasing surplus* (and the consciousness of feasible further increases) enters the picture, *conflict* over a *differential* appropriation (and most unequal *expropriation)* of such surplus by *force*—capable of being *institutionalized* in that way—goes with it.

Paradoxically, the *new modalities of increasing surplus* in history are opened up at the detriment of egalitarian communality. This happens primarily for the benefit of those who gain *control* over the *regulative processes* and *institutionalize* them in a far from egalitarian/communal form. And then, conjointly, the *separate/alienated logic* of the controlling institution itself pursues *its own course* for a long *historical period*. For as long, that is, as the most unequal *institutional logic itself* is capable of pursuing its course, asserting its power all the way to the *historical limit of its viability*.

However, there can be no possibility of its *absolute permanence*, in view of the correlated determinations and constraints of *objective factors.* (To mention briefly some of them: the conditioning force of the available planetary resources, the unfolding changes in science that open up alternative avenues, the development of consciousness, the socially generated and exploding antagonisms, political and social radicalization, etc.) In due course they call for the institution of a *radically different social logic.* That is, they call for the consciously controllable institution of a historically sustainable logic, in contrast to the known forms of more or less *blind* and violently self-imposing/ alienated institutionalization of class exploitation, as happens to be the case under the rule of antagonistically self-imposing and cancerously expansionary capital.

In this sense, it is necessary to stress the vital importance of fully acknowledging both the *objective potentialities* and the historically *unfolding limits,* including in our time the emerging *absolute limits* of the still dominant capital system.

2. THE FETISHISTIC FORMAL DETERMINATION OF SOCIAL LABOR

The *fundamental determinant* in this crucial relationship between the political formations and the expropriation of surplus-labor is the historically prevailing (and of course changing) *production* of social wealth, and the *modality* in which its appropriation/expropriation can be *secured* on a *continuing* basis—in tune with the given historical circumstances as stable as attainable. This kind of development carries with it the necessary activation of the unfolding and coalescing forces of Customs, Tradition, and Legality in the service of the *overall* (comprehensive) *decision-making* process, oriented toward *expropriative appropriation* of the given historical type. This set of relationships constitutes the explanatory ground of the *epochally* meaningful transformations as well as the intelligibility of the *ascending* and *descending* phases of their development.

In order to understand the dynamics of historical development, it is important to focus on the necessary correlation of the internal and external/international economic and political constituents. Internally the different state formations play a crucial role in the enforcement of the required class domination. At the same time, the *international* dimension of this set of relationships is equally important, from the *primitive territorial* self-assertion that generates antagonisms, in the service of the required resources even at a very limited scale, all the way to the *empire-building* forms of self-assertion and expansion, together with their ultimately unavoidable limits, as clearly demonstrated by the fate of *all* past empires, no matter how great at some point in their history.

With the unfolding of capital's power in European history, *major changes* take place on the ground of what can be brought with greater efficacy into the economically exploitable domain. Most important in this respect is the historical change with regard to the *alienability of land,* in contrast to its prohibition in the more remote feudal past, carrying with it significant changes in political formations. This seminal change is paradigmatically encapsulated in the shift from what is called *"nulle terre sans Seigneur"* (no land without its Master, the authoritarian feudal lord, possessor of even the "right to behead his recalcitrant servants") to *"l'argent n'ait pas de maître"* (money has no Master). Such shift calls for a radically different legislative and executive process, in a qualitatively changed overall political decision-making framework. In due course the same considerations must be applied to the *"emancipation of usury"* by being turned into respectable *interest,* in contrast to its past condemnation even by the highest Church authority, although the emancipation of usury (in the service of capital expansion and accumulation) carries with it not far in the future the ironic result of the significant curtailment of the power of the Church itself.[3]

Once the dominant modality of surplus-labor expropriation acquires the form of *universal commodification* (and universal alienability/profitability that must include land and usury/interest), it must carry with it universal equalizability of the commodities offered on the market, and thereby an utterly spurious form of *"universality"* and *"equality."* But such transformation must absolutely exclude both *real universality* (that is, universally shared real determinations of *humanity*) and *substantive equality.* Hence their necessarily *fetishistic formal determination*, premised on the absolute necessity of securing the *structurally entrenched subordination* of labor to capital's commanding force.

Accordingly, we are presented with a totally false "equality," associated with the most iniquitous *economic class determinations* (command and control vested in capital and sanctified by its property) which must be *sustained*—as its ultimate guarantor—by *capital's state formations*. Political activity with regard to the power of effective societal control by the subordinate class is therefore confined to the *formal* level, and *overruled* even at that level at times of *major crises*. It is very important to recall in this respect the *periodic relapse* into authoritarian—and worse, extreme dictatorial—forms of political domination.

3. THE NEW SOCIAL METABOLISM

The *positive counterforce* to these determinations cannot be realized without the *reconstitution of the historical dialectic* that has been perverted and atrophied by capital's fetishistic imperatives, corresponding to the incorrigible necessity of its universal commodification/quantitative equation and unlimitable self-expansion. By contrast to the reductive/impoverishing determinations of universal commodification, *quality* as *human substantiveness* (arising from the enriching resources of unfolding *human need*) must be brought into the foreground and retain its place as a vital *orienting principle*.

This kind of change requires the effective *control* and allocation of real and potential *surplus-labor* not as blindly ever-increasing quantity—predetermined by capital's only practicable imperative of unlimitable/uncontrollable self-expansion, no matter how wasteful in its destination—but as matching the consciously pursued qualitative emancipatory needs of society's freely associated producers.

The *radical qualitative switch* here indicated means the *substantive transformation* of the production of surplus-labor through the vital orienting principle of *disposable time* of each and *every individual*, together with its genuinely equitable distribution. That kind of *real universality* is capable of *qualitative determination* only. As genuine universality, it qualifies in that it embraces *every one* of society's individuals, with their incomparably more resourceful *disposable time*—in contrast to capital's "necessary labor time"—devoted to the realization of their human objectives. In other words, it means the *autonomous self-determination and action* of the totality of particular social individuals, corresponding to their most varied and authentic human needs. Only on such qualitative grounds can we envisage the radical reconstitution—*by* the individuals themselves and *for* themselves—of the fundamental orienting principles and the historically sustainable operative framework of the *new social metabolism*.

Naturally, all this is inconceivable without the effective realization of *substantive equality* and the corresponding supersession of the *state as such* in its historically constituted substance as the *separate antagonistic overall command structure of the decision-making process*. For all such antagonistic command structures, and not only capital's state formations, are by their innermost nature diametrically opposed to the substantive equality of human beings.

At the same time it must be also firmly underlined that the destructive contradictions of the political formations as constituted in history cannot be remedied *within the confines* of the political domain itself, as attempted *and failed* in the past. The historical chronicle of *reformism* speaks eloquently on this score.

It is unthinkable to overcome the *antagonisms* of the known political formations without removing their *common denominator*—the exploitative appropriation of surplus-labor—from their material ground. And for that purpose the *societal reproductive metabolism* itself must be radically reconstituted in its entirety, demanding the *total eradication of capital* and its corresponding state formations from the social metabolic process.

Thus, *real universality* and *substantive equality* are inseparably combined in the necessary reconstitution of the social metabolism in such a way that *all individuals* should be able to *equitably* devote their *disposable time* to the realization of their *shared societal objectives*, in accordance with their creatively fulfilled *human needs*. Without the substantive equality of all human beings the genuine exercise of *disposable time* could not prevail, and the well-known hostile accusations of "leveling down" and the "equitable distribution of misery" would persist. In this sense, the determinations of substantive equality and the creative reality of disposable time are inseparable. Antagonistic political formations, including the modern capitalist state, are *hierarchical* by their innermost substance, and therefore—even if they wanted to do the contrary—cannot help being opposed to any idea of *substantive equality*. They can concede under determinate historical conditions *formal equality* for the sake of securing the reproduction of their own rules and structurally entrenched privileges, in full accord with the antagonistically structured social metabolic order. But the retention of their role as the overall political command structure of the given, antagonistically structured, social metabolism, watching over the continuity of the differential/exploitative exercise of society's reproductive functions, is the overriding condition of their operation. This is why they also must be *eradicated*, together with the radical overcoming of the underlying material processes of the historically long prevailing antagonistic production and allocation of surplus labor.

CHAPTER THREE

From Primitive to Substantive Equality
—via Slavery

Unlike *materially grounded* and strictly determined *primitive equality*, the realization of universally shared substantive equality is feasible only at a highly developed level of social/economic advancement that must be combined with the *consciously pursued non-hierarchical* (and thereby *non-antagonistic*) regulation of a *historically sustainable* social reproductive metabolism. That would be a radically different social metabolism, in contrast to *all* phases of historical development hitherto—including of course the *spontaneous primitive equality* of the distant past rooted in the grave *material constraints* of directly imposed natural necessity and struggle for survival. For the horizon of humanity's consciousness was drastically curtailed and hemmed in under the grave determinations of primitive equality. *Historical sustainability* is therefore totally inconceivable in conjunction with such determinations. "Materiality" of that kind, despite its unquestionable substantiveness, as linked to the corresponding hemmed-in "spontaneity," is obviously not enough to achieve historical sustainability. Other conditions must be conquered in due course so as to be able to turn the *potentiality* of materially grounded substantive equality into historically viable *reality*.

But the requirement of *materiality*, in the case of the human being whose fundamental existential substratum is objectively determined *nature*, is essential. The seminal condition of materiality with regard to equality can be swept aside or wished out of existence—as a rule in a revealingly discriminatory and class-bound self-serving way—only by some *idealist* philosophical conception; one that *predicates* the commendability of some kind of equality (e.g., "in the eyes of God" or "before the Law") and at the same time denies the realizability of materially embodied substantive equality, in its defense of a most iniquitous social order.

The painful truth of the matter is that the vital importance of materiality and its regulatory requirements cannot be overrated as far as the actually unfolding—and in the end either prevailing or doom-laden—historical development of humanity is concerned. The innermost determinations of all-embracing historical development on this planet are always *objective*, even though their carriers are particular human individuals who may well exercise their role under the distorting determinations of false consciousness. For the false consciousness in question is not individualistic fanciful/arbitrary consciousness, as characteristically misrepresented by Max Weber in his projection of the fictitious but socially most apologetic "Private Demon"—decreed to be absolutely insuperable—dominating all individuals. On the contrary, it corresponds to determinate objective interests under the conditions of materially antagonistic historical development. This is a type of historical development characteristic of all social formations in which the overall command structure of decision-making is—for a great variety of identifiable reasons—alienated from the social body as a whole, and is embodied in a separate, superimposed political organ of correspondingly great variety across history, including our present time.

1. ANTAGONISTIC MATERIALITY

The principal forms of antagonistically perpetuated materiality across history are:

1. *slave-owning* early societies, controlled by military force;
2. *feudal serfdom* in which the predetermined and even religiously sanctioned antagonistic rule continues to be imposed, wherever and whenever needed, by force;
3. *"wage slavery"* (in the words of Marx), perpetuating itself by directly material/economic means under the rule of capital, no matter how "advanced" and ultimately safeguarded by political/military force.

In all three of its fundamental articulations, slavery is *structurally entrenched* and peremptorily *hierarchical* with regard to the objective reality of the actual societal decision-making process. This is the case even at the third type of slavery, *wage slavery*, despite the *pseudo-egalitarian* pretenses of political "democracy" that is confined to the more or less vacuously *formal/electoral* level.

Naturally, in all three types of slavery the overall control of the vital materiality of the social metabolic process of reproduction remains divorced from the producers themselves. At the same time, the actual productive functions must be nonetheless performed by those who are not in overall control of the roles objectively assigned to them, while the de facto controllers of the system are of course incapable of accomplishing the necessary reproductive tasks without which society as a whole would collapse. The objective contradiction of such reproductive structure is blatantly obvious, even if it is idealized at the historical phase of wage slavery by the privileged side as the benevolent "Invisible Hand" and not perceived as an untenable contradiction by those at the receiving end.

In any case, this way of controlling the material metabolism of societal reproduction across history cannot be other than *objectively antagonistic* to its inner core, with its dangers of potential instability and even convulsion. In the interest of its ongoing sustainability, the *structurally entrenched hierarchical framework* of the societal complex into which the producers are inserted must be *predetermined* from the outset through *material class determinations*, and it must be *politically safeguarded* as such in the direction of the future. Material entrenchment itself—against which people might *and do* rebel—cannot provide *on its own* the *ultimate guarantee* for its successful perpetuation.

This objective *hiatus* carries with it the *necessity of an ultimate enforcer and guarantor* in the form of the given society's *political command structure*. This command structure articulates itself in history as the "sovereign" power capable of imposing, against all recalcitrance, the potentially endangered requirements of materially exploitative structural/hierarchical entrenchment.

Significantly, *even at the stage of capitalistic wage slavery*—when the primary modality of surplus-labor extraction and its discriminatory expropriation as expanding surplus value is the class determined, and supposedly "neutral," economic material dependency of the workers (combined with the deceitful semblance of their "political equality" and indeed "liberty")—from time to time, in periods of major crises, forms of *directly authoritarian* even extreme dictatorial political control must be imposed on society. Naturally this is carried out by the force of arms, in the interest of securing the capitalist societal reproductive metabolism.

Accordingly, in the immediate aftermath of the First World War, the semi-fascist Admiral Miklós Horthy was imposed on Hungary by the capitalistically most advanced "democratic states" of the United States, Britain, and France, well before Mussolini's "march on Rome" or Adolf Hitler's world adventure–oriented domination in Germany.[1] We see similar developments in the U.S.-manufactured military dictatorship of General Augusto Pinochet in Chile, overthrowing democratically elected President Salvador Allende (remember Henry Kissinger's direct role in it), in tune with the most active support given to other military dictatorships by the United States in Brazil and other parts of Latin America as a matter of course.[2] Material entrenchment must therefore be complemented and safeguarded by the ultimate guarantor of even the most repressive political-military machinery, no matter how "democratic" its ideological justification. An antagonistic societal reproductive order cannot sustain itself without it. The absurdly idealized conditions of capitalist wage slavery—to which "there can be no alternative"—offer no exception to such authoritarian ultimate guarantee. This fact casts a dark shadow on the liberal projections of "controlling the excesses of the state" even when they are genuinely meant by some liberal political philosophers.

Nevertheless, the objective tendency of historical development toward instituting a viable social metabolic order of—materially grounded—substantive equality cannot be denied. The demand for it made itself felt on the historical stage in a most dramatic form at the time of the French Revolution and it had to be acknowledged even by the defenders of the bourgeois order at least in a partial form, as the "equality before the Law." But of course the demand for equality in a harshly contested way goes back in history to countless centuries' earlier ages. As great a philosopher as Aristotle had to dismiss such demand with scathing remarks. Indeed, despite his philosophical genius, he could make pronouncements on the domain of social equality in the most grotesque way, by calling the *slaves* of his time *talking tools*. Obviously, then, class interest can produce staggering irrationality even in the case of the greatest philosophical genius.

2. THE HISTORICAL REALIZATION OF SUBSTANTIVE EQUALITY

The historical realization of consciously pursued substantive equality is dependent on the actual production of its material conditions in the most comprehensive sense. The advocacy of the realization of such a monumental historical achievement could be only a wishful "ought-to-be" if its conditions were to be postulated in the form of "Divine Grace" or the deed of some mysterious "World Spirit," as so much of historical development is projected to be in the idealist philosophical conceptions of the past.

But in actuality this is not the case with regard to the question of substantive equality. For the human natural ground of the unfolding historical process toward the realization of substantive equality is itself material precisely in the most comprehensive sense in which all human beings objectively share the communality of their fundamental natural substratum, with its most varied creative potentiality.

Only the human-made iniquitous metabolic regulatory conditions, arising from self-perpetuating vested interests, can pervert that shared fundamental natural equity into socially discriminatory institutionalized reality, matching the predetermined exploitative requirements of the established hierarchical structural entrenchment, and thereupon outrageously conceptualized in terms of the members of the subordinate class even as the subhuman condition of "talking tools." Indeed, due to the same vested class interests, the socially repressed class of people could be conceptualized in the form of the most absurd racism at a much later stage than Aristotle's ancient Greece, when the great rational dialectical philosopher Hegel could contradict his own truly pathbreaking epistemological democratism by talking about what he called "the African character," with reference to the slaves of his time.[3]

In contrast to Aristotle, in Hegel we find a much more sophisticated justification of the unjustifiable. This is understandable not only because the demand for equality in the French Revolution—in the case of François-Noël Babeuf and his "Society of Equals" even for materially substantive equality—erupted with great force on the historical stage, but also because Hegel himself passionately supported its anti-feudal constituents. However, given his own class horizon, consciously shared in a positive sense with the work of Adam Smith, Hegel could not contemplate any form of social and political order that might be contrary to the emerging and, in the post-revolutionary period, consolidating bourgeois class exploitative substance. His discourse therefore centered on the idea of historically unfolding Freedom, relegating the problem of Equality to the domain of what he described with undisguised contempt and summary negativity as "the folly of the Understanding," setting it in sharp contrast to the idealized domain of Reason itself.[4]

In that way, socially most problematic and indeed antagonistic *materiality* could recede from what Hegel considered the proper philosophical horizon. The underlying problem and dilemma had to be transfigured into the unquestionable ideality of a historically climactic, and in the Hegelian scheme of things forever inseparable, Reason and Freedom, thanks to the postulated good services of Subject/Object identity. At the same time, the structurally prevailing forms of *material antagonism*—both the *internal*, socially exploitative, and the *international*, necessarily warring—could be organically incorporated into his monumental account of World Historical development, characterized by Hegel as "the ways of God," the World Spirit's *Theodicaea*.[5]

To be sure, Hegel did not deny at least the potentiality of social antagonism, as depicted in Smith's great work. But he pushed aside in his *Philosophy of Right* the explosive dangers that might arise from the admittedly harsh predicament of the needy "surplus population" with the fantasy solution of an idealized Europe's colonial expansion, wishfully projected to go on forever in the future. Moreover, the dimension of international antagonism appeared in Hegel's conception from the time of his earliest writings, and remained always predicated in an equally unproblematic way. It took the form of firmly asserting not only the de facto necessity of wars but also their positive commendability, advocated by him for the sake of avoiding moral stagnation. Accordingly, in a passage of five lines from the youthful work on *Natural Law*, repeated by Hegel word for word in the much later *Philosophy of Right*, we learn that thanks to the necessity of purifying war "the ethical health of the peoples is preserved."[6]

In this sense, Hegel was well aware of both of the fundamental dimensions of material antagonism that are inseparable from structurally entrenched substantive inequality. But—given his class horizon—he had to proclaim their full consonance with the World Spirit whose fully realized work in this world could be questioned only by the impatient and "immature Youth" but not by the "mature Man."[7] This is why in Hegel's grandiose historical conception—spelled out in terms of the World Spirit's "Cunning of Reason" (*List der Vernunft*) using the World Historical Persons, like Alexander the Great, Julius Caesar, Martin Luther, and Napoleon as *mere tools* for its own hidden purposes—the *idea of freedom* had to take over the space of *materially substantive equality*.

World Historical Tools of that kind, in the hands of the World Spirit, could be certainly called "talking tools," and indeed eloquent talking tools of the noblest kind. Aristotle would be astounded by such change of meaning, seeing his own pupil, the great Alexander, so defined. Yet thanks to Hegel's overall design in the name of the "Absolutely Cunning World Spirit" (his expression), the newly established iniquitous bourgeois order could acquire its ideal stamp of approval, with no one to be taken to account for its contradictions, not even for the partially acknowledged suffering of the needy.[8] For who would dare to call for taking the wisdom of the World Spirit itself to task at the peak of its fully accomplished *Theodicea*? That would be the greatest of all conceivable philosophical contradictions.

In terms of human emancipation, the demand for equality is inextricably combined with material substantiveness. *Formal* equality in the field of the political domain without structurally equivalent material decision-making *substantiveness*—even if in comparative historical terms it can be considered meaningful in contrast to the feudal or ancient slave-owning past—would be rather vacuous and nullifiable; as indeed it happens to be in its actual operation and also in its own limited terms of reference. Hobbes did not hesitate to call substantiveness without materiality a contradiction in terms. This is how he had put it: "*Substance* and *Body*, signifies the same thing; and therefore *Substance incorporeall* are words, which when they are joined together, destroy one another, as if a man should say, an *Incorporeall body*."[9]

In this sense, any claim as to having realized the workers' equality in the domain of social and political emancipation by granting them some formal rights, while actually denying—on the ground of the structurally prejudged and secured monopoly of the means of production to be vested in the personifications of capital—the *material substance* of controlling the social reproductive metabolism, is exactly like talking about "*Incorporeall body*," that is, a contradiction in terms.

3. IDEALISM AND THE PROBLEM OF MATERIALITY

It goes without saying, no one should accuse Hegel of committing such crude logical inconsistency, with the most deplorable and grotesquely racist exception of his talk about the "African character." In Hegel's case the problems lie elsewhere, with far-reaching consequences for his historical conception as a whole. For by shifting the problem of historical advancement from the materially tangible and substantive issue of Equality, with its objective determinations of potential and real historical advancement, to the ideal postulate of Freedom, as the mysteriously preordained self-objectifying purpose, Hegel is compelled to look for a correspondingly ideal supra-human agency in relation to which the actual human beings—no matter how great in terms of the Hegelian world-historical process—can only appear as mere tools and cunningly used instruments. This is how the unfolding dynamism of historical development is turned into the mysterious World Spirit's Absolute *List der Vernunft* (Absolute Cunning of Reason explicitly admitted to be such by Hegel himself), making the two fundamental concepts of Reason and Freedom organically combined in the monumental idealist architectonic of the Hegelian philosophy.[10]

In one of Hegel's early philosophical works, *Jenaer Realphilosophie*, the dilemma of the "pauper's inequality" appears for a fleeting moment and receives a logically consistent but *totally unreal* solution. He describes the pauper in his miserable *alienated* existence (Hegel's words) as entering the cathedral, and envisages for him a—purely imaginary—"second alienation" from his actual alienated existence. And thus, young Hegel proclaims, thanks to the postulated second alienation, whereby the depicted pauper makes in his mind his real existence disappear as a speck of cloud on the distant horizon, and so in his cathedral-consciousness he "*is the equal to the Prince*" (*er ist dem Fürsten gleich*). But of course the actual life conditions of the pauper did not change in the slightest. Later in his life, "mature Man Hegel" does not offer such—curiously compassionate but utterly imaginary—scenarios and solutions. In their stead, as mentioned before, he dismisses with logical consistency the demand for social equality as "the folly of the understanding"—namely, the kind of folly rightfully condemned in terms of the Hegelian categorial framework on account of emanating from the lower faculty of human reasoning.

The actual historical unfolding of the conditions of real human equality has its identifiable "body" and its "substance" in the Hobbesian sense. Its self-evident agency or subject is the actually existent human being across history. Consequently, historical development assumes a tangible form, irrespective of how antagonistic the actual tendency toward the realization of its objective potentialities might be. By contrast, projecting historical development in terms of "Freedom as such," divorced from its necessary connection with materially substantive human equality, is inevitably idealistic/mystifying. Its claimed self-objectifying conceptuality needs not only a mysterious Newtonian "Prime Mover" but also one who in Hegel's case continues to move it all the way to the final accomplishment of "the ways of God," his *Theodicaea*. Thus, the envisaged historical progression can be depicted in the broad outlines of Hegel's *Philosophy of History* only as a kind of logical/conceptual progression, even if presented with rich—but speculatively selective and idealistically preordained as well as prejudged—historical illustrative material.

Accordingly, Hegel offers us the three principal stages of historical advancement like this:

1. In the oriental world only *one*—the ruler/despot—is free;
2. In classical Greek antiquity *some* men are free;
3. In the modern era, corresponding to "Europe as absolutely the end of history," "*man as man*," or "*man as such*" is free.[11]

As to the explanatory ground of such historical development from "*one*" through "*some*" to the logico-generic "*man as such*," the self-evident Hegelian answer is: the World Spirit itself. But the idea that "*man as such*" is free does not mean in the least that "*all men are free*." Far from it. Structural dependency and subordination must be maintained as the regulators of the societal order. Thus, the projected "universality" of "man as such" devoid of substantively identifiable human historical content is a *pseudo-universality*. As indeed it cannot be other than that in the philosophical conceptualizations envisioned from capital's social metabolic order, when the fetishism of universal commodification—the only practicable, perverse, all-invading "universality"—calls for a merely formal equalization of self-expanding exchange value, subduing use-value and human need.

It is by no means surprising, therefore, that the greatest thinkers of the bourgeoisie had to struggle in vain with the concept of *"universalizability,"* from Kant to Hegel. In their innermost philosophical conception, they could only envisage it in a *separate, otherworldly domain*, with its proclaimed *ideal moral substance*. In Kant's case this view was spelled out in his *Critique of Practical Reason* as the realm of the mysterious *"intelligible world,"* to which human beings were said to *also* belong, making them thereby free and morally responsible for their motivations and actions. And Kant clearly stated, that in the architectonic of his overall philosophical conception, *"the primacy of practical reason"* occupied the overwhelmingly important grounding place. Yet both Kant and Hegel tried to identify in some way the conceived moral otherworldliness with their ideal *postulate* on this earth: in Kant's case with the "ought-to-be" beneficial work of the "moral politician" set in sharp contrast to the rejected "political moralist," and in Hegel's case with the solemnly proclaimed but totally unrealizable class-preserving antagonistic *"ethical state."* Thus, similarly to Kant, in Hegel's conception—from the earliest phase of his talk about "ethical urge" and "ethical totality" to the final summation of his ideas in his *Philosophy of Right* and in his *Philosophy of History*—an ethically idealized political reason occupied the architectonic grounding place. This constituted his own version of the "primacy of practical reason."

4. THE CIRCULAR IDENTIFICATION OF FREEDOM AND REASON

In its fundamental meaning the historical advancement of freedom claimed by Hegel concerned the principal state formations across history as highlighted in his relevant philosophical work. And in that sense the *ultimate* state formation of *"the Germanic world"*—corresponding by no means simply to Germany but to the dominant nation-states of Europe in general—fully matched the postulated final destination of the "ways of God." He said so explicitly in his *Philosophy of History* as well as in his *Philosophy of Right*.

The great difficulty in this respect is that underneath the idealistically transfigured solutions of *otherworldliness*, as offered by the great classical philosophers of the bourgeoisie, we find very real, in fact burning and agonizingly hurtful, determinations, amenable to very different solutions. Humanity's oppressive and in our time most menacing state antagonisms are not curable by even the noblest appeal to the Kantian otherworldly "intelligible realm," nor by the advocacy of the ideal postulates of some imaginary "ethical state." For they arise from the insuperable contradictions of the *self-imposing worldliness* of antagonistic politics itself, embodied in the *separate organ* of the alienating, structurally entrenched overall controlling power of the state in its historical reality. This real-historical state is *necessarily* the enemy of *substantive equality* as a matter of its innermost objective structural/hierarchical determination. No appeal to the ideal of some "moral politician," with his pure "ought-to-be" of Kantian "perpetual peace" in a real world of interminable destructive and self-destructive wars, nor to the even more wishful projection of the "realization of the ways of God on earth" in and through the Hegelian "ethical state," can alter that.

From his earliest writings to his last Hegel was always intensely concerned with the problems of politics. His conception as a whole would be quite unimaginable without that, even if in the 1840s the "Young Hegelians" tried to stress the more radical potentialities of the old master's work.[12] As Georg Lukács also did, almost a century later in one of his greatest works, *The Young Hegel*, written in defense of dialectics against sectarian dogmatism.

As a young philosopher, Hegel projected in support of his vision the benevolent Monster *Briareus*, connecting him with his own ideas about the advocated "ethical totality" and "ethical urge" for the realization of a rather mythical outcome to be brought about by something like "the Nation's God." And even if later Briareus disappeared from his writing, and "the Nation's God" was transmuted into the "World Spirit," Hegel's vision of some kind of ethical solution to the very real—indeed patently antagonistic—problems of the world always remained in evidence. Given his categorical rejection of materially grounded substantive equality, he could offer only an idealistic ethically justified state conception. And that could only be spelled out in terms of a *circular* identification of *Freedom* and *Reason*, because the universally valid demand for equality—whose formal dimension was incorporated in the French Revolution's decree of the "Universal Rights of Man and Citizen," even when some clearly identifiable radical social forces were pressing for much more—had to be swept aside by Hegel's class as absolutely inadmissible.

The identification of Freedom and Reason had to be *circular* because they had to cover and "supersede" (in the Hegelian threefold sense of "*Aufhebung*") the ground of their socially unmentionable antagonistic determinations. In reality "Freedom as such" cannot have a meaning in its own self-enclosed terms of reference. It must be freedom *for* doing or *realizing something* in order to acquire a humanly meaningful content. And that must be linked to some tangibly contested condition of human equality or inequality. Even the one-sidedly limited conception of "freedom from" must be defined in terms of something that promotes or constrains human equality.

However, in Hegel's philosophical development we find the class-determined absence of the historically advancing and materially identifiable—even if in reality sharply contested and "overruled" by the dominant powers—equality in comparison to the more distant past. Yet, the *objectively unfolding trend* is evidenced not only by the writings of some great pre-revolutionary thinkers pointing in the direction of the erupting demand for equality, like Rousseau, well known to Hegel, but also by the actual confrontations of the French Revolution, despite the class-determined limitations of their outcome. As Marx had forcefully underlined it, the class determinations embodied in the emergent bourgeois state started to assume a repressive legal form against the workers at a very early stage of the French Revolution. Thus, most significantly in this respect:

> During the very first storms of the revolution the French bourgeoisie dared to take away from the workers the right of association just acquired. By a decree of June 14, 1791, they declared all coalition of the workers as "an attempt against liberty and the declaration of the rights of man," punishable by a fine of 500 livres, together with

deprivation of the rights of an active citizen for one year. This law which, by means of State compulsion, confined the struggle between capital and labor within limits comfortable for capital, has outlived revolutions and changes of dynasties. Even the Reign of Terror left it untouched. It was but quite recently struck out of the Penal Code.[13]

Under such unfolding developments Hegel could of course happily acknowledge the anti-feudal constituents of the emerging transformations but absolutely not the objectively implied necessity of equality in terms of socially/materially superseding the new type of class domination.

Accordingly, Hegel could only assert that the "triumph of Freedom" consisted in the emergence of the Germanic State as corresponding to the ideality of the World Spirit's "ethical state," proclaimed on the ground that such state is at long last *"organized rationally."* And when he had to prove that in the World Spirit's now realized modern world "man as such is free," he could only do it—again, due to the necessary absence of commendable materially tangible equality from his thought—by claiming that the rationally organized Germanic ethical state is free with full adequacy because *"it is rationally founded on the principle of freedom."* Thus, in terms of the freedom of "man as such" and the fully realized freedom of the state as such, the defining determination of "organized rationally" and "being founded rationally on the principle of freedom" had to coincide and constitute the *"circle of circles,"* eloquently commended by Hegel in that way not only in his massive *Science of Logic* but also in one of his greatest works, *The Phenomenology of Mind*, or—as the same masterpiece is rendered in another English translation—*The Phenomenology of Spirit*.

5. THE HEGELIAN CIRCLE OF CIRCLES

Paradoxically, this circle of circles was not a logical failure but the greatest philosophical achievement conceivable from capital's societal reproductive standpoint. For though leaving the class-determined socially unmentionable unmentioned, it made possible the elaboration of a profound dialectical conception even if in a most abstract form, due to its necessarily missing correlated terms of reference. In truth it can be argued that *Reason and Freedom* not fallaciously but truly should stand for the same thing in historical development, provided that we complement them with their *real ground* of objectively unfolding materiality of ultimately irrepressible *human equality*. In that way there is no need for any separate and mysterious *supra-human Mover*.

To be sure, from capital's social metabolic standpoint this could not be admitted. This is why a logico-metaphysical dialectic—as if floating on purified air, by moving from the earlier mentioned "*one*" of the stipulated speculatively self-realizing world history, through the intermediary category of the logically consistent "*some*," to the abstract philosophical finality of "*man as such*" and "*Freedom as such*"—had to take the place of historically identifiable materiality and real advancement, thereby transfiguring some inconvenient class relations into idealistic yet morally meaningful terms, thanks to the *logico-skeletal validity* of the projected dialectical progression.

In this way so much of speculatively transfigured objective truth could be spelled out in different domains of human experience, from Logic and Aesthetics to an encyclopedic historical knowledge and to the strictly legal dimension of state-legitimatory ideas and practices in the more or less remote past. Even Hegel's absolute insistence on the necessary *ethical determination* of the advocated state has its *relative validity*, provided that it is strongly qualified with reference to the material ground of actually existing society. For historically sustainable human societal interchange is inconceivable without the fully shared acceptance of some vitally important and morally commendable comprehensive regulatory determinations. But, of course, the required normative determinations can and must be set not by some supra-human World Spirit but by the *substantively equal* members of humanity, on the ground of their radically different modality of non-antagonistic social metabolic reproduction, beyond the separate, structurally superimposed political/military states constituted in history.

Hegel was absolutely right in stressing that to be able to talk about historical development one needed some measure in terms of which advancement toward a rationally sustainable condition in history could be expressed. In his case that measure, for the already mentioned reasons of state idealization, could not be other than Freedom itself. The trouble is, though, that "Freedom as such" needs some measure in terms of which it can be properly applied to the advancement, or, on the contrary, retrogression of actual societal development.

No one can deny for a moment the importance of freedom for the realization of human potentialities. But this requirement can only mean in the case of the human being, whose fundamental existential substratum is nature, the objective satisfaction of humanity's *self-realization*, including of course the cultural/intellectual conditions appropriate to the unfolding materially secured and emancipatory historical conditions themselves. Consequently, advancement in history cannot be measured abstractly in the generality of *"Freedom as such"* or *"Freedom itself,"* no matter how fully consistent that might be with the likewise generic determination of *"rationality as such."*

The vital issue in terms of human emancipation and advancement in relation to the admittedly necessary requirement of Freedom is not the inseparability of Freedom and Reason, irrespective of how much we might agree with their inseparability without being trapped by the Hegelian circle. Rather, the crucial issue is the *actual advancement in the substantiveness of freedom*. Only this can provide the appropriate measure of the emancipatory process. In other words, the advancement in the substantiveness of freedom means the historically identifiable *advancement in the objective conditions of its realization*, which is equivalent to the historically unfolding realization of *humanity's substantive equality*.

6. THE STATE AND THE "CUNNING OF REASON"

The Hegelian dual "circle of circles"—that is, humanity as such is free when the state is rationally founded on the principle of Freedom, and the state is ethically realized in tune with the wisdom of the World Spirit's "Cunning of Reason" when it is constituted on the combined rational ground of Freedom and Reason—no longer has any pre-revolutionary bourgeois utopian illusion attached to it. Hegel has no sympathy whatsoever for Rousseau's radical democratic ideas of political decision-making through the "General Will." Also, in the post-revolutionary period, coupled with the turmoil of the Napoleonic Wars, he can only refer in sarcastic terms to Kant's noble postulate of the "Perpetual Peace." In some way Hegel perceives the ironic circumstance that the militarily warring sides are in actual social terms on the same bourgeois side, despite their armed confrontations. In this sense, although he praises Napoleon in a most glowing way as one of the greatest World Historical Persons chosen by the World Spirit as the tool for its own purposes, Hegel has no difficulty including the prominently "colonizing British"—Napoleon's archenemy, called by him *perfidious Albion*—under the idealized Germanic ethical state.

Of course, these are not philosophically corrigible personal misconceptions but the contradictions of a particularly contradictory historical period, even if by no means confined to that period only, given their long prehistory as well as their subsequent historical development up to our time in much the same spirit. As we have seen above, taking the World Spirit to task for the contradictions and failures of its proclaimed insuperable order, instituted through the instrumentality of its World Historical human tools, would be quite outrageous in Hegel's view. And this is far from being as arbitrary as it might appear. For the Hegelian World Spirit's "Grand Design" truly corresponds to a really existing order. A social metabolic order of *institutionalized irresponsibility* in the contradictory sense in which responsibility *can*—and also *must*—be made strictly *partial*, limited to the centrifugally operated *microcosms* of the system. But there can be no *overall responsibility*, as a matter of the fundamental structural determination of capital's social metabolic order.

Hegel is not the only great bourgeois thinker who idealizes that insuperable systemic condition and contradiction. We should remember in this respect Smith's striking projection of the same necessary absence of overall responsibility in his postulate of the—likewise mythical— "Invisible Hand" that is supposed to benevolently sort out everything in the end. The big difference is that Smith sharply rejected the idea of any *political interference* in the operation of the Invisible Hand—by its innermost natural determination ideal—calling that spontaneous social/economic reproductive order "the natural system of perfect liberty and justice."[14]

By contrast, Hegel situated history in his own way firmly above "nature" and had to find the politically reassuring supra-human Subject for his conception of World History. Accordingly, he could not exclude the state and its functionaries from his scheme of things in a historical period of great revolutionary crisis and the collapse of the old reproductive order. For that collapse—deeply implicating the corresponding, far from rational "principle of Freedom constituted" state—was followed by extreme political and military collisions, worsened by the perceived danger that the radical social and political forces, oriented toward materially anchored equality, might even prevail.

This is why Hegel insisted that "the State is the Divine Idea as it exists on Earth."[15] He also made it clear that "the History of the World travels from East to West, for Europe is absolutely the end of History, Asia the beginning," asserting at the same time his perversely "universal" claim regarding the absolute validity of the ultimate Germanic colonizing State formation in the most unashamed sense.[16] Accordingly he wrote, "It is the necessary fate of Asiatic Empires to be subjected to Europeans; and China will, some day or other, be obliged to submit to this fate."[17]

Thus, internally and internationally antagonistic and exploitative *partiality* had to prevail forever in the World Spirit's divinely instituted and sanctioned order as the unalterable *universality* of the fully accomplished Germanic State, *preordained* in that way from the very beginning by the Absolute Spirit's eternalized *circular temporality*. For in Hegel's view:

> The principles of the successive phases of Spirit that animate the Nations in a necessitated gradation are themselves only steps in the development of the one universal Spirit, which through them elevates and completes itself to a self-comprehending *totality*.

... Spirit is immortal; with it there is no past, no future, but an essential *now*. ... The life of the ever present Spirit is a circle of progressive embodiments. ... The grades which Spirit seems to have left behind it, it still possesses in the depth of its present.[18]

7. MONOPOLY AND COMPETITION AS A VICIOUS (GLOBAL) CIRCLE

It is inconceivable to find a solution to these materially constituted and sustained objective contradictions within the antagonistic framework of the capital system. For *neither* dimension of its twofold structural antagonisms—that is, neither the *internal*, class-oppressive, nor the *international*, interminably warring—is capable of being superseded *on its own*, without overcoming the other. The idea commended by Hegel that wars must be pursued because in that way "*the ethical health of the peoples is preserved*" is an apologetic ideological rationalization dressed up in a wishful ethical attire. Wars are actually pursued because no limits are admissible to the expansion-oriented capital system, making thereby the structural imperative of international antagonism systemically insuperable despite its ultimate dangers. Similarly, the internal antagonism of class exploitation is insuperable because the fundamental structural determinations of capital's social metabolic order are constituted in such a way that the *control* of the societal reproductive process—thanks to the monopoly of the means of production vested in the personifications of capital—is *radically alienated from* and *superimposed on* the producers themselves, for the sake of ever-expanding exchange value.

Since the two systemic dimensions of internal and international antagonism *stand or fall together*, in order to find a historically sustainable solution to such ultimately destructive structural antagonisms it is necessary to overcome the *overall structural framework* of the capital system itself. When, however, the dominant vested interests of the system are shared by its thinkers of no matter how great a stature, their envisaged solutions—whether consciously sustaining or just bypassing the insuperable antagonisms in question—can result even in the best of cases only in utterly wishful *deus ex machina* remedies to the missing overall responsibility in the operation of the given social metabolic order. Hence their postulated remedies must be attributed to something like the "Invisible Hand," or the supra-human "Cunning of Reason."

In capital's social reproductive order, *monopoly* is by its nature destructive, and ultimately even all-destructive. For such monopoly arises from the antagonistic self-expansionist centrifugality of the capital system. The *internal* dimension of monopoly over the means of production—in its origin assigned through the blood-soaked "primitive accumulation" to the privileged class of the personifications of capital—is the *necessary primary condition* for the operation of such a system. Consequently, it must be maintained *at all cost*, by the most aggressive dictatorial force of arms by the state, whenever that primary condition is threatened. And since the antagonistic self-expansionary centrifugality of capital's systemic microcosms has no *inherently limiting* objective constituents, the necessary internal exploitative condition must rely for its promoting complementary dimension on the likewise necessary *international* systemic drive toward *all-engulfing monopolistic domination*—on the mad design of global domination, and not only by Hitler—through the political/military agency of the capital state.

It is therefore by no means accidental that the climax of capital's historical development assumed the form of *monopolistic imperialism*, responsible for two devastating world wars in the twentieth century, and equally responsible for countless more or less camouflaged "proxy wars" ever since, restrained in that way only because of the fear of humanity's total self-annihilation through the weapons of mass destruction. In this type of social-economic and political development, contradictorily and dangerously, we find the unholy congruence of *monopoly and competition*.

Competition, in contrast to monopoly, happened to be one of the most dynamic and in more ways than one positive constituents of the capital system in its history. In principle its positive potentiality is applicable also in a non-antagonistic way in the future. However, in capitalist ideology, competition tends to be idolized without the necessary qualifications. Yet the severe problem in this respect is that in our time, due to the activation of some absolute systemic limits of capital's social metabolic order, the antagonistic structural determinations are articulated in the form of the *perverse reciprocity* of monopoly and competition.[19] Perverse because in view of the underlying antagonistic centrifugality on an ever-enlarging scale—due to the increasing concentration and centralization of capital—competition and monopoly constitute a *vicious circle*. Consequently—in a far from benevolent idolizable form—the irrepressible drive toward monopoly produces ever more aggressive competition, and in its turn intensified competition produces the imperative of unlimitable monopoly, with its all-destructive dangers.

Moreover, also very far from the idyllic projections of benevolent globalization, the more globally interconnected capital's material reproductive system becomes, the more dangerous is this vicious circle, in view of the *necessary* absence of a controllable *global* state. For without the now existing and, in their limited setting, to some extent corrective nation-states, the perverse reciprocity of monopoly and competition would produce total uncontrollability even in the particular capitalist countries. And, thanks to the perverse systemic reciprocity of monopoly and competition, the "cutthroat competition" on our horizon for the planet's strategic material resources—imposing also mindless ecological devastation on nature—can only make that danger much worse.

8. CAPITAL'S INSUPERABLE INTER-STATE ANTAGONISMS

One of the most intractable problems of the historically constituted state formations is their insuperable *inter-state antagonism* that carries with it the staggering waste of resources through uncontrollable military expenditure everywhere, in a world of great misery for countless millions.

In Britain alone a major issue of political dispute concerns the planned renewal of the Polaris nuclear submarines, costing dozens of billions of pounds before they multiply, as a rule, in the course of construction. And, of course, they are combined with massive cuts—through the parliamentary reform of the Welfare State's social security system—to the living standard of seven million workers. And the Polaris submarines, with their nuclear weapons, are only one item of the ubiquitous and wasteful military expenditure. Once the squander on armaments is calculated in global terms, it amounts annually to not far from *two trillion* dollars, when hundreds of millions of people must survive on less than two dollars per day. And to underline the mind-boggling irrationality of the established social reproductive order—claimed to be the ideal system of "rational calculation" by Max Weber and many others—the cynically veiled fact is that all of the major capitalist states are hopelessly bankrupt (the United States itself to the tune of nearly $20 trillion), yet continue to subject their populations to such economic and political dictates. Moreover, if we add to all this the official justification for the near-astronomic magnitude of military expenditure—a "justification" spelled out by asserting that in our "dangerously uncertain world" the truly MAD balance of Mutually Assured Destruction provides the "security" and "guarantee of survival," a cynical rationalization in place of trying to *remove the causes* of the deep-seated antagonisms—the materially and politically determined irrationality of capital's ruling order bears no comparison.

It is most important to remind ourselves here that capital's *ultimate sanction* in the past was *war* if the rules of competition could not produce by economic means the results befitting the changing historical conditions in accordance with the advancing monopolistic trends. Just like the idea of the "free market," the projection of the "sovereignty of the states" (large or small) was always a fiction. Hegel was honest enough to declare, together with a presumed justification, that "minor states have their existence and tranquillity secured to them more or less by their neighbors; they are therefore, properly speaking, not independent, and have not the fiery trial of war to endure."[20] Indeed, he could even admit that the wars pursued had, in his view, the welcome effect of strengthening the state's internal dominating function. He did this by praising the view that "successful wars have checked domestic unrest and consolidated the power of the state at home."[21]

Later on, the illusions of universal state sovereignty had to be, of

FROM PRIMITIVE TO SUBSTANTIVE EQUALITY 117

course, unceremoniously brushed aside, even in the form of openly decreeing the virtues of "gunboat diplomacy," by the ruthless assertion of the actual power relations, making a mere handful of big states dominant, as a matter of Right (de jure, not just de facto), over all of the others. In this sense, the trajectory of monopolistic imperialism could not be made at all intelligible without the antagonistic inter-determinations of the expansion-oriented capital system. Imperialist domination and its apologetic rationalization could go very well together. The British Empire ended its long history only a few decades ago, after happily coexisting with *liberal* political theories for two hundred years, and the other way around in the case of thoroughly obliging liberal political theorists.

However, the thorny question in our time is: What happens to the historical viability of the capital system when it loses its *ultimate sanction of fighting out, on the required scale,* its self-expansionary imperatives through the now *suicidal danger* of another global war, exposing thereby also the fictional character of *equitable state sovereignty* that could be made acceptable in the past by the "arguments" of *materially imposed force?*

To be sure, the concept of equality is inapplicable not only to "state sovereignty" but to the state in general. To envisage as *equitable* an overall command system of social metabolic control that must be *structurally entrenched* and *hierarchical* by its innermost determination could only be a contradiction in terms. Much like the "Substance incorporeall" and the "Incorporeall body" sharply dismissed by Hobbes.

The blind overruling of equality enters the picture in our time with all the greater force. For even if the antagonistic *inter-state* relations could be envisaged as equitable—for which it would be necessary to rule out of order the objectively prevailing dynamic force of capital's competitively/monopolistically self-expansionary reproductive order—even in that case the hierarchical/structural rationale of the state command system as historically constituted *internally* would be diametrically opposed to any idea of substantive equality. And that determination calls into question the *global reality* of the state itself, with its insuperable internal and inter-state antagonisms arising from the fundamental structural requirements that are inseparable from the earlier discussed perverse reciprocity between monopoly and competition in the capital system.

Thus, by no means surprisingly, we find in the still-dominant modality of overall political decision-making that the advocacy of capital's ultimate sanction of "fighting out" its self-expansionary imperatives by war cannot be given up. Not even when the most elementary rationality must foreshadow quite catastrophic consequences in its pursuit. But ignoring that, the insane idea of "guaranteeing security by Mutually Assured Destruction"—not only with nuclear but also with chemical and biological weapons of mass destruction—is elevated to the pinnacle of *"strategic thinking."* And who can really guarantee that the "proxy wars" pursued in the last few decades will not be turned into an all-destructive global war sometime in the future? For the relatively limited wars engaged in at the present time are not only not rewarding enough to match the requirements of capital's missing "ultimate sanction." Rather, they may well turn out to be *counterproductive* by not only failing to fulfill their original role— the brutal readjustment of the relations of power in tune with the changing historical conditions—but even on account of their directly ecological and wastefully resource-hungry destructive impact on nature.

If even the danger of humanity's destruction can be ignored by the contemporary state in that way, what are the prospects for a sustainable outcome? Liberalism and social democracy at some point in their history tried to introduce some significant changes into the overall political decision-making process—social democracy by promising the realization of *"evolutionary socialism"*—but both failed in their efforts. The prosaic reality of solemn liberalism turned out to be aggressive *neoliberalism*, and social democracy turned its back, without shame, to its erstwhile creed, siding in most countries with utterly retrograde neoliberalism. Thus, the once projected structural reformability of the state proved to be a hopeless illusion.

In actuality, the big problem is that the state is compatible only with those types of reform that *strengthen* its overall structural framework, and counters with great effectiveness whatever might interfere with the fundamental self-expansionary imperatives of capital's social metabolic order. *Formal* legislative improvements are perfectly acceptable, provided that they do not carry the danger of structural societal change. Kant had already phrased it very clearly: "The general *equality* of men as *subjects in a state* coexists quite readily with the *greatest inequality* in degrees of the possessions men have.... Hence the general equality of men also coexists with great inequality of specific rights of which there may be many."[22]

The "specific rights" in question are of course laid down in protection of private property. For defending the structural framework of the existing order at all cost is the primary function of the state. Smith had put it equally clearly, and he put it in terms that would sound most embarrassing today: "Till there be property there can be no government, the very end of which is to secure wealth and to defend the rich from the poor."[23]

Moreover, the difficulty of significant change is further intensified by the *global* character of the problem itself. For capital's self-expansionary imperative, together with the perverse reciprocity of monopoly and competition, is not confined to some particular country in which it could be remedied. It characterizes the whole of the ruling *social metabolic order* of capital and its state formations, requiring global solutions to the inherent *systemic antagonisms*. The capital system is erected on three supporting pillars: capital, labor, and the state. The three of these are not only deeply connected in particular countries, but also quite unimaginable in our time without their far-reaching global interconnections. And that calls for the socialist alternative as a global transformation.

Another fundamental issue that highlights the global character of the necessary alternative concerns the limitations of introducing major social and political change *within* the limited framework of any particular revolutionary state or states while the surrounding states of capital's social order can exercise their subversive power against the particular states in question, as happened in the past. Not only have the Russian and the Chinese revolutions been subjected to the savage subversive armed interventions of the hostile capitalist states but the

Paris Commune of 1871 had to suffer the devastating consequences of Chancellor Otto von Bismarck's class solidarity with the counter-revolutionary French government when he released the French prisoners of war captured by the German army in order to defeat the common class enemy. Indeed, bourgeois class solidarity had been formally institutionalized in October 1873 through the "Three Emperors League" of Germany, Russia, and Austria-Hungary, explicitly designed against any future "European Disturbance" caused by the working class.

Naturally, we could witness ever since that time, in the last century and a half, countless instances of counter-revolutionary subversion by imperialist powers *all over the world* against socialist attempts to change society. Nor should we expect anything other than the intensification of such efforts as capital's systemic crisis deepens. However, the unavoidable hostility and subversion by capitalist states also carries the danger of adopting ultimately self-defeating strategies by socialists, like the uncritical strengthening of state power that creates its own vicious circle of internally exercised state repression, as happened under Stalinism. V. I. Lenin forcefully and prophetically stressed that any country that represses another country cannot be free. Thus, he advocated for the national minorities "the right of autonomy to the point of secession," sharply criticizing Stalin—who degraded them to "border regions required for maintaining the might of Russia"—as a "Great-Russian bully." The tragic consequences, also for internal repression, are well known.

The state in all of its forms as constituted in history is part of the problem, not its solution on its own, in view of the necessarily intertwined operation of its internal and international self-assertive determinations. There can be no "socialism in one country" also on that score. The crucial issue is the transfer of all powers of decision-making, including those exercised by the state, to the social body. The capital system's internal and inter-state antagonisms can be overcome only together. This is why Marx stressed from a very early period of formulating his revolutionary conception that the state must "wither away." And he remained faithful to that conception until the very end.

9. THE NECESSARY MATERIALITY OF SUBSTANTIVE EQUALITY

After the shock of the French Revolution and the ensuing wars, early nineteenth-century developments had brought with them the stabilization of the bourgeois order. Naturally, the pre-revolutionary bourgeois utopian illusions had to be cast aside. But even so, befitting the circumstances of the immediate post-revolutionary antagonisms, the idea of equality remained in some way "in the air." It could even assume a most baffling form by the proclamation of the highest military honor in Germany in the form of the "socially equitable" Iron Cross, maintained as such ever since 1813 to our own day.

In its own economically most powerful historical specificity (and in due course by far the most wasteful), the socially most iniquitous bourgeois order succeeded in steadying itself early enough in the nineteenth century. There could be no question of granting real equality to the subordinate class of the former "Third Estate" that played a vital role in the relative success of the French Revolution. Only in the *formal* political domain, fully in tune with the material requirements of the bourgeois societal reproductive metabolism, was some form of equality acceptable, thanks to the limited reforming efforts of its leading liberal advocates, from Jeremy Bentham to John Stuart Mill and others. Even the English victor over Napoleon and for some time the Tory prime minister of Britain, the Duke of Wellington, could agree to that—as indeed he had to be asked to do at the time of the limited 1831–32 English Parliamentary Reform Bill. For the structurally entrenched order of class inequality, together with its likewise class exploitative state enforcement, was not significantly changed by such legal adjustments.

Nevertheless, we have seen some advancement in the direction of real equality, even if punctuated by grave antagonisms and disheartening reversals. As a result, there could no longer be any form of open justification for the political/military enforcement of slavery. The blatant contradiction of finding compatible with the aims of the 1776 American Revolution the slave-ownership of its "Founding Fathers" was eventually rectified in the American Civil War, and serfdom also was abolished all over the world. And this was by no means the end of the story. Pressure for revolutionary transformations continued in 1848–49 and 1871, and later on breaking even the "chain of imperialism" in several places not only through the Russian and the Chinese revolutions but also by putting an end to the *traditional colonial* domination in India and Southeast Asia, as well as in Africa.

To be sure, the most powerful form of slavery instituted in all history—capital's *wage slavery*—remains in force. But it must camouflage its rule as being in full consonance with the fundamental requirements of Freedom and Reason. How long can such mystification prevail? That is the difficult question. It used to be genuinely asserted and believed in the most radical social movements of the twentieth century that proper political/ideological enlightenment can sweep away the justification and power of wage slavery. The problems, however, are much more difficult than that. For the real historical stakes are defined in our time as the necessary transformation of the existing social metabolic order of *substantive inequality* into a radically different one of *substantive equality*. No social and political change in the past could be even remotely compared to the monumentality of that task. It requires the total reconstitution of the mode of controlling the material and cultural reproduction of our conditions of existence, from the smallest constitutive cells and microcosms of productive activity to the consciously planned non-hierarchical regulation of the most comprehensive global interdependencies.

As mentioned earlier, the truth is that *freedom* was *parasitic* in history on the objectively available more or less limited ground and potential of *equality* of its time. We should remember that Cyrus the Great granted the relative emancipatory rights of his "Commoners" for fully participating in military campaigns by stressing their *equality*—saying with amazing force that his consideration of their equality applied also to their souls—with the privileged warrior title of "Peers." And that happened nearly two and a half millennia before the time of Hegel.

The great challenge for our time is to turn the historically sustainable new potentialities of substantive equality into humanly self-realizing reality. Inevitably, this calls for the *total eradication* of the historical state—constituted as the structurally entrenched, necessarily hierarchical enemy of substantive equality—along with our increasingly destructive social metabolic order.

CHAPTER FOUR

Capital's Deepening Structural Crisis and the State

When stressing the need for a radical structural change it must be made clear right from the beginning that this is not a call for an unrealizable utopia. On the contrary, the primary defining characteristic of modern utopian theories was precisely the projection that improvement in the conditions of the workers' lives could be achieved well within the *existing structural framework* of the criticized societies. Thus, Robert Owen of New Lanark, for instance, who had an ultimately untenable business partnership with the utilitarian liberal philosopher Jeremy Bentham, attempted the general realization of his enlightened social and educational reforms in that spirit. He was asking for the *impossible*. As we also know, the high-sounding "utilitarian" moral principle of "the greatest good for the greatest number" came to nothing since its Benthamite advocacy. The problem for us is that without a proper assessment of the nature of the economic and social crisis of our time—which by now cannot be denied by the defenders of the capitalist order even if they reject the need for a major change—the likelihood of success in this respect is negligible. The demise of the "Welfare State" even in the handful of the privileged countries where it had once been instituted offers a sobering lesson on this score.

1. DEFINING THE STRUCTURAL CRISIS

The epochal nature of the crisis of our time and the failure of established organs to recognize it can be seen in a recent article by the editors of the authoritative daily newspaper of the international bourgeoisie, the *Financial Times*. Writing about the dangerous financial crisis of 2007–2008—acknowledged now by the FT editors to be dangerous—they end their article with these words: "Both sides [the U.S. Democrats and Republicans] are to blame for a vacuum of leadership and responsible deliberation. It is a serious failure of governance and more dangerous than Washington believes."[1] This is all we get as editorial wisdom about the substantive issue of "sovereign indebtedness" and mounting budget deficits. What makes the *Financial Times* editorial even more vacuous than the "vacuum of leadership" deplored by the journal is the sonorous subtitle of this article: "*Washington must stop posturing and start governing.*" As if editorials like this could amount to more than posturing in the name of "governing"! For the grave issue at stake is the catastrophic indebtedness of the "powerhouse" of global capitalism, the United States of America, where the government's debt alone (without adding corporate and private individual indebtedness) is counted already as well above *14 trillion dollars*—flashed in large, illuminated numbers on the façade of a New York public building—indicating the irresistible trend of rising debt.

The point to stress is that what we have to face is a profound and deepening structural crisis that needs the adoption of far-reaching structural remedies in order to achieve a sustainable solution. It must also be stressed that the structural crisis of our time did not originate in 2007, with the "bursting of the U.S. housing bubble," but at least four decades earlier. I spoke about it in such terms way back in 1967, well before the May 1968 explosion in France, and I wrote in 1971, in the preface to the third edition of *Marx's Theory of Alienation*, that the unfolding events and developments "dramatically underlined the intensification of the global structural crisis of capital."[2]

In this respect, it is necessary to clarify the relevant differences between types or modalities of crisis. It is not a matter of indifference whether a crisis in the social sphere can be considered a *periodic/ conjunctural crisis*, or something much more fundamental than that. For obviously the way of dealing with a fundamental structural crisis cannot be conceptualized in terms of the categories of periodic or conjunctural crises. The crucial difference between the two sharply contrasting types of crises is that the periodic or conjunctural crises unfold and are more or less successfully resolved within the established framework, whereas the fundamental crisis affects the framework itself in its entirety.

In general terms, this distinction is not simply a question of the apparent severity of the contrasting types of crises. For a periodic or conjunctural crisis can be dramatically severe—as the "Great World Economic Crisis of 1929-33" happened to be—yet capable of a solution within the parameters of the given system. And in the same way, but in the opposite sense, the "non-explosive" character of a prolonged structural crisis, in contrast to the "great thunderstorms" (in Marx's words) through which periodic conjunctural crises can discharge and resolve themselves, may lead to fundamentally misconceived strategies, as a result of the misinterpretation of the absence of "thunderstorms," as if their absence was the overwhelming evidence for the indefinite stability of "organized capitalism" and of the "integration of the working class."

It cannot be stressed enough that the crisis in our time is not intelligible without referring to the overall social framework. This means that in order to clarify the nature of the persistent and deepening crisis all over the world today we must focus attention on the crisis of the capital system in its entirety. For the crisis of capital we are experiencing is an all-embracing structural crisis.

The *historical* novelty of today's crisis is manifest under four main aspects:

1. Its *character* is *universal*, rather than restricted to one particular sphere (e.g., financial, or commercial, or affecting this or that particular branch of production, or applying to this rather than that type of labor, with its specific range of skills and degrees of productivity, etc.).

2. Its *scope* is truly *global* (in the most threateningly literal sense of the term), rather than confined to a particular set of countries (as all major crises have been in the past).
3. Its *time scale* is extended, continuous—if you like, *permanent*—rather than limited and *cyclic*, as all former crises of capital happened to be.
4. Its *mode* of unfolding might be called *creeping*—in contrast to the more spectacular and dramatic eruptions and collapses of the past—while adding the proviso that even the most vehement or violent convulsions cannot be excluded as far as the future is concerned: that is, when the complex machinery now actively engaged in "crisis-management" and in the more or less temporary "displacement" of the growing contradictions runs out of steam.

Here it is necessary to make some general points about the criteria of a structural crisis, as well as about the forms in which its solution may be envisaged.

- To put it in the simplest and most general terms, a structural crisis affects the *totality* of a social complex, in all its relations with its constituent parts or sub-complexes, as well as with other complexes to which it is linked. By contrast, a non-structural crisis affects only some parts of the complex in question, and thus no matter how severe it might be with regard to the affected parts, it cannot endanger the continued survival of the overall structure.
- Accordingly, the displacement of contradictions is feasible only while the crisis is partial, relative and internally manageable by the system, requiring no more than shifts—even if major ones—*within* the relatively autonomous system itself. By the same token, a structural crisis calls into question the very existence of the overall complex concerned, postulating its transcendence and replacement by some alternative complex.
- The same contrast may be expressed in terms of the limits any particular social complex happens to have in its immediacy, at any given time, as compared to those beyond which it cannot conceivably go.

Thus, a structural crisis is not concerned with the *immediate* limits but with the *ultimate* limits of a global structure.[3]

Thus, in a fairly obvious sense, nothing could be more serious than the structural crisis of capital's mode of social metabolic reproduction that defines the ultimate limits of the established order. But even though profoundly serious in its all-important general parameters, on the face of it the structural crisis may not appear to be of such a deciding importance when compared to the dramatic vicissitudes of a major conjunctural crisis. For the "thunderstorms" through which the conjunctural crises discharge themselves are rather paradoxical in the sense that in their unfolding they not only discharge (and impose) but also resolve themselves, to the degree to which it is feasible under the circumstances. This they can do precisely because of their partial character which does not call into question the ultimate limits of the established global structure. At the same time (and for the same reason), they can only "resolve" the underlying deep-seated structural problems—which necessarily reassert themselves again and again in the form of the specific conjunctural crises—in a strictly partial and temporally also most limited way. Until, that is, the next conjunctural crisis appears on society's horizon.

By contrast, in view of the inescapably complex and prolonged nature of the structural crisis, unfolding in historical time in an *epochal* and not episodic/instantaneous sense, it is the cumulative interrelationship of the whole that decides the issue, even under the false appearance of "normality." This is because in the structural crisis everything is at stake, involving the all-embracing ultimate limits of the given order of which there cannot possibly be a "symbolic/paradigmatic" particular instance. Without understanding the overall systemic connections and implications of the particular events and developments, we lose sight of the really significant changes and of the corresponding levers of potential strategic intervention positively to affect them, in the interest of the necessary systemic transformation. Our social responsibility therefore calls for an uncompromising critical awareness of the emerging cumulative interrelationship, instead of looking for comforting reassurances in the world of illusory normality until the house collapses over our head.

2. SARTRE AND THE VIABILITY OF ADVANCED CAPITALISM

It is necessary to underscore that for nearly three decades after the Second World War, the successful economic expansion in the dominant capitalist countries generated the illusion, even among some major intellectuals of the left, that the historic phase of "crisis capitalism" had been overcome, leaving its place to what they called "advanced organized capitalism." This can be illustrated by quoting some passages from the work of one of the greatest militant intellectuals of the twentieth century, Jean-Paul Sartre. The fact is, however, that the adoption of the notion that by overcoming "crisis capitalism" the established order turned itself into "advanced capitalism" created major dilemmas for Sartre. This is all the more significant because no one can deny Sartre's fully committed search for a viable emancipatory solution and his great personal integrity. Here it is important to recall that in the important interview given to the Italian Manifesto group—after outlining his conception of the insuperably negative implications of his own explanatory category of the unavoidably detrimental institutionalization of what he called the "fused group" in his *Critique of Dialectical Reason*—he had to come to this painful conclusion: "While I recognize the need of an *organization*, I must confess that I don't see how the problems which confront *any stabilized structure* could be resolved."[4]

Here the difficulty is that the terms of Sartre's social analysis are set up in such a way that the various factors and correlations that in reality belong together, constituting different facets of fundamentally the *same societal complex*, are depicted by him in the form of most problematic dichotomies and oppositions, generating thereby insoluble dilemmas and an unavoidable defeat for the emancipatory social forces. This is clearly shown by the exchange between the Manifesto group and Sartre:

> *Manifesto*: On what precise bases can one prepare a revolutionary alternative?

Sartre: I repeat, more on the basis of *"alienation"* than on *"needs."* In short on the reconstruction of the *individual* and of *freedom*—the need for which is so pressing that even the most refined *techniques of integration* cannot afford to discount it.[5]

Thus Sartre, in this way, in his strategic assessment of how to overcome the oppressive character of capitalist reality, sets up a totally untenable opposition between the workers' "alienation" and their allegedly satisfied "needs," thereby making it all the more difficult to envisage a practically feasible positive outcome. And here the problem is not simply that he grants far too much credibility to the fashionable but extremely superficial sociological explanation of the so-called *refined techniques of integration* in relation to the workers. Unfortunately, it is much more serious than this.

Indeed, the disturbing problem at stake is the evaluation of the viability of "advanced capitalism" itself and the associated postulate of working-class "integration," which Sartre happened to share at the time to a large extent with Herbert Marcuse. For in actuality the truth of the matter is that in contrast to the undoubtedly feasible integration of some particular workers into the capitalist order, the class of labor—the structural antagonist of capital, representing the only *historically sustainable hegemonic alternative* to the capital system—cannot be integrated into capital's alienating and exploitative framework of societal reproduction. What makes that impossible is the underlying structural antagonism between capital and labor, emanating with insurmountable necessity from the class reality of antagonistic domination and subordination.

In this discourse, even the minimal plausibility of the Marcuse/Sartre type of false alternative between continuing alienation and "satisfied need" is "established" on the basis of the derailing compartmentalization of capital's suicidally untenable globally entrenched structural interdeterminations upon which the elementary systemic viability of capital's one and only ruling societal metabolic order is necessarily premised. Thus, it is extremely problematical to separate "advanced capitalism" from the "marginal zones" and from the "third world."

As if the reproductive order of the postulated "advanced capitalism" could sustain itself for *any length of time*, let alone *indefinitely* in the future, without the ongoing exploitation of the misconceived "marginal zones" and the imperialistically dominated "third world"! It is necessary to quote the relevant passage in which these problems are spelled out by Sartre. The revealing Manifesto interview passage in question reads as follows:

> *Advanced capitalism*, in relation to its awareness of its own condition, and despite the enormous disparities in the distribution of income, manages to satisfy the elementary needs of the majority of the working class—there remains of course the *marginal zones*, 15 percent of workers in the United States, the blacks and the immigrants; there remain the elderly; there remains, on the global scale, the *third world*. But capitalism satisfies certain primary needs, and also satisfies certain needs which it has artificially created: for instance, the *need of a car*. It is this situation which has caused me to revise my "theory of needs," since these needs are no longer, in a situation of *advanced capitalism*, in systematic opposition to the system. On the contrary, they partly become, under the control of that system, an instrument of *integration of the proletariat* into certain processes engendered and directed by profit. The worker exhausts himself in producing a car and in earning enough to buy one; this *acquisition* gives him the *impression* of having satisfied a *"need."* The system which exploits him provides him simultaneously with a goal and with the possibility of reaching it. The consciousness of the intolerable character of the system must therefore no longer be sought in the impossibility of satisfying elementary needs but, above all else, in the consciousness of alienation—in other words, in the fact that *this life is not worth living and has no meaning*, that this mechanism is a deceptive mechanism, that these needs are artificially created, that they are false, that they are exhausting and only serve profit. But to unite the class on this basis is even *more difficult*.[6]

If we accept at face value this characterization of the "advanced capitalist" order, in that case the task of producing emancipatory consciousness is not only "*more difficult*" but quite *impossible*. But the dubious ground on which we can reach such an *a prioristic* imperatival and pessimistic/self-defeating conclusion—prescribing from the height of the intellectual's "new theory of needs" the abandonment by the workers of their "acquisitive artificial needs," instantiated by the motor car, and their replacement by the thoroughly abstract postulate which posits for them that "*this life is not worth living and has no meaning*" (a noble but rather abstract imperatival postulate effectively contradicted in reality by the tangible need of the members of the working class for securing the conditions of their economically sustainable existence)—is both the *acceptance* of a set of totally untenable *assertions* and the equally untenable *omission* of some vital determining features of the actually existing capital system in its historically irreversible *structural crisis*.

For a start, to talk about "*advanced* capitalism"—when the capital system as a mode of social metabolic reproduction finds itself in its *descending phase of historical development*, and therefore is only *capitalistically* advanced but in no other sense at all, thereby capable of sustaining itself only in an ever more *destructive* and therefore ultimately also *self-destructive* way—is extremely problematic. Another assertion: the characterization of the *overwhelming majority of humankind*, in the category of poverty, including the "blacks and the immigrants," the "elderly," and, "on the global scale, the third world," as belonging to the "*marginal zones*" (in affinity with Marcuse's "outsiders") is no less untenable. For in reality, it is the "advanced capitalist world" that constitutes the long-term unsustainable privileged *margin* of the overall system, with its ruthless "elementary need-denial" to the greater part of the world, and not what is described by Sartre in his Manifesto interview as the "marginal zones." Even with regard to the United States, the margin of poverty is greatly underrated, at merely 15 percent. Besides, the characterization of the workers' motor cars as nothing more than purely "artificial needs" that "only serve profit" could not be more one-sided. For, in contrast to many intellectuals, not even the relatively well-off particular workers, let alone the members of the class of labor as a whole, have the luxury of finding their place of work next door to their bedroom.

At the same time, on the side of the astonishing omissions, some of the gravest structural contradictions and failures are missing from Sartre's depiction of "advanced capitalism," virtually emptying the whole concept of meaning. In this sense one of the most important substantive needs without which no society—past, present, or future—could survive, is the need for work. Both for the productively active individuals, embracing all of them in a fully emancipated social order, and for society in general in its historically sustainable relationship to nature. The necessary failure to solve this fundamental structural problem, affecting *all* categories of work not only in the "third world" but even in the most privileged countries of "advanced capitalism," with its perilously rising unemployment, constitutes one of the *absolute limits* of the capital system in its entirety.

Another grave problem that underscores the present and future historical unviability of capital is the calamitous shift toward the *parasitic sectors* of the economy—like the crisis-producing adventurist speculation that plagues (as a matter of *objective necessity*, often misrepresented as systemically irrelevant *personal* failure) the financial sector and the institutionalized/legally buttressed *fraudulence* closely associated with it—in contradistinction to the productive branches of socioeconomic life required for the satisfaction of genuine human needs. This is a shift that stands in menacingly sharp contrast to the ascending phase of capital's historic development, when the prodigious systemic expansionary dynamism (including the Industrial Revolution) was overwhelmingly due to socially viable and further enhanceable productive achievements.

We have to add to all this the *massively wasteful* economic burdens imposed on society in an authoritarian way by the state and the military/industrial complex—with the permanent arms industry and the corresponding wars—as an integral part of the perverse "economic growth" of "advanced organized capitalism." And to mention just one more of the catastrophic implications of "advanced" capital's systemic development, we must bear in mind the prohibitively wasteful global ecological encroachment of our no longer tenable mode of social metabolic reproduction on the finite planetary world, with its rapacious exploitation of the non-renewable material resources and the increasingly more dangerous destruction of nature.[7] Saying this is not "being wise after the event." I wrote in the same period when Sartre gave his Manifesto interview:

> Another basic contradiction of the capitalist system of control is that it cannot separate "advance" from *destruction*, nor "progress" from *waste*— however catastrophic the results. The more it unlocks the powers of productivity, the more it must unleash the powers of destruction; and the more it extends the volume of production, the more it must bury everything under mountains of suffocating waste. The concept of *economy* is radically incompatible with the "economy" of capital production which, of necessity, adds insult to injury by first using up with rapacious wastefulness the *limited resources* of our planet, and then further aggravates the outcome by *polluting and poisoning* the human environment with its mass-produced waste and effluence.[8]

Thus, the problematic *assertions* and the seminally important *omissions* of Sartre's characterization of "advanced capitalism" greatly weaken the power of negation of his emancipatory discourse. His dichotomous principle that repeatedly asserts the "irreducibility of the cultural order to the natural order" is always on the lookout for finding solutions in terms of the "cultural order," at the level of the individual's consciousness, through the committed intellectual's *"work of consciousness upon consciousness."* He appeals to the idea that the required solution lies in increasing the "consciousness of alienation"—that is, in terms of his "cultural order"—while at the same time discarding the viability of grounding the revolutionary strategy on *need* belonging to the "natural order." Material need is said to be already satisfied for the majority of the workers and in any case constitutes a "deceptive and false mechanism" and an "instrument of integration of the proletariat."

To be sure, Sartre is deeply concerned with the challenge of addressing the issue of how to increase "the consciousness of the intolerable character of the system." But, as a matter of unavoidable consideration, the leverage itself indicated as the vital condition of success—the power of the "consciousness of alienation" stressed by Sartre—would itself badly need some objective underpinning. Otherwise, the idea (even setting aside the indicated leverage's weakness of self-referential circularity) that it somehow "*can* prevail over against the intolerable character of the system" is bound to be dismissed as a noble but ineffective cultural advocacy. That this is problematic even in Sartre's own terms of reference is indicated by his rather pessimistic words wherein he shows that the need is to defeat the materially and culturally destructive and structurally entrenched reality of "this miserable ensemble which is our planet," with its "horrible, ugly, bad determinations, without hope."

Accordingly, the primary question concerns the demonstrability—or not—of the *objectively intolerable* character of the system itself. For if the demonstrable intolerability of the system is missing in *substantive* terms, as proclaimed by the notion of "advanced capitalism's" ability to satisfy material needs except in the "marginal zones," then the "*long and patient labor in the construction of consciousness*" advocated by Sartre remains well-nigh impossible.[9] It is this objective grounding that needs to be (and in actuality can be) established in its own comprehensive terms of reference, requiring the radical demystification of the increasing destructiveness of "advanced capitalism." The "*consciousness* of the intolerable character of the system" can only be built on that *objective grounding*—which includes the suffering caused by "advanced" capital's failure to satisfy even the elementary need for food not only in "marginal zones" but for countless millions, as clearly evidenced by food riots in many countries—so as to be able to overcome the postulated dichotomy between the cultural order and the natural order.

In its *ascending* phase, the capital system was successfully asserting its productive accomplishments on the basis of its internal expansionary dynamism—still without the imperative of the monopolistic/imperialist drive of the capitalistically most advanced countries for militarily secured world domination. Yet, through the historically irreversible circumstance of entering the *productively descending* phase, the capital system had become inseparable from an ever-intensifying need for the militaristic/monopolistic extension and overstretch of its structural framework. This has led in due course on the internal productive plane toward the establishment and the criminally wasteful operation of a "permanent arms industry," together with the wars necessarily associated with it.

In fact, well before the outbreak of the First World War, Rosa Luxemburg clearly identified the nature of this fateful monopolistic/imperialist development on the destructively productive plane by writing in *The Accumulation of Capital* about the role of massive militarist production: "Capital itself ultimately controls this automatic and rhythmic movement of militarist production through the legislature and a press whose function is to mould so-called 'public opinion.' That is why this particular province of capitalist accumulation at first seems capable of infinite expansion."[10]

In another respect, the increasingly wasteful utilization of energy and vital material strategic resources carried with it not only the ever more destructive articulation of capital's self-assertive structural determinations on the (by legislatively manipulated "public opinion" never even questioned, let alone properly regulated) military plane, but also with regard to the increasingly destructive encroachment of capital expansion on nature. Ironically, but by no means surprisingly, this turn of *regressive historical development* of the capital system as such also carried with it some bitterly negative consequences for the international organization of labor.

Indeed, this new articulation of the capital system in the last third of the nineteenth century, with its monopolistic imperialist phase inseparable from its fully extended global ascendancy, opened up a new modality of (most antagonistic and ultimately untenable) expansionary dynamism at the overwhelming benefit of a mere handful of privileged imperialist countries, postponing thereby the "moment of truth" that goes with the system's irrepressible *structural crisis* in our own time. This type of monopolistic imperialist development inevitably gave a major boost to the possibility of militaristic capital-expansion and accumulation, no matter how great a price had to be paid in due course for the ever-intensifying destructiveness of the new expansionary dynamism. Indeed, the militarily underpinned monopolistic dynamism had to assume the form of even two devastating *global wars*, as well as the total annihilation of humankind implicit in a potential *Third World War*, in addition to the ongoing perilous destruction of nature that became evident in the second half of the twentieth century.

In our time we are experiencing the deepening structural crisis of the capital system. Its destructiveness is visible everywhere, and it shows no signs of diminishing. With regard to the future, it is crucial how we conceptualize the nature of the crisis in order to envisage its solution. For the same reason it is also necessary to reexamine some of the major solutions projected in the past. Here it is not possible to do more than to mention, with stenographic brevity, the contrasting approaches that have been offered, indicating at the same time what happened to them in actuality.

First, we have to remember that it was to his merit that liberal philosopher John Stuart Mill considered how problematic endless capitalist growth might be, suggesting as the solution of this problem the "stationary state of the economy." Naturally, such a "stationary state" under the capital system could be nothing more than wishful thinking, because it is totally incompatible with the imperative of capital expansion and accumulation. Even today, when so much destructiveness is caused by unqualified growth and the most wasteful allocation of our vital energy and strategic material resources, the mythology of growth is constantly reasserted, coupled with the wishful projection of "reducing our carbon imprint" by the year 2050, while in reality moving in the opposite direction. Thus, the reality of liberalism turned out to be the aggressive destructiveness of neoliberalism.

Similar fate affected the social democratic perspective. Marx clearly formulated his warnings about this danger in his *Critique of the Gotha Programme*, but they were totally ignored. Here, too, the contradiction between the promised Bernsteinian "evolutionary socialism" and its realization everywhere turned out to be striking. Not only in virtue of the capitulation of social-democratic parties and governments to the lure of imperialist wars but also through the transformation of social democracy in general—including British "New Labour"—into more or less open versions of neoliberalism, abandoning not only the "road of evolutionary socialism" but even the once promised implementation of significant social reform.

Moreover, a much-propagandized solution to the gruesome inequalities of the capital system was the promised worldwide diffusion of the "Welfare State" after the Second World War. However, the prosaic reality of this claimed historic achievement turned out to be not only the utter failure to institute the Welfare State in any part of the so-called third world, but rather the ongoing liquidation of the relative achievements of the postwar Welfare State—in the field of social security, health care, and education—even in the handful of privileged capitalist countries where they were once instituted.

And, of course, we cannot disregard the promise to realize the highest phase of socialism (by Stalin and others) through the overthrow and abolition of capitalism. For, tragically, seven decades after the October Revolution, the reality turned out to be the restoration of capitalism in a regressive neoliberal form in the countries of the former Soviet Union and Eastern Europe.

The common denominator of all of these failed attempts—despite some of their major differences—is that they all tried to accomplish their objectives within the structural framework of the established social metabolic order. However, as painful historical experience teaches us, our problem is not simply "the overthrow of capitalism." For even to the extent to which that objective can be accomplished, it is bound to be only a very unstable achievement, because whatever can be *overthrown* can also be *restored*. The real—and much more difficult—issue is the necessity of *radical structural change*.

The tangible meaning of such *structural change* is the *complete eradication of capital itself from the social metabolic process*. In other words, the eradication of capital from the metabolic process of societal reproduction.

Capital itself is an all-embracing mode of *control*, which means that it either controls everything or it implodes as a system of societal reproductive control. Consequently, capital as such cannot be controlled in some of its aspects while leaving the rest in place. All attempted measures and modalities of "controlling" capital's various functions on a lasting basis have failed in the past. In view of its *structurally entrenched uncontrollability*—which means that there is no conceivable leverage *within the structural framework of the capital system itself* through which the system itself could be brought under lasting control—capital must be completely *eradicated*. This is the central meaning of Marx's lifework.

In our time, the question of control—through the institution of *structural change* in response to our deepening structural crisis—is becoming urgent not only in the financial sector, due to the wasted trillions of dollars, but everywhere. The leading capitalist financial journals complain that "China is sitting on three trillion dollars of cash," wishfully projecting again solutions through the "better use of that money." But the sobering truth is that the total worsening indebtedness of capitalism amounts to ten times more than China's "unused dollars." Besides, even if the huge current indebtedness could be eliminated somehow, although no one can say how, the real question would remain: How was it generated in the first place, and how can it be made sure that it is not generated again in the future? This is why the productive dimension of the system—namely the capital relation itself—is what must be fundamentally changed in order to overcome the *structural crisis* through the appropriate *structural change*.

The dramatic financial crisis that we experienced in the last three years is only one aspect of the capital system's three-pronged destructiveness:

1. In the military field, with capital's interminable wars since the onset of monopolistic imperialism in the final decades of the nineteenth century, and its ever more devastating weapons of mass destruction in the last sixty years;
2. The intensification through capital's obvious destructive impact on ecology directly affecting and endangering by now the elementary natural foundation of human existence itself; and

3. In the domain of material production an ever-increasing waste, due to the advancement of "destructive production" in place of the once eulogized "creative" or "productive destruction."

These are the grave systemic problems of our *structural crisis* that can only be solved by a comprehensive *structural change* in the system of social metabolic reproduction not excluding the state.

CHAPTER FIVE

Capital's Historic Circle Is Closing

We are now not very far from marking the centenary of President Franklin Delano Roosevelt's First Inaugural Address. In fact, by now more than five-sixths of the time is gone toward that memorable centenary. However, the changes accomplished in all these decades are very far from what were the solemnly declared, and for a long time sincerely believed, original hopeful expectations.

President Roosevelt entered his office in the period of what is customarily referred to as the Great World Economic Crisis, dated 1929–33. His First Inaugural Address was delivered on March 4, 1933, promising a radical change in the world economy, not as a limited conjunctural improvement lasting perhaps a few years, but as a deep-seated and permanent transformation. Major unhindered capital-expansion was thought to be the answer, to be helped along in a significant way by presidential candidate Roosevelt's New Deal program in the United States, announced on July 2, 1932, and contributing, of course, to his overwhelmingly successful election.

Indeed, economic expansion appeared to work almost prodigiously in the United States from the second half of 1933 to the early months of 1937. However, in the second half of 1937 the U.S. economy started to relapse into a stagnant state and in 1938 the country experienced a *deep recession*, with unemployment rising from 14 in 1937 to 19 percent in 1938. Understandably, the outbreak of the Second World War "rescued" the U.S. economy from its recession, carrying with it for the country a massive productive expansion and two decades of successful growth after the end of the global war, in the period of postwar reconstruction all over Europe and in some other parts of the world.

President Roosevelt's original design for a vigorous capitalist economy explicitly advocated the removal of "artificial" protective devices represented by the still existing British and French empires. He made it absolutely clear in his First Inaugural Address that he "shall spare no effort to restore world trade by *international economic readjustment*."[1] And in the same spirit a few years later, he made it quite clear that he advocated the right "to trade in an atmosphere of *freedom from unfair competition and domination by monopolies at home or abroad*."[2] President Roosevelt also made it very clear during the Second World War that he was not only against the British continuing to rule India after the war but equally against the French retaining the territories of Indochina as well as their North African colonies.[3]

Thus, Roosevelt genuinely believed that putting an end to the traditional empires would create the conditions for healthy economic development all over the world. And he projected American leadership as arising not from colonial/military domination, but by virtue of the principles inherent in the U.S. type of economic advancement, oriented by the claimed "freedom from unfair competition and domination by monopolies at home or abroad." Toward the peak of the country's successful expansion under the New Deal he was even talking in heightened positive terms about the work of "*destiny*" in this way: "A better civilization than any we have known is in store for America and by our example, perhaps, for the world. Here destiny seems to have taken a long look."[4]

However, in contrast to such expectations, postwar developments— by which time Roosevelt was dead—had brought with them not "freedom from monopolies at home or abroad" but the assertion of the new power relations of continued imperialism under American domination. Under such conditions the world economy was characterized by the prevalence of the most iniquitous *differential rate of exploitation* of the global labor force, with labor in the capitalistically much more advanced U.S. economy occupying a considerably better position in that respect.

Filipino historian and political theorist Renato Constantino gave a striking example of this gruesome mode of exploitation, which in his country imposed the appallingly low wages of the differential rate:

> Ford Philippines, Inc., established only in 1967, is now [four years later] 37th in the roster of the 1,000 biggest corporations in the Philippines. In 1971 it reported a return on equity of 121.32 percent, whereas its overall return on equity in 133 countries in the same year was only 11.8 percent. Aside from all the incentives extracted from the government, Ford's high profits were mainly due to cheap labor. While the U.S. hourly rate for skilled labor in 1971 was almost $7.50, the rate for similar work in the Philippines was only $0.30.[5]

What is most significant in such matters, however, is that from the early 1970s onward we have been experiencing the capital system's deepening *structural crisis*, instead of the originally projected unhindered expansion of the world economy to the benefit of all. The secondary antagonism of the capital system between the rival competing units for a long historical period contributed to expansion and, in turn, was also greatly supported by continued expansion. This is why it could be idealized in the name of unqualified expansion, ignoring its nature and consequences. With the onset of capital's *structural* or *systemic crisis*, however, things have changed not only for the worse but for much the worst.

Thus, despite the increasingly direct involvement of the capitalist state in the economy, even in the form of injecting in its rescue operations trillions of dollars into the bottomless hole of bankrupt capitalist enterprises, the problems multiplied. At the same time, the neoliberal ideologues of capital hypocritically continued to glorify the insuperable virtues of the "free enterprise system" and even the fiction of "rolling back the boundaries of the state" when in reality we had a propensity to stagger from one crisis to another ever since the 1970s. In our time, however, in contrast to 1939, the potentiality of a *global war* cannot "rescue" the capital system from its deepening structural crisis, because of its suicidal danger. Thus, the primary antagonism between capital and labor—representing also labor's positive hegemonic alternative to the system's modality of societal reproduction—cannot be ignored any longer.

CAPITAL'S CLOSING CIRCLE

With the structural crisis of the capital system as a whole, and by no means only of capitalism, the expansionary historic circle through which capital could dominate humanity for a very long time is perilously closing. That closure brings with it the danger of humanity's total destruction in the interest of capital's absurdly prolonged rule. Since the 1970s I have repeatedly tried to highlight the fundamental differences between capitalism, historically limited to a few centuries, and the much more fundamental frame of reference of the capital system, focusing at the same time on the grave dangers manifest in now-unfolding historical developments.[6]

In stressing the fundamental difference between the capital system as a whole and the limited historical phase of capitalism integrated into the overall capital system it is important to understand that the capital system is not limited to capitalism alone. It cannot be underlined enough that the capitalist private enterprise form of production, with its "personifications of capital" (in Marx's words) in individual capitalists, can be overthrown, and had been, for instance, through the Russian October Revolution in 1917, but not the capital system in its entirety. It must be totally *eradicated* through a fundamental restructuring process and replaced by a radically different socialist metabolic order. Likewise, the *capitalist state* can be overthrown, and had been, but not the *state as such*. The state as *such* must also be *totally eradicated* and replaced by a qualitatively different modality of truly *autonomous overall control* of societal decision-making by the people through the qualitative reconstitution of the social metabolism itself.

The disconcerting historical fact is that whatever can be *overthrown* can also be *restored*. Indeed, private capitalism and the capitalist state had been both overthrown and restored. Restored, for instance in the former Soviet Union, by Mikhail Gorbachev and his associates. And they did not have to restore the capital system itself because they had it already, with themselves as the dominant post-capitalist bureaucratic "personifications of capital" whose role was to enforce the *politically* regulated maximal extraction of surplus labor, in contrast to the *primarily economic* extraction of surplus labor as surplus value under capitalism. For the historically limited post-capitalist transformations of capitalism—like those undertaken in October 1917 and thereafter—are perfectly compatible with the continued rule of the capital system's metabolic order, since no fundamental socialist restructuring is involved in the *political overthrow* of the capitalist state without the eradication of the hierarchically entrenched state structure itself.

This is an elementary lesson for the future. In fact, the difference between the capital system and capitalism is vitally important to us not in relation to the past but in terms of the present and the future. Our grave problem is the danger presented to humanity's survival not simply by this or that particular form of capital's state formations known up to the present time but by any one of its *conceivable* varieties also in the future, as they are *bound* to arise if capital's social metabolic order is not restructured in a historically viable socialist way. It must be also underlined that the idea of a "*global coercive state*," no matter who champions it, borders on insanity.

BREAKING THE BOUNDS OF NATURE

To be sure, capital's personifications of any color must resist at all costs the necessary closure of their system's historic circle in the interest of prolonging its rule. For the globally perceptible social determinations pointing in the direction of that historic closure are both overwhelming and closely intertwined, so that against them the traditionally enforced adjustments and state correctives cannot work any longer.

Let us see the principal factors that indicate the necessary closure of the capital system's historic circle, calling at the same time for a viable alternative.

Perhaps the most obvious—if extremely problematic—global accomplishment that cannot be denied in its all-destructive power even by capital's worst apologists is the ability of the dominant states to annihilate humanity through a global military conflagration. Evidently, this problematic achievement through the now fully operational weapons of mass destruction did not exist in past ages. However, it appeared on our horizon with its menacing finality simultaneously with the closure of capital's historic circle. As we know, in our time, the "strategic thinkers" of the political/military domain do not hesitate to commend and actively "plan the unthinkable," while some presidents and prime ministers decree that, with their politically trustworthy "safe fingers," they would not hesitate to push the *nuclear button* in the event of a global confrontation.

In this way the capital system's ardent defenders put their fate into the safety and viability of the weapons of mass destruction—which include chemical and biological weaponry—as well as into the groundlessly assumed remedy of *Mutually Assured Destruction* (MAD). The alternative would be, of course, to positively overcome the *causes* of lethal antagonisms, which happen to be inseparable from the nature of the capital system itself, especially in the descending phase of its global development. But precisely because such *systemic antagonism* is inherent in capital's social metabolic order, not reducible to its political/military superstructure, the measures traditionally enforced through extreme military violence by the rival states cannot be used under the conditions of potentially total destruction of humanity. That price would be far too high to pay even in terms of the most elementary requirements of rationality.

Advocating MAD as a postulated automatic deterrence is a fundamentally irrational strategy. Its only "rationality" consists in promoting the massive vested interests of the "military-industrial complex," in Eisenhower's memorable phrase. The required and feasible alternative to MAD can only be the elaboration of a qualitatively different social metabolic order. A new order that is not overburdened with systemic antagonisms due to vested interests. The operation of such a qualitatively different social metabolism is the only way to bring under control, and in due course fully eliminate, the now threatening weapons of mass destruction. By contrast, the radical incompatibility of attending to the *causes* of antagonism within the established economic and political order, in view of its insuperably antagonistic systemic determinations, signals the necessary closure of capital's historic circle.

Another literally vital determination on the global scale concerns our planet's *limited material resources*. Naturally, this is also a historical development, accomplished through the spread of the capitalistically ever more advanced mode of industrial production over the entire globe, with more than seven billion people. These conditions of growing resource limitations are sharply differentiated from the past, even the period just before the Second World War. Today it is unavoidable to consider satisfying the needs of *four immense capitalist economic complexes*—the United States, Europe, China, and India—in contrast to a few decades earlier, when a handful of dominant capitalist countries could derive overwhelming benefits from the material resources and services of the "underdeveloped world," treated as the presumed legitimate "hinterland" of their own expansion. As a result of these changes, the working classes of China and India have started to demand a less miserable share of their own products, to be used by themselves, in comparison to the past.

Naturally, of this whole complex of problems, the apologists of capital only notice the greatly increased need for the planet's limited material resources, and even that in a grossly distorted form, under the ideologically most revealing heading of "population explosion." To be sure, no one should deny the increasing relevance of these factors, let alone the absolute legitimacy of the people's need. But it is necessary to highlight some social and economic determinations that inevitably call again for a fundamental structural change in our societal reproductive order. They indicate some heavily aggravating conditions regarding the mode of allocating and utilizing the resources available for the satisfaction of the needs of ever greater numbers who work with, and lay their claim on, our planet's limited material resources as a result of capital's economic conquest of the world.

It is enough to mention here two of the most important aggravating conditions: (1) the perverse imperative of uncontrollable *capital expansion* oriented toward *exchange value*, to the detriment of *use-value*, creating artificial *scarcity*; and (2) the dominance of *destructive production* and concomitant *waste*, combined with the capital system's self-mythology of "creative destruction," made worse in the *descending phase* of capital's systemic development.

In relation to both of these major aggravating determinations, the obvious feasible remedy would be a *positively planned* strategic intervention in the economy, in the interest of maximizing socially required *use-value* and at the same time attending to the strictest control of waste. But that kind of *rationally planned economy*—which is inconceivable without *substantive equality* as its social basis—is totally incompatible with the long-established modality of capitalist production.

Moreover, add to the *general* problem of increased need for the planet's material resources—including the elementary requirement of water—the *special difficulty* arising for the demand for *strategic* material resources among the competing massive capitalist complexes. In the absence of a rationally planned allocation of such resources on a global scale, this can only lead to *belligerent* confrontations among the rival states, with potentially devastating consequences. By now for several centuries the capitalist productive system had very little concern about *economy* as *economizing*, in the original sense of that term. However, in the future the required societal reproduction is bound to be totally unthinkable without the conscious application of the orienting principles of a properly planned and responsibly economizing economy. Accordingly, also in that sense we notice here the necessary closure of the capital system's historic circle.

At least one more problem must be boldly underlined here: the *ecological incompatibility* of capital's mode of social metabolic reproduction with the rationally sustainable demands of our time. This is clearly expressed even in the way in which a new geological epoch is being named to indicate humanity's extremely problematical—indeed most dangerous—impact on our planet. This *new geological epoch* is called the *Anthropocene*, corresponding to the time when some of the capital system's ineradicable damages have been inflicted on our planet, more or less in the last hundred years, beginning with the residues of nuclear explosions and continuing to the present, in permanent plastic deposits in the oceans.

Naturally, capital's ecological incompatibility with the demands of historically sustainable existence goes much further than a few uncontestable and no longer eradicable phenomena that mark a new geological epoch, even if their rate of increase might be reduced or stopped altogether. To the vast range of ecological damages, we have to add, among others, not only chemical pollution and soil erosion, but also, frequently discussed at conferences on "global warming," the increasing acidity in our oceans, as well as the grave disruption of biodiversity and the irresponsible treatment of nuclear waste in the service of profit. Indeed, the earlier mentioned aggravating condition of *destructive production*, in the interest of maintaining uncontrolled growth targets and mindless profitability, is closely connected with capital's enmity to ecological sustainability. Thus, also in this absolutely vital domain the painful evidence points to the closure of the capital system's historic circle. An irreversible closure because the capital system, due to its innermost structural determinations, cannot remedy any of the identified dangerous developments, even if it tries to derive profit from them in some cases, like for instance the grotesquely propagandized "carbon tax" as the claimed solution to global warming.

What are the prospects for the future under these circumstances? That is a very difficult question. For in connection with all of the determinations identifiable in the closure of capital's historic circle we find powerful vested interests inseparable from the mode of overall control characteristic of the Leviathan state. Rational appeal for change would be in this respect naïve. Structurally entrenched overall decision-making powers tend to resort to *adventurism* when they cannot prevail in any other way. Historical evidence for countless centuries tends to confirm that way of responding to fundamental challenges by the rival states when the stakes increase.

THE MARCH OF FOLLY

In relation to the Leviathan state's unavoidable adventurism, it is relevant to distinguish between the unholy imperative of the state's commanding functions in dangerous situations and the role of implementing them by the commanding personnel itself. As mentioned before, in idealist philosophical accounts of historical development, exemplified by the most monumental of them conceived by G. W. F. Hegel, the commanding personnel of the state tends to assume a somewhat mysterious role, under the exalted name of the "World Historical Person"—like Alexander the Great, Caesar, Luther, and Napoleon, repeatedly praised by Hegel—as the instruments cunningly used for its own design and purposes by the "World Spirit" and hidden from the historical individuals concerned.

In his characterization of the paradoxically unhappy fate of such figures, we are told by Hegel that "they attained no calm enjoyment; their whole life was labor and trouble; their whole nature was naught else but their master-passion. When their object is attained they fall off like empty hulls from the kernel. They die early, like Alexander; they are murdered, like Caesar; transported to St. Helena, like Napoleon."[7]

However, the question of *why* the World Historical Persons must suffer a rather unhappy fate in their different historic circumstances remains wrapped up in complete mystery. The assertion that they have *fulfilled* the World Spirit's hidden design and therefore can "fall off like empty hulls from the kernel" seems to be ubiquitously valid by *definition*, thanks to the very nature of the Hegelian explanatory design. The World Historical Persons cannot go wrong even when they go devastatingly wrong, because in doing so, even if their action brings disaster, they actually fulfill the World Spirit's unobjectionable purpose. In this way even the most *irresponsible* deed pursued by them is *responsible* and even *ideal*, because it brings into existence the required World Historical phase of events and developments, together with their objective embodiments.

The particular *institutional* forms and *instruments* through which the World Historical Persons prevail or fail—in the case of the three individuals named by Hegel, Alexander, Caesar, and Napoleon, acting within the particular institutional form of the *antagonistic state* through which they assert their own role—is not mentioned at all, let alone criticized by the great German philosopher, because *they themselves* are said to be the *instruments*. Indeed, they are said to be the instruments not of a potentially objectionable particular state formation but of the World Spirit itself whose *ultimate* design is the institution of the *ethically insuperable* (and therefore absolutely unobjectionable) institution of the Germanic state. Such a state cannot be considered an *instrument* in its human sense. For it is said to be nothing less exalted than "the Divine Idea as it exists on Earth."[8]

The great problem in this respect is that in the really existing world the requirement of successful military action in the interest of the *particular antagonistic state formation* represented by its commanding personnel sooner or later induces them as decision-makers—that is, as Hegel's World Historical Persons—to undertake *extreme risks* and *overreach their own power* in dangerous *adventures* until a greater state power violently counters their efforts. Before that fateful clash, there seems to be *no limit* to their commanding power. They must presume to undertake even the most extreme risks, not because their "whole nature is naught else but their master-passion," but because it is dictated by the objectively required state imperative to succeed on behalf of the state, which they command, and outwit through their chosen extreme designs their adversary or enemy.

The Hegelian World Historical Person nearest to our own time, Napoleon, was undoubtedly an outstanding historic figure. Winston Churchill characterized him as "the greatest man of action born in Europe since Julius Caesar."[9] In truth he was much more than that. He was a great military leader and commander as well as an organizational genius, with his own vision of the state. Napoleon was victorious in fifty-eight of the sixty-five immense military confrontations he fought, often against far superior forces. Even his English military rival, who in the end defeated him at Waterloo thanks to much more powerful military units on his side, "when asked who was the greatest captain of the age, the Duke of Wellington himself replied: 'In this age, in past ages, in any age: Napoleon.'"[10] Moreover, the Code Napoléon, instituted in France in 1804, represented a great advance over its rivals in being the most consistent in eliminating the feudal remnants in the domain of the Law. And yet Napoleon undertook the disastrous Russian adventure in 1812 and was responsible for the almost complete annihilation of his own army. Moreover, he even tried to restore slavery in the French colonies in Latin America as a way of securing military victory, although such an absurdly retrograde social design was undoubtedly contrary to his own conception of political Enlightenment.

Thousands of years earlier, Alexander the Great seemed to be always invincible. However, even he undertook some extreme risks that almost destroyed his army. This happened when he had chosen to follow a route with his vast army through the Makran Desert, although there were alternatives to it, and the army had to suffer nearly catastrophic losses:

> After sixty days in the desert, the survivors...had seen thousands die around them, perhaps half their fellow-soldiers and almost all the camp followers. If 40,000 people had followed Alexander into the desert, only 15,000 may have survived to see Kirman. All such figures are guesses, but there is no mistaking the men's condition. Not even the sum total of all the army's suffering in Asia, it was agreed, deserved to be compared with the hardships in Makran.[11]

And this is not the whole story. For in the course of actual historical development, some conditions today have radically changed in this respect, and by no means for the better. Alexander the Great and Napoleon almost annihilated their own armies through their chosen actions that made them overreach the power presumed by them. But they could do nothing worse than that. Today the situation is incommensurably worse. For irrespective of which side of the social confrontation the commanding personnel might represent—a progressive or a fatefully retrograde one—their overreaching is capable of *destroying humankind* altogether, and potentially even the conditions of life on this planet in its *entirety*.

This is far from being a hypothetical danger. In 1962–63, Soviet leader Nikita Khrushchev installed in Cuba his country's advanced ballistic missiles, capable of raining nuclear warheads on the nearby United States. He was inspired for this action by the fateful misconception that by doing so he might be able to protect Cuba, which was tangibly threatened by the United States also after the Bay of Pigs invasion. The consequence of Khrushchev's action, however, was that the *entire world* was placed in the immediate vicinity of a potential nuclear devastation until those ballistic missiles were withdrawn from Cuba and shipped back to the Soviet Union. Needless to say, no one can exclude today the recurrence, in some form, of a similar potential self-extermination of humankind as a result of adventurous decision-making. It stands to reason that no one should ever have that power. Nevertheless, the fact is that some do. And that kind of danger is bound to persist for as long as the Leviathan state in any one of its conceivable forms survives.

SUBSTANTIVE EQUALITY AND A NEW SOCIAL METABOLIC ORDER

As we have seen, eighty years ago President Franklin Delano Roosevelt was promising the world "a better civilization than any we have known"—in conjunction with a projected unhindered economic development everywhere and the end of imperialism—because "destiny seems to have taken a long look."[12] In reality, however, a few months after President Roosevelt died, shortly after his well-deserved fourth election to the American Presidency, his former vice president and automatic successor, Harry Truman, unleashed over Hiroshima and Nagasaki the atomic weapons of mass destruction, causing the instant death of 130,000 people, mostly civilians. At the same time, contrary to the earlier prognosticated hopeful expectations, countless millions of people all over the world were condemned to remain tied to their earlier conditions of utter misery. Also, imperialism could continue in the same old civilization, as before, even if under new relations of international power, with the United States as its dominant economic, political, and military force.

However, the replacement of one dominant imperialist power by another, redefining thereby the international relation of forces among the former imperialist countries, does not mean that historical development as a whole can be brought to a halt in *epochal* terms, with regard to the *social metabolism* of reproduction in general, in total subordination to the newly dominant state.[13] That kind of absurd political reductionism is proper only to some reactionary pseudo-theoretical empire fantasy. In the really existing world, every mode of social metabolic reproduction has its *historical limits* objectively defined in comprehensive *epochal terms*. It is in that fundamental epochal sense that the *historic circle* of the capital system as a whole is perilously closing in our own time. And that closure has far-reaching objective implications for *every state*, irrespective of its size or its more or less dominant position in the international order, including all known and feasible varieties of the post-capitalist capital system.

Politicians at the top of the established state tend to repeat their view that "there is no alternative." Margaret Thatcher and Mikhail Gorbachev did so in unison, until they had to find out that, after all, there had to be an alternative for both of them.[14] To some extent this assertion of "no alternative" happens to be true, even if not in the way the high-ranking politicians presume, on the basis of their institutionally defined (and confined) position. The changes in this respect under the circumstances of the necessary closure of capital's historic circle are seminally important.

The primary function of the institutionally articulated political/military form of societal control has been for many centuries the protection and enhancement of the established social metabolic order of which it is an integral—both constitutive and self-constitutive—part. This is why periodic attempts made in the past to alter radically that metabolic order had to assume from the start the form of some kind of "revolutionary overthrow" of the established political/regulatory framework. They had to try to "open the gates," so to speak, to a radical change in the social and material *class relations*, from slave revolts and peasant uprisings to the French, Russian, and Chinese revolutions.

However, the consolidation of their initial gains proved to be in general very limited. This had to be the case because the *inertia* of the inherited *structural determinations*—of which the institutionalized political form itself was an integral part, given its own self-constitutive hierarchical structural embeddedness—militated against lasting success. This is why historical development shows the well-known tendency of such revolutionary attempts to turn instead into some form of *change in personnel* only, reproducing the structural determinations of domination and subordination even when there is a significant shift, for instance, from the *feudal* to the *bourgeois* state order.

The emergence of the modern capitalist state alters the form but not the substance of the class determinations of structural domination and subordination. Under the conditions of the *ascending phase* of capital's social metabolic order, materially productive developments can dynamically proceed toward their all-conquering global completion. However, the *descending phase* carries with it some grave negative changes that prove irreversible from capital's social ground, accelerating the closure of capital's historic circle on our planet with its inevitably limited resources. In the material domain such changes bring the consequences of wasteful *destructive production*, due to the unalterable systemic imperative of endless capital-expansion, with its ultimately catastrophic impact on nature. At the same time, on the political/military plane they result in *monopolistic imperialist military destructiveness*, with the danger of humanity's total self-annihilation. And capital's Leviathan state can only *impose* total destructiveness on humanity through its weapons of mass destruction—which it continues to "modernize" and multiply—but not *prevent* it. Thus, the total eradication of the Leviathan state is a vital necessity in our time, in the spirit envisaged by Marx for weighty reasons. This is the course that needs to be followed after the long destructive deviation suffered by humanity since the last decades of the nineteenth century under the conditions of monopolistic imperialism.

This is where we can see the paradoxical truth of "there is no alternative" repeatedly stated by some leading politicians, as confined to the political domain. Certainly, there is no alternative in the sense envisaged by them, because it is impossible to elaborate the much-needed societal reproductive alternative in and through the political/

military framework of state-determinations. By the inherent nature of the fundamental issues at stake, the historically sustainable alternative can only be a radically different *social metabolic order*. For the requirements of sustainability imply a societal reproductive order with its consciously articulated—*autonomously planned and exercised*—mode of overall decision-making, in place of the authoritarian usurpation of power in all of its historically known varieties by the hierarchically entrenched and superimposed antagonistic Leviathan state. Without instituting—uncompromisingly in the form of *substantive equality*— and also safeguarding such order against the restoration of the material and political vested interests of the long class-exploitative past, it is impossible to secure exit from capital's historic circle.

So much must be rectified even in the world of ideas before an order of substantive equality can be secured. Let us confine our attention in that respect to the crucially important dimension of societal restructuring that directly involves the problem of substantive equality. For even Hegel, one of the greatest idealist philosophers of all history, could dismiss the demand for equality in favor of vested interests, with words like these: "Men are made unequal by *nature*, where *inequality is in its element*, and in civil society the *right of particularity* is so far from annulling this *natural inequality* that it produces *out of mind* and raises it to an inequality of skill and resources [wealth], and even to one of *moral and intellectual* attainment. To oppose to this right a demand for equality is a *folly of the Understanding* which takes as real and rational its *abstract equality* and its 'ought-to-be.'"[15]

In reality, the opposite is true of everything Hegel asserts about nature's inequality in relation to human beings. *Difference* is certainly in great evidence in nature, but turning nature's difference into *human inequality* is revealingly arbitrary, when *social institutions* are responsible for it. But the unjustifiable Hegelian ideological legitimation of historically established societal inequality in the name of nature itself arises because some social forces in the course of the French revolutionary turmoil were forcefully struggling over it. This is what Hegel had to reject, with a categorical claim, in the name of the absolute validity of his philosophical categories.

In contrast to the specific antagonisms of the French Revolution, a century and a half earlier, at the time when Hobbes was writing his *Leviathan*, the demand for substantive equality could not appear with its powerful social challenge on the historical agenda. In the Hobbesian philosophical conception, there was no need to assume a retrograde position toward equality and enlist nature in its pretended favor. On the contrary, Hobbes, for his own specific philosophical reasons, could make absolutely clear his view on *nature's full consonance* with human equality:

> Nature hath made men so equall, in the faculties of body and mind; as that though there bee found one man sometimes manifestly stronger in body, or of quicker mind then another; yet when all is reckoned together, the difference between man, and man, is not so considerable, as that one man can thereupon claim to himselfe any benefit, to which another may not pretend, as well as he. For as to the strength of body, the weakest has strength enough to kill the strongest, either by secret machination, or by confederacy with others, that are in the same danger with himselfe.
>
> And as to the faculties of the mind (setting aside the arts grounded upon words, and especially that skill of proceeding upon generall, and infallible rules, called Science; which very few have, and but in few things; as being not a native faculty, born with us; nor attained (as Prudence,) while we look after somewhat els,) I find yet a greater equality amongst men, than that of strength. For Prudence is but Experience; which equal time, equally bestowed on all men, in those things they equally apply themselves unto.[16]

We shall see in the chapters dedicated to Hobbes and Hegel why, in their theories of the state, they adopted such diametrically opposite views.* What is necessary to stress in the present context is that the pressing demand for the establishment of substantive equality that first

---

* The chapters referred to here were to appear in volume 2 of *Beyond Leviathan*. —Ed.

appeared as a historic imperative of social reality during the French Revolution, and was violently defeated in its aftermath, can never be removed from our own historical agenda. For the elaboration and effective societal reproductive operation of the required—fundamentally different—social metabolic order is unsustainable without it. That is the key defining characteristic of the socialist metabolic order. Our success or failure to secure a sustainable exit from capital's dangerously closing historic circle depends on it.

EXITING CAPITAL'S CLOSING CIRCLE

Despite the undeniable dangers on our horizon, is it possible to secure that exit from the capital system's necessarily closing historic circle? That is a painfully difficult but unavoidable question. At the present stage of history, even with the "principle of hope" on our side, this vital question can receive only a conditional and tentative answer.

Toward the end of the Second World War, reflecting on the harrowing vicissitudes of the war years, Sartre wrote a great one-act play, translated into English under the title *No Exit*. He wanted to convey in it the feeling of absolutely paralyzing powerlessness that seemed to dominate people under the conditions of ostensibly uncontrollable war.

At first, he thought to set the stage in a caved-in bomb shelter where the escape routes have been blocked. But then he realized that in a situation like that the force of *solidarity* among the people buried in that shelter could begin to operate, urging them to work together to *find an exit*. And that would undermine the meaning Sartre intended to convey in his play. Thus, thanks to a brilliant dramatic insight, he set his play in *hell*, from which there could be no escape. And this is how his intended message sounded from the mouth of one of the three fatefully trapped people:

> Yes, now is the moment; I'm looking at this thing on the mantelpiece, and I understand that I am in hell. I tell you, everything has been thought out beforehand. They knew I would stand at the

fireplace stroking this piece of bronze, with all those eyes intent on me. Devouring me. [*He swings around abruptly.*] What? Only two of you? I thought there were more. Many more. [*Laughs.*] So this is hell. I would never have believed it. You remember all we were told about the torture-chambers, the fire and brimstone, the "burning marl." Old wives' tales! There is no need for red-hot pokers. *Hell is other people!*[17]

That was the final summation, which stressed the irreconcilable antagonism among the three people whose mutually tormenting bad conscience defined their relationship of hell among themselves throughout their interchanges in the course of the play, giving its nightmarish meaning to the riveting Sartrean words: "*Hell is other people!*"[18] Those words referred in general to "other people," wherever they might be, who have brought, and might also in the future bring, the war upon others and themselves, engaging uncontrollably in similar acts of hell and trapping others as well as themselves in hell by their own acts.

This vision was conceived by Sartre in his haunting play just months before Truman ordered the instant destruction of the people of Hiroshima and Nagasaki in the name of democracy and freedom. For several decades thereafter, Sartre continued to fight with passionate determination and courage against the very real danger of nuclear inferno being imposed upon the earth. In all those decades, the tormenting words of warning about the acts of hell brought into this world by people, the ubiquitous "other people," could always be felt behind Sartre's indefatigable protests, even when they were not directly uttered.

Unpunished state-determinations continue to be responsible today for countless acts of hell, when unjustifiable justifications can be twisted around at will in endless self-legitimating contradictions. In many ways feudal reactionary Saudi Arabia can continue to bomb, unpunished, countless civilian targets in Yemen, even the hospitals clearly marked by the organization Médecins Sans Frontières, and the infernal destructive weaponry is supplied for such acts of hell by the leading "democratic states," violating thereby their own supposed international commitments. And when this is made clear in public, they can cynically retort that there is "insufficient evidence" that the Saudis use the weapons against civilian targets. The "democratic states" can do that unpunished because they are the judge and jury also over what should be considered, as defined by their own view, the "sufficient evidence."

The same kind of self-legitimating self-contradiction can prevail over the infernal weapons of mass destruction in general. The military-industrial complex may be criticized on occasion, but its highly profitable products—for which the funds are supplied by the state from taxes imposed mostly on the working people—cannot be seriously challenged. The dominant states cannot consider abandoning such weapons. Once upon a time a leading left-wing British politician of the Labour Party, Aneurin Bevan, declared that he "would not walk into the negotiating chamber naked"—that is, if the highly debated issue of British nuclear disarmament would be adopted as party policy— and therefore he was rejecting it as future foreign secretary. Bevan was betraying thereby the reactionary nature of his taking for granted the permanent discriminatory inequality of international power politics. And he could not be considered an exception in that respect. In their international agreements, the politicians of the dominant states agree to reduce their nuclear arsenal by a few hundred bombs and at the same time order the manufacture of thousands of them from their own military-industrial complex. Thus, many thousands of such nuclear weapons are available to be unleashed on our planet, while as few as two hundred of them would be sufficient for the destruction of humanity altogether, according to the relevant scientific assessment.

It is perfectly true, of course, that some of the major states are less dominated by the vested interests of their own military-industrial complex than some others. But that is quite irrelevant in the present context. None of the dominant states are likely to give up on their own nuclear weapons, not only in view of the now generally acknowledged role of such weapons of mass destruction in asserting military strength in the international power structure, but also because of their own likely fear of being more exposed through unilateral nuclear disarmament to nuclear destruction. Thus, the now existing huge nuclear arsenals are likely to be with us for the foreseeable future. At the same time, as capital's historic circle is getting nearer to its irreversible closure, the intensifying internal and international economic and social antagonisms are bound to carry with them increasing dangers. And since materially grounded globalization inexorably proceeds under the present circumstances, nation-based antagonistic political/military determinations can only aggravate the systemic antagonisms. The best one can hope for in that respect is that the dominant states do not engage in a fundamental direct confrontation, with its catastrophic consequences.

These challenges cannot be resolved within the paralyzing confines of the necessarily hierarchical and antagonistic framework of the political/military domain. For finding a solution, as mentioned before, a radical transformation of our modality of decision-making is required, affecting no less the elementary constitutive cells of our societal reproduction than the most comprehensive level of the global interdependencies. And the fundamental guiding principle of that kind of transformation can only be the universal adoption of the positive principle of productive work, on the basis of substantive equality, inseparable from the total eradication of the *hierarchical* and *necessarily antagonistic state formations*.

Nearly two centuries ago, Johann Wolfgang von Goethe with wonderful, subtle irony, depicted in his *Faust* the final moments of his hero, who was modeled by him in some way on the great historic figure of Paracelsus. In that final scene, Goethe's hero, blinded by *Sorge* (Anguish) because he refused to yield to her, mistakenly greets the noise of the Lemurs—who are in fact digging his grave—as the welcome noise of canal digging, in realization of his great social project and self-fulfillment for which he is destined to lose his wager with Mephistopheles, the devil. These are Faust's final words:

> A swamp along the mountain's flank
> Makes all my previous gains contaminate;
> My deeds, if I could drain this sink,

Would culminate as well as terminate:
To open to the millions living space,
Not danger-proof but free to run their race.
Green fields and fruitful; men and cattle hiving
Upon this newest earth at once and thriving.
Settled at once beneath this sheltering hill
Heaped by the masses' brave and busy skill
With such a heavenly land behind this hedge,
The sea beyond may bluster to its edge
And, as it gnaws to swamp the work of masons,
To stop the gap one common impulse hastens.
Aye! Wedded to this concept like a wife,
I find this wisdom's final form:
He only earns his freedom and his life
Who takes them every day by storm.
And so a man, beset by dangers here,
As child, man, old man, spends his manly year.
Oh to see such activity,
Treading free ground with people that are free!
Then could I bid the passing moment:
"Linger a while, thou art so fair!"
The traces of my earthly days can never
Sink in the aeons unaware.
And I, who feel ahead such heights of bliss,
At last I enjoy my highest moment—this.[19]

In *Faust*, Divine Providence rescues the hero from the clutches of the devil Mephistopheles. We cannot count on such solution in our references to the legitimately updated contemporary meaning of historic Paracelsus. The ground of Goethe's understandable irony, depicting also the fateful mistake of Faust in his wishful self-fulfillment, noble and deserved as it is in favor of his hero, must be removed in the actually existing world.

Under the conditions depicted by Goethe, Faust/Paracelsus could not possibly achieve his historic dream. Goethe in his greatness supremely conveyed that. Even in our time, the earlier indicated question marks still remain. This is because historic achievement of the magnitude involved in positively oriented and truly autonomous human decision-making absolutely needs the enduring foundation of substantive equality. This is feasible only on the condition of fully articulating the required radical mass movement in the spirit of globally extendable solidarity. Combined with substantive equality, that is the only basis on which the necessary critique of the Leviathan state can succeed in historically sustainable terms.

PART TWO

The Mountain We Must Conquer: Reflections on the State

CHAPTER SIX

The Mountainous State

Under the conditions of the capital system's deepening structural crisis, the problems of the state loom, inevitably, ever larger.* For in the long-established mode of overall political decision-making processes, the state is expected to provide the solution to so many problems that darken our horizon, but it fails to do so. On the contrary, attempted state remedial measures—from dangerous military interventions to addressing grave financial collapses on a monumental scale, including rescue operations of private capitalism undertaken by ever-escalating state debt to the tune of trillions of dollars—seem to aggravate the problems, despite vain reassurances to the contrary.

The difficult questions that must be answered today are these: what is happening in our planetary household in the present critical times? Why do the traditional state remedies fail to produce the anticipated results? Is the state as it had been historically constituted capable of solving our acute problems, or has the state as such become a major contributor to the worsening problems themselves

---

* Part Two of *Beyond Leviathan*, "The Mountain We Must Conquer," is based on lectures on the state that Mészáros delivered in November 2013 in Brazil at four universities. —Ed.

and to their chronic insolubility? What are the requirements of a radically different alternative? Are there any viable prospects for the future if a substantively different way of controlling the social metabolism cannot be instituted against the preponderance of the perilously failing state determinations? Is there a way out from the vicious circle to which we are confined by capital's incorrigible structural determinations of social metabolic control in the material reproductive domain and within the framework of its necessary state formations?

All these questions are painfully difficult to answer in light of past developments. For the vital corrective function of capital's historically constituted state formations was always the maintenance and strengthening of the system's irrepressible material self-expansionary imperatives. And the state continues to have this same function even in our own historical time when such self-expansionary imperatives have become suicidal to humanity. Thus, the challenge today calls for a radical critique of the state in its fundamental terms of reference, as the historically established modality of overall decision-making more or less directly affects the totality of societal reproductive functions, from the elementary material productive processes to the most mediated cultural domains. At the same time, it must be stressed that the critique is viable only if it carries with it a historically sustainable alternative. In other words, it is not enough to "wipe the slate clean," as it were, in the form of simply rejecting the existing modality of capital's overall decision-making processes. Only the self-interested apologists of the capital system can accuse the advocates of the socialist alternative with asking for "utopian lawless anarchy." Nothing could be further from the truth. Indeed, the complacently claimed continuing success of the past modality of state practices is precisely what turns out to be false on closer inspection. For what used to work within the more limited framework of the nation-states in the past proves to be badly wanting in a world in which the fundamental material structures of capital's social metabolism are poised toward their global integration without their feasible equivalent at the state-legitimated political plane.

THE CENTRIFUGALITY OF CAPITAL'S ANTAGONISTIC SOCIAL ORDER

The real issue is that the decision-making processes of capital's state formations by their very nature—due to the social metabolic ground of material reproduction upon which they have been historically constituted—can represent only the paradigm of alienated superimposition in their incorrigible mode of operation. To envisage anything meaningfully contrasting to that it would be necessary to postulate a substantively different social metabolic ground for the established social order's overall decision-making processes. For given the necessary centrifugality of their material microcosms, which are expected to secure the conditions of societal reproduction as a whole—and given that they do this precisely through their antagonistic structural determinations—the state formations of the capital system could never fulfill their required corrective and stabilizing functions, and thereby prevail over potentially disruptive tendencies, without superimposing themselves on all encountered resistances as an alienated body par excellence of overall decision-making. This is the case irrespective of whether we are talking about the liberal-democratic institutional framework or about any of capital's openly dictatorial state formations. As separate/alienated organs of overall political control they are all under the overwhelming requirement to assert "might-as-right" in the interest of fulfilling their state-legitimated overruling and corrective functions, as we shall discuss in the course of this study.

In this sense, far from being guilty of advocating some "utopian lawless anarchy," the socialist alternative is concerned with the overall conception and practical establishment of a qualitatively different mode of societal interchange, a mode in which the constitutive cells or microcosms of the given social metabolism can truly cohere into a historically sustainable whole. The reality of "globalization," much idealized in our time, is bound to remain a dangerously one-sided trend, pregnant with explosive material antagonisms, for as long as the constitutive cells or microcosms of our planetary household are internally torn by the ultimately irreconcilable contradictions of their prevailing centrifugality. For the centrifugality characteristic of the innermost determinations of the capital system as such carries with it the structurally entrenched imperatives of antagonistic capital-expansion and their separate/alienated state-legitimated defense. Consequently, given its absolutely crucial function in the global societal reproduction process, the kind of state-legitimated defense of the established social metabolism cannot assume any other form than superimposition at all costs. And this amounts, whenever necessary, even to the most violent assertion of the interests of the contending forces at the level of political/military decision-making in the domain of interstate relations.

Naturally, the most disturbing truth in this matter is that "the Law" instituted by capital's state formations on the antagonistic material ground of its own constitutive microcosms, internally as well as internationally, cannot work, and indeed does not work. It works de facto only, by asserting itself as force—or "might-as-right"—arising and prevailing as state-legitimated imposition over against all potential resistance and recalcitrance. In that sense the Law imposes itself on the basis of categorically decreeing the constitutional viability of itself in its symbiosis with the established relation of forces, and continues to provide their state-legitimation with the same categorical claim rooted in force, until there is a major change in the relation of forces themselves. Thus, the constitutional proclamation and legally unchallengeable imposition of "might-as-right" can continue, whether it is done in the most ruthless dictatorial fashion or with the "smiling face" of the liberal-democratic state formations of the capital system. But despite all attempts at the unhistorical eternalizations of the state, the imposition of might-as-right over society cannot go on forever. The moment of truth arrives when the absolute limits of the capital system are activated in a historically determinate form, undermining the necessary corrective viability of the system's state formations in all of their given and conceivable forms. For the states of the capital system are not intelligible at all in and by themselves, but only as the required corrective complementarity to the otherwise unmanageable structural defects of their expansion-oriented mode of social metabolic reproduction. And that structural imperative of expansion can be driven forward by the successful accumulation process only for as long as it can prevail in its material terms of reference confronting nature without destroying humanity itself. This means that the insuperable limits of the established state formations reside not simply at a politically corrigible level, as vainly attempted and justified in traditional jurisprudential discourse, but in the absolute limits of capital's ultimately suicidal mode of social metabolic control, activated through the structural crisis of the overall system.

Clearly, such considerations cannot enter capital's horizon either at the level of its incorrigible centrifugal material reproductive determinations or under the state-legitimated ideological rationalizations of its political regulatory practices. That makes the historically well-known modalities of imposing might-as-right in the name of "the Law," together with their jurisprudential idealizations, extremely problematical. In this sense the law, as alienated imposition over the individuals who constitute society as a whole, cannot work *de jure*, namely as the law right and proper. By contrast, the only law that can work as law (on capital's material ground unrealizable sense of *de jure*), and indeed must work in the interest of cohesion as the absolute requirement of any historically sustainable social metabolic control in a truly globalized world in our future, is "the law we give ourselves." This is not a question of counterposing the "rule of law" as the necessary regulatory framework of societal interchange to some abstract imperative of ungrounded *morality*. That kind of counterposition happens to be the convenient escape clause of liberalism and utilitarianism when, in view of their unacknowledged idealizations of the antagonisms inseparable from the reality of the nation-states, they fail to fill the categories of "universal law" and "international law" with real content.[2] No such self-serving opposition between law and morality is sustainable on any rational ground.

The real opposition that must be firmly asserted is between, on the one hand, law *autonomously determined* by the freely associated individuals at all levels of their life, from their most immediate productive activities to the highest regulatory requirements of their cultural and overall societal decision-making processes and law *superimposed* over them, on the other. Such a superimposition can only occur through the *apologetic codification* of the established relation of forces by a separate body, be that body the most "democratic" in its *formal state-legitimated* sense. Accordingly, the false opposition between morality and law must be rejected, and not only in the form of the liberal/utilitarian escape clause. We find a similar opposition of morality and law also widespread among the various, more or less openly authoritarian adherents of "real-politics," and this time at the expense of morality, mindlessly condemned by the "realists of power" as "mere moralizing." In both cases, the false opposition of law and morality can be rejected only on the ground of a *substantively equitable* socialist metabolic order, based on the kind of productive microcosms in which the (social) individuals can—and do—*set the law in themselves*. But that order is conceivable only by *eradicating* capital from the social metabolic process and thereby superseding the necessary *centrifugality* of the long-established constitutive cells of societal interchange.

It is necessary to consider in the same context the characteristic misrepresentation of another issue of major importance. It concerns an a priori judgment repeatedly asserted in a shallow condemnatory sense against "direct democracy" even by some genuine believers in the once progressive liberal tradition. And, of course, this negative judgment is at the same time circularly used in favor of the claimed self-evident validity of "representative democracy," in virtue of its contrast, by definition, to the condemned "direct democracy." Moreover, we are expected to agree with the soundness of that view even when the writers in question are willing to admit the painfully evident actual failure of the type of state regulatory system they nevertheless continue to idealize. The trouble is that even apart from the overwhelming evidence for the failure of representative democracy in every country, not to mention its periodic transmutation into dictatorial forms, the great weakness of the advocated position is twofold. First, because it suffers from the fetishistic mechanical quantification of asserting that in historical circumstances different from the characteristics of extremely small states—like the Athenian democracy at the time of its decision-making *agora*—it is inconceivable to have other than representative democracy. And second, because the propounders of this approach narrowly confine the problem itself—again in the interest of asserting a circularly self-referential and self-validating position—to the *political/ institutional domain*, although in reality it is incomparably broader and more fundamental than that.

The crucial issue concerns the second weakness of this position, which has a bearing also on the first. For it is totally beside the point to debate the *size* of the advocated regulatory framework without addressing the much more relevant and fundamental question of the *type*—and thereby the *qualitative determinations*—of the decision-making structures and corresponding forms of control. What makes the state formations of the capital system perilously unsustainable under the present historical conditions is the *antagonistic centrifugality* of the constitutive cells of the established order of social metabolic control. That kind of state regulatory framework, in view of its innermost antagonistic determinations, is unworkable not only on an all-embracing global scale but in how small a size it might be scaled down to.

The real challenge is, therefore, the historically sustainable overcoming of the structurally entrenched antagonisms in the *constitutive cells* of capital's social order, which are responsible for the *centrifugality* of its incurable systemic determinations. This is the only way to provide an alternative type of cohesive regulatory framework which can be *laterally coordinated* and *cooperatively structured* from its smallest societal reproductive microcosms to its absolutely unavoidable all-embracing forms of decision-making in the future. The fundamental stakes of our time—in all domains, from the elementary material reproductive processes to the gravest potential interstate collisions that resulted in catastrophic wars in the past—call for the *qualitative redefinition*, in a practically sustainable sense, of the constitutive cells of our social order, in the sense of superseding its ever more destructive centrifugality by eradicating capital itself from the ongoing metabolic process.

Accordingly, the real stakes concern the modality of *decision-making as such*, which should not be—with self-serving tendentiousness—confounded with the necessarily self-legitimated decision-making organs and processes of the *state* itself. The apologists of "representative democracy" want to confine the solutions of our grave problems to the strictly *formal* equality and most obvious *substantive iniquitousness* of the state-regulated *political* domain, where it cannot be found. One must get out of that self-defeating vicious circle, with its alienated decision-making processes superimposed on the people. The real issue is not "direct democracy" or "representative democracy" but the effective and self-fulfilling regulation of their mode of existence by the individuals under the conditions of *substantive democracy,* in contrast to the political legislative vacuity of easily curruptible "representative democracy." And the only viable way of making democracy substantive—and not "representative" in a most remote way, and at the same time of course more or less intensely resented—is by instituting a form of decision-making from which *recalcitrance* is absent because the social individuals (or associated producers) *set the law in relation to themselves,* so as to be able to *autonomously modify* it whenever the changing circumstances of their self-determined societal metabolic processes so require. But that is feasible only if the overall conditions of their existence are materially grounded on *constitutive cells qualitatively different* from capital's social order, because antagonistic cetrifugality itself is consigned to the past. This is the positive requirement of a truly cohesive, globally sustainable overall societal metabolic structure that can overcome in its state formations the destructive implications of superimposing *false universality*—inevitably by the force of arms, as fatefully experienced in the past—on its internally torn antagonistic material constituents. It has been reported that in a conversation with Margaret Thatcher on nuclear disarmament Gorbachev quoted a Russian proverb according to which "once in a year even an unloaded gun can go off." No one in their right mind should seriously expect from the existing state-legitimated forms of regulation any guarantee for the future against the grave implications of that.

THE CHALLENGE OF SUBSTANTIVE EQUALITY

The contradictory determinations of these problems had been exposed to public scrutiny well over two and a quarter centuries ago, way back at the time of the American and the French revolutions, which coincided with the onset of the great Industrial Revolution.

The line of demarcation was ineradicably marked by the appearance of the problem of *substantive equality* on the historical agenda under the conditions of the revolutionary turmoil itself. The militant advocates of substantive equality could not put it in sharper terms than condemning with utter contempt the past and present political evasions of this seminal issue: "From time immemorial they hypocritically repeat: *all men are equal;* and from time immemorial the most degrading and monstrous inequality insolently weighs upon the human race." And they could also clarify their vital concern in a most tangible way by adding: "We need not only that equality of rights written into the Declaration of the Rights of Man and Citizen; we want it in our midst, under the roofs of our houses." In this way the rejection of the purely *formal/legal* measures of all projected remedies—which plagued not only in those times but continued to plague all the way down to our own days the traditional state-legitimated approaches to these problems—was combined with the necessary requirements of any practically viable solution, by looking for answers in the economic and social domain. Naturally, by focusing attention on the missing dimension of political decision-making, the role of the state itself had been subjected to critical scrutiny, even if at the time of the French Revolution only in an embryonic form. This crucial issue could only assume its overriding importance half a century later, in the Marxian conception.

Looking back in the history of political thought we find that the fundamental concern of the debated theories of the state, from Plato and Aristotle onward, was always the different *forms* in which the modalities of overall decision-making, with rival benefits or drawbacks, could be praised or blamed. One form or another of the state—or of the rival constitutions in Aristotle's overview—was always taken for granted as the overarching mode of decision-making. The same goes for the theories of "ideal states" in Ancient Greece and also much later. Thus, in this respect we could witness a significant change toward the end of the eighteenth century, when the state as such started to become the object of critical reflection, in contrast to questioning only the relative merits of the state's different ways of superimposing itself on social life as the ultimate arbiter in all major matters. Understandably, the revolutionary upheavals of the late eighteenth and early nineteenth centuries had to bring with them not only a growing awareness of classes and class antagonisms, as well as of the impact of some major interstate wars, but also the crisis of politics itself and the acknowledgment that the old ways of dealing with such crises could no longer work. Ultimately this circumstance confronted the major thinkers of the age with the almost prohibitive problem of addressing the *legitimacy* or not of the *law itself.* Some, like the Romantic philosophers, did it in an apologetic and retrograde way, conceptualizing history in a most reactionary fashion by wanting to turn its wheels backwards. Others, like Immanuel Kant, projected their noble but utterly wishful "ought-to-be" of a *"perpetual peace,"* and of course to no avail. However, the most grandiose solution, spelled out in full conformity to his bourgeois class horizon, was offered by Hegel, in his *Philosophy of Right.* Accordingly, while acknowledging the fundamental and potentially most disruptive and far-reaching social antagonisms of his age, Hegel nevertheless reasserted with the firmest class-bound justification the unquestionable legitimacy of the law. He did that in world historical terms, appealing to nothing less than the authority of the *Weltgeist* (world spirit). But he could only provide such answer in the name of his grandiloquent *Theodicaea:* the "justification of God in history" at the price of arbitrarily terminating at the same time history itself in his postulated "Europe as the end of history," with the necessary national wars of the European "Germanic" states, including empire-building England, warmly commended by Hegel.

Liberalism entered the historical stage in the same period of late eighteenth-century revolutionary upheavals, but in a more prosaic garb. It always assumed the totally unproblematical, indeed self-evident validity of its own attitude to legislation and societal management as representing "the whole of society." At the same time, it was willing to contemplate and institute ameliorations, in view of the erupting problems and conflicts of the revolutionary turmoil, but always well within the established structural framework of the existing order, subjecting it only to marginal critique. Neither the historical dimension of the constitution of the states, nor their questionable legitimacy represented any problem to liberalism. The boundless self-commending assumptions in its own approach, coupled with partial reformatory sympathy, seemed to be enough for its self-justification. In other words, liberalism was characterized both by the systematic evasion of the fundamentals, including the question of legitimacy of law-making in other than technical/procedural terms, and in a positive way by the advocacy of limited social and political improvements, including the extension of the franchise for parliamentary elections. Such combination of "balanced" conflict-evasion and structurally containable reform—the telling hallmarks of liberalism—may well explain its relative success among all of capital's state formations in the past. But in no way could it amount to significant changes.

Liberalism could never advocate an *equitable* society; only a *"more equitable"* one, which always meant *far less than equitable*. Even at its most progressive phase of development, liberalism confined its reformatory views and corresponding practical efforts strictly to the sphere of the *distribution* of the goods produced—naturally with negligible lasting success. For liberalism always closed its eyes to the embarrassing fact that meaningful improvement toward an equitable society could only result from a fundamental change in the structure of *production* itself. This could not be otherwise because the sphere of distribution was *structurally predetermined* by the unalterable consignment of the class of labor to a necessarily subordinate position in society, given the state-legitimated and forcefully protected allocation of the means of production to the class constituted by the personifications of capital. Accordingly, to have a more iniquitous system of distribution than the structurally entrenched capital system was quite inconceivable, condemning thereby liberal enlightenment even at its best to purely marginal efficacy. The same went for the liberal advocacy of "state restraint," which always had to be accommodated well within the structurally prejudged framework of the unquestionable overall defense of capital's societal reproductive order. And that had to be—and indeed had been—unquestioningly state-legitimated by all forms of liberalism. Not surprisingly, therefore, simultaneously to the unfolding of the capital system's *structural crisis*, the once-upon-a-time reformatorily-inclined liberalism speedily metamorphosed itself into a most aggressive form of state-apologetic *neoliberalism*. This is how the moment of truth turned Bentham's "greatest happiness or greatest felicity principle" into an accusing finger toward neoliberal liberalism in our historical time.

Naturally, these were not redressable historical contingencies but necessary developments, dramatically unfolding in conjunction with the activation of capital's absolute limits through the maturation of its systemic crisis. For a very long time it was the gratuitous promise of all kinds of capital-apologetics—from the disingenuous postulates of now completely abandoned "evolutionary socialism," and from the "modernization" theories for overcoming "third world underdevelopment" all the way to the fiction of globally instituting the "welfare state," which is now vanishing even from the handful of its privileged countries—that the *"cake to be distributed"* will *eternally grow*, bringing full happiness to absolutely everyone. Abundant *distribution* will take care of everything, no one should therefore worry about the problems of *production*. But the cake simply refused to grow so as to match any variety of the projected "greatest felicity." Capital's structural crisis had put an end to all such fantasies. It is said that during the French Revolution, when it was reported to Marie-Antoinette that the people were starving because they had no bread, the ill-fated Queen responded with "Why don't they eat cake?" In the light of the deepening structural crisis and its customary justifications, Marie-Antoinette could be credited with an infinitely more realistic solution than the defenders of the capital system in our time.

The radical shift from the self-apologetic concern with totally unrealizable "more equitable" distribution—when in reality the tiniest percentage expropriates to itself much more than the lion's share of wealth, forcefully protected by the state—to a radical change in the structural determinations of production is essential. For the objective trends of development in our time indicate worsening conditions everywhere, with austerity policies ruthlessly imposed by capitalist governments on their working population even in the richest capitalistically advanced countries. The class of labor is gravely affected by the measures to which it must be subjected in the interest of maintaining the profitability of a fetishistic and cruelly dehumanizing system.[1] Thus, the great challenge for the realization of an equitable social order that erupted on the historical stage in revolutionary turmoil toward the end of the eighteenth century haunts our historical time. This is because no solution is feasible to our ever-aggravating problems without the adoption of the vital orienting principle of *substantive equality* as the fundamental regulator of the social metabolic process in a truly globalized world.

But, of course, nothing could be more alien to the operation of the capital system in its structural crisis than the institution of equality. It is constituted as a system of structurally entrenched hierarchies that must be protected in every way by its state formations. On capital's side the structural crisis of our age activates the demand for an ever greater direct involvement of the state in the continued survival of the system, even if that runs counter to the self-mythology of the superior "private enterprise." *"Save the System,"* as the London-based capital-apologetic weekly journal *The Economist* demanded on its front page in 2009, at the time of the eruption of the global financial crisis. Naturally, the major capitalist states all duly obliged with trillions devoted to their rescue operations.

However, the underlying issue is far greater than the periodic emergencies. The most serious objective trend of development in this respect in the political economic domain, going back to the end of the 1960s, is the *"equalization of the differential rate of exploitation."*[2] This deeply affected the living conditions of the working classes even in the most privileged capitalist countries. Displaying the true meaning of "globalization," this is an incurable objective trend—a veritable political economic law—inseparable from the imperative of profitable capital accumulation on a global scale. Accordingly, the changing share of labor in overall social wealth must indicate an inevitably downward trend through increased exploitation everywhere, including the former beneficiaries of colonization and imperialism. True to the nature of the established social metabolic order, nothing could be more *perverse* a trend of global development, asserting itself as one of the greatest ironies of modern history, after promising greater equality through "progressive taxation," than the growing iniquities due to the *downward equalization of the differential rate of exploitation* in which all of the capital system's state formations are deeply implicated with their actively pursued policies. And given the deepening structural crisis of the system, the role of capital's state formations can only get worse on this score, as it will on the military and ecological plane.

THE MOUNTAIN BEFORE US

In view of all these considerations, a radical critique of the state in the Marxian spirit, with its far-reaching implications for the withering away of the state itself, is a literally vital requirement of our time. The state as constituted on capital's antagonistic material ground cannot do other than protect the established social metabolic order, defending it at all costs, irrespective of the dangers for the future of humanity's survival. This determination represents a mountain-size obstacle that cannot be bypassed in attempting the much-needed positive transformation of our conditions of existence. For under the unfolding circumstances of capital's irreversible structural crisis the state asserts and imposes itself as the mountain we *must* climb and conquer.

To be sure, this cannot be a leisurely recreational climb. The fundamental reason in this respect is that the grave problems arising from the political reality of the state, even when they assume the form of devastating wars, are only part of the challenge. The capital system has three interconnected pillars: capital, labor, and the state. No one of them can be done away with on its own. Nor can they be simply abolished or overthrown. The particular varieties of the capitalist state can be overthrown, and also restored, but not the state as such. The particular types of the historically given personifications of capital and wage labor can be juridically abolished, and restored, but not capital and labor as such, in their substantive sense of constitution as encountered in capital's social metabolic order. The sobering truth should be remembered that whatever can be overthrown can also be restored. And it has been done. The *materiality of the state* is deeply rooted in the antagonistic social metabolic ground upon which all of capital's state formations are erected. It is inseparable from the substantive materiality of both capital and labor. Only a combined view of their *threefold interrelationship* makes the state-legitimated functions of the capital system intelligible.

Thus, the problems now at stake on the plane of overall political decision-making as necessarily managed by the state cannot be solved without attending to their deepest social metabolic ground. And in that broader and more fundamental sense, it is not enough to *climb* the mountain in question, envisaging one-sidedly the overthrow of the given capitalist state as the answer to the destructiveness unfolding in every sphere of our social life under the conditions of capital's deepening structural crisis. Such problems are not amenable to a viable solution within their limited institutional terms of reference. The perilous mountain confronting humanity is the combined totality of capital's structural determinations that must be *conquered* in all of their deeply integrated dimensions. The state is, of course, a vital constituent in this set of interrelationships, in view of its now overpowering direct role in the necessary modality of overall decision making. Politics often played a key role in initiating major social transformations in the past. That is bound to remain with us also in the foreseeable future. But the mountain in all of its dimensions must be—and can only be—*conquered* if the deep-seated structural antagonisms at the roots of the state's insoluble contradictions are brought under historically sustainable control.

CHAPTER SEVEN

The End of Liberal-Democratic Politics

Let us consider in the first place a most revealing quotation from a distinguished British prime minister, Sir Anthony Eden, who belonged to the Liberal Democratic wing of the Conservative Party and played an honorable role—together with Winston Churchill and Harold Macmillan—in opposing the Conservative "Appeasement of Hitler" in the 1930s.

No one should have any doubt about the accuracy of this quote, because it is fully authenticated by another prime minister of the same political orientation, Sir Edward Heath, who always proudly stressed that he took his political inspiration from "Winston Churchill, Anthony Eden and Harold Macmillan," and on that ground he strongly opposed Margaret Thatcher's right-wing conservatism to the end of his life.[1] Indeed, at the time of entering Parliament, Heath was one of the leading figures and Conservative Manifesto writers of the post–Second World War "One Nation Politics," which is today adopted and promoted in a most unprincipled way by the "New Labour Party."[2]

The circumstances referred to in this letter are far more important than a particular historical event, no matter how dramatic such an event might be. For in this case, we are confronted by a veritable line of demarcation that indicates the end of a long historical tradition and the collapse of its customary way of managing international conflicts with the methods of righteous conspiratorial diplomacy, pursued in the name of once genuinely held and successfully asserted by now epochally outdated liberal-democratic ideology. The circumstances in question speak for themselves. They are as follows.

On October 21, 1955, shortly before the clamorous collapse of the Suez adventure, Conservative prime minister Anthony Eden told future prime minister Edward Heath—at the time the Chief Whip of his party, whose job was to "whip" its Members of Parliament into line for supporting the government—that his great political success in bringing about the imminent military invasion of Suez by Britain, France, and Israel amounted to *"the highest form of statesmanship."*[3] Nothing less than that, as no doubt such outcomes used to be considered and hailed in the past. The event was described by Edward Heath in his autobiography like this:

> I went into the Cabinet Room as usual shortly before Cabinet was due to start, and I found the Prime Minister standing by his chair holding a piece of paper. He was bright-eyed and full of life. The tiredness seemed suddenly to have disappeared. "We have got an agreement!" he exclaimed. "Israel has agreed to invade Egypt. We shall then send in our own forces, backed up by the French, to separate the contestants and regain the Canal." The Americans would not be told about the plan.[4]

As it turned out, the military adventure, prepared by the secret intrigue between Britain and its partners, humiliatingly failed as a result of American opposition under the presidency of General Eisenhower. Soon afterward Sir Anthony Eden had to give up politics altogether, with the customary excuse of "health reasons."

What Eden called *"the highest form of statesmanship"* was supposed to deserve its great political accolade because this infamous deal was prepared in the well-tried diplomatic way behind the stage, combined with "negotiations" for public consumption (for added secret diplomatic hypocrisy, conducted in New York City) with the usual cynical pretense of avoiding precisely any military conflict over the issue of the Suez Canal. However, Eden and company made the big mistake of presuming to be able to impose their *fait accompli* as *"the highest form of statesmanship"* on the American administration. They were deluding themselves. For, as Paul Baran rightly emphasized in his pathbreaking book about postwar power relations: "The assertion of American supremacy in the 'free' world implied the reduction of Britain and France (not to speak of Belgium, Holland and Portugal) to the status of junior partners of American imperialism."[5]

In this way the historic line of demarcation, which asserted itself in the form of the humiliating collapse of the Suez war adventure, highlighted the naked reality of *power relations* that could no longer be embellished either by liberal-democratic wishful thinking or its hypocritical pretenses. The old ways could not work any longer, no matter which power tried to assume the role of imposing its internationally dominating aspirations on the rest of the world in the name of historically anachronistic liberal-democratic aspirations—that is, only in *formal* democratic and universalistic terms.

Naturally, despite the British conspiratorial failure nothing was actually solved at the time in *substantive* terms about the real causes of the Suez conflict and about some of the deep-seated contradictions inseparable from the once successful colonial domination of North Africa, which still continue to surface in our own time, even if in 1955 a new imperial power managed to call back to their senses the "junior partners of American imperialism." Nor should it be denied, in subservience to the new international power relations, that the historic line of demarcation in question also highlighted that the *formal-democratic* pretenses of continued neocolonial domination, masquerading as liberal-democratic generosity and advancement, have become destructive *historical anachronisms*. The dramatic protests erupting not only in the form of the "Arab Spring" but *worldwide* call for fundamental *substantive* changes. And the call was not simply for some readjustment *within* the framework of the established power relations, which would leave everything substantively in its place, as it happened in the past. Far from it. Indeed, the protestors call for a radical change in the *structural framework of the exercise of power itself*—including the modern state—and thereby for a change in substance from the hierarchically entrenched and enforced *domination* of the working classes by capital's social and political order to an alternative order of genuine self-determination.

To be sure, the once successfully prevailing varieties of liberal democratic state conceptions differed only with regard to their *internally* less authoritarian aspirations from the openly class-oppressive types of state domination. And they did that precisely in the interest of securing more general national support for their international—and even for their most ruthlessly empire-building—adventures. In terms of *external* domination they were perfectly happy to resort, by all means at their disposal, to the most violent imposition of their rule wherever they could do that as self-righteous *nation-states* and exploitative *colonizers*. This constituted the perverse *normality* of the antagonistic social order about which I argued a very long time ago:

> Growth and expansion are inner necessities of the capitalist system of production and when the local limits are reached there is no other way out except by violently readjusting the existing relation of forces. The relative stability of the leading capitalist countries—Britain, France, and the United States—was in the past inseparable from their ability to *export* the aggressiveness and the violence *internally generated* by their systems. Their weaker partners—Germany, Italy, and others—after the First World War found themselves in the middle of a grave social crisis and only the Fascist promise of a radical readjustment of the established relation of forces could bring a temporary solution acceptable to the bourgeoisie, through diverting the pressures of internal aggressiveness and violence into the channels of a massive preparation for a new world war. The small capitalist countries, on the other hand, simply had to subordinate themselves to one of the great powers and follow the policies dictated by them, even at the price of chronic instability.[6]

THE IRREPRESSIBLE GLOBAL ASSERTION OF RULE

The difficult question for us is: How long can the perverse normality of an antagonistic social-economic and political order, with its irrepressible tendency toward the global assertion of its rule, maintain its domination without destroying humanity itself? This is the size of the mountain we *must* climb and conquer.

One of the gravest problems in our time is the structural crisis of liberal-democratic politics and the advocated solutions feasible from the vantage point of the existing states. Wherever we look and whatever remedies we are offered, their common defining characteristics always display the contradictions and the limitations of the historically constituted nation-states. This also happens to be the case when the claimed justification for the pursued policies is full of the rhetorics of universally commendable "democracy" and the unavoidable "globalization," coupled with the projection of answers in conformity to such determinations. At the same time, the claimed solutions are explicitly or by implication always based on the assumption that the historically long-established alienation of overall political decision-making, embodied in the modern states, must remain permanently the only feasible framework of overall societal management.

As we know, Marx had a radically different view on this issue. His conception of the required socialist change of the social order is inseparable from his critique of the *state as such,* and not simply of the capitalist state. This approach is spelled out in the form of his advocacy and anticipation of not just the established state's major transformation but of its complete *withering away*. On this matter, just like on so many others, he offered a fundamentally different conception than even the greatest and most representative thinkers of the bourgeoisie.

The painful circumstance is that since the time when Marx formulated his views on the imperative of historically sustainable societal change, embracing in every way the whole of society, we could not see any sign of the state's withering away. Rather, we could witness the opposite. Yet this circumstance should not divert attention from the fundamental validity of Marx's advocacy. For the innermost determinations and destructive contradictions of the capital system in its deepening structural crisis today are intelligible and surmountable only if the modern state formations' overbearing role in the modality of all-embracing decision-making in the social metabolic process under the rule of capital is fully taken into account. No historically sustainable remedy is conceivable without that. It is therefore no exaggeration to say that the continued historical significance of the Marxian theoretical framework hinges on the realizability (or not) of his concern with the withering away of the state.

HOBBES AND HEGEL

In the course of modern history, the intellectual giants of the bourgeoisie produced two truly great works on the state, which have never been equaled, let alone surpassed, since their creation. They are *The Leviathan* by Thomas Hobbes, conceived in the middle of the seventeenth century, and *The Philosophy of Right* by Hegel, created in the first third of the nineteenth century. Naturally, neither of the two had the slightest interest in the projections of liberalism. Indeed, Hegel provided a scathing critique of the liberal illusions that fallaciously transfigured the realizability of *partial privileges* championed by their far from universal beneficiaries into totally untenable claims to *universal validity*.[7] But of course the conceptual horizon of both of these great thinkers was circumscribed by their different, nevertheless forceful, idealizations of the nation-state.

We have to return in due course to Hobbes and Hegel as the unrivaled peaks of the bourgeois theorizations of the state. At this point it should suffice to indicate a striking contrast. The contrast in question is clearly visible between the Hobbesian and Hegelian substantive theoretical assessment of the vital issues involved in evaluating the problems of the state, with all of their complexity and relevance to the functioning of the society of their own epoch, and in our time, the self-deluding disorientation of even some relatively progressive liberal-democratic politicians, like Sir Anthony Eden—not to mention their *neoliberal* and *neocon* colleagues—in the pursuit of policies capable of producing only disaster, and doing that in the name of *"the highest form of statesmanship."*

CHAPTER EIGHT

The "Withering Away" of the State?

Marx never abandoned his view that the necessary radical change of capital's social metabolic order is inconceivable without fully overcoming the preponderant power of the established material reproductive system's state formations. Not even when the unfolding historical events pointed, dishearteningly, in the opposite direction.

It is equally important to stress that when he stressed the necessity of the state's "withering away"—and for the same reason remaining faithful to acknowledging fully the requirements of *epochal* social and historical viability—he made it abundantly clear that to envisage the state's *abolition* by any form of conspiracy, or even by some more broadly based juridical *decree,* could only be a voluntaristic pipe dream. He never stopped insisting about that.

In this sense, the actual feasibility of the advocated radical societal change had to be conceived by Marx as arising from the historically sustainable unfolding of appropriate social processes, accounting for them in their tangible reality as they assert themselves in accordance with the dialectical mediatory transformation of their multifaceted objective and subjective requirements. The obstacles and massive constraints emanating from the existing relations of power as linked to the role of the state in the preservation and potential further development of the capital system as a whole, could not be simply wished out of existence, contrary to the way in which not only his primarily anarchist opponents but even some of his long-standing friends and comrades projected the course of events and the strategies to be followed. This is why Marx tirelessly stressed in his pronouncements that foreshadowed the prospects of development on the terrain of political action and *all-embracing* decision-making—without which, and this must be firmly stressed, no conceivable social metabolic order could function—that the future not only *must* but *can only* bring with it the *withering away* of the state. Thus, both terms of "can" and "must" had to remain pivotal points of any historically sustainable socialist orientation in this matter, whatever might be the temptations to exclude one or the other as we have experienced them up to the present time.

It is well known that, together with his plan to write a relatively short work on dialectics, one of the important projects Marx was hoping to accomplish, particularly in his early years, was a theoretical overview of the thorny problems of the state. However, as a result of his ever-deeper engagement in the radical critique of political economy, which required a monumental effort—and even painfully health-consuming— this project more and more receded from his horizon.

But this is only a partial explanation, even if in strictly personal terms well understandable. Much more important was the objective historical development after the revolutionary wave of the late 1840s, which subsequently—following the serious economic crises of the late 1850s and the 1860s when Marx and Engels had so much hope for the possibility of a fundamental societal change—resulted in the relative stabilization of capital's social order in the European "little corner of the world."[1] Moreover, the European economic and political crises of the late 1850s and the 1860s had brought not only the social explosion manifesting itself in the 1871 Paris Commune but the military defeat and savage repression of the participants in that Commune, and simultaneously the strengthening of bourgeois class solidarity against the "common enemy."[2]

Inevitably, all this had a major impact on the prospects of development of the working-class movement with which Marx was closely associated on personal terms, both as a militant intellectual and as the political leader of the movement's organizational articulation, the First International. The ongoing developments took a turn in the direction of the particular working-class movements beginning to occupy increasing political institutional ground in their national setting, but this happened at the price of abandoning some of their earlier revolutionary tenets for the sake of operating within the bourgeois class-oriented legal framework of their capitalist state.

CRITIQUE OF THE GOTHA PROGRAMME

This problem presented itself in a most acute form in Germany with the Gotha Program, which was written for the purpose of promoting the unification of the radical wing of the movement with the opportunistic accommodators of the German working class. The "Eisenachers" constituted the radical wing of the working class, whereas the "Lassalleans"—whose inspirer Ferdinand Lassalle was for quite a long time "probably in secret understanding with Bismarck," as Marx correctly suggested in 1865—were trying to integrate the class movement into the established state regulatory structure.[3] To counter that Marx produced in April (or early May) 1875 a devastating *Critique of the Gotha Programme,* which pointed out not only the inner contradictions of this particular program but also the disastrous prospects for the future of the socialist movement if it adopted the strategy foreshadowed by such unprincipled unification. But all this was to no avail and the fateful unification went ahead.

Under the given historical circumstances, political accommodation prevailed, inducing the working-class participants to "follow the line of least resistance" in their relations to the ruling order. This course of development emerged thanks also to the newly opened prospects for capital expansion favored by imperialistic developments, with Bismarck's Germany as a most powerful contestant in the international arena. Understandably, there could be no question of the state's *withering away* for a long time to come, even if its necessity had to be reasserted, as indeed it had been done by Marx in his *Critique*. The objective trends of development favored opening up a road to a more aggressive reassertion of capital's power, paralyzing the principled socialist aspirations of the working-class movement for a painfully long time to come, as perceived by Marx. Significantly, he concluded the *Critique of the Gotha Programme* with these resignatory words: *"Dixi et salvavianimammeam"*—I said it and saved my soul.

Naturally, Marx's radical critique was hidden from public view by the leadership of the new party for sixteen years. When in the end it was allowed publication, two decades after the Paris Commune—and even then only as a result of the forceful intervention by Engels, threatening to reveal it himself if his request continued to be denied—there was no way of reversing the fateful course of events. By that time things had gone too far. Revealingly, Engels himself insisted in 1875, in his letter to August Bebel, who belonged to the Eisenacher wing of the party at the time of its unification, that the road bound to be followed by the advocated reorientation of the German working class inevitably meant that "the principle that the workers' movement is an *international movement* is, to all intents and purposes, *completely disavowed*."[4] The grave implications of this prophetic judgment for the movement being trapped by a tragically chosen blind alley were clamorously confirmed at the outbreak of the First World War when German Social Democracy ignominiously identified itself with the imperialist war adventure of their state.

Marx always clearly emphasized that the great historical transformation of the future is inconceivable without the sustained revolutionary work of what he called the *"practical critical agency,"* that is, the organized international working class. However, more or less simultaneously with the negative impact of the Gotha Program in Germany, and in the same disheartening way, the First International also went through a major crisis and had to cease functioning in 1875. To theorize under such conditions about the proximity of the "withering away of the state" would be indeed naive, to say the least. Imperialist developments in the last two or three decades of the nineteenth century put on the order of the day the ever more aggressive confrontations for the radical redefinition of the *relations of power* among the dominant international forces. And that meant not the weakening but, on the contrary, the imperative of *strengthening* of their states.

It goes without saying that the immense destructive consequences of the unfolding imperialist developments and their corresponding military implications, which had to result in due course even in two *global conflagrations,* and on the economic plane the deep-seated and ever more dominant *monopolism,* as the socioeconomic corollary of such transformations, were beyond Marx's horizon. The proper theorization of the new imperialism, with its necessary impact on the nature of capital's state formations, was left to the age of Lenin. And even then, it had to be affected by transient historical specificities, carrying with them somewhat optimistic overtones by defining imperialism, with regard to its several lethally warring state antagonists, as the "last phase of capitalism." The subsequent formation of *global hegemonic imperialism,* with the United States of America as its overwhelmingly dominant power, was constituted only after the Second World War and so far also succeeded in managing its affairs without a global collision of the potentially contending states of the global capital system. Moreover, another radically different attempt at controlling capital's antagonistic modality of social metabolic reproduction, which appeared in history well beyond Marx's horizon, was the Soviet-type economic and political system, with the *politically regulated* maximal extraction of surplus labor under the rule of its state formation, in contrast to the *primarily economic* extraction of surplus labor as *surplus value.*

THE CHALLENGE TODAY: THE STATE AND THE GLOBAL SYSTEM OF CAPITAL

In view of all these considerations, we may recall that "since capital in Marx's lifetime was very far from its present-day articulation as a truly global system, equally, its overall political command structure as a system of globally interconnected states was far less visible in its precise mediatedness. It is therefore by no means surprising that Marx never succeeded in sketching even the bare outlines of his theory of the state, although the latter was assigned a very precise and important place in his projected system as a whole. Today the situation is quite different, in that the global system of capital, under a variety of very different (indeed contradictory) forms, finds its political equivalent in the totality of interdependent state- and inter-state relations. This is why the elaboration of a Marxist theory of the state is both possible and necessary today. Indeed, it is vitally important for the future of viable socialist strategies."[5]

CHAPTER NINE

The Wishful Limitation of State Power

But can we assert with confidence that there is a proper Marxist theory of the state in the more recent literature?
Let me quote on this issue Norberto Bobbio, who left us a most valuable body of theoretical work on the law, conceived by him in the best tradition of the original, and in its own time undoubtedly progressive liberalism. Moreover, Bobbio as a scholar was not only a passionate anti-fascist, he also professed deep social reformatory sympathies for, and consistently voiced solidarity with, the gravely disadvantaged in capitalist society. This is clearly testified by many of his enlightened interventions in postwar political debates and by his legislative role as Senator for Life under the presidency of Sandro Pertini, in the old Italian Socialist Party that was led for a long time by Pietro Nenni, well before its corruption by Berlusconi and its disintegration under Bettino Craxi. I always considered Norberto Bobbio a very dear friend and a great ally of our cause.

Bobbio's answer to the question: "Is There a Marxist Theory of the State?"—the title of one of his prominent articles—is an emphatic No. He states that view at times with forceful sarcasm, as, for instance, when he comments on the debate between John Lewis and Louis Althusser:

Lewis has written that "man makes history." Althusser unleashes a pamphlet at him, maintaining that such is not the case. "Ce sont les masses qui font l'histoire." I challenge anyone to find a social scientist outside the Marxist camp who can seriously pose a problem of this type. [Bobbio adds in a footnote:] Of the two assertions, Lewis's at least has the merit of being clear, even though general, and of having a precise polemical aim: that history is made by men means that it is not made by God, providence, etc. Althusser's claim, on the other hand, which pretends to be a scientific proposition, is likewise general but unclear. Indeed, one need not be an admirer of analytic philosophy to consider the proposition meaningless, since to give it meaning would require defining what the masses are, what "making" means, and what history is—an extremely simple undertaking![1]

Naturally, the last few words are meant in biting irony. Bobbio is the last person to deny the major theoretical difficulties involved in the satisfactory solution of such problems. If anything, he tends to argue in the opposite sense, putting the stress on the overwhelming difficulties. In any case, Bobbio is also right in stating that some Italian Marxists who claim that there is a fully worked out theory of the state in Marx's writings continue to repeat twenty pages of his text—from the *Civil War in France,* as Umberto Cerroni does in his *Teoriapolitica e socialismo*—and fail to account for the reality of the state. In his highly popular book, *Quale socialismo?,*[2] Bobbio offers the same negative stance about the debated problems of socialism, in the form of a multiplicity of unanswered concluding questions,[3] as in his article from *Telos* quoted above.

Nevertheless, Bobbio's appreciation of Marx as a dialectical thinker cannot be denied. This is clearly visible in a major article published in one of his most important collection of essays, *Da Hobbes a Marx.*[4] In an article of this volume, "La dialettica in Marx," first published in 1958, he singles out a vital question concerning the relation of Hegelian Logic to Hegel's theory of the state. In the spirit of his own preference for the liberal democratic conception of the state Bobbio quotes Marx in full agreement: "Logic does not serve to prove the state but the state serves to prove Logic."[5] In this way Marx describes the process of mystification of reality, which consists in overturning an empirical position into a metaphysical proposition.

At the same time, in a somewhat conflicting way, Bobbio comments that "in my view what counts about Marxism in the history of thought is the materialistic theory of history."[6] Here, too, despite agreeing with Marx in his critique of Hegel, and in indicating his sympathy for the Marxian dialectical view of history while rejecting the dialectic of nature, there is no sign of Bobbio approving even in principle the Marxian conception of the state, although in this 1958 essay his reasoning is spelled out on the basis of debatable methodological considerations that, in view of our limitations here, cannot be discussed now.

THE QUESTION AS TO WHY THE STATE AS A CATEGORY IS TREATED CRITICALLY IN MARXIAN THEORY

However, this issue goes well beyond a particular historical controversy. It also highlights a more fundamental theoretical problem. For even if we agree with Bobbio about the absence of a proper Marxist theory of the state up to the present time, there is something very problematical with regard to his own general position, which he shares with the liberal tradition in general. It is highly relevant in this connection that Bobbio firmly *asserts* the nonexistence of the Marxist theory of the state but never investigates *why* it does not exist, if that is the case. Indeed, Bobbio simply *stipulates*—both in the way in which he argues his own case and also by fully siding with the liberal-democratic conception of the state—that the Marxist theory of the state not only *does not exist* but also that it *cannot exist* at all. And in that way there is no need for asking the crucially important question of *why*, because the *assertion* and *stipulation*—from the ground of *assuming* the liberal-democratic state's permanent validity—settles the issue as a matter of course.

This position is firmly expressed in Bobbio's categorical rejection of *any* alternative to *representative democracy*, which means, of course, the corresponding dismissal of Rousseau. Naturally, the rejection of the Marxian idea of the *withering away of the state* is a necessary corollary of all that. Bobbio, in fact, adopts Adam Smith's views on the required limitations of state power, in sharp contrast to Hegel's idea of the ideal universality of the fully adequate *"ethical state."* Paradoxically, in unacknowledged conflict with some of his own tenets, Bobbio embraces the position of even the conservative wing of the liberal democratic theory represented by Luigi Einaudi,[7] the first postwar president of the Italian Republic. Not surprisingly, in this approach the question of *why* is never asked about the objective constitutive grounds, and consequently the future viability (or not), of the liberal democratic state itself.

Yet, without a *historical/genetic* account and prognosis of past, present and future there can be *no validly sustainable* theory of the state, indeed of any state. There can be only its *assumption* and—with regard to the future—the more or less peremptory *assertion* of its permanence, complemented by a Theory—or Philosophy—of the *Law*. Such *Theory of the Law,* represented as the *Theory* (or *Philosophy*) *of the State,* can explain only the *modality* of the *given* legal framework's *operation*—like, for instance, the parliamentary functioning of "representative democracy"—and do that in a rather idealized form. This is the case even when the believers of the liberal approach are willing to advocate to "restrain the state from excessive interference with civil society," in general with very little, if any, success in such efforts.

This connection indicates a major concern that is as a rule obscured or even completely ignored. For the investigation of the problems of the state is often *identified with*, or—in more precise terms—*reduced to* theories of *Law* and *Right*. In German, as we know, the same word, *Recht,* covers both Law and Right. In fact, Hegel's *Philosophy of Right* is also his *Philosophy of the State* and sometimes this work is translated as one and sometimes as the other. The serious trouble in this respect is that identifying the state with the Law and the Right fundamentally distorts and apologetically rationalizes and justifies the actually existing *reality of the state* by projecting—explicitly or by implication—the *ideal coincidence* of rightful Law with the far from self-evident unquestionable coincidence of "The Law" with "The State." For the actually existing state—including the modern capitalist "democratic state"—is characterized not only by *Law* and *Right* but also by utterly destructive *Lawlessness* and thereby by the diametrical opposite of *rightful law*.

INTERNATIONAL LAWLESSNESS AS LIBERAL IDEALISM

Under some circumstances of particularly acute crises, this is even recognized by liberal legal theoreticians. But even when it is done, this embarrassing admission happens in a characteristically one-sided way, without examining the questionable assumptions of the advocated liberal framework despite its crisis. A very good example is a politically well-meaning but theoretically rather doubtful book by Philippe Sands, titled *Lawless World: America and the Making and Breaking of Global Rules*.[8] What makes Sands's book on recent grave violations of international law quite inadequate is that the author simply postulates the *exceptionality* of the state's lawlessness, without investigating the underlying *causes* that make *state lawlessness* the *recurrent rule* at times of *major crises*. When Sands tries to explain what he calls "one of the *great enigmas* of modern British political life"[9]—which in this case, far from enigmatically asserted itself in the British prime minister's total subservience to the unlawful military adventures of American imperialism under President George W. Bush in Afghanistan and in Iraq, exposed and honorably condemned with regard to international law by the author of *Lawless World*—Sands is willing to seriously entertain as an explanatory idea Blair's "idealism" and his "well-intentioned" attitude to international politics.[10] But of course state lawlessness condemned by some liberal legal theorists in the name of the law continues unabated in the international arena when Bush and Blair vacate their seats in favor of their successors. And there is nothing *enigmatic* about that.

CHAPTER TEN

The Assertion of Might-as-Right

The deepest underlying truth and causal determination of these matters—valid for *all states*, including the customarily idealized "modern democratic state"—is that *"right is might"* because *"might is right,"* and not the other way round, as groundlessly postulated even by some genuine believers in liberal theory. Naturally, the particular *modality* of asserting, through state legislation, the presumed imperative for imposing and legitimating *might-as-right* changes historically. But the fundamental determinations remain the same for as long as the state itself exists in *any* form.

This is also true of the particular *phases*—changing "back and forth" from time to time, of the modern capitalist state, e.g. liberal-democratic, Bonapartist, colonial imperialist, Nazi-Fascist, neo-con dominated, etc. Moreover, the post-revolutionary capital system also produced its historically varying phases of more or less directly authoritarian state formations, from Stalin to Khrushchev and from Gorbachev and Yeltsin to Putin, or the forms named "Peoples' Democracies" from Rákosi to Gomulka and Kádár, or in another setting, the state regulatory forms under Tito. Naturally, the historically distinct Chinese varieties, from the time of Mao to the present, must also be remembered in this context.

Nor did Marx entertain any illusion about the character of the feasible transitional state formation concerning the inherited "might-as-right." He envisaged it with the explicitly stated orientation of turning "might-into-right." Marx made that very clear by talking about the transitory *dictatorship of the proletariat* precisely in his *Critique of the Gotha Programme* while forcefully stressing the necessary withering away of the state.

Max Weber's *state-apologetic* formula that assigns *"the monopoly of violence"* to the state—often hailed as a great insight—is in fact a shallow pseudo-explanation and a cynical evasion of the real problem. It is on par with another profundity by Weber that grotesquely asserts that the state is the "creation of Occidental Jurists." Neither of the two propositions has even a minimal explanatory value regarding the conditions under which the modern state formation comes into being and historically changes its forms from the institution of consensually liberal-democratic measures at a certain stage of development to the adoption of openly dictatorial rules of control.[1] The serious problems of *why* the state *must resort* to violence, when it does, and even more important, *how far* a system of societal management like that exercised by the alienated decision-making processes of politics can be historically sustained, remain complete *"mysteries"* (or "enigmas," as naively suggested by Phillipe Sands, quoted in the previous chapter), even when the ludicrous Weberian suggestion is propagandized that purports to explain the antagonistic reality of the state through the birth pangs of the brains of more or less drunken Occidental judges.

STATE VIOLENCE AND STATE RIGHT

In the past, the self-serving idealization of the liberal democratic state relegated the problem of state violence to the domain of the *"despotic state."* This continued to be done later when some liberal state theorists were willing to acknowledge violence (of course, strictly marginal violence) in their own states as "aberration," occasional executive "excessiveness," emergency "exceptionality," or administrative "failure," and the like, all of which were expected to be properly corrected by the future "state restraints" wishfully projected by liberal political theory.

Under the impact of sharpening contradictions and antagonisms, in the twentieth century the notion of *"despotic state"* was "modernized" in the form of *"the totalitarian state."* This definition functioned as a convenient but rather absurd umbrella term under which so many thoroughly different—not to say diametrically opposite—determinations could be lumped together, without explaining anything, yet proclaimed and sustained through the adopted definitional/tautological self-evidence of pretendedly "descriptive" assertion. Moreover, the *definitionally* established claim to *self-evidence*, was not only supposed to constitute a *fundamental critique* of the denounced "totalitarian" state forms, but also, at the same time, and even more problematically, it was seen as constituting the equally self-evident justification assumed by "anti-totalitarian" theorists who defined themselves in terms of their circularly self-commending dismissal of what they simply rejected.

In Hegel's philosophical system the problem of the *despotic state* was solved by the "Absolute Spirit" unfolding and disclosing itself in terms of world historical development by confining Oriental despotism irretrievably to the past, and bringing to light the true "ethical state" as *"the image and actuality of reason."*[2] That is, World Spirit was said to establish the real kingdom of *Recht* in the fullest dual sense of the term, covering both the State and the morally commendable Right. But, of course, this could not mean the end of violence. For Hegel, to the credit of his intellectual consistency, simultaneously maintained both the ideality and unalterable actuality of the *nation-state,* which meant for him the morally justified acceptance of *war* as the ultimate guarantor of the idealized nation-state's *sovereignty*.

Naturally, in the philosophy of Hobbes there could be no question of the supersession of violence. Far from it. Indeed, in any theory of politics oriented toward the nation-state, the standpoint of such state can only be adopted with *consistency* by the theoreticians involved if the nation-state's necessary implications for *war*—in view of the potentially most destructive antagonistic *interstate* relations that must be carried to their logical conclusion—are also accepted. That can be opposed only by the wishful Kantian *Sollen*—his projected "ought-to-be" of the postulated, but on capital's social ground never realizable, *"perpetual peace,"* which was dismissed with biting sarcasm by Hegel.

A MONOPOLY ON LAWLESSNESS

In truth, the real problem is not *generic violence* but quite tangible, socially grounded, and sustained *state lawlessness* that regularly surfaces and asserts itself as a matter of *systemic crisis determinations*. The question of violence, no matter how grave, is only a part of the more general and also much more fundamental problem. The pretended "value-free" descriptive assertion about the state's monopoly of violence is only a circular triviality at the claimed descriptive level. In fact, the unacknowledged purpose of the Weberian pronouncement is the apologetic *legitimation* and *justification* of the capitalist state and its *lawlessness* as violence. This could not be further removed from the author's claims to *Wert-Freiheit* (value-freedom). In its proper meaning the Weberian assertion states that even the violence of the state is legitimate because the state itself cannot be *held responsible* for its lawlessness and violence by anyone, hence its *monopoly*.

However, on closer inspection such a proposition turns out to be not simply vacuous but utterly false on two counts. First, because at times—like the Nuremberg war criminal trials, when former power relations suffered a well-deserved shock and reversal—the state's postulated *exemption from responsibility* is emphatically *and rightly* denied, with obvious consequences for the commanding personnel of the guilty state. And second, because the pretended "monopoly of violence" in its terms of reference to exemption from being held responsible for the act in question applies also to the *madman* who kills another human being, and receives as the implicit acknowledgment of his own Weberian "monopoly of violence" the judgment of being sent to a medical institution or "lunatic asylum," instead of being executed, or jailed for life in a prison.

Thus, talking about the monopoly of violence, apart from being factually false as a claimed exclusivistic monopoly, is also an ideologically self-serving blatant evasion of the essential problem. That is to say, it is the state-apologetic evasion of the vital fact that what we are really concerned with is *state lawlessness*—even when it is not manifest in a violent form but rather as state-promoted fraudulence in legally protected and indeed legally facilitated tax evasion, for instance—and not generic violence, which can assume a virtually infinite number of more or less directly hurtful forms. Evidently, the prevalence of violence in state practices can be more or less intense, according to the changing circumstances. But the changing modality of state violence should be the subject of serious historical investigation, instead of obfuscating the matter with the state's generic identification with its decreed monopoly of violence.

ERNEST BARKER ON THE STATE AND LAW

It is worth quoting here at some length Ernest Barker's views on the state and law. A former professor of political science in the University of Cambridge, Barker is, tellingly, still part of the general university curriculum.

We find in his theory of the state a most revealing idealization of both the state and the law, by asserting their ideal unity in terms of a mysteriously proclaimed notion of "purpose." This is how Barker presents that view:

> Each national society is a *unity*. ... But each society is also a *plurality*. It is a rich web of contained *groups*—religious and educational; professional and occupational; some for pleasure and some for *profit*; some based on neighbourhood and some on some *other affinity*; all dyed by the national colour and yet all (or most of them) with the capacity and the instinct, for associating themselves with similar *groups* in other national societies, and thus entering into some form of international connection. ... The state, we may say, is a national society which has turned itself into a legal association, or a juridical organization, by virtue of a legal act and deed called a *constitution*, which is henceforth the norm and standard (and therefore the

THE ASSERTION OF MIGHT-AS-RIGHT

"Sovereign") of such association or organization.... Constituted by and under this constitution, and thus created by a legal act (or series of acts), the state exists to perform the legal and political *purpose* for which it was constituted.[3]

The word conspicuously absent from such political science and its theory of the state is *class*. In its stead, we have the universal vaguery of "groups." The result of the adoption of this tendentiously "lowest common denominator"—through which the capitalist class exploiters of the class of labor appear as members of a "voluntary association interested in profit" and in which the laborers do not appear at all—is the declamatory genericity concerning "groups" that are supposed to make up the "national society." And then, of course, we are also presented with the customary circularity of such political theories in Barker's attempt to define "the constitution of the state"—upon which so much else is supposed to hinge—through its "constitution," begging thereby the question in the service of social and political apologetics. Thus, we are also told a few pages further on:

> The *state* is essentially *law*, and *law is the essence of the state*. The state is essentially law in the sense that it exists in order to secure a *right order* of relations between its *members*, expressed in the form of declared and enforced rules. Law as a system of declared and enforced rules, is the essence of the state in the same sort of sense as his [the political philosopher's] words and acts are the essence of man.[4]

Barker's only concern is to abstractly postulate the wishful reality of the "law-observing-state," namely British law idealized by him, in contrast to the authoritarian German/Italian/Fascist state. But, as frequently happens, this approach is not at all interested in a critical analysis of the origin, nature, and transformation of the idealized "law-abiding state" that it circularly assumes, on the shaky ground of the temporarily established relation of forces.

The underlying intent and practical usefulness of treating the state as a "group," like the other "groups," is manifest in Barker's way of *legitimating* the state in his discourse on the *"state's purpose."* These are his words:

> It [the state] is a group or association; and it stands on the same footing as other groups or associations. Its essence or being consists in *its purpose,* just as the essence or being of all other groups consists in their purpose. Not only is purpose the essence of the groups contained in the state; it is also the essence of the state itself. . . . The characteristic of the purpose of the state is that it is the *specific purpose of law.* Other purposes, so far as they concern or affect this purpose, must necessarily be squared with it. This is the same as to say that other groups, so far as they hold or assume a legal position, must necessarily be adjusted to the legal group which we call the state. They are not thereby adjusted to its *will:* they are adjusted to its *purpose* which is *law.* The state would be failing to attain its purpose and thereby to discharge its *duty,* if it failed to secure such adjustment. But the adjustment is not a matter of discretion, and it is not absolute: it is controlled by the purpose of the state, and it is relative to that purpose. To reject the theory of the real personality of groups is not to fall into worship of the omnicompetent or absolute state. It is to find the essence of the state in its purpose of law, and *to subject it to its purpose,* just as we find the essence of other groups also in their *particular* purpose, and just as we make them too the servants and the ministers of their purpose.[5]

In this way, the wishfully idealized "purpose" reveals its apologetic substance when Barker asserts that the state's *purpose* is also its morally commendable *duty* to *enforce the necessary adjustments* to its own "purpose." Accordingly, opposing disembodied "purpose" to actually operative *will,* as adopted by Ernest Barker—while insisting on the *duty* of the state to *enforce conformity*—amounts to no more than apologetic sophistry. At the same time, Barker's talk about *"subjecting the state to its purpose"* is utterly vacuous. At best it is only a wishful collection of words without practicable content. For who is going to lawfully *"subject* the state to its purpose" when the whole discourse is centered on the necessary—and in Barker's own words constitutionally sanctified—subjection of "all groups and associations" to the state's overbearing "purpose," legitimated by him in the name of the categorically asserted *identity of the state and law* defined as their mutual "essence"?

THE STATE ABOVE THE LAW

The trouble with all such apologetic misrepresentations of the state and law is that the difficult question of justifying the actually prevailing relationship between *might and right* under capital's state formations is either avoided or more or less consciously taken for granted as the right and proper way of managing societal interchange in all conceivable systems of overall political decision-making. Consequently, the thorny issue of *state lawlessness* cannot even be considered, no matter how grave. The mere assumption of *might* as the more or less implicitly but always arbitrarily decreed legitimate ground of *right itself* justifies everything by definition. It justifies even the crudest and most violent suppression of *internal dissent* and its search for some viable alternative, not to mention the wars pursued against the *"external enemy"* in the interest of temporarily exporting the accumulated internal antagonisms of the established social metabolic order.

Moreover, by treating might-as-right in this apologetic self-justifying way, the champions of such state-legitimated ideology also turn into a complete *mystery* how and *why* the postulated, and by them morally commended "law-abiding state," *becomes* under determinate historical circumstances the kind of "German/Italian/Fascist state" criticized by Barker. The political theorists who assume might as the self-evident legitimate ground of right cannot possibly have an answer to such an embarrassing question. They either close their eyes to it, ignoring painful historical evidence, or—worse still—come to terms with it when such developments take place while maintaining their pretenses to political enlightenment, as Max Weber does. In this respect it is by no means accidental that Weber as a "man for all seasons"—notwithstanding his liberal claims—could be an enthusiastic military defender of the aggressive interests of German imperialism during the First World War, and could find himself in full agreement with the proto-fascist General Ludendorff's cult of "the leader," also in the aftermath of that war.

The necessary relationship is between *state lawlessness* as such and the assertion of *might-as-right* as the practical modality of overall political decision-making under the rule of capital. The historically given state formations of the capital system must be asserted as the effective *enforcers* of the rules required for the maintenance of the established societal reproductive order. Naturally, "the law" must be defined and modified accordingly, so as to suit the changing power relations and the corresponding modifications of the fundamental antagonisms that are inseparable from capital's metabolism of societal reproduction. That way of imposing state legitimacy is at times feasible in tune with "constitutional rules" and at other times feasible only through the suspension and violation of all such rules. Historical development decides which of the two must prevail under the given—and rule-changing—circumstances. Hence it is totally arbitrary to postulate either ideal constitutionality or its necessary suspension or abolition as the *norm*. The two of them go—or, rather, *come and go*—together, with bewildering regularity.

Since, however, *might-as-right* must always take the upper hand, at least as the "reserve powers" of idealized sovereignty, and it must do so even under the least conflictual circumstances of any "trouble-free democratic golden age," any postulate of the "law-abiding state"—or of the liberal-democratic formulations of the same idea as "state restraint" in relation to "civil society"—can be no more than unadulterated fiction. Thus, *state lawlessness,* as the necessary assertion of *might-as-right* under the historically changing circumstances of self-legitimated determinations, is inseparable from the reality of the state as such. In other words, might-as-right and state lawlessness are in a sense synonymous, in view of their *necessary correlation*. What is contingent in this necessary relationship is the form or modality—that is, the nonviolent or, on the contrary, in the most brutal way, violent—assertion of the state-legitimated imperative of might-as-right.

A very good example of the formally changing but in its substance continuing relationship between state lawlessness and might-as-right in British history was provided by the authoritarian assertion of state power in the name of the "defense of democracy" under the premiership of Margaret Thatcher during the miners' strike of 1984. The secret state documents released in January 2014 in conformity to the "thirty years' rule" of legalized concealment made it clear that the British government not only systematically lied in the media about the contested issues, denying the already adopted secret policy of closing seventy-five coal pits and the necessary mass unemployment resulting from that decision, but also resorted to the unlawful action of state violence against the miners and their supporters, cynically violating its own constitutionally regulated statutes. Margaret Thatcher's government ordered the police force to intervene against the miners on a prolonged strike, thereby violating not only the professed democratic rules in general but, paradoxically, the rules constitutionally laid down to the police for the purpose of ideologically palatable "democratic law enforcement." This course of events had to be imposed under the circumstances despite the fact that the police force wanted to conform to its constitutionally prescribed rules and statutes. Naturally, the police wanted to do this not for defending constitutionality but in the interest of maintaining a more easily manageable relationship with the public at large. This, rather than expose itself as being the party directly responsible for the bitterly acrimonious adversariality resulting from the action dictated unlawfully, and indeed unconstitutionally, by the "democratic" government.

The state, with its power of lawlessness, was *above the law* in the first place, thanks to the self-legitimated reality of might-as-right. Otherwise, it could not act unlawfully even over its own police force, violating the relevant constitutional statutes when it suited the changing circumstances. Being *above the law*—not as an "aberration" but by the capital state's always given inherent determination, revealed only at times of major conflict—is the fundamental meaning of *incorrigible state lawlessness*. The state's incorrigible lawlessness resides in its innermost constitution as sovereign *arbiter* over the law, and is therefore *above the law*. Everything else is consequential or secondary to that, including the apologetically hailed technicality of the "separation of powers," depending on whether the enforcement of the objective implications of being above the law calls for violent or nonviolent modalities of action. "States of emergency" can be decreed whenever the conditions of intensifying crises make such courses of action the "proper way," even without any military involvement. The ideologically embellished cynical lies spelled out in the name of the "defense of democracy" should not be confused with reality. In state practice the vainly pursued justification of the unjustifiable adds insult to injury by first acting in a most unlawful/unconstitutional way against the miners, and then denounces them—in Margaret Thatcher's own words—as *"the enemy within."*[6]

This is not a "personal aberration" nor "excessive interference with civil society," as traditional liberal-democratic theories of the state would argue. What matters here is the perverse *objective continuity* between being above the law, thanks to the state's structurally secured position, and its ability to decree "states of emergency"—including even the most authoritarian modes of action—in the name of the "defense of democracy." The only way to make this kind of development intelligible is to underline the structurally determined inseparability of might-as-right and state lawlessness asserting itself, of all things, in the name of "the rule of law." The same goes for the slippery road starting from the claimed "defense of democracy," proceeding through the proclamation of "states of emergency," and going all the way to the recurrent imposition of dictatorial forms of government, as *organically* linked to one another. Transformations of this kind can be made intelligible only on the same ground of the structurally determined inseparability of might-as-right and state lawlessness as the self-legitimated privilege of the state. This is why we can ignore only at our peril the prevalence of state lawlessness—often constitutionally sanctified in theories of the state as such—as the overbearing reality of the state, irrespective of how violent or not the form in which it manifests is under the changing historical circumstances.

However, it is an equally important consideration in this respect that even when state lawlessness assumes a most violent, catastrophically destructive form, the contradiction manifest in it could not be explained simply with reference to the *state alone*. The state may well be the executor of such violence, going as far as a massively destructive *global war,* but it cannot be identified as the deepest *cause* of such events *in and by itself.*

In our societies the causally determining ground of violence is the social metabolic order of *the capital system itself.* The state, to be sure, is an *integral part* of this system as a mode of social metabolic control, and it functions as the active agency of both *state law* and *state lawlessness* in the service of the overall maintenance of the established social metabolic order. The state's responsibility in promoting and enforcing the *objective imperatives* of the capital system is *colossal* but by no means *exclusive*. This qualification is required not for exempting the state from its responsibility but, on the contrary, for making possible a genuine and historically sustainable *critique* of the state. For without *disentangling* so many things on this terrain it is impossible to define the strategic lines of *what is to be done* as well as *what can be done* in terms of the *reality of the state* as an integral part of the capital system.

CHAPTER ELEVEN

Eternalizing Assumptions of Liberal State Theory

What needs to be *disentangled* is not simply a question of highlighting some characteristic theoretical distortions and their underlying motivations. It is much more difficult than that, because it requires *practical disentangling* through a radical change of society. For the revealing theoretical representations of these vital issues of social life in the annals of social theory and philosophy are firmly rooted in the social realities themselves. The theories in question articulate the underlying social interests and values, in accordance with the standpoint of the *ruling order*, which their ideologically motivated authors adopt even in their partial criticisms of what they consider corrigible in the given order. Thus, the necessity of *disentangling* itself, in the interest of historically sustainable transformation, and the structurally entrenched difficulties encountered in attempting to do that, clearly indicate the *practical embeddedness* of the problems themselves as they have historically arisen, and have become strengthened, even encrusted, by the force of social inertia.

At this point of our engagement with the subject only a brief reference can be made to what requires, with regard to these thorny issues, a fuller critical analysis in due course. A whole range of problems must be confronted that not only *did* but also *had to* remain entangled in bourgeois theories of the state, even in the greatest of them. To name a few, it is enough to think of the relationship between right and the state, right and the law, the state and the law, right and might, and its often mystifyingly camouflaged corollary, might asserted as right, at one level, and the spurious claims to self-evidency in the advocated classifications, legislations, and codifications at another.

Moreover, the objective historical changes that result in contrasting theoretical transformations must always be borne in mind. The conceptions of Hobbes and Hegel represented great theoretical accomplishments in their own time, even though they were by no means justifiable as permanent solutions to the problems at hand, as often claimed by these authors. However, these conceptions become extremely problematical at a later stage. This is because at a significantly altered later stage some articulated structural antagonisms in historical reality bring forward self-assertive social subjects who foreshadow the likelihood—or at least offer the practical feasibility—of a qualitatively different solution. At some point in time this includes, as directly relevant to us, the hegemonic alternative to capital's social metabolic order embodied in the historical force of labor.

In this sense, understandably, the customarily hidden or apologetically rationalized contradiction between right and the law, or the actually existent state and its claimed enforcement of right, or indeed for that matter the necessary relationship between might and right, could not represent any problem whatsoever to Thomas Hobbes under his conditions of historical development. But, of course, the same kind of historical exemption could not apply to Hegel who, at a later stage, could not help confronting the prohibitively difficult conflicts at the roots of these issues. And he did that with utmost integrity, no matter how problematical his adopted stance had to be in view of the changing class relations. He theorized them without evading the challenging reality of the new historical antagonisms because he could perceive them from the standpoint that could remain in tune with his own class horizon.

Accordingly, in his grandiose scheme of things Hegel produced—in the form of an unintended swan song—the last great bourgeois philosophy of the state. He did that by depicting the advocated "ethical state" as the rationally accomplished supersession of capitalist "civil society" (though in his own way not only acknowledging but *preserving* its contradictions) as an integral part, and even as the climax, of the unfolding world historical process.[1] He called that process a *Theodicaea: "a justification of the ways of God."*[2] In this way, Hegel projected the historically fully adequate realization of the *state as such* as *"Spirit's perfect embodiment."*[3]

JOHN AUSTIN ON LAW AND RIGHT

In much the same historical period as the completion of Hegel's philosophy of the state and right, the contrast to the Hegelian vision could not be greater in the conception of a strange but, in his own field of study, certainly most remarkable English utilitarian legal theorist, John Austin.

In his case so much—far too much—had to be taken for granted as unquestionably self-evident on the terrain of the allegedly fully legitimate political relations, in his view to be simply classified by jurisprudence, and therefore in no need of further analysis and, heaven forbid, critical explanation. In that sense, Austin could conveniently relegate some of the thorniest of theoretical difficulties and political contradictions of legal theory to the domain of linguistic considerations, "explained" by him as mere "ambiguities" and "confusions." Not surprisingly, Austin has been warmly acknowledged as a most distinguished ancestor to a characteristic approach to the problems of jurisprudence in the twentieth century, favored by some leading analytic linguistic philosophers, such as Oxford professor H. L. A. Hart. In this spirit, with regard to the issues of Right and the Law as discussed in legal philosophy in Austin's time under the German term "*Recht*," this English liberal/utilitarian thinker insisted:

> Since the strongest and wariest of minds are often ensnared by ambiguous words, their confusion of those disparate objects is a venial error.

Some, however, of these German writers are guilty of a grave offence against good sense and taste. They thicken the mess which that confusion produces, with a misapplication of terms borrowed from the Kantian philosophy. They divide "*recht*," as forming the genus or kind, into "*recht* in the objective sense" and "*recht* in the subjective sense," denoting by the former of those unapposite phrases "law."[4]

Austin claimed at the same time, with self-serving firmness, that "*the confusion of 'law' and 'right,' our own writers avoid.*"[5] Although, directly contradicting himself, he had to concede in a manuscript note connected with the same judgment that "Hale and Blackstone are *misled by this double meaning* of the word *jus*. They translate *jus personarum et rerum*, '*rights* of persons and things,' which is mere jargon."[6]

Naturally, Austin could have only words of insult for those who addressed themselves to the problems of "right-is-might" or "might-is-right," dismissing them as "shallow scoffers and buffoons" whose ideas are "either a flat truism affectedly and darkly expressed, or thoroughly false and absurd."[7] Strong words from a legal theorist who claims for his own position nothing less than the virtues of strict analytic objectivity and maximal linguistic accuracy, guided by the rigorous pursuit of logical perfection and positively commendable conscious design to guard against the intrusion of potential valuational distortions. In other words, the whole arsenal of "ideology-free" establishment self-mythology.

Austin, as a liberal utilitarian legal theorist and philosopher, differed to a large extent from his most distinguished predecessor, Jeremy Bentham. This difference manifested itself by no means for the sake of a more enlightened approach to the unfolding social conflicts and the attempted English parliamentary reforms connected with them. On the contrary. Though acknowledging that "the *innovating age* before us" is associated also with "*sinister interests*,"[8] and consequently called for appropriate legislative measures, after 1832—which was not only the year of reform but also the year of Jeremy Bentham's death—Austin firmly rejected the extension of the franchise promoted by his neighbor Bentham. Indeed, he attributed Bentham's political radicalism to what he considered the complete ignorance of the real character of the lower classes by his great utilitarian ancestor whose principal philosophical ideas he himself embraced.

UTILITARIANISM, LAW, AND THE STATE

But these problems are not confined to the questionable claims and more or less progressive political stance of particular legal theorists at a determinate phase of historical development. Undoubtedly Bentham worked with much greater sympathy for the relative advancement of the socially disadvantaged than Austin. But that was not enough to enable him to overcome the major limitations of their shared utilitarian/liberal stance. Also, Bentham operated with the political conceptual arsenal of *huge assumptions* about the nature of the *established* social order, which he wanted to improve without altering in the least its fundamental structural framework.

As an example, we may recall his characterization of constitutional law. This is how it reads:

> The constitutional branch [of the body of law] is chiefly employed in conferring, on particular classes of persons, *powers*, to be exercised for the *good of the whole society*, or of considerable parts of it, and prescribing *duties* to the persons invested with those powers. The powers are principally constituted, in the first instance, by discoercive or permissive laws, operating as exceptions to certain laws of the coercive or imperative kind. . . . The duties are created by imperative laws, addressed to the persons on whom the powers are conferred.[9]

The word *classes* appears in this text but simply as the overall designatory term for determinate individuals (like "a tax-gatherer" or "a judge" a few lines later) without any indication of the real nature of *class society*. At the same time Bentham's huge assumption assigns the reason of constitutionality to the traditional fiction of its dedication to the *"good of the whole society."* Moreover, the prevailing modality of the distribution of *powers* and *duties* is also fictionalized by Bentham, for the same reason and as a result of eliminating their real *class determinations*. For in actuality, powers and duties are *most iniquitously* distributed in the established socioeconomic, and not simply political/constitutional, order.

Naturally, in such conceptions that *idealize* constitutionality, there can be no room for even the slightest hint that most constitutions emerge in the course of actual history *unconstitutionally*, compared to the very different constitutions of the past, with their once equally idealized claims. And, of course, such changes are established through the more or less violent overturning of the formerly dominant *relations of power*. Historical considerations of genesis and transformation in this kind of liberal/utilitarian conception are nonexistent. Not surprisingly, therefore, the difficult problems of international law and universal law receive a rather vacuous treatment, with generic references to the great variety of nations and languages,[10] and taking the established legislative settings for granted, maintaining that "there remain the mutual transactions between *sovereigns* as such, for the subject of that branch of jurisprudence which may be properly and exclusively termed international."[11]

The same goes for John Austin's view on the subject. It is relevant to quote Austin's partial acceptance of his utilitarian ancestor's approach. This is how he comments on Bentham's position regarding Universal Law:

> Mr. Bentham is of opinion that it must be confined within very narrow bounds. That is true, if by expository Universal Jurisprudence he intended Jurisprudence expository of that which *obtains* universally as Law. For assuming that the systems of all nations, wholly or in part, exactly resembled each other (i.e., that all or many of the provisions to be found in those several systems were exactly alike), still we could not speak of them with propriety as forming a Universal Law: the sanction being applied *by the government of each community*, and not by a superior common to all mankind. And this ranks international law with morals rather than with law.[12]

At the same time Austin idealizes "refined communities" and their "matured systems of law," corresponding of course primarily to his own.¹³ He adds in the same spirit: "It is only the systems of two or three nations which deserve attention: the writings of the Roman Jurists; the decisions of English Judges in modern times; the provisions of French and Prussian Codes as to arrangement. . . . Whether the principles unfolded deserve the name of Universal or not, is of no importance. Jurisprudence may be universal with respect to its subjects: Not less so than legislation."¹⁴ Thus, the problem of legal universality is left in a suspended state of animation, accompanied only by an apologetic hint at the way of getting away from its embarrassing reality by an approving summary reference to the prevailing internal and international power relations.

In regard to the problems of "sovereignty and subjection," we are offered by Austin the same, utterly fictitious, atomistic/individualistic conception of the established relations of domination and rule on both sides of the socioeconomic and political divide. In this sense we are told:

> If a *determinate* human superior, *not* in a habit of obedience to a like superior, receives *habitual* obedience from the *bulk* of a given society, that determinate superior is sovereign in that society, and the society (including the superior) is a society political and independent. . . . Upon that certain person, or certain body of persons, the other members of the society are *dependent:* or to that person, or certain body of persons, the other members of the society are *subject.* . . . In order that a given society may form a society political, the generality or bulk of its members must be in a *habit* of obedience to a determinate and common superior.¹⁵

When Rousseau and those in Rousseau's spirit speak of sovereignty as belonging to the people, that view has a deep significance, pointing in the direction of the proper understanding of the underlying problem itself, with far-reaching implications for the future of historically sustainable societal decision-making. In contrast, the Austinian kind of liberal/utilitarian approach, with its atomistic/individualistic stance, can only produce obfuscation even in its own terms of reference. For even the pseudo-explanatory postulate of the "habit" of the individuals on one side, and the claimed "absence of the habit of obedience" on the dominant side, needs some explanation in order to acquire any meaning and credibility. Once, however, the historically conditioned and changing class determinations and antagonisms are exiled from the legal and political discourse, or travestied as individual motivations and individually rewardable or punishable acts and habits of "persons" or "bulks and bodies of persons," both the process of legislation and of its structurally prejudged framework become a complete mystery, confounding the debated issues instead of clarifying them, as claimed for its "analytical rigor" by Austin's twentieth-century inheritors.

In a similar vein of confounding individual and class determinations, in the interest of idealizing his individually enjoyable utilitarian "happiness" principle as the postulated real ground of a legitimate political order, Bentham fictionalizes the established framework of government. He writes: "The business of government is the *happiness of society*, by punishing and rewarding.... What happiness consists of we have already seen: enjoyment of pleasures, security from pains."[16]

In the same way, the sense in which the question of "materiality" is said to be relevant, "or of importance," as added in a footnote by Bentham, to the utilitarian vision of regulating societal interaction and regarding the consequences of the individual's act to be rewarded or punished, we are presented with this judgment: "Now among the consequences of an act, be they what they may, such only, by one who views them in the capacity of a *legislator*, can be said to be material, as either consist of pain or pleasure, or have an influence in the production of pain or pleasure."[17] By adopting this line of reasoning, massively loaded with unmentioned assumptions, we learn absolutely nothing about the actual constitution of the legislative process, including the mode of assigning the regulatory functions of society to the "legislator," nor about the structurally determined most unequal distribution of "pleasure and pain" in the established social and economic order. The "business of government" defined as the production of the "happiness of society" by punishing or rewarding the individuals through the "materiality of pain and pleasure" can only be pure wishful thinking, precisely because the reality of class antagonisms and corresponding power relations that determine both the production and distribution of *real materiality* among the social classes is totally obfuscated. This obfuscation is accomplished by the falsely assumed individualistic terms of reference of both the legislators and the "individual persons" who must be fictitiously "rewarded or punished," thanks to the idealized "business of government."

The same kind of individualistic orientation and corresponding assumption, at the expense of the comprehensive class-determined dimension of the problems—without which, however, no state theory can be made intelligible—vitiates liberal utilitarian philosophy in general. We can see this graphically exemplified when Bentham asserts: "The *community* is a *fictitious body,* composed of the *individual persons* who are considered as constituting it as it were its *members*. The interest of the community, then, is what?—the *sum* of the interests of the several members who compose it."[18] Here again we are offered a big assumption and distortion, worsened by its fetishistic stance and mechanical quantifying assertion. For the vital *qualitative* considerations required for understanding the relationship between the individuals and their communities—and making meaningful the philosophically valid proposition according to which "the whole is greater than its parts" precisely on *qualitative* grounds—are nowhere in sight.

THE ABSOLUTE TABOO OF QUESTIONING THE FOUNDATIONS OF THE STATE

Benthamite utilitarian principles and their more or less amended varieties exercised a lasting influence on the development of liberal political theory, especially in the Anglo-Saxon world. In the present context, we cannot be concerned with their details. What greatly matters, however, is the dominance of the unquestioned—and in terms of the liberal/utilitarian theory, unquestionable state-apologetic assumptions, together with their presumed justification. To quote Bentham again, this time on the postulated self-evident validity of the fundamental utilitarian moral and political principle, he asks and answers his own question about that principle in this way: "Is it susceptible of any proof? It would seem not: for that which is used to prove everything else, cannot itself be proved: a chain of proofs must have their commencement somewhere. To give such proof is as impossible as it is needless."[19]

If it is true that "the chain of proofs must have their commencement somewhere," the question still remains: but *where?* For if the function of the allegedly valid commencement of the chain is to prevent inconvenient questioning—because it is incompatible with the given theory—that is very far from justifiable.

Here we have a very serious problem confronting us, which rules "out of order" the major task of theoretical and practical disentangling without which it is impossible to understand the real nature of the state, not to mention the problems of its much-needed transformation. Yet the characteristic tendency of liberal/utilitarian theory (and, of course, by no means only of that) is to use its manifold assumptions to *exclude* the legitimacy of further fundamental questioning, conceding only the acceptability of ameliorating some details of the overall structural determinations of the established order and, at times of major crises, not even that. The "commencement of the chain" thus assumes the role of constituting the self-evidently legitimate *barricade* in defense and in justification of that order. This is how the theoretical viability and the practical feasibility of questioning the *state as such* are condemned as *absolute taboos*, because the established reality of the state lies, and must remain, by definition, beyond the proclaimed "commencement of the chain."

In truth, the real question is not which particular point should be designated as the "first member of the chain"—its commencement. This way of approaching the matter can be considered only as fallacious self-assuming arbitrariness. The proper subject in terms of which the "susceptibility of the proof" denied by Bentham must be decided concerns the very nature of the chain itself, its self-servingly *excluding* or, in complete contrast, its critically questioning *inclusive* character. If, therefore, on the vital issues of the state, with its antagonistic contradictions, the established actual configuration of the "members of the chain" is what is preventing the required critical enquiry, as it happens to be in the self-assuming liberal/utilitarian theory of politics, in that case one must *step outside* of that chain instead of accepting its *presuppositions* by declaring them to constitute the "necessary commencement of the chain." For *within* the established structural framework of the assumed liberal state formations, only the *operational* and *procedural* characteristics are open to examination, as dictated, by definition, in the name of "the commencement of the chain," but not the historical viability and sustainability of the *state itself.*

In conclusion, it must be stressed that the same considerations apply to *any state,* and by no means only to the liberal-democratic state. No conceivable state formation can assume itself as permanently given and forever sustainable in virtue of its chosen links of the chain.

CHAPTER TWELVE

Hegel's Unintended Swan Song and the Nation-State

The Hegelian conception of political philosophy addresses the substantive issues of the state as such, and not only its operational framework. This is undoubtedly a valid comparative ground for the assessment of its achievements.

However, emphasizing this vital difference cannot mean that one should consider Hegel's philosophy of the state and right as representing the final summation of the intricate problems of the political domain, as claimed by this great German philosopher. Nevertheless, by comparing the relative merits of the rival approaches it must be emphasized that, in contrast to liberal/utilitarian or liberal-democratic philosophy, Hegel examines the *state itself* as a substantive historical reality, without any attempt at hiding the antagonistic "civil society" upon which it is erected as its constitutive and indefinitely continuing material ground. Liberal/utilitarian as well as various other post-Hegelian political theories tend to be satisfied with addressing even the gravest issues of the political domain within the unquestioned operational confines of the given state formation, explicitly or by implication excluding—as a matter of self-evidently proper admissibility or not to a valid theoretical discourse on the legislative process itself—the problems both of the origin and the historical sustainability of the existing state reality as such.

Under the dramatic circumstances of Hegel's time, from the American and the French revolutions as well as the Napoleonic Wars to the emergence of, at first embryonic, working-class militancy and its continued extension, the challenging problems of the state assume ever greater intensity. Indeed, the modern state of the capital system asserts an increasingly greater role in the overall control of the societal reproduction process in the course of subsequent historical developments. The new historical stage reflected in Hegel's political philosophy synthesizes in a most paradoxical way both an *end* and a *beginning* in relation to the *contending* social classes of the age. The *end* in question is the historical supersession of the *feudal* class relations in the revolutionary storms of the late eighteenth century, followed with passionate interest and understanding (his words) by Hegel himself. The *beginning*, however, represents a much more complicated matter for him, in that it marks the appearance of the working classes on the historical stage. Not surprisingly, we thus find an incomparably more sustainable understanding of the *end*—the truly irreversible *historical closure* of the feudal order, manifest in the collapse of the *ancient regime* welcomed by Hegel—than in the emergent forces of the historical *beginning*.

Nevertheless, Hegel attempts to synthesize them both in his conception of the relationship between his "civil society" and the "ethical state." Undertaking such a synthesis represents his philosophical greatness in the field. At the same time, the way in which he accomplishes it, by *subsuming* the new beginning under the proclaimed permanently enduring overall framework of the idealized state—which in his view is destined to reconcile the contradictions of civil society—marks the historical limitations of his approach. For Hegel's grandiose unintended swan song offers a conceptualization of the two in the form of enclosing the forces of the radically new beginning under the dominance of the unalterable *historical closure* in his philosophy of the state and law. This is done because it provides the only way in which the unique Hegelian synthesis of antagonistic civil society and antagonism-resolving ethical state can offer a perspective compatible with his own class horizon.

Tellingly, with the help of a powerful poetic imagery, Hegel rationalizes in a categorically self-justifying way—the only viable philosophical stance in general—the adoption of the perspective of the historical closure when he writes about the paradigmatic "owl of Minerva" in the penultimate paragraph of the Preface to his *Philosophy of Right*:

> Philosophy in any case always comes on the scene too late. . . . As the thought of the world, it appears only when actuality is already there *cut and dried after its process of formation has been completed.* The teaching of the concept, which is also history's inescapable lesson, is that it is only when actuality is mature that the ideal first appears over against the real and that the ideal apprehends this same real world in its substance and builds it up for itself into the shape of an intellectual realm. When philosophy paints its gray in gray, then has a shape of life grown old. By philosophy's gray in gray it cannot be *rejuvenated* but only *understood*. The owl of Minerva spreads its wings only with the falling of the dusk.[1]

In this respect the trouble is not only that the emerging social forces of the new beginning evidently cannot be there under the novel circumstances as "cut and dried after their process of formation has been completed." That is the secondary consideration in this matter, because it requires very complicated historical conflicts and social confrontations, with advances and reversals as the conditions permit, before the social subject that assumes the role of being the carrier of the "new beginning" can achieve its full maturity and realize its historical potentiality and corresponding mandate. And that may take a very long time indeed. But it is far from legitimate to exclude "rejuvenation," on a self-serving a priori ground, in favor of resigned *"understanding."*

The real issue at stake is much more fundamental than the maturity (or not) of a social force to the point of being cut and dried, so as to become visible from the perspective of the owl of Minerva. For in addition to the *relative* historical differences in the determination of the embryonic working-class militancy in the young Hegel's time—evidenced in the great turmoil of the revolutionary explosions themselves, including attempts like the formation of organizational forces that try to assert themselves as, for instance, Babeuf's *"society of the equals"* (and being savagely repressed for it)—there is also an *absolute, qualitatively novel* dimension to this complex of problems. It consists in the *total impossibility* of emancipating the forces of *capital's hegemonic alternative: labor*—the members of which in sheer numbers constitute by far the overwhelming majority of society. In the past, that traditional form always resulted in the emergent new forces imposing themselves as privileged social exploiters on the rest of society. There are not enough people in the rest of society to make that feasible. In other words, the *absolute radical novelty* of the revolutionary turmoil in Hegel's time, which was never conceivable in the past, defined itself in this: *class exploitation* must be relegated forever to the historical past, asserting in that contrasting form the elementary requirements of the new beginning. And the "owl of Minerva" could offer no help for that. For the *qualitative uniqueness* of the age of these great revolutions was to turn into an irreversible historical anachronism the traditional solution of pressing problems through the customary *"change in personnel"* from one class of exploiters to another. Such radical novelty in history could not be conceptualized by adopting the perspective of *historical closure* in the name of the owl of Minerva. On the contrary, a historically sustainable vision of the *present and the future* also had to be an integral part of such historically arising change in perspective.

THE WITHERING AWAY OF THE STATE AS A SEPARATE ORGAN ABOVE SOCIETY

But then, if one takes seriously the objective determinations of unfolding historical changes, together with their fundamental implications for the great cause of human emancipation in terms of the qualitatively different imperatives of the "new beginning," the question of state theory must also be deeply affected by the shift in perspective. For the conception of the *classless society* as the real condition of human emancipation in all-embracing terms is *totally incompatible* with the continued existence of the state—of *any state*—as the *separate organ* of overall political decision-making in the societal reproduction process. This is why the Marxian approach to the same problems inextricably had to link the radically new modality of *communal* social metabolic control—under the *planned* management of the conditions of their life by the freely associated producers, guided by the vital orienting principle of *substantive equality*—to the equally necessary determination highlighted under the name of the withering away of the state. For it was *inconceivable* to envisage the required radical emancipatory transformation of not this or that particular social class but the *whole of humanity*—and the qualitative novelty historically unfolding in the great revolutionary period was precisely the *inseparability* of the two—without the supersession of the *state as such*. Not simply its *overthrow,* as often projected in vain, because whatever can be overthrown can also be *restored,* and all too frequently had been, but its complete *withering away* and irretrievable consignment to the historical past.

The greatness of Hegel in the field of sizing up the huge problems of the state was manifest in his monumental scheme of proclaiming the organic relationship between existent civil society and the projected ethical state. In this way Hegel could devise, in the face of the social antagonisms he *had to* and *did* concede, a solution presented in the form of his systemic depiction of the *contradictory actualization* of the *historic closure*, which itself put under question the continued viability of the longtime dominant *class exploitative order* of society. And in that sense Hegel conceptualized an objectively crucial line of *historic demarcation* that dramatically defined in its novelty the turn of the eighteenth to nineteenth centuries.

However, the historic closure objectively marking the end of the class exploitative order in general could not "actualize itself" (one of Hegel's frequently used explanatory categories) *by itself.* It was also pregnant with the objective imperatives of a qualitatively different order, assuming the form of a radical challenge unknown in past history and representing the vital objective and subjective conditions of an effective supersession of the class exploitative order as such. Thus *past, present,* and *future* were inseparably combined in the unfolding new historical challenge. The qualitatively and radically new of the revolutionary age, putting on the historical agenda as the necessary condition of emancipating labor the inseparable combination of that imperative with the emancipation of all of humanity, was *already there* in Hegel's time. Indeed, it represented the *greatest challenge* in all history for the whole of humanity.

To be sure, the forces involved in promoting change could not be said to be there "*cut and dried after their process of formation has been completed,*" as the owl of Minerva would demand. The relevant historical forces only started to embark on their process of formation through—by its very nature necessarily contested, deeply antagonistic—historical course of development. But the *challenge* itself was—and remains all the way to our own time—absolutely irrepressible, destined to decide whether humanity is to survive or perish.

Facing it, Hegel consciously adopted the perspective of the *past* in the form of turning the unfolding *present,* in the name of his definition of the absolute fulfillment of the reconciliatory self-actualized World Spirit as "right from the beginning" eternal present, and transformed the three dimensions of temporality into a permanent *historical closure.*[2] Moreover, he also *justified* the eternalized present from the nostalgic vantage point of the owl of Minerva, projected as the paradigmatic embodiment of historic closure. He did it also in this respect because doing so provided the only way for him to reconcile, in tune with his own class interests, the forceful condemnation of past exploitative privileges (especially highlighted in his early writings) with the transfigured variety of class domination in general sanctified by his *Theodicaea.*[3] And he conceived the latter as the proclaimed imaginary transcendence of the antagonisms of civil society thanks to the supreme role of the idealized state, which itself was said to embody nothing less than *"the image and actuality of reason,"* as we have seen. This is why Hegel's grandiose philosophy of right and its projected "ethical state" as the fulfillment of the ways of God could only be realized in its resignatory references to the owl of Minerva as an unintended swan song.

Nevertheless, within the adopted philosophical framework of the state and the law, Hegel proceeded to explore with the greatest consistency and intellectual rigor the necessary requirements of the operation of the projected state formation in the given world order. In this sense he characterized the only feasible state reality to be the world historically constituted but from now on untranscendable *nation-state*. He thought through even the most perilous implications of such a state formation—both *internally* and *externally*, regarding the determinations of *sovereignty* and the forever recurrent antagonisms of *interstate relations*—to their logical conclusion. Accordingly, he insisted:

> The nation-state is mind in its substantive rationality and immediate actuality and is therefore the *absolute power on earth*. It follows that every state is *sovereign* and autonomous against its neighbours. It is entitled in the first place and without qualification to be sovereign from their point of view, i.e. to be recognized by them as sovereign.[4]

But, of course, it depended on the actually prevailing *power relations* that a particular state could successfully assert its "right to sovereignty" against its weaker neighbors. Hegel did not preach idealistic illusions on this subject. On the contrary, verging on cynicism in the rationalization and justification of his arguments in embracing the necessary implications for large-scale wars among nation-states, he proclaimed:

> A state through its subjects has widespread connexions and many-sided interests, and these may be readily and considerably injured; but it remains inherently *indeterminable* which of these injuries is to be regarded as a specific breach of treaty or as an injury to the honour and autonomy of the state. The reason for this is that a state may regard its infinity and honour as a stake in each of its concerns, *however minute,* and it is all the more inclined to susceptibility to injury the more its strong individuality is impelled as a result of *long domestic peace* to seek and create a *sphere of activity abroad*.[5]

In plain language this meant that the legitimate ground of war could be arbitrarily decided, "however minute," in the interest of countering the "undesirable" effects of "long domestic peace" by creating a successful "sphere of activity abroad." Just like we have actually experienced it in the last two centuries. In Hegel's vision, the nation-state was inseparable from the necessity of peculiarly legitimized wars that could only mock Kant's postulate of "perpetual peace" by saying that "corruption in nations would be the product of prolonged, let alone 'perpetual' peace."[6] International law, with its unavoidable universalistic claims, was always the weakest domain of modern bourgeois theories of politics and morality.[7] The objective imperatives of capital's social metabolic order asserted themselves without ceremony, and their pseudo-universal justificatory theorizations could only be shabby and feeble even in the case of an intellectual giant like Hegel.

A far too long period of history after the death of Hegel—and also in that same year of 1831 the death of his outstanding Prussian military contemporary, General Carl Marie von Clausewitz, who famously defined war as *the continuation of politics by other means*—seems to have fully confirmed Hegel's views that the nation-state is the *absolute power on earth*, and therefore as an absolute can assert its sovereignty through the necessity of its wars, no matter how destructive. Forty years after Hegel and General von Clausewitz, the new imperialism, with its lethally contending nation-states, among them in a prominent place the Prussian Bismarck's Germany, *began* a period of ever more intensive military confrontations, bringing with it in due course the formerly inconceivable conflagrations of two world wars, with countless millions perishing through their devastation.[8]

THE STATE AND THE "ABSOLUTE END OF HISTORY"

If Hegel is right in his judgment about the nation-state constituting the historically insurmountable absolute power on earth, is there a way out from this fateful course of destructiveness, which even today seems to prevail in different parts of the world? If the answer is "No," Hegel's unintended swan song left to us in his philosophy of the state would have to be also the swan song for humanity itself.

It is true, of course, that the nation-state dominates our life everywhere, despite the wishful projections of benevolent "globalization." In fact, the grave historical defect of capital's social metabolic order, representing one of its structurally determined absolute limits, is that it failed to produce the *all-embracing political state* of the capital system in general, while continuing its irrepressible drive toward *global integration* of its *material* reproductive structures. The nation-state thus remained to our own days perilously "absolute" in that sense. But that is not—and by itself cannot be—the end of the story. The limits in this respect also unfold through the modality of objective historical developments.

The limits of the Hegelian philosophy of the state, in the same way, are not simply internal-philosophical but *objective historical* and by no means evident in their author's lifetime. However, they become painfully clear when we set the Hegelian conception of the state in its claims to *timeless* validity against the reality of our present. The Hegelian timelessness of the state is predicated in his work through the notion of the "eternally present," which is paradoxically transfigured into *absolute finality*, thanks to the "right from the beginning completed" being of rationality itself in the shape of the divine World Spirit, evocatively combined by Hegel with the self-explanatory mythological authority of the owl of Minerva. Naturally, the real agency of history and the state in this vision could not be the self-conscious human being. It had to be the divine World Spirit, with its "cunning of reason."[9] Hegel described the particular states, nations, and individuals as "the *unconscious tools* and organs of the world mind at work within them,"[10] and characterized them as "the living *instruments* of what is in substance the deed of the world mind and they are therefore directly at one with that deed though it is *concealed* from them and is *not their aim and object.*"[11]

To be sure, Hegel was not alone with this view. He shared its conceptual design with the whole of the bourgeois philosophical tradition in its ascending phase of historical development, when it was still concerned with confronting real dilemmas and offering from the shared standpoint of the giants of bourgeois thought some feasible and compatible solutions, displaying at the same time the social and historical limitations of such standpoints. Thus, we find the philosophical equivalents of accounting for the absence of self-consciousness in the historical actors and their deeds defined by Hegel as the "cunning of reason" (*List der Vernunft*) in Vico's "providence," in Adam Smith's "Invisible Hand," and in Kant's providential "plan of nature." All these rather mysterious explanatory schemes, intended to illuminate the real nature of historical aims, were postulated with the corresponding powers of their realization. And the postulated powers were said to be capable of asserting and imposing themselves with unquestionable legitimacy *over against* the intentions, desires, ideas, and conscious designs of the historically existent human beings.

Even in the ascending phase of capital's historical development, it was quite *inconceivable* to envisage from the standpoint of the bourgeoisie—which *had to* eternalize "civil society" under its continued domination—a materially identifiable and socially efficacious *alternative collective subject* as the carrier of sustainable historical transformations. This is why there could be no *trans-individual* (communal) historical subject in all such conceptions of history and the state, but only *supraindividual* and consequently also *suprahuman*. Not even when Adam Smith intended to offer something tangible, in the form of the market, but had to indicate as its mysterious benevolent regulatory force the "Invisible Hand."

Hegel could only acknowledge the temporality of the past as already fully accomplished. There could be no question of the actually given—and idealized/eternalized—present becoming one day past history. In this sense he wrote: "The History of the World travels from the East to the West, for *Europe is absolutely the end of History.*"[12] Accordingly, there was a past before History succeeded in traveling from the East to the West but never more. Consequently, the violence and imperialist expansion of the dominant nation-states could never be consigned to the past because its presentness represented being perfectly in tune with the ultimate reality of the self-disclosing World Spirit as the "Principle of the North" assigned to the *Germanic realm* and to the Germanic (not narrowly German) state. For the Hegelian Germanic state included the highly praised empire-building English state under its determinations. And Hegel summed up the supreme ideality of what has been accomplished with these words:

The realm of fact has discarded its barbarity and unrighteous caprice, while the realm of truth has abandoned the world of beyond and its arbitrary force, so that the *true reconciliation* which discloses the *state as the image and actuality of reason* has become objective. In the state self-consciousness finds in an organic development the actuality of its substantive knowing and willing.[13]

This is where the historical untenability of Hegel's grandiose conception and resignatory swan song, in its nostalgic appeal to the owl of Minerva which excludes any possibility of "rejuvenation," becomes absolutely striking. For the postulated unity of the realms of fact and truth, and the decreed reconciliatory solution of the underlying contradictions—through the claimed self-disclosing actualization of the World Spirit as Reason embodied in the ethical state's forever sustained symbiotic relationship with the given bourgeois civil society—reveals its extremely problematical character right from the beginning. A conception of the state and history that was acclaimed to be valid not only by many of Hegel's contemporaries but also by his much later followers.

HEGEL AND THE WORLD SPIRIT AS A SUPRAHUMAN HISTORICAL AGENCY

The Hegelian Philosophy of history and the state suffered a great prospective derailment when its author opted for the track he actually followed through to its limits with unfailing logical consistency. With penetrating insight worthy of a philosophical genius, in a period of epochal revolutionary turmoil, Hegel perceived that a "new beginning" had objectively entered the historical horizon, asserting itself as the *impossibility* to settle the contending historic claims by emancipating only a *part* of the social divide in the old form of imposing it on the rest of society as the "changed personnel." There was an objective alternative to that traditional form, arising in the same revolutionary situation, even if far from "cut and dried," but only in its embryonic process of formation. However, siding with that alternative would not just logically *imply* but also inevitably *require* the necessary elaboration of a radically different historical perspective, premised on the indispensable, and historically in truly epochal terms sustainable, supersession of all fundamental social antagonisms. Choosing that avenue appeared to be too prohibitive to Hegel, given the actual relation of social forces and the turn of historic events subsequent to the French Revolution.

Yet the question remained: Could one deny that the epochal antagonisms highlighted by the revolutionary turmoil do not exist or do not matter, as some Romantic philosophers did? The grotesquely biased position of such Romantics, assuming the form of pretended divine justification, was inseparable from conservative, indeed profoundly reactionary, social interests. Thus Friedrich Schlegel, for instance, unashamedly argued in the same epoch that produced the historical conception of Hegel—the age not only of the French but also of the Industrial Revolution:

> The Creator has not reserved to Himself the beginning and the end alone, and let the rest follow its own course; but in the middle, and *at every point* also, of its progress, the Omnipotent Will can *intervene at pleasure.* If He pleases He can instantaneously stop this vital development, and suddenly *make the course of nature stand still;* or, in a moment, give life and movement to what before stood motionless and inanimate. Generally speaking, it is in the divine power to *suspend the laws of nature,* to interfere directly with them, and, as it were, to intercalate among them some higher and immediate operation of His power, as an exception to their development. For as in the *social frame of civil life,* the author and *giver of the laws* may occasionally set them aside, or, in their administration, allow certain cases of exception, even so is it, also, with nature's Lawgiver.[14]

The reactionary intent behind Schlegel's arbitrary assertions is fairly obvious. It becomes even clearer when he draws a direct parallel between the "wisdom of the divine Order of Things" and of the "divine Order in the History of the World and the Relation of States" to justify the principle according to which "power emanates from God" and therefore strictly forbids us to *"violate or forcibly subvert any established right,* whether essentially sacred or hallowed only by prescription."[15] It would be difficult to make the association of such an absurd position more transparent—which goes as far as denying even the continued validity of elementary natural laws—with blindly backward-looking restoratory social interests in any age, let alone in an epoch of revolutionary upheavals.

Obviously, this kind of blind alley could not be followed by a philosophical genius of great integrity like Hegel. He realized and positively endorsed the dramatic transformations whereby the politically repressive conditions of the *ancient regime* had been overthrown by the French Revolution and, accordingly, must belong to the historical past. But his class interests could not allow him to side with the emerging new potentialities of the unfolding historical development. This is why he opted for the track that both displayed the structural antagonisms of civil society and at the same time stipulated their *reconciliation* through the grandiose—in the Hegelian conception of the *"eternally present,"* from the beginning of time preordained but not at any time arbitrarily "at his pleasure Omnipotent" and natural-law-denying—intervention of the World Spirit itself, thanks to its worldly institution of the established *ethical state,* proclaimed by Hegel as "the image and actuality of reason," and "the absolute power on earth."

The Hegelian approach constituted a monumental vision, even if in the long run it could only lead to derailment. For the track opted for and followed through with great consistency by Hegel happened to be a very long track. The magnitude of the task of *universal* emancipation, which never before appeared as objectively feasible in the course of historical development, was in a strange but meaningful form incorporated and retained in the Hegelian conception, in a form compatible with his chosen track. This could be because Hegel refused to offer some pedestrian earthly reconciliation and accommodation to the depicted structural antagonisms in mean prosaic terms. Nothing less than the divine World Spirit's suprahuman historical agency, embodied in the proclaimed "rationality of actuality," could match up to the acknowledged magnitude of the stakes as perceived and depicted by Hegel. And the train itself, commandeered by him, could travel on the chosen track for a very long historical time. Indeed, it could travel throughout the entire modern epoch of antagonistic history; for as long as fighting out the broadest societal conflicts remained under the—even in our time still prevailing supremacy—of the "sovereign" nation-states.

Nevertheless, the derailment to come, which was foreshadowed from the very beginning when Hegel opted for the ultimately fateful track while turning his back to the "immature" new beginning, is bound to inexorably "actualize itself" when the train of capital's national state formation, glorified by Hegel, "hits the buffers." But will it be a catastrophic derailment, destroying the whole of humanity, or can the train itself be slowed down in time, so that only its driverless front engine carriage is crushed by the impact when the train hits the buffers? This is the question for us.

The derailment is bound to happen in our own historic time. The Hegelian ideal "actualization of the rational" could not be accomplished, notwithstanding Hegel's postulate pronounced in wishfully past temporality, according to which "the realm of truth has abandoned the world of beyond and its arbitrary force." In sharp contrast to that, the actual violation of truth in the interest of enforcing capital's social metabolic control over our conditions of existence is ubiquitous, and state-legitimated arbitrary force is the ultimate guarantor and enforcer of the requirements of such mode of control. At the same time, the "actualization" of the underlying historical potentialities proceeds, but it is very far from its idealized Hegelian sense. On the contrary, it assumes most threatening forms. Accordingly, set against the truly and gravely actualized, and indeed ever-intensifying dangers of our own historical predicament, the Hegelian theory of history and the state brings itself down to earth. For the reckless pursuit of the antagonistic imperatives of the nation-state that we witnessed and continue to endure in different parts of the world, and that in its proclaimed timeless configuration and absolute permanence had to be idealized by Hegel, in our actually existing reality could only be *suicidal to humanity*. And no conceivable postulate of any imaginary *suprahuman* historical agency—be it Adam Smith's "Invisible Hand" or Hegel's World Spirit with its "Absolute Cunning of Reason"—could offer a reconciliatory solution.

For this reason, under the conditions of the deepening structural crisis of our system of social metabolic reproduction, the problems at stake could not be greater in the now unfolding process of capital's antagonistic globalization, wedded to the interests of the necessarily contending nation-states. They bring to the fore a whole range of contradictions directly concerned not with the remediable operational and procedural defects of some particular state formations but with the *reality of the state as such*. For the state itself, as constituted in the last five or six centuries, is grounded on global capital's far from historically sustainable material development, due to the inherent destructive imperatives of the capital system's now pursued modality of reproduction.

"Grow or perish" continues to be the order of the day, and the meaning of growth, in the spirit of the prevailing order, is fetishistically reduced—by violating *truth* and absurdly imposing its destructive transfiguration as *falsehood*, not in the *"world of beyond"* but in the actually existing one, through the naked instrumentality of state-legitimated *"arbitrary force"*—to its fallaciously asserted identity with *wasteful capital-expansion*. And the state formations of the capital system sustain that kind of development on all continents. As a result, the structurally generated social and political crisis and the much needed, though as yet slowly unfolding, protest is visible everywhere in our planetary household, wherever we look. The direct material determinations of capital's reproductive order are fully complemented by the all-embracing political command structure of capital's state formations, constituting thereby the structurally intertwined and enmeshed reality, and the practical vicious circle, of the capital system as a whole.

Is there a way out from the perilous maze of this system's antagonistic contradictions? Where are the gaps to be exposed and what are the effective leverages to be taken hold of in the interest of the required systemic change? What is to be done and what can be done at this juncture of history with regard to the great problems of the state? These are the problems to which we must now turn.

CHAPTER THIRTEEN

Capital's Social Metabolic Order and the Failing State

The necessary critique of the state, to be sure, cannot mean the advocacy of turning our inevitably global modality of societal reproduction into some kind of utopian bucolic village community. Socialists who assert the validity of the communal productive interchange of the freely associated individuals, with Marx among them, are crudely accused of indulging in such idle fantasies. The truth of the matter is the diametrical opposite. For the gravest problem of capital's state formations—from which many potentially lethal antagonisms arise, demonstrating the total failure even of the most violent and aggressive attempts of monopolistic imperialism to solve them in the past, by imposing through the force of arms one or two of the temporarily most dominant powers over the rest of them (like Germany and Japan in the Second World War)—is that capital, due to its innermost structural determinations, could not produce the *state of the capital system in general*. But this great historic failure, to which there can be no feasible remedy on capital's material ground, cannot be wished out of existence, nor can it be swept under the proverbial carpet. The problem remains, and with the passing of time can only become more acute, until a historically tenable solution is elaborated to the underlying antagonistic determinations. In this sense, the radical socialist critique of the state, far from orienting itself toward the dream world of some utopian bucolic village community, must also take on board this great, chronically unresolved global problem.

Solution in this respect can only be envisaged from the long-term perspective of the other road that could not be adopted by Hegel. As we know, it was Marx's historic merit to bring to the forefront of debate—in the period of the new revolutionary wave of the 1840s— the far-reaching implications and the practical imperatives of this new epochal perspective, elaborating in his great work the overall strategic horizon of its prospective international unfolding. But he was by no means the first to passionately engage in the struggle for the realization of the advocated aims and objectives. Indeed, as far back as half a century before Marx, Babeuf and his comrades, in their "conspiracy of the equals," clearly voiced some of the principal requirements, and their movement was brutally liquidated in the aftermath of the French Revolution. Even the Marxian definition of the significant difference between the lower and the higher stage of socialist transformation, formulated in his *Critique of the Gotha Programme* in terms of the fundamental societal orienting principle of human need, recalls Babeuf's eloquently stated views on real equality:

> Equality must be measured by the *capacity* of the worker and the *need* of the consumer, not by the intensity of labor and the quantity of things consumed. A man endowed with a certain degree of strength, when he lifts a weight of ten pounds, labors as much as another man with five times the strength when he lifts fifty pounds. He who, to satisfy a burning thirst, swallows a pitcher of water, enjoys no more than his comrade who, but slightly thirsty, sips a cupful. The aim of the communism in question is *equality of pains and pleasures,* not of *consumable things and workers' tasks.*[1]

Moreover, the "Manifesto of the Equals" by Babeuf and his comrades explicitly and most forcefully condemned the hypocritical exploitation and domination of the overwhelming majority of the human race in the actually established order, as divided into "masters and servants" and "rulers and ruled." They condemned the social order that had no shame of justifying such domination in the name of "equality before the law" and of the "Rights of Man."[2] In other words, they condemned the cruelly enforced realities of Babeuf's time, which remain the burning issues of state domination even today.

However, despite the violent repression of Babeuf's movement, the new historic trend emerging from the great revolutionary turmoil at the turn of the eighteenth century continued to slowly advance and in due course assumed a variety of forms well before Marx and the revolutionary explosions in the 1840s. In its most difficult course of unfolding, due to the established relations of power and the corresponding exercise of repression by the dominant forces, advancement for this trend could only be made for quite some time through "capillary changes" and in a subterranean form, at first in different parts of Europe. Nevertheless, through the survival of socialist secret societies and through their passionate advocacy of equality some progress continued to be made, which in its turn had brought with it even some most surprising ramifications.

We should remember in this respect a social connection of major importance not confined to the early nineteenth century but reaching all the way deep into our own historical present. It appeared through the dramatic and far-reaching historical developments in Venezuela under the presidency of Hugo Chávez Frias. As we all know, the inspirer of President Chávez was *El Libertador*, Simón Bolívar, who not only defeated the army of the Spanish Empire in Latin America but also liberated the slaves in the face of violent opposition by his own class—even his loving sister describing him as "crazy"—several decades before that issue could even be raised and partially settled in North America. And Bolívar insisted that equality was and had to be respected as *"the law of laws,"* adding that "without equality all freedoms, all rights perish. For it we must make sacrifices." Indeed, in his magnificent Address to the Congress of Angostura he singled out the liberation of the slaves as the most vital of all of his orders and decrees, saying: "I leave it to your sovereign decision to reform or revoke all of the statutes and decrees enacted by me; but I plead with you to confirm the *absolute liberty of the slaves,* as I would plead for my life and for the life of the Republic."³

What is also relevant in this context is that Bolívar's legendary teacher, Simón Rodriguez, who was much admired by Bolívar not only in his childhood but all his life, was a passionate believer in equality. He took Bolívar to Monte Sacro in Rome in August 1805 and was a witness to his solemn oath for the liberation of his country from Spanish rule; he lived in Paris for decades after leaving Rome and, like Marx in the early 1840s, frequented socialist secret societies in Paris, returning to South America in 1823. Thus, the subterranean trend assumed this most unusual form, linking faraway continents and enlisting for the cause of real equality and the corresponding liberation of the slaves a great historic figure, Bolívar, who was supposed to be destined by his social origin to fight on the opposite side of the class barricade. Obviously Hegel, who on the "African character" propagandized the most absurd racist views in his *Philosophy of History,* never expected his divine *List der Vernunft* (Cunning of Reason) to play such dirty tricks and indulge in such "subversive acts of history."

EQUALITY AND DISPOSABLE TIME

Another vitally important dimension of the same trend to define human emancipation in truly universal and substantively equitable terms concerns the relationship between the way we reproduce our direct material conditions of life, through the hours we dedicate every day to work, and the hours we allocate for other activities. Naturally, there is an important individual aspect to this question, enabling particular individuals to assign determinate portions of their time for this rather than that kind of activity. But there are some vital social preconditions in operation before the individuals can even begin to think about how to allocate their own time. These preconditions are determined by particular individuals' place in the social order, giving to some of them much more "liberty" (or "freedom") while curtailing with the same stroke the equality of the others. This is why Bolívar was absolutely right to insist that *"without equality all freedoms, all rights perish."*

The fundamentally social question of allocating our time is, of course, modifiable through the historical advancement in society's productive powers and the adopted orienting principles that can be used for regulating the social metabolism of reproduction. And not only the historically attained degree of productive advancement but also the adopted orienting principles of metabolic control require an overall societal frame of reference to acquire their proper meaning. Certainly we are limited by the historically attained degree of productive advancement. But we are no less limited—on the contrary, rather more so, and potentially even crippled—if we do not elaborate and adopt the appropriate orienting principles of social metabolic control, because that could nullify the realization of the objectively attained degree of scientific and other productive advancement. And this is precisely where the vital question of the state's role enters the picture. For the societal reproduction process, with the multiplicity of its material productive and various decision-making enterprises, must *cohere* in some way, otherwise the society in question could not survive.

Thus, the healthy functioning of society depends, on the one hand, on the *nature* of the material productive enterprises, according to the specific historical conditions that define and shape their character, and on the other hand, on the *modality* of the *overall* political decision-making process that *complements* the societal metabolic process as activated in the multiplicity of the particular material reproductive units, helping them to *cohere* into a *sustainable whole*. Under some historical conditions—especially under the rule of capital as a social metabolic order of reproduction—this cohesion is workable only if the political controlling dimension is constituted as the *separate/alienated* decision-making organ of some of the most vital functions. The state formations of the capital system must act as the *necessary corrective*—for as long as they are historically capable of fulfilling such corrective functions—to *structural defects* identifiable in the nature of the *material reproductive structures* themselves. However, and this cannot be stressed enough as the other side of the same coin, the need for *cohesiveness* is an *absolute* societal requirement, and therefore cannot disappear even with the "withering away of the state."

Two important consequences follow from this absolutely necessary consideration:

1. The radical critique of capital's state formation in our time is directly related to its—ever more dangerous—*historic failure* to fulfill its vital *corrective functions,* which are called for by the antagonistic material reproductive process itself. As a result, the now *failing state* (the painful actuality of our time, irrespective of how many debt-ridden trillions are poured into capital's bottomless hole) can only endanger the societal metabolic process, instead of remedying the crisis. This is because the state is *integral* to the structural determinations of the capital system, and its required corrective/remedial functions can only be *internal* to it. Thus, the state cannot *exempt itself* from the unfolding *structural crisis* of the capital system as a whole.
2. The relative primacy in this inextricable interrelatedness between capital's material reproductive structures and its state formations—which at a certain point of history becomes a vicious circle—belongs to the former. It is therefore impossible to envisage the necessary withering away of the state without simultaneously confronting the critical problems of radically altering the global material reproduction process. The painful historical failure to make any progress so far in the direction of the state's withering away envisaged by Marx acquires its intelligibility on this ground. And the same consideration applies not only to the evaluation of the past, concerning the forces that prevented the realization of the original expectations, but also to the prospects for the future.

With regard to point 1, it is highly relevant that the current advocates of "liberal imperialism" arrogantly define the territories of their wishful colonial reconquest as the "failed states." No explanation is given why the so-called failed states are supposed to have failed. It is simply asserted with declamatory arbitrariness that such states must be considered failed states. This view is combined with the equally arbitrary declamation—a total logical non sequitur conveniently stipulated by the self-interested propounders of such "theories," according to which the peremptorily condemned failed states must be brought under the rule of the dominant capitalist states, without even asking the elementary question of the practical feasibility (in terms of material and human costs and unavoidable destructiveness) of the advocated "liberal imperialist" undertaking. Throwing in the word *liberal* is expected to take care of all such concerns. And what is even worse, the "strategic thinkers" and their high-ranking politician sponsors who promote such "vision" of humanity's future also refuse to admit that *the failing states are their own*—still dominant—*core states* of the capital system. One of the most acute signs of the failure of the core states is that with their continuing war adventures, proclaimed in the name of "human rights," "democracy," and "liberty," they try to impose the historically anachronistic and dramatically failed modality of direct colonial domination on the arbitrarily denounced "failed states."

We must have a closer look at the deep-seated causal determination of these literally vital problems of our unfolding historical development in the final pages of this chapter. Regarding point 2, there can be no escape from the vicious circle of capital's inherently antagonistic determinations—which endanger the survival of humanity not only in military terms but also on the ecological plane—without radically altering our modality of social metabolic control by completely *eradicating* capital from the societal reproduction process.

SOCIALLY DISPOSABLE TIME

The challenge in this respect, which has acquired monumental proportions in our time, was *embryonically* conceptualized a quarter of a century before Marx, as an integral part of the far-sighted new trend that raised the question of emancipation in universal and substantively equitable terms, extended to the whole of humanity. In relation to the essential question of *how* we could and should meaningfully allocate our time—the one and only lifetime of all human beings—for the appropriate purposes among the competing demands, with vital implications for the most relevant issue of the individuals' "free time," the answer was given in an anonymous pamphlet far back in 1821 in this way:

> Wealth is *disposable time* and nothing more.... If the whole labor of a country were sufficient only to raise the support of the whole population, there would be no *surplus labor*, consequently nothing that can be allowed to accumulate as capital.... *Truly wealthy a nation*, if there is *no interest* or if the *working day* is six hours rather than twelve.[4]

Thus, the crucial category of *disposable time* is brought forward by the anonymous writer, in addition to "no interest," "surplus labor" and the "working day," advocating for the future—and for the really meaningful wealth of any nation—the reduction of the working day to *six hours*. But, of course, this perspective anticipates even today a radically different world. For capital can only be interested in the reduction of *necessary labor time* in the service of capital-accumulation and for maximizing profit.

The addressee of this anonymous pamphlet was Lord John Russell, a progressive Whig political figure (Earl Bertrand Russell's ancestor), who in the 1820s had sympathy for social reform and later to some extent for the reduction of the long working day. But a whole world separated him from the general perspective of the pamphlet itself. The idea of making *disposable time* the orienting principle for the regulation of societal reproduction implied the creation of a radically different social order. Not only in 1821, when it was suggested, but a few years short of two hundred years from the original idea, in our time, it is still a major challenge for the *future*, without which the socialist mode of social metabolic reproduction could not be considered historically sustainable.

But how is it possible to institute in reality the orienting principle of *disposable time* as the effective regulator of the societal reproduction process? Who can rightfully decide *how much disposable time* is available to be allocated for the diverse productive and humanly fulfilling functions that can *rightfully* claim an appropriate share of it? Indeed, who can decide what is the real amount of both the quantity *and the quality* of the disposable time of the particular individuals and of their society as a whole? Under the rule of capital this is inconceivable. But even between the transitional lower stage and the higher stage of the advocated socialist societal reproductive order the contrast is still striking. For the principle of distributing the social product among the members of society according to their quantitatively measurable *contribution* to the total social product can be regulated with relative ease by a *general policy*, possibly even under the supervision of a separate authority instituted as temporary. But the proper way of distributing the social wealth *"according to the needs of the individuals"*—indicated in Babeuf's case by the example of his thirsty men who need a pitcher of water or only a cupful—calls for the fully equitable acknowledgment of the social individuals' own decision-making authority on the subject. For only the socially conscious individuals can truly judge what can be considered not only the quantitatively (measured in hours) but also in a *qualitative* sense (concerning the *intensity*) the true amount of their freely available *disposable time*, so as to be rightfully allocated by the individuals concerned for productive purposes as well as for their own fulfillment. At the same time, this issue involves deciding this question: What are the genuine human *needs*—in contrast to capricious wants and "artificial appetites" capable of endless multiplication, like the monetary figure inserted into bank accounts—to be enjoyed by the social individuals on a substantively equitable basis? No *separate authority* can claim legitimacy on these matters.

Naturally, none of these questions are practically compatible with the horizon of the capital system whose objective material imperatives—which must be supported, and indeed they are, by the system's corresponding state formations—press for the reduction of *necessary labor time only*, and thereby for the inevitable production of *superfluous people*, together with the now officially acknowledged and cynically justified "structural unemployment." For the potential increase of real wealth through the conscious adoption of *disposable time* as the overall regulator of production—in contrast to the dehumanizing imperative of endless capital accumulation—and the immense amount of *free time* generated by the utilization of disposable time when the working day is reduced to six hours or even considerably less than that, could only function as *social dynamite,* blowing the capital system sky high in the absence of meaningful creative activity at the disposal of individuals.

This orienting principle of societal reproduction is incompatible with the capital system, including its state formations, on the ground of three vital considerations. First, because the adoption of *disposable time* calls for *qualitative* determination of the social metabolism, in place of the fetishistic domination of quantity under the conditions of capital's rule over society. Second, because, in its *appeal to the future,* this regulatory principle is *open-ended,* both regarding the realization of the *genuinely planned* productive objectives of society at large (without which humanity could not survive) and the *self-determined aims of life fulfillment* of the particular individuals whose disposable time is made to prevail for the chosen objectives on the basis of their *substantive equality.* And third, because even under the best of conditions, during the ascending phase of systemic development, the required *corrective* functions of capital's state formation—in view of the relative primacy of the material reproductive structures over the political dimension in their inextricable interrelatedness—cannot significantly *change* the overall framework. These corrective functions can only adjust its operational effectiveness in tune with the unalterable *absolute premise* of the structurally entrenched subordination of labor. The structural defects of the direct material determinations must be *preserved* stronger than ever through the *contradictorily corrective* functions of the state, because capital could not survive without them. And that means imposing on history the destructive imperative of an ultimately quite untenable *stunted dialectic* of failed *Aufhebung* (superseding preservation) in which *preservation* must prevail *at all cost,* at the expense of vitally needed *supersession.* Hence in the longer run its historically unfolding and ever-intensifying *destructiveness.* And in that sense, again, the predetermined imperatives of the *past,* with the established contending nation-states, dominate the *present.*

Thus Hegel, who was a great dialectical thinker, on the most general philosophical terrain could highlight more than anybody else the *conceptual requirements* of *Aufhebung*. But he violated his own principle when he refused to acknowledge the *stunted realization* of necessary *Aufhebung* under the actually existing conditions. In a paradoxical sense he was right to assign the accomplished reality of his modern capitalist nation-states in his philosophy of history to the *temporality of the past*, insisting that the Germanic states constituted "absolutely the end of history." Where he had to be fundamentally corrected by Marx was the Hegelian scheme—the prosaic reality of unresolved contradictions that he could only commend by sanctifying them in the name of the World Spirit—according to which the subsumption of the antagonisms of "civil society" under the wishfully proclaimed "ethical state" represented *Theodicaea,* the *"justification of the ways of God,"*[5] and at the same time the final stage of *"Spirit's perfect embodiment,"*[6] as we have seen.

In this stunted dialectic, the ultimate guarantor of the fictitiously projected "positive actuality" of societal reconciliation, the capitalist state had to be idealized even under its most devastatingly problematical aspects. Accordingly, even the technology of modern warfare had to be promoted, in a most astonishing way, by Hegel. We can hardly believe our eyes when we read in his *Philosophy of History* the kind of social-apologetic idealization of the mass-produced instruments of destruction when he presents us with the "philosophical deduction" of modern warfare from what in his explicitly stated view must be accepted as the apex of the ideally most commendable determinations: *"thought and the universal."*

This is how Hegel tries to convince his readers with the help of a most peculiar philosophical deduction about the "superior form of human bravery" displayed in the modern warfare of his idealized nation-states:

> The principle of the modern world—thought and the universal—has *given courage a higher form,* because its display now seems to be more mechanical, the act not of this particular person, but of a member of a whole. Moreover, it seems to be turned not against single persons, but against a hostile *group,* and hence *personal bravery appears*

impersonal. It is *for this reason that thought had invented the gun,* and the invention of this weapon, which has changed the purely personal form of bravery into a more abstract one, is no accident.[7]

In this way, through its direct derivation from "the principle of the modern world," the material contingency of ever more powerful modern warfare, rooted in globally expanding capitalist technology, acquires not only its "ideal necessity." It is simultaneously also set above all conceivable criticism in virtue of its full adequacy — "the rationality of the actual"—to that principle. And since morally commendable courage as "intrinsic worth" is inextricably linked by Hegel to the "absolute, final end, the sovereignty of the state," the apologetic circle of history reaching its culmination in the Germanic "civilizing" state of the capital system, with its ruthlessly efficacious modern warfare "invented by thought" for the sake of realizing, in a suitable "impersonal" form the "image and actuality of reason," is fully closed. One can only wonder how Hegel could justify, in the name of "being invented by thought and the universal" at an even "more advanced" stage of capitalist development, the use of the *most cowardly* weapon ever produced in human history: *drones*, by which destruction is imposed on countless victims of imperialist aggression, operated by the push of an electronic button from a comfortable office thousands of miles away from the murderous explosions. And how could Hegel ascribe, even with his stunted dialectic, such magnitude of moral depravity to the supreme historical agency of his World Spirit (*Weltgeist*) and its "Absolute Cunning of Reason"?

THE SUBSTANCE AND FORMS OF ALIENATION

Understandably, in the Marxian approach both the material reproductive structures of capital's "civil society" and the corresponding state formation in its entirety had to be subjected to a radical critique, instead of metamorphosing the no longer sustainable past into the insuperable "eternal present" of a stunted dialectic. Given the requirements of not partial but *universal emancipation*, in contrast to the past historical modalities of "change in personnel," this task could be accomplished only by focusing attention on the vicious circle of capital's material reproductive structures and the corresponding state formations. Accordingly, the radical critique had to be addressed to the *state as such*, and not only to a historically specific form of the state that would leave the underlying structural determinations standing. This is why the *withering away of the state* had to be envisaged (on the basis of disposable time) as an essential requirement of the global socialist transformation, beyond the structurally entrenched subordination of labor and the destructive antagonisms of the nation-states, be they "Germanic" or whatever else.

One of Marx's great insights into understanding historical development was summed up with his analogy that asserted: "Human anatomy contains a key to the anatomy of the ape." In this sense Marx insisted:

> Bourgeois society is the most developed and the most complex historic organization of production. The categories which express its relations, the comprehension of its structure, thereby also allow insight into the structure and the relations of production of all the vanished social formations out of whose ruins and elements it built itself up, whose partly still unconquered remnants are carried along within it, whose mere nuances have developed explicit significance within it, etc.[8]

Marx went on to emphasize a few paragraphs further on that "the categories express the forms of being, the characteristics of existence."[9] The same consideration can be applied, *mutatis mutandis*, to the problems of the modern state and to the decision-making modalities of the social body in general in past formations. The subject is always humanity in its unfolding history, moving ahead on the insuperable material ground of nature that compels it to reproduce the conditions of its existence within a framework of rules and regulations that can be favorable or, on the contrary, most detrimental to an objectively feasible advancement. The vital importance of the nature of the organs of overall decision-making, in relation to the actually given or feasible mode of controlling the metabolism of societal reproduction, enters the historical picture on this score.

This is not a question of any "ideal state," although it is far from irrelevant that the projection of some ideal overall regulatory system has been a *stubbornly recurrent* theme in the entire history of human thought. The past conceptions of the ideal state cannot be discussed at this point. What matters in the present context is to underline the brutal fact that ever since the prevalence of class exploitation in any form the expropriation and appropriation of the fruits of *surplus labor* provided the material ground on which historical advancement was perversely premised. The regulatory organs of overall decision-making—from slavery and feudal serfdom to the capitalist wage slavery of our time—had to be articulated and consolidated around that *core category* of humanity's social being, which must obviously remain the material ground of societal advancement and human accomplishment in the future. But to be historically sustainable in the future, humanity's usable disposable time must be liberated from its class integument.

Regarding the historical past, the deciding factor was not the particular *form* in which surplus labor had been most iniquitously expropriated and appropriated for their own primary benefit by the ruling classes. Under capitalism this process assumed the form of the economically regulated extraction and conversion of surplus labor into surplus-value, and the corresponding, ultimately untenable and lethal imperative of its ever-expanding accumulation as destructively self-imposing capital. This specific historical form could be changed under the post-capitalist capital system into the *political extraction* and discriminatory allocation of surplus labor, still at the expense of labor. What mattered always, and continues to matter for as long as the system of superimposed expropriation and domination of surplus labor *in any form* survives, is the *substance* that changes its form. And the overall regulatory framework is inseparable from it. The fundamental issue, therefore, in its material terms of reference, is the expropriation and alienated appropriation of *surplus labor as such,* not just this or that particular form of it, and, in terms of the overall political command structure of regulatory determinations today, the *state as such.* The two of them *stand or fall together*. Humanity's *disposable time* cannot be liberated without it. This is the mountain we *must* climb and conquer.

CAPITAL'S STUNTED DIALECTIC

The particularly acute problem for our time is the necessary and ever more dangerous failure of the *correctives* instituted by the political dimension of societal interaction in the past. As a result of such increasing failure, we are now subjected to the attempt to lock everything into the ever-narrowing vicious circle between capital's structurally entrenched material reproductive determinations and its political command structure.

The correctives of capital's state formation were always *problematical*, even in the ascending phase of the system's development, but in the descending phase they have become ever more *adventurist*. Their function in the first place was to keep within manageable limits, that is, to guard against internally destructive excesses, the *inherent centrifugality* of capital's material determinations, as manifest from the smallest *microcosms* of the material reproductive units that must "follow their own course," to the most gigantic transnational corporations intent on dominating everything. The *structural defects*[10] of the capital system's material determinations could never be overcome without weakening, and even undermining, the effectiveness of the material system itself, which is by its innermost nature *expansion-oriented* and *driven by accumulation*, and of course vice versa, according to the prevailing circumstances. In this sense, the state's correctives were always problematical, even if in the ascending phase *systemically constructive*. For they could intervene only within well-marked limits, since their primary mandate was not the *supersession* but the *preservation* of *capital's competitive centrifugality*, on account of its *dynamic* side, which for a long historical period constituted the material force of its irresistible drive forward and successful demolition of all obstacles that stood in the way, to the point of global systemic domination.

Given the *insuperable centrifugality* of capital's material reproductive units, the *cohesiveness* as the *absolute* requirement of *any* social metabolic order could only be achieved, and in the course of massive economic expansion maintained, through the corresponding *all-encroaching* expansion of the system's state formation. Since such cohesion could not be produced on the *substantive* basis of the self-expansionary microcosms of capital's material reproduction, only the *formal universality* of the *state imperatival* determinations could complete capital's mode of social metabolic reproduction as a system. But even this unique way out was feasible only on a *strictly temporary* basis. Until, that is, the *overall systemic limits* of this kind of societal reproduction had to be reached in the course of historical development. Then the limits had to assert themselves with a vengeance both in terms of the necessary *material* requirements of the system's *unlimitable* self-expansionary productive microcosms—deeply affecting in a most *destructive way nature itself*—and of the totalizing political plane of *global interstate relations*, foreshadowing the potentiality of catastrophic destructiveness in the form of yet another all-out military conflagration as witnessed twice in the twentieth century. For the inexorable drive of capital's material structures is not brought to a point of rest by being contained within the *national boundaries*.

The wishful projection of *unproblematical globalization*, most powerfully promoted today by the United States as the dominant *aggressive nation-state*, is the obvious manifestation of this contradiction. But even if the existing nation-states could be somehow put under a common umbrella—by military force or by some kind of formal political agreement—that could only be ephemeral, leaving the underlying contradictions unresolved. For it would still maintain the innermost structural defect of the capital system in its place, that is, the *necessary self-expansionary centrifugality* of its material reproductive microcosms. In other words, even in that way the capital system would today remain totally devoid of an effective and *cohesive operational rationality*.

For several decades the monopolist imperialist stage of capital's descending phase of systemic development was still able to provide a perversely corrective "advancement," in the sense of securing the temporary military triumph of the dominant power or powers, although such "corrective" had to assume an increasingly more destructive form because of its ever-greater wars. Thus, what used to be only *problematical* but still assertable in the more distant past started to become under the conditions of monopolistic imperialism more *prohibitive*, due to its ever-increasing *stakes* coupled with necessarily *diminishing returns*. Inevitably, this kind of development, with its increasing stakes and diminishing returns, pointed toward the prospect of rendering *totally untenable* the assertion of capital's ultimate sanctions against the *externally* denounced, but in its deepest centrifugal structural determinations *internal*, systemic antagonist.

It cannot be stressed strongly enough that only the characteristic false consciousness of capital's personifications—which conveniently also provides "self-evident justification" and state-legitimation for the pursued wars—can misrepresent the insoluble *internal* structural determinations and contradictions of the established social and political order as the *externally produced* and militarily disposable contingent threats of an enemy to be subdued. Here again the actual *causal order* is presented upside down, indicating the necessary *consequences* of the underlying systemic determinations as if such consequences were the *real cause* of the periodic conflagrations morally justified in the name of defending the state from "external threat." And, of course, the logical conclusion arising from such upside-down conceptions of "external threat" also predicates that the necessary collisions in question are perfectly manageable by the customary military conflicts of the "sovereign" nation-states. In reality, the causal determinations and contradictions are *internal* to the very nature of the capital system's unalterable mode of social metabolic control. This is because the incorrigible centrifugality of capital's material determinations, in their irrepressible drive for global extension and domination, could not be contained by—and limited to—any given national boundary. Consequently, sooner or later the irresistible *self-expansionary drive* must assume the form of *interstate collisions*, no matter how destructive they might be, to the point of the two actually experienced global conflagrations in our historical past.

Once the prospect of humanity's total destruction enters the historical horizon, through the nuclear, chemical, and biological weapons of mass destruction, the military solution of the fundamental problems of interstate antagonisms—with their deep-seated roots in capital's centrifugal material ground—is made impossible on the *required scale*. Wars can be pursued, *and indeed they are*, on a more limited scale, but not an *all-out war*, which in the past could successfully subdue the adversary, extracting from it subsequently its resources for the benefit of the victor. Moreover, the unavoidable *all-round destructiveness* inseparable from an *all-out war* fought with the weapons of mass destruction would be so immense that *no rational meaning* could be assigned to the notion of "victor." For under such conditions there could be no more victors. There could be only the *universally defeated*. Thus, even this long-established dimension of the *state corrective functions*—namely the ultimate sanction for "enforcing sovereignty by war" in Hegel's idealized state-apologetic sense—which was so vital for the viability of capital's centrifugal order, now totally loses its practicability and meaning. Accordingly, with the *structural crisis* of the capital system in our time we have in this respect also reached the limits.

Naturally, the most extreme neoliberal and neo-con "strategic thinkers" of imperialism refuse to take any notice of such developments and continue to indulge in the most absurd projections of waging war in the future, sometimes in the name of openly glorified "liberal imperialism." I discussed some of this in the past,[11] and there is no need to repeat their views here. However, what is particularly striking in all such openly imperialist advocacy of military domination is that the authors fail to understand even the elementary difference between the past economic reality of *all-out wars* and the implications of the necessarily *limited wars*— which must remain limited, short of collective suicide. For the limited wars are not only incapable of bringing the expected returns to the victor, namely to the militarily preponderant United States, but they are in economic terms *counterproductive*. They are counterproductive even if for the time being they provide high profits—at the cost of the state's catastrophic indebtedness and ultimate bankruptcy—to the national/transnational military-industrial complex. It is enough to remember the sum of more than one *trillion dollars* that the United States had to spend on the Iraq War alone, not to mention all of the other wars envisaged and happily promoted by these "strategic thinkers." The once practicable economic logic of the *all-out wars* has become totally insane as "economic rationality"—even in General Carl Marie von Clausewitz's sense of "the continuation of politics by other means"—and cannot be made to prevail any longer. For it is simply inconceivable that *any particular country*—no matter how powerful in its military imperialist aspirations—could dominate on a sustainable basis the *entire world*. Yet, that kind of logic is the only "sense" that could be attributed to the aggressive empire-building aspirations propagandized by all such mindless "strategic thinking," projecting the economic viability and commendability of "imperial overstretch" against "imperial understretch," and sloganizing about "premodern failed states" and the "evil axis," as well as promoting at the same time "no exit from occupied territories," and unashamedly glorifying "death and destruction" to be inflicted upon the "failed states."

It would be tempting to dismiss the advocacy of all such nightmarish adventurism on account of its *total irrationality*. To be sure, it is true that the irrational projections of these "strategic thinkers" do not matter in themselves. But they are *symptomatic* of some fundamental contradictions that cannot be ignored. The real concern is the vicious circle of alienated interchange between the material/economic and the political domain of the capital system. This vicious circle counterposes itself to any attempt at finding rationally sustainable solutions to our grave problems. For the reciprocal interchange between the material/economic and the political domain assumes the form of an incorrigibly stunted dialectic, because *one side* in the material ground of the social metabolic process must dominate the other—that is, exchange value must prevail over use value, quantity over quality, abstract over concrete, formal over substantive, command over execution, and of course, capital over labor. This kind of necessary one-sidedness generates correspondingly one-sided remedies in the political corrective domain, like not only the *facilitating* role played by the state in support of giant transnational corporations (while cynically criticizing monopolism) but also undertaking state-promoted *monopolistic imperialist expansion at all costs,* including the advocacy of all-out war, instead of rational limits to be set to wasteful and—beyond a certain historical stage even all-destructive—inadmissible capital expansion.

There can be no solution to this fundamental problem within the parameters of the antagonistic nation-states constituted through the vicious circle of capital's *stunted historical dialectic.* The key to removing the *causes* of global conflagration can be found in the necessity to overcome on the plane of the *social metabolism itself* the fetishistic domination of one side by the other just mentioned, founded on the structurally entrenched domination of labor by capital and its expropriation of the vital controlling functions of the social metabolism.

Capital's centrifugal material ground *could not and cannot* have a historically sustainable overall command structure. Accordingly, the various state formations of the capital system have been constituted in the course of history out of the need to provide a remedy—no matter how contradictory, indeed antagonistic—to this structural defect of the system's social reproductive metabolism by bringing the incorrigibly centrifugal and potentially most disruptive units under some kind of control. This solution could be offered only by maintaining the *separate/alienated* character of capital's state formations as the overall command structure of the system, without *any* prospect of integrating the material reproductive and the political state-legitimated control functions. At the same time, the *material reproductive* determinations of the capital system continue their unrelenting drive toward *global* integration that *cannot be matched* in a historically sustainable way by capital's state formations, despite all wishful projection of globalization.

Thus, the integrative tendencies as a whole remain truncated on capital's actually existing ground, and the political dimension remains characterized by the antagonistically confrontational overall command structure of the nation-states. In this sense, what was in its original constitution a temporarily (even if for a long historical period necessary) practicable corrective to capital's disruptive material centrifugality becomes a *potentially all-engulfing catastrophic centrifugality* on the global plane, in need of an appropriate global corrective. But a global corrective is inconceivable without overcoming the structural defect of capital's material centrifugality and opposition to a mode of decision-making in which the autonomously chosen objectives of the freely associated individuals can be combined with, and truly integrated into, a rationally planned and historically sustainable overall framework.

CHAPTER FOURTEEN

Himalayan Obstacle: Conclusion to Part Two

This is the size of the mountain we *must* climb and conquer. Some time ago I spoke of the "Himalayan obstacle." This seems like a real understatement. Our mountain is many Himalayas on top of one another. And there are no native Sherpas to be exploited for the hard work. We must do it ourselves, and we can do it only if we are willing to confront the real stakes and the real obstacles.

The contingencies of our situation, highlighting the limits of our social metabolic order, are not only painful, they are inalterably *global contingencies*, with their sobering implications. For if the size and resources of our planet were, say, ten times bigger than they happen to be, in that case capital's destructiveness could be carried on for quite some time. But *they are not* ten times bigger, but only as big as they actually are. If nothing else, the ongoing domination and *destruction of nature* should make it palpably clear that *there is a limit to everything*. And capital's absolute limits demonstrate their destructive untenability not only in this respect but also on several other scores.

No ideal or utopian states can be envisaged under the urgency of time. The longing for ideal solutions constantly recurring in the past may tell us something irrepressible about humanity's legitimate aspirations. But they need to be set on more secure foundations.

Despite distorting accusations, no unrealizable claim is involved in the advocacy of the necessary socialist alternative. What that alternative appeals to is the tangible requirement of *historical sustainability*. And that is also offered as the *criterion* and *measure* of its feasible success. In other words, the test of validity is defined in terms of historical viability and practical sustainability, *or not*, as the case might be.

Naturally, no social metabolic order can function without its orienting principles. Indeed, their historical sustainability depends on the *practical viability* of their *rival orienting principles*. This is why the socialist order can only be envisaged on the material ground of the *rationally planned* and determined appropriation of *surplus labor* produced by *each and every one* of society's *freely associated* individuals, who realize and *fulfill their aspirations* in the spirit of their *disposable time*, on the basis of their *substantive equality*, in full *solidarity* with one another and with their *socially shared aspirations*.

This is what makes feasible the *conquest* of the mountain we must climb.

PART THREE

Ancient and Modern Utopias

CHAPTER FIFTEEN

From Plato's Cave to the Sombre Light of The Laws

Ever since the publication of a much-celebrated book in the sixteenth century it has been customary to call *"utopian"* the idealized visions of the social and political order. As we know, it was Sir Thomas More who gave the title *Utopia*—meaning "Nowhere"—to his book published in 1516.[1] In this seminal work he offered both a sharp critique of the socioeconomic and political conditions of his own times and an idealized counter-image to them as their projected practicable alternative in the tongue-in-cheek world of *Nowhere*.

The savage excesses of early capitalistic developments constituted the critical targets of Sir Thomas More. They were famously summed up in his graphic imagery according to which *"sheep are eating men."* This striking expression was meant to underline the complete *absurdity* of anything comparable to that. But, as a matter of undeniable fact, what was sarcastically condemned as *absurdity* by the author of *Utopia* fully corresponded to the painful *reality* of the historically prevailing conditions at the time.

The undeniable inhumanity highlighted in that graphic way by Sir

Thomas More was due in actually existing society to the state-imposed *enclosure* of the common land, under the conditions of "primitive capital-accumulation." Such enclosure was pursued in the interest of the highly profitable production of wool at that stage of early capitalistic developments, and the extermination of hundreds of thousands of human beings—a truly mind-boggling figure in terms of the size of the country's population in the early sixteenth century—who were condemned as dangerous "vagabonds." In this way the figurative but profound truth of the expression "sheep are eating men," made very clear through its striking power the brutality of the unfolding socioeconomic transformation.

It goes without saying that the overwhelming majority of the human beings denounced and eliminated by state violence as destructive "vagabonds" were people mercilessly chased away from their former productive livelihood on the common land. But the vested interests of the victoriously advancing capitalist societal reproductive order and its authoritarian state formation had to find a palatable justification for the state-enforced cruelty of mass extermination by calling the people concerned destructive and parasitic vagabonds.

To be sure, the more or less evident idealization of the depicted social and political order did not start with the work of Sir Thomas More. It goes back thousands of years. Indeed, it goes back in social and political theory as far as we can find structurally entrenched hierarchical state formations and their antagonistic modalities of overall decision-making wedded to a correspondingly antagonistic material reproductive order. For all such socioeconomic and political systems by their innermost determinations ruthlessly dominate the great masses of the people. This is why they must be idealized in the world of ideology for as long as such conditions can historically prevail.

For our own purpose in this work it will be sufficient to go back in history as far as the philosophical ideas on the state advocated by Plato and Aristotle, conceived by them not far from two and a half thousand years ago. For from that time onward, we could witness the most telling *continuity* of not only European but all Western social and political thought in that sense.

Unsurprisingly, due to the dominant class relations and the pivotal role exercised by the state in safeguarding their stability, even the state theories of the most important philosophers envisaged for a very long time the assumed ability to remedy within the decision-making framework of the state the economic and political contradictions that the thinkers could identify in their societies. They projected this kind of a solution in the interest of the continued maintenance of the order that customarily proved to be successful in their given societies. This happened to be the case even when the philosophers in question were able to put into relief some of the grave contradictions they had to experience. Understandably, advocating the institution of the required fundamental changes as an alternative to the existing mode of production and societal reproduction proved to be prohibitive in terms of their general conceptual framework.

Accordingly, for thousands of years the explanations put forward by the major thinkers retained the state itself as the overall horizon of decision-making even when the negative impact of a number of fundamental social and political contradictions in their societies could not be denied. Indeed, paradoxically, the outstanding political thinkers continued to retain the wishfully state-oriented horizon even when they themselves offerred some highly insightful interpretations pointing to the eruption of the state's contradictions. This is why Marx could underline in one of his *Theses on Feuerbach*, with full justification, that even the greatest philosophers in the past have "only interpreted the world: the point is to change it."[2]

We had to wait for thousands of years before the *nature of the state* as historically constituted in its *necessarily hierarchical* and *structurally entrenched* unchangeable character could be identified as one of the *root causes* of the problems to be overcome, rather than capable of providing the historically sustainable solution to those problems. Nevertheless, such root causes had to be confronted at some point in history because the character and the role of the state for countless centuries *precluded* the solution of the vital problems in social advancement by its unalterable modality of decision-making. That is what could not be carried on indefinitely. For the state continued to usurp the role of necessary arbiter over all of the fundamental issues of social life, from the elementary material conditions of reproduction all the way to the most complex and bewilderingly intertwined political and cultural issues.

In due course, this state of affairs had become untenable. And that was not a question of *"whether or not"* but *"when,"* due to the unfolding historical conditions both in terms of the inevitable social conflicts and the potentially catastrophic ultimate ecological limitations that at some point in history had to assert themselves. For the overall modality of the state's decision-making could not be significantly altered precisely in view of the *hierarchical structural entrenchment* of the *state as such* in the antagonistic societal reproductive order, no matter how destructive the consequences might be.

The untenable antagonistic determinations underlying this relationship between the fundamental societal metabolic order of reproduction and the state's decision-making power were not of a limited temporary and contingent character. On the contrary, the state's structurally entrenched and necessarily hierarchical/self-imposing nature and mode of operation was inseparable from the prevailing modality of material production and reproduction that itself was structurally dominated by *irreconcilable class antagonisms*. This is why the overall decision-making modality of the state had to match in its own antagonistic way its counterpart in the class-repressive material reproductive order.

Obviously, this kind of contradictory interchange between societal reproduction and the state could only constitute a veritable *vicious circle* whose constitutive parts reciprocally reinforced—and were bound to reinforce—one another. Inevitably, with regard to the future, the two of them stand or fall together, in the sense that the antagonisms of the state and the antagonistic material metabolism of society can only be overcome by consigning both of them to the past in a historically sustainable way. In other words, the fatefully negative impact of their vicious circle can be overcome only by radically superseding both the entrenched state and society's exploitative class-antagonistic material metabolism as it has been historically constituted over thousands of years.

THE IDEAL SOCRATIC STATE

Plato lived a long and at times dramatically eventful life, between 429 and 347 BCE. Although he was a member of a most distinguished and privileged aristocratic family, and of course a supporter of slavery, ironically he had to suffer the indignity of being sold as a slave in Sicily. He was rescued by Anniceris who bought his freedom with the considerable expenditure of twenty minas,[3] according to the account provided to us by Diogenes Laertius.[4]

Plato wrote not just one but several utopian visions of the ideal state. Two of them—especially *The Republic* but also *The Laws*—are very well known, but the third is hardly ever considered. This is to some extent understandable because the third survived only as a small fragment, interrupted in the middle of a sentence. Nevertheless, it is significant for us, because in this work Plato attempted to exemplify "in the world of reality" the Socratic account of the ideal state in the same spirit in which he represented it in *The Republic*. Plato tried to do that in this fragmentary dialogue with reference to the victory of ancient Athens 9,000 years prior to Plato's own time—claimed by *legend*—over the equally legendary island of *Atlantis*, described as part of the original kingdom of the God Poseidon in Greek mythology.

We find references to this fragmentary utopian vision in two of Plato's dialogues, *Timaeus* and *Critias*. They both belong to what is usually called Plato's "Late Period," to which also the most extensive of his work on the state, titled *The Laws*, undoubtedly belongs. By contrast, *The Republic* is the outstanding dialogue on the ideal state written in the years designated as Plato's "Middle Period."

In the dialogue *Timaeus*, as in *Critias*, there are three participants in addition to Socrates: Critias, Hermocrates, and Timaeus himself. At the beginning of *Timaeus*, we are offered the briefest possible summary of the "chief theme" of *The Republic*, as discussed one day earlier by the four of them and reiterated in some detail by Socrates himself. As he puts it in *Timaeus*, "The chief theme of my yesterday's discourse was the State—*how constituted and of what citizens composed it would seem likely to be most perfect*."[5]

However, the main purpose of these dialogues was meant to assert the practicable validity of the account presented the day before by Socrates in his long tale on *The Republic*. That objective is spelled out in the words of Critias, who explains that the Socratic tale reminded him of what he heard from his grandfather—also named Critias—as actual history about ancient Athens. These are the relevant words of grandson Critias:

> I am ready to tell you the whole tale. I will give you not only the general heads, but the particulars, as they were told to me. The city and citizens, which you yesterday described to us *in fiction*, we will now *transfer to the world of reality*. It shall be the ancient city of Athens, and we will suppose that the citizens whom you imagined were our veritable ancestors . . . ; they will perfectly harmonize, and there will be no inconsistency in saying that the citizens of your republic are these ancient Athenians.[6]

Regrettably, because of the fragmentary character of the dialogue presented by young Critias, his account never amounts to what he promises in his words of introduction: "the whole tale," with "all the particulars" as they were told to him by his grandfather. Nevertheless, we learn that his grandfather's story concerned the way in which ancient Athens was originally constituted, with much the same defining characteristics as the vision presented the day before in the tale of Socrates; and both of them coinciding by "some mysterious coincidence,"[7] as we are told later by young Critias, with the "narrative of Solon," the great law-giver and poet. And indeed, such noble constitution is said to have enabled the ancient Athenians to heroically triumph, "9,000 years earlier," over the immense power of the rulers of Atlantis.[8] Thus we are assured not only of the practicable viability of the Socratic state but also of its highest moral worth. At the same time, we also learn that the reprehensible (because unprovoked) invader, the mighty island of Atlantis, soon after its defeat following violent earthquakes and floods, as if it were the result of some divine justice, completely disappeared in the depth of the sea.

In this way we are in a twofold sense expected to be satisfied about the ideal character of the state projected by Socrates. In one sense, according to the assurances given by the younger Critias, there can be no disharmony between the two accounts given by Plato when the *"fiction"* of Socrates is *"transferred to the world of reality,"* thereby asserting that the Socratic *Republic* is a *practically viable* and successful mode of regulating the societal order. And in the second vital sense, we are also assured that there could be absolutely no conflict between the commended *value system* of the ideal Socratic state and the *world of reality* both in the present and in the future. In other words, in the vision offered by these two tales there can be no conflict between the reality of "is" and the world of "ought-to-be." And that underlines their unquestionable validity.

NATURE AS JUSTIFICATION

In philosophy and social theory we often find appeals to some higher authority—something like "Divine Providence" or "Nature"—advanced as a claimed support for the position of the thinkers arguing their own case. As we have seen, Hegel presented his conception of historical development not simply as his own view of the world but as the *Weltgeist* (World Spirit) unfolding *its reality* in the form in which we all experience it as the actual course of history. Not surprisingly, Kant appeals in his forceful way to the Providential "great artist *nature*"*("natura daedala rerum")* in support of his own views.[9] Indeed, in a similar mode of assertion one of the greatest representatives of the Scottish Enlightenment, Adam Smith, characterizes the capitalist social and economic order that he passionately supports as "the *natural system* of perfect liberty and justice."[10]

In the same respect, we must remember in social and political theory those approaches that postulated an original *"state of nature"* for humanity's development. Nor should we overlook in the various conceptions of the state the advocates of *"Natural Law,"* irrespective of how debatable the legislative order erected on that foundation might be. For all such self-commending assumptions can lead to extremely problematical conclusions. Sometimes they can lead to no less dubious a result than the affirmation of the diametrical opposite of the real state of affairs. That can happen even in the case of some very great thinkers. To take only two of them from among the greatest, let us consider briefly the views of Kant and Hegel in the domain of classical German philosophy.

Hegel's way of using *Nature* in favor of the earlier mentioned self-commending purpose is all the more revealing about the—unacknowledged—antagonistic *class character* of the underlying structural determinations at work in the societal order, duly reflected in social and political theory. This is precisely because his curious postulate of the claimed authority of "Nature" in the name of his socially biased dismissal of equality had to be integrated into a monumental *idealist* philosophical conception, together with the "World Spirit." For if a materialist philosopher—like Thomas Hobbes, for instance—appeals to the unchallengeable authority of nature in support of his own views, that would seem to be well in tune with his general philosophical position. But when a great idealist thinker, like Hegel, adopts the same approach, whose ultimate frame of reference is nothing less than the World Spirit, one must look into the reasons for that. And the answer is readily provided when we consider the Hegelian passage in question. This is how it reads:

> Men are made unequal by *nature*, where *inequality is in its element*, and in civil society the *right of particularity* is so far from annulling this *natural inequality* that it produces *out of mind* and raises it to an inequality of skill and resources [wealth], and even to one of *moral and intellectual* attainment. To oppose to this right a demand for equality is a *folly of the Understanding* which takes as real and rational its *abstract equality* and its "ought-to-be."[11]

Clearly, the motivating force of Hegel's utterly perverse appeal to the authority of "Nature" is his determination to assert—in line with a fallacious conversion of nature's undeniable diversity into socially produced human inequality, so as to be able to ascribe the latter as "natural inequality"—the inalterability of nature itself. This then, in its turn, is supposed to dominate forever "civil society" by some kind of natural fatality in all respects, even including "moral and intellectual attainment." This is a most outrageous mode of reasoning, corresponding to extreme ideological prejudice, made only worse by the circumstance that it is produced by the pen of a philosophical genius.

As we have seen earlier, Thomas Hobbes refuted the Hegelian reasoning about the claimed nature-determined inequality of human beings nearly two centuries before Hegel. It is well worth repeating the way he had put it:

> Nature hath made men so *equall,* in the faculties of body and mind; as that though there bee found one man sometimes manifestly stronger in body, or of quicker mind then another; yet when all is reckoned together, the difference between man, and man, is not so considerable, as that one man can thereupon *claim to himselfe any benefit,* to which another may not pretend, as well as he. For as to the strength of body, the weakest has strength enough to kill the strongest, either by secret machination, or by confederacy with others, that are in the same danger with himselfe. And as to the faculties of the mind, (setting aside the arts grounded upon words, and especially that skill of proceeding upon generall, and infallible rules, called Science; which very few have, and but in few things; as being not a native faculty, born with us; nor attained, (as Prudence) while we look after somewhat els,) I find *yet a greater equality* amongst men, than that of strength. For Prudence is but Experience; which *equall time, equally* bestowed on all men, in those things they *equally apply* themselves unto.[12]

Thus, the Hegelian way of using an utterly travestied "Nature" for his self-commending purpose turns the actual state of affairs, concerning real and potential human equality, into its diametrical opposite, in the service of a most retrograde social and philosophical position. Blindly unquestioned ideological vested interests constitute the foundation of such reasoning. Inevitably, Hegel's theory of the state suffers its consequences.

Kant's case is somewhat different. It is, of course, true that his view of human equality is fatally flawed because it is based on an upside-down vision of the societal reproductive order. It is conceived in a way that totally ignores the structurally entrenched exploitative and therefore necessarily class-antagonistic social determinations, and at the same time unforgivably justifies the blatant inequalities of the ruling order by simply asserting, with unqualified claim, that "the poor are dependent on the rich and the one who is dependent must obey the other, just as one man has command over another, as one man serves and another pays, etc."[13] Here the class-imposed and structurally entrenched *real dependency relations* of the social metabolism of production are *completely reversed*. Thus the class-exploitative social order in which "one man serves and another pays" is not just blindly misrepresented, hiding the *parasitic dependency* of the "rich who can pay" on the work of those who actually produce even the elementary material conditions of their livelihood, but also peremptorily taken for granted *without the slightest criticism* as inalterable in the future, according to the author of the *Critique* of both "Pure Reason" and "Practical Reason." That makes the lofty Reason most problematical, masterfully though it is articulated in those *Critique*s within their own terms of reference. Nevertheless, Kant's advocacy of what he calls "the moral duty of eternal peace" under the historical conditions of the Napoleonic Wars that were engulfing the whole of Europe for decades is by no means reprehensible. Rather the opposite. For even today, well over two centuries after the passionate Kantian advocacy, the constantly threatened cause of securing and successfully safeguarding peace is absolutely vital for the survival of humanity.

However, the trouble arises with Kant's assumption of what he calls *"nature's mechanical course"* projected by him for the purpose of making *"nature's teleology"* appear triumphant. For he presents this *assumption* as the Providential *solution* of the identified contradictions. In fact, the Kantian assumption is postulated as the solution unfolding in actual history for which we must thank the benevolent "great artist *nature*" ("*natura daedala rerum*"), who provides us with nothing less than the "*guarantee*" that we reach in the future the moral end of eternal peace that is "axiomatically" stipulated by Reason itself. This kind of *wishful misrepresentation* of the actual state of affairs could not be more *unfounded*, against the very real prospects for the potential self-annihilation of humankind that we must starkly confront in our time, in sharp contrast to the a prioristically projected moral good of eternal peace that is supposed to be miraculously *promoted*, and even *guaranteed*, by the "mechanical course of nature's teleology."

Such nobly motivated but palpable misrepresentation of the historically encountered perilous antagonisms, including decades of destructive wars in the eighteenth century and countless more of them up to the present time, including two *global wars*, is not an accidental or corrigible part of Kant's reasoning. On the contrary, it is the *necessary consequence* of his fundamental misconception of the *inherent character* of the antagonisms in question. For he reduces the actually operative antagonisms—in much the same way as we find that in bourgeois philosophical conceptions in general—into purportedly corrigible *individualistic "selfish propensities and conflicts*," thereby ignoring their *irreconcilable class determinations* that *must prevail* in capital's social metabolic order as if they had the power of a potentially all-destructive "*natural law.*"

Indeed, Kant's wishfully envisaged solution of the contradictions analyzed by him—a solution projected in *positive terms* on the claimed ground of the benevolent intervention of the "great artist of nature"—is explicitly stated in Kantian philosophy to be concerned with the "*selfish propensities themselves*" in such a way that *within the framework of the state itself* those selfish propensities and forces should be cunningly "*directed against each other*" by the Providential mechanism of nature. And of course the result being that one selfish propensity *balances* the other (yet another ubiquitous wishful postulate of the bourgeois conceptual universe) so that their providentially regulated interaction should miraculously "suspend and eliminate the otherwise devastating effects" of the condemned selfish propensities.

To be sure, individualistic "selfish propensities" are amenable to such treatment and solution, embodying in that conception even a philosophical predecessor to Hegel's "List der Vernunft," that is, his "Cunning of Reason," instituted in world history by the "World Spirit" in much the same way as they are said to be realized by nature's Providentially teleological mechanism in the Kantian account. In total contrast, the materially grounded *exploitative class antagonisms* that are objectively and deeply rooted in insuperable vested interests, thereby destined to decide and allegedly also to legitimate *"who commands and who obeys"* in capital's antagonistic social metabolic order, are certainly not amenable to a similar treatment. And that makes a fundamental difference. For, understandably, once the constituent parts of the societal contradictions are characterized in the Kantian way, reduced without rhyme or reason into "selfish individualistic propensities" that in principle must be manageable by the state, there can be no real obstacle envisioned to their asserted utterly wishful solution. They can even be depicted in paradoxically positive terms as the absolutely fundamental dynamic forces of the otherwise unachievable historical development of humanity.[14]

All this is very different when we consider objectively class-determined social antagonisms. For in terms of their structurally entrenched innermost determinations they can be so devastating as effectively to foreshadow nothing less than humanity's total self-destruction through some global war, fought to the bitter end with the abundantly available weapons of mass destruction. And in that objectively grounded social metabolic setting, the traditional wishful postulate of idealized remedial *"balancing"*—which, characteristically, happens to be well in tune with the requirements of an *established iniquitous* societal order—becomes totally meaningless.

Defining the contradictions and antagonisms in terms of individualistic "selfish propensities" can still offer a margin of benevolent intervention for the work of successful balancing generously guaranteed, as Kant assures us, by the "great artist of nature." However, there can be no margin of action whatsoever for such intervention when the potential social antagonists confront one another—on the material ground of irreconcilable class contradictions that correspond to rival conceptions of their envisaged social metabolic order—in their global collision of total destruction. Nonetheless, these are the ultimate real stakes concerning the literally vital necessity of "eternal peace" in our time, and not the "selfish propensities" of individual conflicts conveniently balanceable by the *"mechanical course of nature's teleology."*

Another crucial aspect of the claimed Kantian solution of the identified contradictions directly concerns the *state as such*. In that important aspect the state is represented by Kant as the provider of a most welcome solution because he can characterize the realization of the demands to which the state is subjected as being *"within the ability of man"* and therefore as being well in keeping with his own self-commending conception of *nature*. As we can see in Kant's analysis of these thorny issues, he does not hesitate to assert that in order to achieve the cunning balancing of the selfish propensities for the purpose of eliminating their devastating societal effects, what is necessary in his words "is only to *organize the state well*, which is indeed within the ability of man," contrasted by him to man failing to be *"a morally good man"* by his *natural* constitution.[15]

Accordingly, what was considered by Kant in the first place as the practical limitation of the otherwise praiseworthy "general will" is now said to be properly overcome because *"Nature* comes to the aid of this revered but practically ineffectual general will which is founded in reason," and it "directs the selfish forces *against each other* in such wise that the result for reason is *as if* both selfish forces were *nonexistent."* Thus, thanks to the "good organization of the state itself," in the service of its successful balancing of the potentially devastating effects that arise from the propensities of the selfish individuals, man is *"compelled to be a good citizen"* and thereby the well-organized state compensates also for man's original failure with respect to being "a morally good man."[16]

Unfortunately, Kant's optimism and noble disposition to come to the aid of what he calls, as we have just seen, the "revered but practically ineffectual general will which is founded in reason," completely bypasses the principal difficulty involved in finding a historically sustainable solution to the identified problems through any direct appeal to the assumed authority of Providential *"nature"* with regard to the *state*. For Kant's revealing assertion that in order to obtain the required historically valid outcome it is necessary "only to *organize the state well*, which is indeed within the ability of man" is *never established*. It is never established either in this particular work, where it is categorically proclaimed, or anywhere else.

In truth, in the light of our actual historical experience it is much easier to be convinced of the *diametrical opposite* to what is categorically asserted by Kant on the claimed ability of human beings to properly *control the state*. For, contrary to Kant, to say that thanks to the claimed positive outcome "man is *compelled to be a good citizen"* in reality does not even touch the surface, let alone the potentially most destructive, even *catastrophic*, dimension of the *problem* represented and imposed by the *state as such* in its character as itself happens to be historically constituted. Not only because the advocacy of *"good citizen"* is a *characteristically loaded term* whose meaning—far from being an acceptable compensation for defining man as *by his nature prevented* to be a "morally good man"—can be most arbitrarily *decided by the state itself*, prejudged in the interest of its own mode of necessarily self-imposing operation.

In reality, the state, which by the innermost characteristics of its structurally entrenched objective determinations *usurps overall societal control*—and indeed, as the institutionally secured *alienation* of the power of ultimate decision-making from time immemorial, *it must usurp* overall societal control—stands in fateful contrast to Kant's belief that for the solution of the perennial destructive antagonisms of known history "it is necessary only to *organize the state well.*" In other words, the state as historically constituted for the *hierarchically exercised usurpation* of overall societal control, in the interest of securing and safeguarding structurally determined class-exploitation, is *not controllable at all* by human beings without radically overcoming the necessarily antagonistic determinations of the societal order in *all* of its dimensions.

This is the point where we can clearly see the *derailing consequences* of confining the analysis of the contradictions—indicated by Kant himself—to the *political domain*. For the crucial impediment in this respect is not the institutional framework of the state, said to be remediable if it is *"well organized,"* on the ground of—by the state circularly/self-servingly defined criteria of—"good citizenship." Rather, in actually existing reality that crucial impediment is the *antagonistic material metabolism of societal reproduction itself.*

Moreover, to make matters worse, "this has not been invented by capital," to use a Marxian expression, but has been the case for countless centuries before capital's rule, and it continues to be so today. Indeed, it can continue to be the case for as long as the organ of overall societal decision-making, fatefully embodied in the state, is *objectively* structured in a *class-exploitative* way, and therefore necessarily dominated in its innermost structural determinations by insuperable contradictions. The *political antagonisms of the state as such,* corresponding to the state's historically constituted reality up to the present, are inextricably *grounded* on such materially irreconcilable structural determinations. Thus, not the more or less improvable political organizational framework of the state but the structurally entrenched antagonistic forces of the materially grounded societal reproductive metabolism are the real determinants that fatefully militate against the claimed Kantian solution that advocates a better organization in the political domain.

In all ages up to the present, the political reality of the state as such can be made intelligible only in terms of the historically established social metabolism in which the state is deeply embedded. This is why it cannot be stressed enough that the state and the given social metabolic order stand and fall together. Finding a historically sustainable solution to their antagonisms is *inconceivable* without the *eradication of the state itself from the antagonistic social metabolism,* on the one hand. And, of course, on the other hand, that means a conscious engagement in a sustained historic process of eradication of the state as such that must be organically combined *at the same time* with a *radical restructuring of the social metabolism itself* in a *non-antagonistic* way. These are the necessary constituents of an objectively structured and inseparable historical dialectic. Confronting the two vital constituents of this objective dialectic together is the only way to irretrievably consign to the past their *mutually reinforcing destructive vicious circle.*

Kant's optimistic characterization of the ability of the state itself to solve in its own terms of reference the identified contradictions is utterly uncritical of the state. In his arguments on these issues, we are always restricted to the political domain of the state itself, envisaging only its partial *organizational transformation* for the beneficial outcome postulated by the great German philosopher. The social metabolism of the established material reproductive order is never even remotely subjected to the required critical questioning. This is why Kant must assume in his commended explanatory framework both the *Providential teleology* and the corresponding beneficial *mechanism* of a most problematical conception of "nature" in order to be able to envisage the much-needed resolution of the destructive contradictions. Those two *quasi-miraculous forces*—one of them a *Providential agency* and the other its postulated *"natural mechanism"*—are expected to function in the desired way in his philosophy *in place of* the absolutely essential radical *critique of the state*.

The revealing Kantian representation of his commended vision of Providential "nature," in support of a state critically unexamined on its inextricable social metabolic ground, can be fully contrasted with the striking way in which Herodotus characterized, thousands of years before Kant, some painful social and political developments, including above all war itself, in terms of really existing nature. These were the words in which the great historian Herodotus of Halicarnassus ironically highlighted a fundamental change, manifest in the form of a *complete reversal* of the normal course of nature in human life through the eruption of war, with its far from welcome consequences: "In peacetime it is sons who bury their fathers—but in times of war, it is fathers who bury their sons. Somewhere in the heavens there is someone smiling at what has happened."[17]

Indeed, the striking contrast between the two conditions—one originally in evidence in human society and the other its *overturning* in one way or another, for one reason or another—could not be put better and more pointedly than it is done here by Herodotus. In his undisputable presentation of actual conditions of life and their utterly bewildering subversion the historian of ancient Greece powerfully puts into relief the divergent impact of peacetime and the time of war on the normal course of human affairs. Herodotus's way of depicting with subtle but sharp irony the contrast between the obvious course of nature regarding the life span of human beings and its complete overturning by war, can be rightfully considered to match the order of actually existing nature, in its perfectly straightforward reality, not travestied in any way by ideological vested interests. An order of nature represented, however, for a variety of weighty social and political reasons, in characteristically different, and indeed frequently in tendentiously biased fashion, with totally unjustifiable appeals to the authority of "nature," throughout several millennia of philosophical development; and in a most baffling way depicted even by some of the greatest philosophers.

LAW AND THE STATE AS SUPERIOR AND BEYOND CONTESTATION

Returning to the utopian state theories of Plato, recall here the way in which the dialogue *Critias* is interrupted in the middle of a sentence and becomes a fragment. These are the last words of the surviving fragment:

> Zeus, the god of gods, who *rules according to law,* and is able to see into such things [such as virtue and vice, righteousness and unrighteously exercised power, etc.], perceiving that an honourable race was in a woeful plight,[18] and wanting to inflict punishment on them, that they might be chastened and improve, collected all the gods into their most holy habitation, which being placed in the centre of the world, beholds all created things. And when he had called them together, he spake as follows.[19]

Thus, we are told that Zeus "rules according to law" but we never learn what the law-giving god of gods had to say to the assembled gods. Nevertheless, what is clear enough from the projects pursued by Plato in his so-called Late Period is that the seminal problems of the Law and the state were central to his concerns in this phase of his creative life. In that sense, it is perhaps not a coincidence or an insurmountable loss, that *Critias* is interrupted and becomes a fragment in the middle of a sentence precisely at the point at which Zeus is expected to address the gods in terms of the necessary Laws. For by far the longest dialogue of Plato's Late Period has for its title *The Laws,* to which we shall return in the next section of this chapter.

One of the rather neglected dialogues representing the last days of Socrates offers the reflections of the condemned Socrates on Law and Justice in his conversation with his friend Crito, whose name gives the title to this dialogue. The conversation in which Crito tries to persuade Socrates to save himself by escaping in disguise to Thessaly, immediately precedes the time when the philosopher, condemned to death, has to drink the fatal poison. Socrates firmly rejects his friend's request, with eloquent arguments about the full right of the Laws and the State to execute him even if the punishment is unjust, though in his view unjust not through the fault of the Laws but because of the groundless accusations levelled against him as a result of which he becomes *"a victim not of the laws but of men."*[20] The arguments of Socrates sustained by him in defense not of himself but of the Laws and the State are thoroughly significant to warrant a rather long quotation.

Plato in a dramatic way represents the Laws in this dialogue as directly addressing Socrates with their accusing fingers, and talking to him in this manner:

"Tell us, Socrates," they say, "what are you about? Are you not going by an act of yours to *overturn us—the laws and the whole state,* as far as in you lies? Do you imagine that a *state* can subsist and not be *overthrown,* in which the *decisions of law have no power,* but are set aside and trampled upon by individuals?' What will be our answer, Crito, to these and the like words?. . . [The Laws continue:] "And was that *our agreement* with you, or were you to *abide by the sentence of the state?* . . .

"Since you were brought into the world and *nourished and educated* by us, can you deny in the first place that you are *our child and slave, as your fathers were* before you? And if this is true you are *not on equal terms with us*; nor can you think that you have a *right* to do to us what we are doing to you. Would you have any right to strike or revile or do any other evil to your father or your master, if you had one, because you have been struck or reviled by him, or received some other evil at his hands?—you would not say this? And because we think right to destroy you, do you think that you have any right to destroy us in return, and *your country* as far as in you lies? Will you, O professor of true virtue, pretend that you are *justified* in this? Has a philosopher like you failed to discover that our country is more to be valued and *higher and holier* far than mother and father or any ancestor, and more to be regarded in the eyes of the gods and of men of understanding? Also to be soothed, and gently and reverently entreated when angry, even more than a father, and *either to be persuaded*, or if not persuaded, to be *obeyed?* . . . Consider, Socrates, if we are speaking truly, that in your present attempt you are going to do us an injury. For, having brought you into the world and nurtured and educated you, and given you and every citizen a share in every good which we had to give, we further proclaim to any Athenian by the *liberty which we allow* him, that if he does not like us when he has become of age and has seen the ways of the city, and made our acquaintance, he may *go where he pleases* and take his goods with him. None of us laws will forbid him or interfere with him. Any one who does not like us and the city, and who wants to *emigrate* to a colony or to any other city, may go where he likes, *retaining his property*. But he who has experience of the manner in which *we order justice* and *administer the state*, and still remains, has entered into an *implied contract* that he will do as we *command* him. And he who disobeys us is, as we maintain, *thrice wrong;* first because in disobeying us he is disobeying his parents; secondly, because we are the authors of his education; thirdly, because he has made an agreement with us that he will duly obey our commands; and he *neither obeys them nor convinces us* that our commands are *unjust;* and we do not rudely impose them, but give him the *alternative of obeying or convincing us;* —that is what we offer, and he does neither. . . . You,

Socrates, are *breaking the covenants and agreements* which you made with us at your leisure, not in any haste or under any compulsion or deception, but after you have had seventy years to think of them, during that time you were *at liberty to leave the city,* if we were not to your mind, or if our covenants appeared to you to be unfair. You had *your choice.*"[21]

It should be of no surprise to us, in the light of what we know about subsequent developments in European political philosophy, that Crito could find nothing to counter the Socratic discourse depicted with such dramatic force by Plato in the eloquent submission of the judgment of the proclaimed "threefold aggravated guilt" pronounced by the Laws against him. For the arguments expressed in this curious way by the condemned Socrates were reverberating in the same sense across ages of political theory, even if as a rule without any explicit reference to him. They were fully integrated into the philosophical conceptions of Hobbes and Locke on the extremely problematical commanding force of *"tacit consent"* which *by definition* condemned all those who tried to dissent—arguably well justified by some of the weightiest social and political reasons—from the judgment of the state and its Laws against them. Indeed, these and some related political doctrines were reaffirmed in the much later works of political philosophy that claim to justify the perhaps even more problematical "smiling face" of the Liberal Democratic political theorists on their own unacknowledged Leviathan state.[22] Naturally, Crito could not have an idea of any of that.

All the same, it is necessary to emphasize here that the views expressed by Socrates in the *Crito*, in his humble acceptance of the harsh accusations levelled against him by the Laws in the name of the *safety of the State* and its proclaimed *"justice,"* represent an *unreserved recantation* on his side, compared to the Socrates beautifully depicted in Plato's *Apology*, for instance, where he is represented as a falsely and unjustly accused and condemned martyr. And yet, it would be too hasty and totally unjust to consider this undeniably sharp contrast between the two images of Socrates—and perhaps much more than just a contrast; rather: a veritable contradiction—as simply a philosophical inconsistency on Plato's part.

To be sure, we are talking about a *real contradiction*. And again, much like in the earlier discussed Kantian claim about a wishfully and arbitrarily projected "nature," which had nothing to do with really existing nature—and, moreover, fundamentally for the same materially grounded reasons—it is not a contradiction *corrigible* within the Platonic conceptual framework, nor should it be considered as anything like a philosophical *inconsistency*. The heart of the matter is encapsulated in the paradoxically/contradictorily *absolving*, and at the same time readily *accusatory/self-accusatory* sentence according to which Socrates is "a victim not of the laws but of men," and therefore he must accept the guilty verdict and the death penalty by Law associated with such "guilt" once the State itself so *proclaims* the validity of its *"justice"* through its legal enactments and thereby *so commands*.

In this vision, the Laws and the State are *by definition* superior to all admissible contestation. This is why accepting the judgment of dissenting individuals—no matter how firmly and deeply their dissent might be *grounded* in its rationally defensible objective terms—must be defined as inadmissible, in pointed contrast to the absolutely unquestionable validity of the Law and "Justice" *as commanded* by the State and its *self-serving* Laws. For, as we are told by Plato in the passage quoted from *Crito*, "A state cannot subsist in which the decisions of law have no power, but are set aside and trampled upon by individuals." And to make matters worse, agreeing to be subservient to such Law and "Justice" carries with it the necessary consent to the absurd political principle that apologetically *counterposes men to the Law*, turning thereby the Law itself into a totally mysterious entity by asserting that the *victim* of such self-contradictory but peremptorily self-serving system—which claims rational self-evidence to its own legitimacy by definition—is *"a victim not of the Law but of men,"* as we have seen it proclaimed by Plato through the capitulating figure of his Socrates in *Crito*. This is accompanied by the assertion that Socrates "neither obeys [our commands], or convinces us that our commands are *unjust;* and we ... give him the *alternative of obeying or convincing us.*"²³ Though this is utterly *vacuous*, because the claimed "alternative" is no alternative at all. For it is the *state itself* that *decides* whether or not it is *"convinced"* of what is *just or unjust in the views of the people* who might challenge its proclaimed "justice" and Law, ruling on the matter in the interest of *its own commands*.

Accordingly, in terms of the total capitulation and recantation by the Platonic Socrates in *Crito*, we are already confined to the *short-circuited political domain*, thousands of years before Kant. For the *absolute taboo* of the materially constituted *class-antagonistic* social order and its state, misrepresented as "individuals trampling upon it"—and indeed in Plato's case a *slave-owning society*—cannot be subjected to any criticism. On the contrary, it must be idealized as not only "fiction" (in the words of Critias, with his reference to the Socratic tale of *The Republic*, as we saw it in *Timaeus)* but also when that fiction is "transferred to reality" through the even more fictitious/legendary tale of the heroically defeated island power of Atlantis "9,000 years earlier." It is most significant in this respect that the *slavery* operative in the materially grounded social metabolism of his society must be defended by Plato even with the dubious "weapons" of *philosophical inconsistency*. This is in most telling contrast to the sharp contradiction between the two images of Socrates, where Plato is *fully consistent* with his own *state-idealizing* conceptual framework. As Hegel rightly pointed out, "Plato in his *Republic* makes everything dependent on the Government and makes *Disposition* [an *ex animo acquiescence in the laws*, that is, a fully positive acceptance of the Laws by everyone] the principle of the State; on which account he lays the chief stress on Education."²⁴

The inconsistency arises, however, because *slavery as such* must be depicted in *positive terms* when it suits Plato. That is, when both the soon to be executed Socrates and everybody else *must accept* that they are the *slaves of the state*.²⁵ At the same time, in relation to actually existing and structurally determined class-antagonistic slavery, by a most telling contrast, the Platonic judgment must be pronounced in forcefully *negative terms*, as *inadmissible slavery*, when it suits Plato in the opposite sense. That is to say, when the defeat of a *state-enslaving design by a rival state* ("Mighty Atlantis")[26] must be hailed as the greatest heroism of legendary and forever idealized Ancient Athens. Accordingly, the *structurally entrenched class-antagonistic slavery* as the *necessary material ground* of the social metabolism—prevailing, of course, also in Athens contemporary to the time of Plato—cannot be subjected to any real criticism. Not even to *"implied* criticism," despite the fact that the legitimatory ground of "contractual agreement" in the service of the state (proclaimed ever since Plato and voiced by him as an accusation [made by the Laws] against the Socrates we see in *Crito*) is the concept of *"implied contract."* Also in this case, the state-apologetic philosophical rule on "implied guilt" and implied agreement, or for that matter on "tacit consent," is: "if it suits me, it stands, and if it does not suit me, you better forget it."

Most important, is the traditionally false definition of *"Sovereignty"* in class-antagonistic political theory, such that it is *positive* in its full approval of *defeating the external rival* that attempts to impose *slavery* of some kind upon a *state,* including the *nation-state* glorified as "the *absolute power* on earth" by Hegel,[27] while remaining *tendentiously ignorant* of the *internal class-antagonistic* slavery. Moreover, this is the case even though the total domination of the class of slaves is vital in the materially grounded metabolism of societal reproduction as well as in the domain of the Law and the State in Plato's Athens. Naturally, the issue itself goes well beyond Ancient Athens, since *under the rule of capital* it is metamorphosed into *wage slavery.* That is, into the most powerful form of slavery ever invented in the course of history. And indeed, the materially grounded and structurally entrenched class-antagonistic slavery represents the *necessary precondition* of successfully asserting *externally* viable state *"Sovereignty"* articulated against *rival states.* Inevitably, therefore, the overwhelming majority of the members of society in this sense are *excluded from Sovereignty.* In actuality, *Sovereignty,* contrary to all ideological mystification, must be usurped by the inevitably *belligerent State,* through its *personifications* constituting the authoritarian command structure of the ruling class as the necessary organ of *overall societal decision-making.* An authoritarian command structure is then enforced with the historically varying but *always hierarchically entrenched rules* of the self-perpetuating Law and its arbitrarily proclaimed self-justifying "Justice."

The philosophical inconsistency and self-contradiction of operating with a *double standard*—in Plato's case with his contradictorily positive and at the same time negative view of slavery itself, and everywhere else in class-apologetic social and political theory in a variety of different but structurally no less intertwined forms—is the reflection of the objective *social antagonism* that *must prevail* in the materially grounded *social metabolism*. Because such antagonism *must* objectively prevail in the elementary *social metabolism* of class society, it is for precisely that reason why it cannot be overcome simply within the *state-legitimated political domain*. Within that domain it is possible to identify some major problems, even without finding a *solution* to them. We have seen Plato pinpointing in an *admirably farsighted* way the absurd multiplication of legal statutes as a disease, evident also in our time in the ever denser *legal jungle* of our states, as mentioned in the preface to this book with reference to Plato's great insight. But the explanatory grounds of the identified contradictions in politics and the law remain hidden from him, because they *necessarily arise* from the effectively uncriticizable social metabolic ground itself. Thus, the possibility of actually superseding the denounced contradictions, including their manifestation in the ever-extended legal jungle, must be out of the question.

We have seen that Kant in a similar way had to confine his diagnosis and projected solution of the identified contradictions to the *short-circuited political domain,* proclaiming totally in vain as the remedy to the uncontrollability of the belligerent state the "better organisation of the state." But, as we know, the problem is much more ancient than the Kantian age. For we became locked into the *short-circuited antagonistic political circle* in the loftiest works of political philosophy in Plato's time, not very far from two and a half thousand years before Kant and Hegel. A circle which, of course, cannot be other than an insurmountable *vicious circle* within the confines of the unavoidable short-circuit that results from the untouchable self-serving class-antagonistic social metabolism. For the self-perpetuating state-apologetic Law and its unjustifiable *"Justice"* must be correspondingly constituted from time immemorial as the alienated organ of hierarchically entrenched overall decision-making on the basis of such material ground.

How desperately ironic it is, then, that the great philosophical martyr, Socrates, must end his life as a state-apologetic defender of oppressive "Justice," in total submission to the usurping Law, meekly accepting that he is "thrice guilty."[28] That must be the case because the alienated usurping short-circuit of the self-justifying political domain, in its embeddedness in the antagonistic material ground of societal reproduction, cannot be superseded without a radical critique and a fundamental practical restructuring of the social metabolic ground itself. This is the only way to transfer the alienated power of overall decision-making to the social body itself, where it truly belongs.

THE STATE AND THE PARABLE OF THE CAVE

In his much-admired metaphor of the cave, Plato attempts to combine the epistemological aspects of his theory with their ethical dimension, linking them organically to his vision of a far from egalitarian "human nature" corresponding to a fundamental metaphysical conception of the "soul." Indeed, his vision of the *ideal state* is meant to arise from the organic foundation of the deeply intertwined relationship of these constitutive parts.

For us, the best way to enter into the central core of this most influential ancient theory of the ideal state will be to start by reading Plato's own words on the meaning of his striking metaphor of the "cave" (or "den," as the Greek word can also be translated into English). The first person "I" is Socrates who tells the long tale to his friends; at this particular point to Glaucon who responds to him.

This is how Plato presents the cave in *The Republic*, in the reported conversation between Socrates and Glaucon:

> And now, I said, let me show in a figure how far our nature is enlightened or unenlightened: Behold! Human beings living in an underground den, which has a mouth open towards the light and

reaching all along the den; here they have been from their childhood, and have their legs and necks chained so that they cannot move, and can only see before them, being prevented by the chains from turning round their heads. Above and behind them a fire is blazing at a distance, and between the fire and the prisoners there is a raised way; and you will see, if you look, a low wall built along the way, like the screen which marionette players have in front of them, over which they show the puppets.

"I see."

And do you see, I said, men passing along the wall carrying all sorts of vessels, and statues and figures of animals made of wood and stone and various materials, which appear over the wall? Some of them are talking, others silent.

"You have shown me a strange image, and they are strange prisoners."

Like ourselves, I replied, and they see only their own shadows, or the shadows of one another, which the fire throws on the opposite wall of the cave?

"True," he said, "how could they see anything but the shadows if they were never allowed to move their heads?"

And of the objects which are being carried in like manner they would only see the shadows?

"Yes," he said.

And if they were able to converse with one another, would they not suppose that they were naming what was actually before them?

"Very true."

And suppose further that the prison had an echo which came from the other side, would they not be sure to fancy when one of the passers-by spoke that the voice which they heard came from the passing shadow?

"No question," he replied.

To them, I said, the truth would be literally nothing but the shadows of the images.

"That is certain."

And now look again, what will naturally follow if the prisoners are released and disabused of their error. At first, when any of them is liberated and compelled suddenly to stand up and turn his neck round and walk and look towards the light, he will suffer sharp pains; the glare will distress him, and he will be unable to see the realities of which in his former state he had seen the shadows; and then conceive someone saying to him, that what he saw before was *an illusion*, but that now, when he is approaching nearer to being and his eye is turned towards more real existence, he has a clearer vision—what will be his reply? And you may further imagine that his instructor is pointing to the objects as they pass and requiring him to name them—will he not be perplexed? Will he not fancy that the shadows which he formerly saw before are truer than the objects that are now shown to him?

"Far truer."

And if he is compelled to look straight at the light, will he not have a pain in his eyes which will make him turn away to take refuge in the objects of vision which he can see, and which he will conceive to be in reality clearer than the things which are now being shown to him?

"True," he said.

And suppose once more, that he is reluctantly dragged up a steep and rugged ascent, and held fast until he is forced into the presence of the sun himself, is he not likely to be pained and irritated? When he approaches the light his eyes will be dazzled and he will not be able to see anything at all of what are now called realities.

"Not all in a moment," he said. . . .

This entire allegory, I said, you may not append, dear Glaucon, to the previous argument; the prison-house is the world of sight, the light of fire is the sun, and you will not misapprehend me if you interpret the journey upwards to be the *ascent of the soul into the intellectual world* according to my poor belief, which, at your desire, I have expressed—whether rightly or wrongly God knows. But whether true or false, my opinion is that in the world of knowledge *the idea of good appears last of all*, and is seen only with an effort; and when seen, is also inferred to be the universal author of all things beautiful and right, parent of light and of the lord of light in this visible world, and the immediate source of reason and truth in the intellectual; and that this is the power upon which he who would act rationally either in public or private life must have his eye fixed.

"I agree," he said, "as far as I am able to understand you."

Moreover, I said, you must not wonder that those who attain to this beatific vision are unwilling to descend to human affairs; for their souls are ever hastening into the upper world where they desire to dwell; which desire of theirs is very natural if our allegory may be trusted.

"Yes, very natural."

And is there anything surprising in one who passes from divine contemplation to the evil state of man, misbehaving himself in a ridiculous manner; if, while his eyes are blinking and before he has become accustomed to the surrounding darkness, he is compelled to fight in courts of law, or in other places, about the images or the shadows of images of justice, and is endeavouring to meet the conceptions of those who have never seen absolute justice?

"Anything but surprising," he replied....

Our argument shows that the power and capacity of learning *exists in the soul already;* and that just as the eye was unable to turn from darkness to light without the whole body, so too the instrument of knowledge can only by the movement of the whole soul be turned *from the world of becoming into that of being,* and learn by degrees to endure the sight of being, and of the brightest and best of being, or in other words, of *the good.*

"Very true."[29]

In this way everything needed by Plato for the establishment of the ideal state is fully harmonizable, in terms of both theory of knowledge and ethics, grounded on the metaphysical order of the soul, because "the power and capacity of learning *exists in the soul already,*" as the allegory of the cave made the underlying difficult concepts graphically clear and comprehensible. The convincing allegory was needed because a few passages earlier Plato's talk about *"the power of the dialectic"*—through which real insight into the proper constitution of the ideal state, as expressed in *The Republic*—sounded prohibitively difficult. These are the crucial underlying concepts that had to be illuminated in Plato's view, referring to the assumptions and hypotheses of "geometry and arithmetics and kindred sciences" in the first place:

> And do you know also that although they make use of the visible forms and reason about them, they are thinking not of these, but of the *ideals* which they resemble; not of the figures which they draw, but of the *absolute square* and the *absolute diameter,* and so on—the *forms* which they draw or make, and which have *shadows and reflections in water of their own,* are converted by them into images, but they are really seeking to behold the *things themselves,* which can only be seen with the *eye of the mind?*
>
> "That is true."
>
> And of this kind I spoke as *the intelligible,* although in the search after it the soul is compelled to use hypotheses; not ascending to a *first principle,* because she is unable to rise above the region of hypotheses, but employing the objects of which the shadows below are *resemblances* in their turn as images, they having in relation to the shadows and reflections of them a greater distinctness, and therefore a higher value.
>
> "I understand," he said, "that you are speaking of the province of geometry and the sister arts."
>
> And when I speak of the other division of the intelligible, you will understand me to speak of that other sort of knowledge which *reason herself attains by the power of the dialectic,* using the hypotheses not as *first principles,* but only as hypotheses—that is to say, as steps and points of departure into a world which is *above hypotheses*, in order that she may soar beyond them to the *first principle of the whole;* and clinging to this and then to that which depends on this, by successive steps she descends again without the aid of any sensible object, *from ideas, through ideas, and in ideas she ends*.
>
> "I understand you," he replied, "not perfectly, for you seem to me to be describing a *task which is really tremendous,* but at any rate I understand you to say *that knowledge and being, which the science*

of dialectic contemplates, are clearer than the notions of the arts, as they are termed, which proceed from hypotheses only; these are also contemplated by the *understanding* and not by the *senses;* yet, because they start from hypotheses and do not ascend to a *principle,* those who contemplate them appear to you not to exercise the *higher reason* upon them, although when a *first principle* is added to them they are cognizable by the *higher reason.* And the habit which is concerned with geometry and the cognate sciences I suppose that you would term *understanding* and not *reason,* as being intermediate between *opinion and reason.*"

You have quite conceived my meaning, I said; and now, corresponding to these four divisions, let there be *four faculties* in the soul—*reason* answering to the highest, *understanding* to the second, *faith* or *conviction* to the third, and *perception of shadows* to the last—and let there be a *scale* of them, and let us suppose that the several faculties have *clearness* in the same degree that their objects have *truth.*

"I understand," he replied, "and give my assent, and accept your arrangement."[30]

Accordingly, in Plato's view everything required in terms of trustworthy knowledge and commanding values for the establishment of the ideal state—to be ruled by the *Philosopher King* who is assisted by the class of properly educated *Guardians* well versed in philosophy—is flawlessly integrated in this vision. For "the power and capacity of learning *exists in the soul already,*" and the Platonic *"science of the dialectic"* can provide access to the "intelligible world," and the things in themselves characterized as the *Forms,* in contrast to the customary reliance on deceptive appearances and shadowy illusions. Thus, the effective rulers of the state can grasp *"the first principles of the whole"* that make it viable to control the *parts.* In this orientation, of course, the combination of fully adequate knowledge and the corresponding value system, based on the insights yielded by the "power of the dialectic" in its drive "from becoming to being," perfectly in tune with the categories and faculties identified by Plato, is said to culminate in the ability "to endure the sight of being, and of the brightest and best of being, or in other words, of *the good.*"

The Platonic conception of the categories and faculties has been immensely influential in the course of philosophical development, from the time of Plato's equally influential direct pupil, Aristotle, all the way to the enthusiastic commentators on his work in our own time. Some of the greatest philosophers were deeply indebted to his categorial framework and views on the corresponding human faculties of knowledge, displaying their power at times in the most unexpected way. As Lukács highlighted it in one of his major works, "Hegel pours scorn in a number of places on Kant's 'soul-sack' in which the different 'faculties' (theoretical, practical, etc.) are lying and from which they have to be 'pulled out.'"[31] However, at times the Critic is guilty of the same "sin," which he negatively attributes to his adversary. Thus, Hegel does not hesitate to use his own "faculty soul-sack" when it suits him in the service of his extremely prejudiced rejection of *equality*. As quoted earlier in this chapter, he sharply condemns the advocacy of *social equality* by saying that its supporters argue from the standpoint of the *inferior faculty of the understanding,* instead of the *superior faculty of reason,* thereby violating both "natural inequality" (falsely claimed by Hegel), and the proper order of importance among the faculties of knowledge, and consequently advocating an abstract and totally inadmissible "ought-to-be."[32]

In the "middle period" of his life, approximately two and a half thousand years ago, Plato wrote by far the most influential of his works, of nearly three hundred large pages, *The Republic,* on the ideal state. But he did not stop there. For in the "late period" of his creative activity he had written an even more extensive, though far less influential book on the ideal State than *The Republic*, giving it the title: *The Laws*. Despite the great difference in the impact of these two massive works on the ideal State, some of the problems raised in *The Laws* are important enough for us to take a brief look in the final pages of this section.

In *The Laws*, Plato spelled out in minute detail the framework of the Law that should be adopted by law-makers in places where the state could not be ruled by a Philosopher King. The adoption of his own legal code was meant to be a practically workable approximation to the philosophically ideal system.[33] In relation to the constitutions of states known in his age Plato in *The Laws* was advocating a "compromise" between two fundamental types by insisting that *"a compromise between a monarchical and a democratic constitution is precisely the sort of compromise a constitution should always be."*[34]

His overwhelming concern was the *safety* of the state and its defense against being *subverted* and *overturned* under the historical conditions of great upheavals and wars all too dominant in his time. He was convinced that only a coherently articulated legal grounding that extends over all aspects of the state could remedy the encountered contradictions, enabling thereby the state *"to survive"* against internal and external challenges.[35]

This is how Plato stressed the absolute rigor required in order to be able to achieve that vital aim:

> The state is just like a ship at sea, which always needs someone to keep watch night and day: as it is steered through the waves of *international affairs*, it lives in *constant peril* of being captured by all sorts of *conspiracies*. Hence the need of an *unbroken chain of authority* right through the day and into the night and then on into the next day, guard relieving guard in endless succession.... [The members of the state's executive committee] must be particularly concerned with the *constant revolutions of all kinds* that are apt to occur in a state; if possible, they must *prevent* them, but failing that they must see that *the state gets to know* as soon as possible, so that the *outbreak* can be *cured*. That is why this executive committee has to be in charge of convening and dissolving not only statutory meetings but also those held in some *national emergency*.[36]

Moreover, in terms of securing the state *internally* against *quarrels, subversion, and overthrow*, he was stressing the need to guard against what he called *"indiscriminate equality,"*[37] in the name of his social-apologetically conceived idea of *"justice"* which was tellingly adopted by his great pupil Aristotle, as we shall see in the next chapter. Thus,

Plato was insisting that the quarrels which presented immense danger to the state were inevitably arising from such "indiscriminate equality" and must be forcefully rejected because *"complaisance and toleration. . . . are the enemies of strict justice."*[38]

One of the eternally debated problems in political theory concerns the difficulty to decide what is preferable: the rule of Men or the rule of Law itself? Plato's answer to an Athenian in *The Laws* was unhesitating:

> Such people are usually referred to as "rulers," and if I called them "servants of the laws" it is not because I want to mint a new expression but because I believe that the success or failure of a state hinges on this point more than on anything else. Where the law is subject to some *other authority* and has none of *its own*, the collapse of the state, in my view, is not far off; but if law is the master of the government and the government is its slave, then the situation is full of promise and men enjoy all the blessings that the gods shower on a state.[39]

Plato was most emphatic against *political subversion,* making it very clear that "we should treat as the biggest enemy of the entire state the man who makes the *laws into slaves,* and the state into the servant of a particular interest, by subjecting them to the *diktat* of mere men. This transgressor of the law uses *violence* in all that he does and stirs up *sedition....* Every man who is any good at all must *denounce the plotter* to the authorities and take him to court on a charge of violently and illicitly *overthrowing the constitution.* The court should consist of the same judges as for *robbers from temples,* and the procedure of the entire trial should be the same as it was for them, a majority vote being sufficient for the *death penalty.*"[40]

With regard to all these problems total respect had to be paid to what Plato called *"The Pantheon of the State,"* with its far-reaching and immensely severe implications. Thus, the grave offenses against it had to be punished with nothing less than the *death penalty.* One of the momentous instances underlined by him was the conscious violation of the rules laid down for the proper and the improper way of observing religious shrines. Plato insisted: "If a man is proved guilty of a serious act of impiety typical of an adult, and not just the peccadillo of a child, either by establishing a shrine on *private land* or by sacrificing on public *land* to gods not included in the pantheon of the state, *he must* be punished by death for sacrificing by impure hands."[41]

This was a matter of truly great relevance in Plato's age. As we know, in the 1840s Feuerbach's book on "the Holy Family" was in the forefront of the philosophical debates engaged in the critique of theology and society. Given the religions of Plato's time, such debate was inconceivable. However, the connection highlighted by Plato was of utmost significance, regarding the ties that had to be established and observed between the *state and the dominant religion*. A tie that became later vital to the states, as well as to the relevant churches, for *thousands of years*.

Plato's approach expressed in the last quotation was all the more important because in his time Greek religion was still rather distant from becoming *monotheistic,* that is, eminently suitable to provide the most powerful support for the state, including its ability to be imposed later, in Roman times, as the *compulsory state religion*. Nevertheless, Plato's rule about devotion to the *Pantheon of the State,* with its direct linkage to the most severe punishment by the state itself against the violation of the rules laid down in favor of that Pantheon, clearly pointed in that direction.

In Plato's time, in view of the great upheavals and turmoil, the crucial issue was the consolidation of the rival states. Everything in terms of law-giving and law-making had to be in the service of that overwhelmingly important requirement. The move in Greek Mythology—with its many gods who were among themselves actual or potentially quarrelling law-makers—to some kind of more orderly conception had to be accomplished sooner or later. Thus *"The Pantheon of the State"* had to be defined and regulated by the state's strictest laws in terms of the gods who can be rightfully included in the Pantheon of the State, in the interest of the necessary all-round stability. That is how the state-imperatives and the trend toward religious monotheism—with its powerful institutional articulation in the form of a dominant religion and its state-regulated rituals—acquired their common ground. The categorical rules pronounced by Plato in *The Laws* about *"The Pantheon of the State"* were most insightful about this unfolding development.

Finally, it is also a matter of considerable relevance that in *The Laws* Plato is emphatic about the power of theology for safeguarding the state. Accordingly, in his efforts to clarify in the final pages of this work the vital requirements to be considered when selecting the members of the ultimate guarantee for the state's untroubled survival, the *Nocturnal Council*, he insists that "one of the finest fields of knowledge is *theology*.... We must never choose as a Guardian of the laws anyone who is not preternaturally gifted or has not worked hard at theology, or allow him to be awarded distinctions for virtue.... No one who is unable to acquire these insights and rise above the level of the ordinary virtues will ever be good enough to *govern* an entire state, but only to *assist* government carried on by *others*."[42]

In this way, true philosophy was judged inseparable from theology according to Plato, and by no means only according to him. Indeed, many people might be astonished to learn that one of the greatest philosophers of all time who lived thousands of years later in Germany, between 1770 and 1831, Georg Wilhelm Friedrich Hegel, defined philosophy as *"rational theology."*[43] And, as we have seen it before, he repeatedly characterized historical development itself as *"Theodicaea, the justification of the ways of God."* [44]

CHAPTER SIXTEEN

Equality in the Broken Mirror of Justice: The Meaning of Aristotelian Politeia

One of the most fundamental questions of philosophy across the ages is the *evaluation and justification* of the relationship that prevails among particular human beings, together with the classes to which they belong, in terms of the historically constituted social hierarchy. The issue cannot be simply ignored because that would sharply contradict philosophy's necessary concern with, and claim to, *universal validity*. Yet, the *power relations* in society at large inevitably intervene in this matter. Not surprisingly, therefore, in a slave-owning society like Ancient Athens, it would be naive to expect the advocacy of *substantive equality* from the greatest philosophers. Indeed, in Plato's writings the judgment over this question assumes a shocking form, amounting to a dismal insult, when he declares that "even if you proclaim that a *master and his slave* shall have equal status, friendship between them is *inherently impossible*. The same applies to the relations between *an honest man and a scoundrel.*"[1]

From Aristotle we receive an even worse judgment. For a scoundrel is still a *human being*, no matter how grotesque Plato's identification of the masters/slaves relationship with that between honest men and scoundrels is, whereas the characterization of slaves by Aristotle deprives them of their humanity as well. For he treats slaves as nothing more than living pieces of property and tools. This is how he puts it:

> Tools may be animate as well as inanimate; for instance, a ship's captain uses a lifeless rudder, but a living man for watch.... So any piece of property can be regarded as a tool enabling a man to live, and his property is an assemblage of such tools; *a slave is a sort of living piece of property;* and like any other servant is *a tool in charge of other tools.*[2]

And, of course, Aristotle decrees both masters and slaves to be *justifiably* made masters and slaves by *nature itself*. He asserts: "The element that can use its *intelligence* to look ahead is *by nature ruler* and *by nature master*, while that which has the *bodily strength* to do the *actual work* is *by nature a slave,* one of those who are *ruled*. Thus there is a *common interest uniting master and slave*."[3] In this way, to make matters even more astounding, after denying intelligence to the slave and granting him only bodily strength for "doing the actual work"— as if the slave's ongoing multifaceted tasks could be accomplished without the burdensome and constantly challenging intelligence inseparable from the realization of those tasks—the *"common interest"* declared here by Aristotle is between the ruling *human master* and his—thanks to the established power relations of society appropriated and dominated—*"living piece of tool."* This is indeed an utterly peculiar conception of "common interest." It reveals a perversely transfigured *class interest* that we find throughout history camouflaged even in the writings of some of the greatest philosophers, not only Aristotle but also Hegel.

Accordingly, as we can see, the painfully difficult problem of *inequality* versus *equality* enters the horizon of philosophy in Ancient Greece, and *immediately* finds its social-apologetic justification there. The proclaimed philosophical *"rationality"* offers—in complete conformity with the structurally determined great power relations with their deeply entrenched conditions of inequality—only the *ideological rationalization* of the established order.

This is, in fact, a very difficult issue on account of its given or potential resonance among the great masses of the people. The recurrent concern with equality cannot be dismissed as irrelevant because of the far too obvious connection between *equality and justice*. Indeed, as we find in the history of political philosophy, the connection between equality and justice is at times even admitted to exist by the debating philosophers. However, in view of its highly complex and thorny character it requires considerable philosophical ingenuity to come to terms with the connection between equality and justice by way of both acknowledging and spiriting it away more or less at the same time, and for countless centuries to come, including our present time.[4]

The way in which this ideological rationalization is paradigmatically accomplished by Plato and Aristotle takes the form of firmly asserting that *inequality is really justifiable equality,* because "indiscriminate equality for all amounts to *in*equality," as Plato had put it in *The Laws,* threading the pathway to be followed by his great pupil Aristotle.[5] As a result, by taking notice of the undeniable connection between equality and justice, and at the same time spiriting it away by turning the rationally sustainable value-determinations upside down, philosophy succeeds in its own domain in "rationally" *justifying the unjustifiable.*

Aristotle's words are most revealing in this respect. This is how he argues his case:

> Thus it is thought that *justice is equality;* and so it is, but not for all persons, only for those that are *equal. Inequality* is also thought to be *just;* and so it is, but not for all, only for the *unequal.* We make bad mistakes if we neglect this *"for whom"* when we are deciding what is *just....* So, as justice is relative to people, and applies in the same ratio to the things and to the persons (as pointed out in my Ethics),[6] these disputants, while agreeing as to equality of the thing, disagree about the *persons for whom,* and this chiefly for the reason already stated, that they are judging their own case, and therefore badly.[7]

The most problematical aspect of this way of arguing is that by highlighting the notion of *particular persons* "for whom" equality or inequality should be correctly considered justifiable equality or inequality, makes the real *power relations* that dominate the established societal order completely disappear.[8] Aristotle's definition of the slave as a "living piece of property and tool"—and moreover as property *justly possessed* by the master and ruler—avoids the vital question of how such property is actually *acquired* on the one side and totally denied on its opposite side, all in unquestionable conformity to the requirements of "equality and justice for the unequal." In place of indicating the contradictory *acquisition/expropriation/ retention* of property on the ground of the prevailing power relations, we are offered by Aristotle the arbitrarily decreed class-mythology of the pretended *"master and ruler by nature"* and its fitting counterpart of the *"slave by nature,"* who is therefore said to be ruled fully in accordance with *nature*. And even this is far from being enough. Another piece of class-mythology must be added to it, and of course we receive it from Aristotle through his revealing postulate of the *"common interest"* between the ruling master and the ruled slave.[9]

Thus, the real or potential social antagonisms cannot be acknowledged at all because the full consonance of equality and inequality with pretendedly nature-determined justice must be taken for granted in the name of *the good of everyone* in the whole of society. Aristotle cannot help acknowledging that circumstance even explicitly, in the interest of *ideological justification,* by acknowledging that the notion of "common interest" is meaningful *"insofar"* as the relationship among the people "contributes to the *good life of each. The good life is indeed their chief end both communally and individually.*"[10] But at that point the *ideological mystification* must also enter, so as to justify the really existent *gruesome inequality* between master and slave in terms of which the claimed "good life" on the side of the slave means only *mere survival,* and even that *primarily* for the purpose of the master's continued domination, as Aristotle has to concede it. For, in his own words, "although the *natural slave* and the *natural master* really have the *same interest,* rule of master over slave is exercised *primarily* for the *benefit of the master* and only *incidentally* for the benefit of the slave, because if the slave deteriorates the master's rule over him is inevitably impaired."[11]

Accordingly, though earlier the natural purpose of constituting the state was "for the *good life of each,*" applicable to them as *"their chief end both communally and individually,"* now it must be altered to the ideologically rationalizing dictum of "for the sake of *life itself.*"[12] This is why and how the social-apologetically used concept of *"justice"* must come to the forefront and *overrule* the claims to real *equality*, in the interest of proclaiming that the structurally entrenched *inequality* all too obvious in the constitution of the state should be considered the *veritable equality*. The nature of "good" as such therefore must be *redefined* in relation to the state from "for the good of each" to stand for the pretended "justice." Indeed, we can read on another page of Aristotle's *Politeia: "In the state the good is justice."*[13]

JUSTICE IN PLATO AND ARISTOTLE AS THE LIQUIDATION OF THE IDEA OF HUMAN EQUALITY

Understandably, in Plato's philosophy we find the same approach to equality and justice. In the utopian state project detailed in *The Laws*—despite the advocacy of strict hierarchy and unquestionable slavery—Plato's claim to *"proper equality"* is maintained, so as to *legitimate* the acclaimed state for its *universalizable ideality*. In this sense Plato insists that proper equality is

> to grant *much* to the great and *less* to the less great, adjusting what you give to take account of the real nature of each.... We maintain, in fact, that *statesmanship* consists of essentially this—*strict justice*. This is what we should be aiming at now, Cleinias: this is the kind of *"equality"* we should concentrate on as we bring our state into the world. The founder of any other state should also concentrate on this same goal when he frames his laws, and take no notice of a bunch of dictators, or a single one, or even the power of the people. He must always make *justice* his aim, and this is precisely as we have described it: it consists of *granting the "equality" that unequals deserve to get.*[14]

In this way, by defining "equality for the equals" and "inequality for the unequals" through the pretended "justice" to be *aimed at* (without indicating the crucial criteria of its feasible realization) as the claimed and *by definition justified measure*—naturally in the service of the socially well entrenched *inequality*—we end up with a *colossal self-serving circularity* visible in philosophical judgments over equality and justice to our own days. In Plato, the underlying social-apologetic purpose can be successfully accomplished because the adopted concept of "justice" can be conveniently twisted and turned around in tune with even the most iniquitous requirements. For "justice" is *decreed* to be the *ultimate measure* itself and therefore in no need of an ascertainable measure to sustain it. And this is possible because the concept of "justice" in such discourse can be used without any *substantive* qualifications, as it is indeed used also at the historical climax of such philosophical developments, in bourgeois conceptions of political philosophy and jurisprudence, by insisting—as we have seen it in Kant's conception, for instance—that the law "concerns *the form and not the matter of the object* regarding which I may possess a right."[15] Thus, thanks to the missing requirement of substantive qualifications, the declamatory *"strict justice"* postulated by Plato in actuality amounts to be the total *negation of justice* as well as to the arbitrary and a prioristic *legitimation of injustice*.

As the groundlessly proclaimed semblance of something that is supposed to sustain justice, we are offered by Plato the wishful requirement that the statesman's judgment *should be* made by "taking account of the *real nature of each*" of the people involved in the affected cases.[16] But even such a wishful requirement, envisaging the viability of the law in the projected ideal state, is bound to remain only a self-serving facade justifying the unjustifiable. For the *"real nature* of each" is invariably what suits the maintenance and continuing domination of the structurally well entrenched iniquitous social order—*class slavery*—in the name of nothing less challengeable than *"nature itself."* This is the absolutely necessary *social premise* on the basis of which the statesman's judgment must be made and unquestioningly legitimated according to Plato. For the declared "real nature" as the justifier of slavery is supposed to be the *self-evidently final authority* in these matters. The same is true of Aristotelian discourse in which both the masters and their slaves are declared to be masters and slaves *by nature* and therefore justifiably *the ruling and the ruled by nature* in explicitly stated terms, as we have seen above. Consequently, the possibility of *human equality* for Aristotle is totally out of the question. And that view must be claimed by him to be in full conformity to the requirements of *"justice."* Thus the role of "justice" in Aristotelian discourse, much like in the Platonic conception, is the socially prejudged *liquidation of the idea of equality,* combined with the claimed *self-evidency* of such judgment in its appeal—on the groundlessly asserted claim of the ruling order and its ideological rationalizations—to the ultimate authority of nature itself in this matter.

The Aristotelian clause of *"for whom"* added to evaluating and justifying equality and inequality in terms of the admissible *persons* as being one (equal) or the other (unequal) as particular persons, ignoring their actual belonging to the structurally dominant (or not) *social classes*, is the hammer used to break the mirror to pieces in which the nature of *equality*—now transfigured into "justly" unalterable *inequality*—must be fragmentarily reflected. This is how we end up with equality offered to us in a fatefully distorted form in the necessarily broken mirror of incontrovertibly class-determined "justice." To put it in other words, when equality in fundamental social matters is proclaimed to be *by nature* impossible (remember Plato's "scoundrel" and Aristotle's "living tool"), *justice must suffer its consequences.* Accordingly, the role of *"justice"* becomes the *categorical denial of justice.* And, of course, nothing can be a more fundamental social matter than the structurally entrenched and safeguarded division of society into antagonistic classes, appearing in actual history in the form of *masters and slaves.*

However, as we have seen earlier, in the work of the outstanding English philosopher Thomas Hobbes, the authority of nature is advocated in the diametrically *opposite* sense. In his view, human beings are said to be *equal in terms of nature itself* and therefore the *legitimacy* of the established political order must be considered on very different ground. Thus, it should come as no surprise to us that Thomas Hobbes submits Aristotle's philosophy to the sharpest criticism in his *Leviathan.*

What is directly relevant to us at this point is the assertion by Aristotle that

> those of *noble birth* or who are *free* or have *wealth* are *quite right* [fully justified] to lay *claim to honours*, since the members of the state must be *free* and must have *taxable* property *(you could no more make a state out of paupers than out of slaves)*. But obviously something more is needed besides: I mean *justice*, and the virtue that is proper to citizens. For without these additions it is not possible for the state to be managed. More exactly, whereas without free population and wealth there cannot be a state at all, without justice and virtue it cannot be *managed well*.[17]

What is questionable in this analysis is the Aristotelian treatment of pairing the "pauper" (or "the needy" in another translation) with the *slave* as the *justification* of the advocated state. Pairing them with each other can only be a tendentiously prejudged false analogy. For in referring to the pauper and the needy we are talking about *relative degrees* of socio-historical specificity, and possibly of the all-round prevailing hardship imposed on society as a whole by the extremely harsh conditions of really existent nature,[18] and not by the fictitiously stipulated self-justifying Platonic or Aristotelian social-apologetic concept of "nature." Thus, under such conditions it is not only *possible* but indeed *unavoidable* to "make a state out of paupers" and the needy.

This case is *categorically* different when talking about the slaves. For the concept of the slave—also in its Aristotelian usage—necessarily involves its ruling master, or whatever else might be the structurally dominating force over the specific type of the slave, as it prevails elsewhere, for instance in the form of "wage-slavery" under the *rule of capital*. It makes no sense at all to envisage the society of the slaves *in and by itself*. And in that sense Aristotle is absolutely right in claiming that you could not make a state out of slaves alone. But he uses the *false analogy* of pairing the slave with the pauper and the needy *precisely* in order to be able to proclaim on that ground the self-evident necessity of the slave's conceptually unavoidable counterpart in the established society, *the ruling master*. Further—thanks again to the same false analogy between the slave and the pauper—what makes plausible the legitimacy of the pauper's and the needy's counterpart everywhere is the state's domination over societal decision-making in tune with Aristotelian "justice": that is, the *noble* and the *rich* and *wealthy*.

In Plato's philosophy we find four fundamental virtues: *"courage, restraint* [or temperance/moderation], *justice and wisdom."*[19] One of the four of them—justice—seems to be the odd one out. The other three can stand confined to individual actions and characteristics, or refer to particular individuals confronting for instance extreme circumstances in their struggle with the harsh adversity of nature. By contrast, justice is an *inherently social determination* when it designates the actions of particular individuals. In that sense justice can be considered a subclass of *wisdom* in the relevant domain, that is, when talking about its role in shaping society and its historically constituted state formations in conformity to the fundamental requirements of commendable practical wisdom.

What we find in the major qualification made by Aristotle in the last quotation is indeed alignable to the sense of justice as *wisely pursued practical judgment,* when he says that without justice and virtue the state cannot be *managed well,*[20] even if it can be somehow established in the first place, and therefore, arguably, in that very different sense managed, although badly. But, of course, that qualification is no guarantee that those who are aware of the difference in general terms between managing the state and managing it well will be disposed to advocate the *socially commendable implications* of state management. Far from it. The vested interests of *antagonistic class domination,* like the privileges obtained in a slave-owning society, tend to push even the greatest thinkers in the opposite direction, as we know from past history.

ARISTOTLE AND THE POLITICAL ANIMAL

Aristotle famously declared in his reflections on the purpose of human association that the state exists by nature. These were his words on the subject:

The *final association*, formed of several villages, is the state. For all practical purposes the process is now complete; *self-sufficiency* has been reached, and while the state came about as a means of securing life itself, it continues in being to secure the *good life*. Therefore *every state exists by nature,* as the *earlier associations* too were *natural*.... Moreover the *aim and the end* is perfection; and self-sufficiency is both an end and perfection.[21]

And this is how his most enduring reflections on the state continue:

It follows that the state belongs to the class of objects which exist by *nature*, and *man is by nature a political animal*. Any one who by his nature and not simply by ill-luck has no state is either *too bad* or *too good*, either *subhuman* or *superhuman*.[22]

Thus the Aristotelian profound insight firmly underlines the inherently *social character* of the human being as a *zoon politicon* [political animal] who must be living *in association* with other human beings, stressing this condition as an insuperable determination of nature. In that sense, the concept of "nature" is not arbitrarily posited by Aristotle because he both refers to the zoon politicon's nature-established connection with the *animal world* and at the same time contrasts the human form of associated life with that of the *bees* and with what he calls the other *"gregarious animals."*[23] He highlights the specificity of human beings as their ability to communicate among themselves with *speech* that enables them to differentiate between "what is *useful* and what is *harmful*, and so also what is *just* and *unjust*.... It is the *sharing* of a *common view* in these matters that makes a household and a state."[24]

However, what is utterly problematical at this point is the Aristotelian assertion that "the *sharing* of a *common view*" can be equally applied to the *household* and the *state*. A shared common view is in truth meaningfully applicable to the household, in terms of the genuine *shared interests* of the household's members, but it is most questionable about the state. In the really existing state that is constituted on the ground of antagonistic social classes the Aristotelian claim is not true. For in the case of the historically constituted state—not only because of its immensely greater complexity and ramifications compared to the household but also in view of the fact that according to even Aristotle the slave's "common interest" with the master's interests is only "life itself" as nothing more than his *"mere survival,"* and not the totally different *"good life"* of his master.[25] Thus it is arbitrary to talk about *"sharing* a *common view"* in the *state as a whole* where we find *diametrically opposed class-interests* that should be "well managed" by the state as the overall command structure of society, with its full authority/sovereignty (again in Aristotle's words) to take on board or to completely overrule/reject the views of its subjects. Most tellingly, Aristotle likes to talk about the more "flexible" and much more easily "stretchable" as well as quite readily assumed and postulated term of *"common* interest" rather than the potentially much more relevant concept of *"shared* interest."

Once, however, the state's conformity to nature is stipulated on the ground of the declared nature-based analogy of the household and the state, it is easy to assert the corresponding unquestionably happy relationship between justice and the state. Accordingly, we can read in Aristotle's *Politeia* at the end of the section that discusses the relationship between the state and the individual: "The virtue of justice is a feature of a state; for justice is the arrangement of the political association, and a sense of justice decides what is just."[26]

Thus, the most problematical aspects of managing the (unacknowledged) inherent antagonisms of class society through the claimed "justice" of its antagonistic state formation are brought into "well-managed" harmony by Aristotle, thanks to the state's wishfully declared conformity to "nature" by a questionable analogy with the "natural household," under the proclaimed all-round *beneficial*—encompassing "unequal equality"—proper ruling organ of the state. The necessary and successful working presence of virtue and justice in the state is in no way established by Aristotle. It is simply asserted to be a "feature of the state" on the basis of another unestablished assertion, according to which "justice is the arrangement of the political association," coupled with the conveniently declared claim that "a sense of justice decides what is just," when in reality it is the state itself that decides through its enforced legal and judiciary system what it considers justifiable or not.

In this way, even the limited truth of some natural characteristics encountered in the household—like the male members' higher brute physical force in comparison to the average strength of women—is tendentiously distorted by Aristotle, in the spirit of the same social-apologetic interests of hierarchical domination, when he eagerly metamorphoses relative physical strength into absolutely unalterable social and human superiority by writing that "as between *male and female*, the former is *by nature superior and ruler*, the latter *inferior and subject*. And this must hold good of *mankind in general*."[27]

Under the conditions of subsequent historical development not less torn by class antagonisms than ancient Greece, the Aristotelian characterization of the claimed "natural" order and hierarchy is echoed directly or indirectly. Also, Christianity for a very long time embraces it in its own way. Thus, for instance, the outstanding theologian/philosopher St. Augustine talks about the necessity of authority and obedience in this way:

> St. Paul says that: "If any does not take care of his own, and especially of his own household, he has denied the faith and is worse than an unbeliever." From this care arises that peace of the home which lies in the harmonious interplay of *authority and obedience* among those who live there. For, those who have the care of the others give the orders—*a man to his wife, parents to their children, masters to their servants*. And those who are cared for must obey—*wives their husbands, children their parents, servants their masters*.[28]

And that is by no means the end of the story. For, as we have seen earlier, many centuries after St. Augustine in the Kantian philosophy we find the same advocacy of unjustifiable authority and inequality when Kant writes that "the one who is dependent must obey the other as a *child obeys his parents or the wife her husband*."[29] And later in the same work Immanuel Kant goes as far as to deny even the possibility of conceding the right to vote to women as much as to children.[30]

To be sure, Aristotle has no inclination to construct utopian state conceptions of the Platonic type, like *The Republic* and *The Laws*. For a variety of well-grounded reasons, including his passionate involvement in some fields of experimentally sustained natural science, especially zoology, Aristotle likes to keep his feet more firmly on the ground.[31] Nonetheless, what Aristotle considers the positive and fully realizable—and indeed more than that, the *one and only* long-term sustainable—determinations that must be instituted by any ruler who wishes to manage a state well, are thoroughly utopian in character. They are utopian even if in a very different way from Plato's characterization of the ideal states, as we shall see in the final pages of this chapter.

However, before discussing that problem, it is important to mention a couple of major concerns put into relief by Aristotle on the relationship between the state and the individual. First, his insistence that "it is preferable that *law should rule* rather than any single one of the citizens. And following this same line of reasoning further, we must add that even if it is better that *certain persons* rule, these persons should be appointed as *guardians* of the laws and as *their servants*.... Therefore he who asks law to rule is asking *God and intelligence* and no others to rule; while he who asks for the rule of a human being is importing a *wild beast* too; for *desire* is like a wild beast, and *anger perverts rulers* and the very best of men. Hence *law is intelligence without appetition.*"[32] In this sense, rule by the law itself without being subverted by desire and passion could hardly be advocated with greater devotion than it is done here by Aristotle.

The other Aristotelian concern is also crucially important. The practical considerations about it are turned by Aristotle from their immediate connection with the state and the household into a fundamental orienting principle of dialectical thinking in general, with its far-reaching social-ontological as well as methodological significance.

This is how that concern is spelled out by Aristotle in his *Politeia* in the context of his ground-breaking assessment of the defining characteristics of the zoon politicon and the overall structural determinations of the unique association inseparable from such zoon politicon:

The state has a *natural priority* over the household and over *any individual* among us. For *the whole* must be *prior to the part*. Separate hand or foot from the whole body, and they will no longer be hand or foot except in name, as one might speak of a "hand" or "foot" sculptured in stone. That will be the condition of the spoilt hand, which no longer has the *capacity and the function* which define it.... It is clear then that the state is both natural and prior to the individual. For if an individual is not *fully self-sufficient* after separation, he will stand in the same relationship to the *whole* as the *parts* in the other case do. Whatever is incapable of *participating in the association* which we call the state, a dumb animal for example, and equally whatever is perfectly self-sufficient and has no need to (e.g. a god), is not part of the state at all.[33]

This Aristotelian elucidation of the seminally important relationship between the *whole* and its *parts* would represent a tremendous dialectical insight for any age, let alone for being made two and a half thousand years before our time. We had to wait for a very long time to find any philosopher able to match it at the turn from the eighteenth to the nineteenth century. For the way in which Aristotle grasps this crucial relationship between the whole and its parts, the sharp conceptual-dialectical analysis, with its decisive methodological relevance encountered in philosophy ever since Plato, is inseparably combined with throwing the necessary light on the fundamental *substantive aspects* of the issues at stake. In the work of the great German dialectical thinker Georg Wilhelm Friedrich Hegel, we witness the conscious attempt to do the same in his major works of synthesis. Indeed, Hegel is directly indebted to Aristotle in that respect, including the centrality assigned by him to the substantively as well as methodologically critical relationship between the whole and its parts in all analyzed domains.

ARISTOTLE'S BROKEN MIRROR

Now we can turn to Aristotle's far from Platonic utopia. As a quick anticipation, it can be summed up as the Aristotelian *idealization of the middle condition.* But no one should imagine that this is as simple and straightforward as it sounds. When stressing the utopian character of some major Aristotelian ideas, it should be immediately added that not only have they been very influential in history but also that they are almost prohibitively multifaceted, extending over many domains of human life with the strict evaluational rigor stressed by their originator.

In terms of the far-reaching influence of Aristotle on account of the idealization of the middle condition, we need not do more for the moment than to remind ourselves of the most radical eighteenth-century theory of Rousseau in favor of the middle condition. However, it is necessary to go into much greater detail about the multifaceted reasoning of Aristotelian utopia, which is concerned with the question of how to organize the zoon politicon's unique association in such a way as to make it best suited to the requirements of both the parts and the whole, that is, both to the particular individuals and to their state.

We can start in this respect by quoting a point made by Aristotle with direct reference to his own *Nicomachean Ethics*.[34] It reads as follows:

> If we were right when in our *Ethics* we stated that virtue is a *mean*, and that the happy life is a life without hindrance in its accordance with virtue, then *the best life must be the middle life* consisting in a mean which is open to every man of every kind to attain. And the same principle must be applicable to the *virtue or badness of constitutions and states*. For the constitution of a state is in a sense the way it lives. In all states there are three state-sections: the very well-off, the very badly off, and thirdly those in between. Since therefore it is agreed that *moderation* and a *middle position are best,* it is clear that, in the matter of the goods of fortune also, *to own a middle amount is the best of all.* This condition is most easily *obedient to reason*, and following *reason* is just what is difficult both for the *exceedingly* rich, handsome, strong and well-born, and for the *opposites*, the extremely poor, the weak, and those grossly deprived of honour. The former incline more to arrogance and crime on a large scale, the latter are more than averagely prone to wicked ways and petty crime.[35]

Thus the middle condition, in sharp opposition to all extremes, is forcefully recommended as the most appropriate for the fulfillment of *virtue* and at the same time as being fully in tune with *reason itself,* both regarding the individuals and the state as a whole. And Aristotle continues his analysis in the same spirit by adding that "It is clear both that the best partnership in a state is the one which operates through the *middle people,* and also that those states in which the *middle element is large,* and *stronger if possible than the other two together,* or at any rate stronger than either of them alone, have every chance of having a well-run constitution."[36]

Aristotle's enthusiasm for the constitution oriented toward the middle people is so great that he even proclaims, quite unrealistically, that it is bound to result in a social-political order free from factions. This is how he puts it: "The superiority of the middle constitution is clear also from the fact that it alone is free from factions. Where the *middle element* is large, there least of all arise factions and divisions among the citizens. And big states are freer from faction, for this same reason, namely that their middle element is large.... An indication of the truth of what we have been saying is to be found in the fact that the *best lawgivers* have come from the *middle citizens*—Solon, for example, whose middle position is revealed in his poems, and Lycurgus, who was not a king, and Charondas and most of the rest."[37]

Naturally, in tune with his enthusiasm for the middle condition, Aristotle argues that *"at all times* the legislator ought to endeavor to include the *middle people* in the constitution."[38] Indeed, he does not hesitate to insist that both the *oligarchic* and the *democratic* legislator should do that. For "if he is framing laws that are oligarchical in character, he should have the middle people always in view; if democratic, he should again make them attractive to those in the middle.... The better mixed a constitution is, the longer it will last."[39] Aristotle also confesses his relative preference for democracy over oligarchy on the ground of its greater proximity to the constitution of the middle people, while declaring the latter the safest of them all with these words: "A constitution of the middle people is nearer to democracy than is a constitution of the few, and is of all such constitutions the safest."[40]

Aristotle is well aware of the troubles that can and do arise from extreme forms of inequality, again in tune with his preference for the middle condition, corresponding to the same spirit in which he earlier stressed that "to *own a middle amount* is the best of all." In another context he recommends the same rule even more forcefully by saying, "Exceptional prosperity in one section of the state is to be guarded against. . . . An endeavor should be made either to *merge* the poor population with the rich or to *augment the middle;* this *dissolves the factions* that are due to the inequality."[41] In the same way, when talking about the requirement of *"constitutional safeguards,"* Aristotle lays great stress on what he calls *"the principle of the middle way."*[42]

Unfortunately, Aristotle can also be trapped into a laughable corner on account of allowing himself to be carried away by his enthusiasm for the middle condition. This is well illustrated by the sharp contrast he arbitrarily makes between the Asiatic and the Hellenic nations. It is hard to believe our eyes when we see an assertion made by Aristotle in this respect. The passage in question reads like this: "The Asiatic nations have in their souls both intellect and skill, but are lacking in spirit; so they remain *enslaved and subject*. The *Hellenic race,* occupying a *mid-position geographically,* has a measure of both, being both spirited and intelligent. Hence it continues to be free, to live under the best constitutions, and given a single constitution, to be *capable of ruling all other people.*"[43] This is as bad as the quotation by Hegel, seen above, in which he decreed that the Chinese people will one day be necessarily subjected to rule by the *Germanic state*. Indeed, it would come as no surprise to learn that Hegel derived his direct inspiration for that groundless idea from what we have seen in our last quotation from Aristotle—as he was certainly in the deepest sense inspired by Aristotelian philosophy for some of his own pathbreaking conceptions.

To be sure, advocating preference for the middle condition is well understandable in that it represents the rejection of extremes in a form that seems to be on the face of it more practicable than any alternative to it, like the immediate adoption of *substantive equality,* for instance. But being *"more practicable"* does not make the advocated "middle condition" *practicable* at all, in the same sense in which claiming to be *"more equitable"* is indeed very far from being *truly equitable* at all. And this is not simply a question of social radicalism. Even a giant radical thinker like Rousseau had to be deeply disappointed on the same score. For, as we have seen in chapter 1, Rousseau passionately argued: "Under bad governments equality is only apparent and illusory; it serves only to keep the pauper in his poverty and the rich man in the position he has usurped. In fact, laws are always of use to those who possess and harmful to those who have nothing: from which it follows that the social state is advantageous to men only when *all have something and none too much*."[44] The necessary failure in such advocacy of the middle condition was due not only to the inherent difficulty in defining the magnitude of Rousseau's *"something"* and also his *"not too much"* but above all to the illusory character of expecting a viable solution from some change in the *distribution* of the social products without radically altering their mode of *production*. For the structurally entrenched and dominant mode of production and societal reproduction is always bound to operate in its own favor. And that is a common feature of the advocated and idealized "middle condition" both in Rousseau and in Aristotle. No wonder, then, that despite its repeated championing even by some outstanding thinkers we are as far from its projected all-round realization as countless centuries ago.

In the Aristotelian utopia everything appeared to be able firmly to support the idealized middle condition. For a start, it was commended by Aristotle on the ground that it was built on the mean/middle/moderate *virtue* itself. And that condition was *eo ipso* bringing with it for the particular individuals who shared the middle condition *"happy life without hindrance."* For the grounding of their *"state-section"* on virtue was said to harmonize fully with *reason itself*, in the sense of reason being properly *obeyed by them* due to the absence of the temptations wedded to the extremes. Moreover, the same principles were said to apply over the corresponding middle constitution, and happily indeed because "the constitution of a state is in a sense *the way it lives*."

However, saying all that and calling the social classes *"state-sections"* whose contradictions can be overcome within the political domain of the idealized constitutional framework was too much to expect. Thus, inevitably, the Aristotelian utopia projecting the realization of the zoon politicon's idealized and constitutionally secured "middle condition" had to remain a world of utopia.

As to the Aristotelian broken mirror, it is *inconceivable* to put the fractured pieces together. To be sure, using *justice* as the decreed measure of *equality* had to be an *absolute premise* for Plato and Aristotle. That was their only way to proclaim *justifiable* in the name of misrepresented *nature* the gruesome inequality of slave-owning society. In reality, it is the other way around. For the appropriate measure of *justice itself* can only be *substantive equality* on all fundamental issues of the state, not least its antagonistic social metabolic foundation necessarily unacknowledged by Plato and Aristotle.

CHAPTER SEVENTEEN

Primitive Accumulation of Capital and the World of More's Utopia

Sir Thomas More, knighted by King Henry VIII in 1514, died as a martyr for his faith because he refused to acknowledge the *supremacy* of the King over the Church proclaimed by an Act of Parliament in 1534, and therefore was condemned, guilty of "High Treason." Since 1935—the fourth centenary of his execution on the order of the same King Henry who once highly favored him—Sir Thomas More is revered as a saint of the Roman Catholic Church.

Yet, in his final years More confessed his own feelings of guilt and remorse for ordering on behalf of the state the most severe punishment of people judged to be holding the wrong religious beliefs. Such "guilty people" were condemned through Sir Thomas More's authoritarian judicial power by the same state that executed him in 1535. And the state executed him despite being earlier served by Sir Thomas with utmost devotion, under the same King Henry VIII, who was in the end responsible for his death sentence.

Contradictions of this kind in the world of politics are by no means unique, as the chronicle of the troubled relationship between the Church and State reveals throughout their long history. What is unique, though, is that Sir Thomas More is also the immortal author of a rigorously critical book on the state and its politics, titled *Utopia*, written in Latin by him in Brussels in 1515[1] and published in 1516 in Louvain under the editorship of Erasmus, who was a leading light of the most progressive intellectual forces of their greatly tormented historical period.

Thomas More's book became immensely influential in the course of the history of progressive social and political thought, even giving its defining name to a brand of socialist orientation. Not surprisingly, one of the outstanding figures of late nineteenth-century utopian socialism in England, William Morris, published a beautiful edition of More's *Utopia* in 1893 at his still much-admired Kelmscott Press. As to the highest praise shown by Erasmus for the work of Sir Thomas More,[2] it is well known that in 1517 Erasmus advised one of his own correspondents to send for a copy of *Utopia* "if he wished to see *the source of all political evil*." In those words, Erasmus gave a most fitting evaluation and appreciation of the truly great merits of More's striking achievement. For the story line of *Utopia*—meaning in Greek "nowhere"—cannot compete with the extremely powerful critique of the *actually existing* political systems of the cruel age of land enclosure in England as highlighted in More's work in the most explicit terms, fiercely exposing the repressive state systems in general, represented by him as the sharply condemned counter-image of the *idealized imaginary island Utopia*. Naturally, a work of that kind could not be published in England in its author's lifetime.

"A MAN FOR ALL SEASONS"

The author of *Utopia*, Sir Thomas More, was born in Milk Street, London, on January 7, 1478. His father was a very successful barrister who later became a judge at the King's Bench. Thanks to his father's influence, the young Thomas acquired the privileged position of joining the household of Cardinal Merton, the Archbishop of Canterbury and Lord Chancellor, who praised before his guests to the highest degree the young boy's remarkable gifts and promised for him a great future. As we know, the Cardinal's generous judgment proved to be abundantly justified.

Thomas More studied in Oxford under the enlightened renaissance scholars Colet and Linacre and completed his legal studies at New Inn and at Lincoln's Inn. His political carrier started at the early age of twenty-four, in 1502, when he became a member of Parliament, and he was also appointed in that year Under-Sheriff of the City of London, which happened to be an important judicial office. In Parliament he gained an exceptionally high reputation by forcefully opposing in 1504 the demand for more money by King Henry VII—whose reign ended five years later, in 1509—and indeed he did that with astonishing success for a young parliamentarian. Understandably, the soon to become King of England, Henry VIII—paradoxically at that time, by way of Cardinal Wolsey's advice—took notice of More's extraordinary parliamentary oratory and potential political service. Thus, after the death of King Henry VII, when Henry VIII. became the King of England, the return to a public role by Thomas More could not be delayed for very long.

His knighthood in 1514 was combined with being elevated also to the King's Privy Council and from that time onward his influence on King Henry VIII grew constantly. In the same year of 1514, Sir Thomas More became Master of Requests, and his appointment as Treasurer of the Exchequer, in 1521, represented a very high office. But even higher offices were still to follow. In 1523, he was elected Speaker of the House of Commons and in 1525 he was appointed Chancellor to the Duchy of Lancaster. Yet, as mentioned before, the strangely somber crowning of his high political carreer came in 1529, at the time of Cardinal Wolsey's demise, when he was elevated by Henry VIII to the highest office of Lord Chancellor, replacing the disgraced Cardinal Wolsey. But it was not a happy appointment for him. His resignation from that high office was accepted by the king in 1532, and in that same year began his irreconcilable dissent from the unfolding conflict between the King and the Church, still under the Pope's traditional authority. As a result, Sir Thomas More's unforgivable dissent from royal convenience and dictates carried with it his descent toward a fateful tragic end in 1535. That is how a most illustrious political carreer, with all its personal contradictions, was consummated exactly two decades after the completion of Sir Thomas More's biting exposure of *"the source of all political evil"* in his *Utopia*.

UTOPIA VERSUS THE SIXTEENTH CENTURY

Sir Thomas More's literary masterpiece has for its story line his alleged encounter and ensuing conversations, in Brussels, in the year 1515—when he had been living there for some time, fulfilling the mission assigned to him by Cardinal Wolsey—between himself and a somewhat mysterious figure called Raphael Hythloday, whose name (again with a touch of irony) in Greek means "knowing in trifles." This man, the invented Hythloday, was supposed to have traveled to the Americas with Amerigo Vespucci on three of Vespucci's sea journeys, but traveling also on his own on another sea journey somewhere in the same part of the world. Hythloday claimed that when he was traveling alone he had the extraordinary good fortune of experiencing a very different way of life on the legendary island of Utopia, which he describes in great detail to Sir Thomas More in their long conversations. What was of course factually known at the time when More was writing his book was that Amerigo Vespucci truly traveled in the Americas between 1499 and 1503, and his account of those sea journeys was also printed in the year 1507 and was available to all interested to read it. That tangible evidence of Vespucci's journeys was in a way meant to provide authenticating background to the story of Hythloday's claimed sea journeys.

To be sure, the original inspiration for such utopian visions of life in European philosophy and political thought goes back all the way to Plato's *Republic* and his other writings on an idealized conception of society and *The Laws*. However, in the historical period of Sir Thomas More's *Utopia* there were also some very different inducements for engaging in that kind of imaginary projections. After all, Christopher Columbus encountered the Americas only a little more than two decades earlier, in 1492, and the continent of Australia was not yet known at all. Moreover, despite the four-year-long exploratory journeys of Amerigo Vespucci, the North and South American Continents and the numerous nearby islands were still very far from being properly known at that time. Besides, even as late as the middle of the eighteenth century the exploring sea captains could still report their experiences about seeing people living on faraway islands in very different ways, in contrast to Europe. As I indicated in my book *Beyond Capital*, European explorers were at times struck in the newly discovered parts of the world by the total absence of the possessive value system they took for granted in their own countries. Indeed, one of the most radical and far-sighted thinkers of the French Enlightenment, Denis Diderot—the same philosopher who insisted that "if the day worker is miserable, the nation is miserable"[3]—offered a profound critique of capitalist alienation by favorably contrasting the manner of living of the formerly unknown tribes of some Pacific islands to that of his own country. In an imaginative commentary on a community discovered by a famous French explorer, sea captain Bougainville, Diderot indicated as some of the basic contradictions of the socioeconomic system dominant in Europe "the distinction of *yours* and *mine*" (le distinction du *tien* et du *mien*), the opposition between "one's own particular utility and the general good" (ton utilité particulière et le bien général), and the subordination of the "general good to one's own particular good" (le bien général au bien particulier).[4] Most remarkably, we find similar thoughts in Thomas More's *Utopia* more than two centuries earlier.

It is also relevant to mention in the same context that Sir Thomas More was not alone in his attempt to project some kind of an idealized vision set in contrast to the unfolding historical developments in the world. We should remember here that in the sixteenth and seventeenth centuries a fundamental social and economic transformation—through the immense dynamism of the capitalist societal reproduction process—asserted itself not only in Europe but started to bring under its power the entire world. Inevitably, this transformation could only be an intensely contradictory process. So much had to be overturned before the inherent determinations of the new social reproductive metabolism could fully stabilize itself, ruthlessly demolishing everything that stood in its way. This is why the so-called primitive accumulation of capital is inseparable from utmost cruelty on a formerly unimaginable societal scale.[5]

The brutal antagonisms of the highly profitable land enclosures pilloried in More's *Utopia* are a paradigm of both the scale of such transformations and of the inhumanity involved. We shall see More's critical assessment of them in a moment. But it is also necessary to emphasize that in the course of a historic transformation of such monumental dimensions some vision of the future as a potential alternative appears—even if rather hazily—on the horizon, before the overall process is firmly consolidated. This is why Thomas More is not the only one in this historic period to come forward to offer his utopian projections. To name only two more of such examples to be considered later, we must bear in mind the names of the English Sir Francis Bacon of Verulam and the Italian Tommaso Campanella, who both sketched their own utopian visions well before a century after the execution of Sir Thomas More on the arbitrarily proclaimed ground of "High Treason."

"SHEEP DEVOURING MEN"

In the words of Raphael Hythloday, the imaginary island of Utopia was conquered by "Utopus" whose original name was "Abraxa." He became the *"Lawgiver"* of that island and was revered in the same way as the legendary Lawgivers of the Ancient World were in the works of Plato and Aristotle, among others.

Right in the first major conversation between More and Hythloday, represented in the form of an unmistakable critique of the political intrigues and customs of England, Hythloday makes it clear that he could not serve any prince because "most princes apply themselves more to *affairs of war* than to the *useful arts of peace*; ... they are generally more set on *acquiring new kingdoms*, right or wrong, than on *governing well* those they possess. And among the ministers of princes, there are none that are not so wise as to need no assistance, or at least that do not think themselves so wise that they imagine they need none;

and if they court any, it is only those for whom the prince has much personal favor, whom by their fawnings and flatterings they endeavor to fix to their own interests."[6]

Moreover, soon enough More's interlocutor offers us a sharp condemnation of the absurdly severe punishment of thieves who are themselves the victims of the grave material conditions to which they are subjected, saying:

> This way of punishing thieves was neither *just* in itself nor *good for the public;* for as the severity was *too great*, so the remedy was not effectual; simple theft not being so great a crime that it ought *to cost a man his life,* no punishment how severe soever being able to restrain those from robbing who can find *no other way of livelihood.* ... There are dreadful punishments enacted against thieves, but it were much better to make such *good provisions* by which every man might be put in a method how to live, and so be preserved from the *fatal necessity of stealing and of dying for it.*[7]

Naturally, the author of *Utopia* does not stop at simply expressing his sympathy for the unjustly executed thieves but goes on to expose the underlying economic and political causes of the mindlessly ineffectual but cruel capital punishment imposed on the victims of "fatal necessity" by the state. This is done in a conversation that Hythloday claims to have had in England with the same Cardinal Merton who once so highly praised the young Thomas More. This is how Hythloday describes those causes, in his devastating indictment of the whole system, as directly arising from the state-enforced *land enclosures*:

> "I do not think that this necessity of stealing arises only from hence [the requirement of having in reserve numerous idle hands for war]; there is another cause of it more peculiar to England."
>
> "What is that?" said the Cardinal.
>
> "The *increase of pasture*," said I, "by which your sheep, which are naturally mild, and easily kept in order, may be said now *to devour men, and unpeople not only villages, but towns;* for wherever

it is found that the sheep of any soil yield a softer and richer wool than ordinary, there the nobility and gentry, and even those holy men the abbots, *not contented with the old rents* which their farms yielded, not thinking it enough that they, living at their ease, *do no good to the public,* resolve to do it hurt instead of good. They *stop the course of agriculture,* destroying houses and towns, reserving only the churches, and *enclose grounds* that they may lodge their sheep in them.... They turn the *best inhabited places in solitudes*; for when an insatiable wretch, who is a plague to his country, resolves to enclose many thousands of acres of ground, the *owners* as well as *tenants* are *turned out of their possessions,* by tricks, or by main force, or being wearied out with ill usage, they are *forced to sell them* [for little money]. ... When that little money is at an end, for it will be soon spent, what is left for them, but either to steal and so to be hanged (God knows how justly), or to go about and beg? And if they do this, they are put in prison as *idle vagabonds;* while *they would willingly work,* but can find none that will hire them; for there is no more occasion for country labor, to which they have been bred, when there is no arable ground left. ... This likewise in many places *raises the price of corn.* The *price of wool* is also so risen that the poor people who were wont to make cloth are no more able to buy it; and *this likewise makes many of them idle....* But suppose the sheep should increase ever so much, *their price is not like to fall;* since though they cannot be called a *monopoly,* because they are not engrossed by *one person,* yet they are in so few hands, and those are so rich, that as they are *not pressed to sell them* sooner than they have a mind to it, so they never do it *till they have raised the price as high as possible.*"[8]

Thus we see clearly identified a whole range of contradictions absurdly generating and reinforcing one another. Indeed, a few paragraphs further on Thomas More also highlights the bad effects of the *scarcity* generated by *misery* as well as the moral consequences of *luxury* also in senseless contradiction to misery. To quote the sharp condemnatory words of Hythloday again:

Luxury likewise breaks in apace upon you, to set forward your poverty and misery; there is an excessive vanity in apparel and great cost in diet; and that not only in noblemen's families, but even among tradesmen, among the farmers themselves, and among all ranks of persons. You have also many infamous houses, and, besides those that are known, the taverns and alehouses are no better; add to these, dice, cards, tables, football, tennis, and quoits, in which *money runs fast away*; and those that are initiated into them, must in the conclusion betake themselves to *robbing for a supply*.

Banish these plagues, and give orders that those who have dispeopled so much soil, may either rebuild the villages they have pulled down, or let out their grounds to such as will do it; restrain those engrossings of the rich, that are as bad almost as *monopolies;* leave fewer occasions to idleness; let *agriculture* be set up again, and the *manufacture of the wool be regulated*, that so there may be *work* for those companies of idle people whom *want forces to be thieves*, or who, now being idle vagabonds or useless servants, will certainly grow thieves at last. If you do not find a remedy to these *evils*, it is a vain thing to *boast* of your *severity in punishing theft*, which though it may have the *appearance* of justice, yet in itself is *neither just nor convenient*. For if you suffer your people to be *ill-educated*, and their manners be *corrupted from their infancy*, and then punish them for those crimes to which their first education *disposed them*, what else is to be concluded from this, but that *first you make thieves and then punish them?*[9]

To be sure, none of the recommendations voiced by Raphael Hythloday could be seriously expected to be adopted under the conditions exposed by Sir Thomas More. What made matters even more difficult to disentangle and remedy was that though some of the contradictions highlighted by More were due to the long prevailing determinations of the established social and political order, others—including the frightful inhumanities graphically encapsulated in the sentence *"sheep are now devouring men"*—signaled the triumphantly advancing power of capital, manifest in its ruthless accumulation, irresistible concentration and all-encroaching self-expansionary domination. To imagine that some well-meaning political authority could effectively counter all such problems by means of its benevolent *"regulation"* would be totally illusory, given the magnitude of the problems at stake, even if some political force—perhaps a truly enlightened prince and his uncorrupted advisers, like Sir Thomas More himself—could be allowed to work in favor of positive changes. Not surprisingly, therefore, the final lines of *Utopia*, when the author speaks about the constitution of the legendary island described by Hythloday in his own voice, reads like this: "I cannot perfectly agree to everything he [Raphael Hythloday] has related; however, there are many things in the Commonwealth of Utopia that I rather *wish*, than *hope*, to see followed in our governments."[10] In this way *wish* contrasted with *hope*—but even so, genuinely felt *wish*—is presented as the reluctant resigned final message of More's *Utopia*.

THE CONSPIRACY OF THE RICH

Given the socially very different character of the old and new contradictions identified in More's *Utopia*, the remedies proposed against them also had to be very different. In relation to those characteristic of the long established social order, we find in *Utopia* the straightforward recommendation of measures in principle adoptable by any politically enlightened government. Many of the earlier quoted critical remarks made by Hythloday fall into that category. Moreover, most of More's critical comments in *Utopia* about law and justice can be added to them. At times Thomas More's strictures assume sharply explicit form. Thus, for instance, he explicitly condemns the law as *obviously absurd* when it puts thieves to death.

This is how the author of *Utopia* formulates his critique in that respect:

> I think putting thieves to death is *not lawful*; and it is plain and obvious that *it is absurd,* and of *ill consequence* to the *commonwealth*, that a thief and a murderer should be equally punished; for if a robber

sees that his danger is the same, if he is convicted of a theft as if he were guilty of murder, this will naturally incite him to kill the person whom otherwise he would have only robbed . . . so that *terrifying thieves* too much, *provokes them to cruelty*.[11]

In the same sense, More's recommendation to abandon the endless multiplication of laws is in principle perfectly adoptable by any rational government. For, as mentioned earlier, Plato protested against the grotesque illusion of legislators who continue with their laws to cut off some heads of Hydra without realizing, or caring about it, that by doing this they only help Hydra to grow several more heads.[12] However, it is doubtful that the idea of "Good Constitution and few laws"[13] as positively complementing the fully justifiable critique of the perverse proliferation of laws offers a viable solution in that matter. A historically sustainable solution would call for incomparably more radical transformation of the social and political order than what could be envisaged by the impact of such legislative adjustments. But "juridical illusions" are maintained far too long because they are closely associated with powerful materially vested interests.

In a similar respect, when we think of another important recommendation in More's *Utopia*, concerning the way in which the Utopians treat religious attitudes, it is again easy to agree that its adoption would be in principle beneficial to any enlightened government. In that respect, More no doubt had in mind the troubles of his own country and age. As we know, in the end Thomas More had to fall victim to the irreconcilable contradiction between the state of Henry VIII and the Church of Rome. In contrast to the religious tribulations of his age, More praised the circumstance that in Utopia, where there were said to be several distinct religions, no one was ever punished for their religious convictions.[14]

By comparison to the irrationalities of the old order, the contradictions wedded to the societal determinations of capital at its early stage of development, at the time of More's *Utopia*—corresponding to the brutal vicissitudes of primitive accumulation and land enclosure—could not be confronted and cast aside in a relatively straightforward way. The contrast of the unfolding socioeconomic savagery of capital was too great and shocking for that, especially when set against the conceptions reminiscent of the utopian visions of classical antiquity, mostly in relation to Greece, and the attempted mediation of the values exemplified in More's time by enlightened Renaissance scholarship, including that of Erasmus, Linacre, and Thomas More himself.[15]

This contrast is explicitly spelled out by More through the words of Hythloday toward the end of *Utopia* when he says:

> I have described to you, as particularly as I could, the constitution of that commonwealth which I do not only think *the best* in the world, but indeed *the only commonwealth* that *truly deserves that name*. In all other places it is visible, that while people talk of a commonwealth, every man only seeks *his own wealth*; but there, where *no man has any property*, all men zealously pursue the *good of the public*: and, indeed, it is no wonder to see men act so differently; for in other commonwealths, every man knows that unless he provides for himself, how flourishing soever the commonwealth may be, he must die of hunger; so that he sees the *necessity of preferring his own concerns to the public;* but in Utopia, where every man has a *right to everything*, they all know that if care is taken to keep the *public stores full*, no private man can want of anything; for among them there is *no unequal distribution*, so that *no man is poor*, none in necessity; and though *no man has anything*, yet *they are all rich;* for what can make a man so rich as to lead a serene and cheerful life, *free from anxieties*.[16]

In this way the tale of More's utopian island is put forward as a feasible remedy to the fundamental incompatibilities of the unfolding fetishistic trends of early capitalistic developments. The Utopians are depicted by More as commendable in terms of human values fully in tune with the best ideals of Greek antiquity. The critical views expressed either through Hythloday's comments or in Thomas More's own voice amount to a very loud shouting of *"No"* to the experienced inhumanities and to the capitulation of even "those holy men the abbots, who are not contented with the old rents," callously ignoring the good of the public, and thereby they "resolve to do it hurt instead of good."[17]

For More there is no sign in the existing world of any socially powerful movement that could provide a historically viable *positive alternative* to the denounced trends. Thus, he can only say an emphatic *"No"* to the encountered evil. The *positive counter-image* to it can only be depicted by Thomas More in the form of a "ready-made" *imaginary society* claimed to be ideally functioning on a legendary island. All the more so because the fetishistic manifestations of the unfolding malevolence—like "sheep that devour men and unpeople not only villages but also towns"—are even more absurd than the obviously absurd law that punishes in the same way the minor thieves as the murderers.

The malevolent force condemned by Thomas More—pinpointed by him in the shape of the rule of *private property,* as well as in the vicious pursuit of *money* and *gold*—seems to be rather mysterious in terms of their apparently uncontrollable power, but ripe in More's view for their necessary abolition, because they favor only the rich and harm in so many ways the laboring poor who are "depressed by a *barren and fruitless employment.*"[18] The unavoidable result of the destructive rule of private property and money is extreme hardship for those who deserve much better. But despite their vital contribution to the public good, they "must lead so miserable a life, that the condition of the beasts is much better than theirs."[19] Thus the words of Raphael Hythloday toward the end of *Utopia* assert an absolute indictment of the existing totally unjust order and its oppressive laws:

> The richer sort are often endeavoring to bring the hire of laborers lower, not only by their *fraudulent practices*, but by the *laws* which they *procure* to be made to that effect; so that it is a thing *most unjust in itself,* to give such small rewards to those who deserve so well of the public, yet they have given those hardships the *name and color of justice,* by *procuring laws* to be made for regulating them. Therefore I must say that, as I hope for mercy, I can have no other notion of all the other *governments* that I see or know, than that they are a *conspiracy of the rich,* who on *pretence* of managing the *public,* only pursue

their *private ends*, and devise all the ways and arts they can find out; first, that they may, *without danger, preserve all that they have so ill acquired*, and then that they may engage the poor that they toil and labor for them at *as low rates as possible*, and *oppress them* as much as they please. And if they can but prevail to get these contrivances established by the *show of public authority*, which is considered as the *representative of the whole people*, then they are *accounted laws*.[20] Yet these wicked men, after they have, by a most insatiable covetousness, divided that *among themselves* with which *all the rest might have been well supplied*, are far from that happiness that is enjoyed among the Utopians: for the *use* as well as the *desire of money* being *extinguished*, much anxiety and great occasions of mischief is *cut off with it*. And who does not see that the frauds, thefts, robberies, quarrels, tumults, contentions, seditions, murders, treacheries, and witchcrafts, which are indeed rather *punished* than *restrained* by the severities of law, would all fall off, *if money were not any more valued by the world?* Men's fears, solicitudes, cares, labors, and watchings, would all perish in the same moment with the *value of money*: even *poverty itself*, for the relief of which money seems most necessary, *would fall*.[21]

In this way, thanks to the ready-made utopian island's exemplary customs and institutions, *equity* and *true justice* can be claimed to exist as tangible and rewarding realities somewhere in the world discovered by Hythloday, in striking contrast to the miserable conditions of existence of "those employed in labor so necessary that no commonwealth could hold out a year without them."[22]

The key issue identified by More in terms of the required remedy is the absence of *property* and *money* among the Utopians, in contrast to the established world in which private concerns prevail over the public good and the measure of everything is *money* coupled with the adoration of *gold*. They value gold only in proportion to its *use*, and prefer *iron* to gold.[23] To counter the corrupting influence of gold, it is treated by them with contempt, as a badge of infamy, and their rejection is illustrated by the example of making their *chamber pots* from gold.[24]

Moreover, since there are no idle hands in their society as regulated on the basis of equal distribution without the possibility to expropriate by anyone private property, they have an *abundance* of what they *need*, although they only work six hours per day.[25] "The chief end of their constitution is to regulate labor by the necessities of the public and to allow all the people as much time as is necessary for the improvement of *their minds*, in which they think the *happiness* of life consists."[26]

The virtues of equal distribution are also illustrated by the reported example of a famine in some other country where many people lost their lives needlessly. As Thomas More puts it: "Many thousands have died of hunger; and yet if at the end of that year a survey was made of the *granaries of all the rich men* that have *hoarded up* the corn, it would be found that there was enough among them to have prevented all that consumption of men that perished in misery; and that if it had been distributed among them, none would have felt the terrible effects of that scarcity; so easy a thing would it be to supply all the necessities of life, if that blessed thing called *money*, which is pretended to be invented for procuring them, was not really the only thing that *obstructed their being procured*"![27]

All this adds up to the famous definition of government in *Utopia* as the *"conspiracy of the rich."* It is a striking phrase that encountered countless positive resonances in the history of political thought since its first formulation. Indeed, this definition of government had become the most memorable sentence of Thomas More's early sixteenth-century work among all of the major representatives of utopian socialism.

Thomas More talks several times in his *Utopia* with great disapproval about *"monopoly."* Naturally, the socially most harmful kind of monopoly is the monopoly of production-controlling legally sanctified property, inseparable from the legislative practices of "procuring laws by the rich for themselves" in the interest of protecting their property and the exploitation of the laboring people at the lowest possible pay rate. At the time of writing *Utopia,* no positive alternative was visible to regulating societal reproduction in that way in the actually existing world, as forcefully condemned by Hythloday's and More's words.

This is why the positive counter-image to the denounced evil had to be located by Thomas More on a faraway imaginary island.

THE LIMITS OF MORE'S *UTOPIA*

The trouble is that despite the numerous enlightened aspects of Thomas More's utopian vision we find in his work a maze of contradictions. This even includes his suggestion, resembling some kind of "overseas aid" in the "welfare state" terms of today that *one-seventh* of the surplus wealth of the Utopians should be given away to the poor of other countries.[28] The contradictions can be summed up under two main headings. First, the retrograde hierarchical character of some of More's cherished ideas, also inherited from Plato and Aristotle, and second, the utterly naive projection of the socioeconomic solutions recommended by him.

Concerning the retrograde hierarchical nature of some of More's ideas in *Utopia*, we must recall that *slavery* exists in that society, and it is perfectly acceptable to More for a variety of functions, from serving the utopian families to performing the dirtiest work everywhere, as well as to provide extreme forms of punishment by consigning condemned persons into slavery. And that is by no means all in terms of enforced hierarchy. Deplorably, much like in idealized Greek antiquity, *"Wives serve their husbands, and the children their parents,"*[29] and "Husbands have the *power to correct their wives*."[30] Indeed, More tells us also that "no beauty recommends a wife so much to her husband as the *probity* of her life, and *her obedience.*"[31] At the same time, in terms of the regulation of all aspects of the life of the Utopians, the most important rules are preordained by the fundamental constitution of their society laid down by the "Lawgiver Utopus," in absolute authority. And, of course, to question any part of that would be not only inadmissible but quite inconceivable. Thus the power of decision-making in crucial matters is completely divorced from the social body. Also the senators, magistrates, and priests have their mandates assigned to them in terms of enforcing the idealized dictates of the original lawgiver.

As to Thomas More's naive projections about instituting an equitable and just socioeconomic order, it is enough to mention that

- his main concern is the healthy reconstitution of *agriculture* heavily damaged by the devastating impact of absurd and cruel land enclosure;
- he imagines that *"equal distribution"* of the goods taken from the common store *"without money or exchange"* can secure equitable and happy life;
- he pairs *abundance* for the people in Utopia with the fact that "among them no man is poor *in necessity,"* which may well amount only to the *equal distribution of misery*;
- he advocates the abolition of *money* but self-contradictorily retains it for all kinds of *warfare* purposes;
- he has no insight, due to being captivated by the notion of "equal *distribution,"* into the great relevance of *production* combined with the antagonistic dynamism of the unfolding, early capitalistic trends of development.

To be sure, we must also remember here the historical age that imposed on the utopian thinkers such limitations. To quote the classic assessment and appreciation of their work by Engels: "The utopians were utopians because they could be nothing else at a time when capitalist production was as yet so little developed. They necessarily had to construct the elements of a new society out of their own heads, because within the old society the elements of the new were not as yet generally apparent; for the basic plan of the edifice they could only appeal to reason, just because they could not as yet appeal to contemporary history."[32]

Indeed, it is also most relevant to mention that Engels discusses in this place the work of three early nineteenth-century great utopian thinkers: Saint-Simon, Fourier, and Robert Owen. When we read Thomas More we should remember that the world of *Utopia* was depicted by him *three centuries earlier.*

CHAPTER EIGHTEEN

Machiavelli and Campanella on the Road to Giambattista Vico

With the dynamically unfolding power of capital, some major new challenges appeared on the horizon of philosophy. In a crucial sense this had to mean the end of the long prevailing *value system* of *scholasticism* that could rely for its own support, under the conditions of the Middle Ages, on the vast educational-institutional network of the Church. This had to radically change with the unfolding of the capital system. At the same time, the *technological* achievements and requirements of the ever more powerful capitalist economic order inevitably promoted, in the interest of the system's increasing *productivity,* the concomitant reorientation of philosophy toward *secular scientific* pursuits. Naturally, this kind of material transformation had to carry with it the critical questioning of many religious dogmas in the sharpest terms, together with the redefinition of *morality* and *politics* in all domains, from the everyday life of the individuals to the broadest framework of their national communities and their interactions with one another, including of course their *state* organizations and *warfare.*

In this sense, understandably, since they were active contemporaries to such developments, all three of the great thinkers whose names are indicated in the title of this chapter—Machiavelli, Campanella and Vico—had to represent a dangerous contrast to the dominant ideological tenets and corresponding rules and institutional settings designed to impose them.

As we have seen in the preceding chapter, the author of *Utopia*, Sir Thomas More, had to die as a martyr for his faith, on account of the irreconcilable conflict associated with that faith and its institutional links with royal authority. However, the often-violent conflictual relationship between church and politics could and did indeed assert itself the other way around. In his lifetime, Machiavelli suffered from it, though, unlike some others, not by way of execution, but in the form of torture and imprisonment, as well as banishment. And more than that, after his death he was for centuries grossly misrepresented and violently denounced for his profoundly insightful political and moral principles.

A few decades after Machiavelli's death, the philosopher Tommaso Campanella had to spend no less than twenty-seven years of his life in prison, several of them under the politically ordained religious authority of the Spanish Inquisition. Moreover, Campanella shared his admiration for natural philosophy with perhaps the greatest philosopher of his time, Giordano Bruno, who was executed in Rome under Church order by immolation. Tellingly, one of Machiavelli's heroes, Girolamo Savonarola, was also executed by immolation, this time in Florence, under the arbitrary order of the same Church of Rome.

And the third of our great philosophers, Giambattista Vico, no doubt unforgivably in the view of the religious bigots, highlighted in his pathbreaking work *The New Science* the inherently *historical character* of social development and the power of humanity. He did so in a way meant to be analogous to God, described by Vico as the *maker of nature*, by characterizing human beings as the *makers of their own history*.

In its far-reaching implications nothing could be considered more sinfully heretical than projecting social transformation as potentially controlled by human beings. For it glaringly contradicted the vision of an eternally predetermined and unquestioningly obeyed order as administered by an authoritarian Church. Indeed, *horribile dictu*, the idea of history being made and consciously controlled by human beings could in due course even become an acknowledged and revered precursor of the materialist conception of history.

MACHIAVELLI'S *PRINCE* AND *DISCOURSES*

The Italian Niccolò Machiavelli was a contemporary very close of the English Sir Thomas More. He was born in Florence, nine years before More, in 1469, and died in 1527, just a few years before More's execution in 1535. Thus, Thomas More lived for fifty-seven years and Machiavelli for fifty-eight.

Machiavelli's two fundamental works directly relevant to us are *The Prince*, a short book completed in 1513, two years before Thomas More's *Utopia*, and the much longer *Discourses on the First Decade of Livy*, written by the banished Machiavelli between 1512 and 1517.

It is hard to imagine a more crudely misrepresented and condemned thinker than Niccolo Macchiavelli in the history of philosophy and political thought. The word "Machiavellian" was in fact used for a long time not for referring to a body of identifiable political and moral ideas but as a *term of abuse*, condemning with it not only Niccolo Machiavelli, the Devil Incarnate, but also those who might be in any way sympathetic to the thoughts arbitrarily proclaimed to be absolutely reprehensible by the abusers, as expressed from their pretended moral height, often wearing their self-important religious attire. Nothing more was required to obtain the desired condemnatory effect *by definition* than the abusive term itself. Such method of *circularly fallacious* procedure was expected to work, *as usual*, both for decreeing what was supposed to be rejected and simultaneously also for asserting the rightfulness and wisdom of the position from which the rejection was proclaimed.

We can see the total contradiction between Machiavelli's abusive accusers and the real state of affairs by looking at some passages on religion written by the Italian philosopher and political actor. For, in truth, Machiavelli most eloquently supported the *positive role* that religion played in his judgment in the Roman Republic, thanks to the *proper use* to which it was put in his view by its rulers. Thus Numa Pompilius, the successor of Romulus chosen by the Senate, receives the highest praise from Machiavelli. Accordingly, he writes in his *Discourses on the First Decade of Livy,* that "Numa, finding the people ferocious and desiring to reduce them to *civic obedience* by means of the arts of peace, turned to *religion as the instrument necessary above all others* for the maintenance of a *civilized state,* and so constituted it that there was never for so many centuries so great a *fear of God* as there was in this republic. It was religion that facilitated whatever enterprise the Senate and the great men of Rome designed to undertake.... Citizens were more afraid of *breaking an oath* than of *breaking the law.*"[1]

Machiavelli continues his *Discourse* on the role of religion in the same spirit. This is how it reads: "It will also be seen by those who pay attention to Roman history, how much religion helped in the control of armies, in encouraging the plebs, in producing good men and in shaming the bad. So that if it were a question of the ruler to whom Rome was more indebted, Romulus or Numa, Numa, I think, should easily obtain the first place.... Romulus did not find it necessary to appeal to divine authority; but to Numa it was so *necessary* that he *pretended* to have private conferences with a nymph who advised him about the advice he should give to the people. This was because he wanted to introduce *new institutions* to which the city was unaccustomed, and *doubted whether his own authority would suffice.*"[2]

As we can see, some vitally important objective conditions of viable political decision-making are emphasized here, fully in agreement with commendable moral views expressed in the interest of the Roman Republic and its people. And the same goes for Machiavelli's continuing analysis of Numa's predicament, set in line with other historically admired great legislators in this way:

> Nor in fact was there ever a legislator who, in *introducing extraordinary laws to a people*, did not have *recourse to God,* for otherwise *they would not have been accepted,* since many benefits of which a prudent man is aware, are not so evident to *reason* that he can *convince* others

of them. Hence wise men, in order to escape this difficulty, have recourse to God. So *Lycurgus* did; so did *Solon*, and so have many others done who have had the same end in view. Marvelling, therefore, at Numa's goodness and prudence, the Roman people accepted all his decisions.... All things considered, therefore, I conclude that the *religion* introduced by Numa was among the *primary causes* of Roma's success, for this entailed *good institutions*; good institutions led to *good fortune*; and from good fortune arose the *happy results of undertakings*. And, as the *observance of divine worship is the cause of greatness in republics*, so the neglect of it is the cause of *their ruin*. Because, where the *fear of God* is wanting, it comes about either that a kingdom is ruined, or that it is kept going by the *fear of a prince*, which makes up for the *fear of religion*.[3]

Equally, "Those princes and those republics which desire to remain *free from corruption*, should above all else maintain incorrupt the ceremonies of their religion and should hold them always in veneration; for there can be no surer indication of the decline of a country than to see *divine worship neglected*."[4]

We should recall that Machiavelli speaks with the highest terms of praise of Savonarola. He writes about this defeated and burned priest: "It did not seem to the people of Florence that they were either ignorant or rude [*rozzi*], yet they were persuaded by *Friar Girolamo Savonarola* that he had converse with God. I do not propose to decide whether it was so or not, because of so great a man one ought to speak of reverence; but I do say that vast numbers believed that it was so, without having seen him do anything out of the common whereby to make them believe; for his life, his teaching and the topic on which he preached, were sufficient to make them trust him. Let no one despair, then, of being able to effect that which has been effected by others; for, as we have said in our preface, *men are born and live and die in an order which remains ever the same*."[5]

The assertions in the last two lines are not "erratic" or "marginal aberrations," to be safely and rightly ignored, as some modern interpretations suggest, including Bernard Crick in his otherwise in many ways praiseworthy Introduction to the Penguin edition of Machiavelli's *Discourses*. They are deeply believed by Machiavelli and others, not least by Hobbes, even when they insist that full attention must be paid to *changing circumstances*. The real issue for them—and they stress how difficult it is to solve that issue satisfactorily and sustainably—is how to find the *necessary remedies* fitting to both the changing historical events and circumstances, and at the same time to the "permanent *order*" and "*nature*," which must be *respected*, and through its proper respect turned into the necessary *guiding principle* under the necessarily changing circumstances.

In this sense Machiavelli forcefully underlines—as a vital operating principle of politics—that "the *security of a republic*, or of a kingdom, therefore, does not depend upon its ruler governing it prudently *during his lifetime*, but upon him so ordering it that *after his death*, it may *maintain itself in being*."[6] Thus, in an age of great turmoil—just like the age of Hobbes was—the vital concern is *securing and maintaining continuity*. This is the way in which these great thinkers conceptualize under their own historical conditions the immensely complex and difficult *dialectic of change and continuity*, grasping as the "*übergreifendes Moment*"[7] for their time the *imperative of continuity* that corresponds in their view to the requirements of "nature" and "human nature" under the prevailing circumstances.

The role of *religion*—as the necessary "*institution*" and "*instrument*"—is "proper" for this purpose, even if the legislators and the philosophers do not believe in the particular religious tenets, let alone in the religiously claimed *miracles*.[8] For Machiavelli, "Every religion has the basis of its life rooted in some one of its *main institutions*." The rulers should encourage religious observance "even though they be *convinced that it is quite fallacious*."[9] According to this view, it is utterly *grave* that at the time when Machiavelli writes his work, "Italy has lost all devotion and all religion," and that the Church "has kept, and keeps Italy divided," resulting in "disunion and weakness."[10]

Obviously, then, Machiavelli's value system is intensely concerned with remedying the grave contradictions of the age to which the retrograde forces supported by his detractors in effect wantonly contribute. Hence their self-justifying hostility toward him. Indeed, Machiavelli firmly asserts the positive role of religion not only in the Roman Republic, but he also advocates it for his own historical conditions troubled by grave crises. Religion worked in Machiavelli's view most beneficially in the Roman Republic, because there it was put to its *"proper use,"* in sharp contrast to his own times when the power of the Church "keeps Italy *divided,*" resulting in *"disunion and weakness."* Nevertheless, Machiavelli insists on maintaining a *positive perspective,* by saying, "*Let no one despair* of being able to effect that which *has been effected by others*." Meeting the challenge has been accomplished successfully in the past, as the historical records of Rome prove, and it can be accomplished again in the future. The perilous conditions of Italy call—in the interest of the country's successful defense—for unity and strength. If religion fulfills its role, in its proper way, in accord with its right institutional setting, instead of causing disunion and weakness, one can be assured of a happy outcome. The cause of *defending one's country* is an absolutely undeniable good cause. This is what Machiavelli asserts with great passion toward the end of his *Discourses*.[11] And no one should accuse Machiavelli of recommending *fraud*. For the term used by him for the admissible methods against one's enemy is *"astuzia,"* wrongly translated into English by the Jesuit priest Leslie J. Walker as *"fraud,"* and thereby creating a totally false picture. For in Italian *"astuzia"* means not "fraud"—*"fraudulenza"* is the Italian word for "fraud"—but *"astuteness"* or *"cunning"*—which is perfectly acceptable as a strategic weapon when the stakes are as vital as the successful defense of one's country.[12] By contrast *"fraud"* would be morally reprehensible and also politically unstable in Machiavelli's own terms.

The same goes for the views expressed in Machiavelli's other great work, *The Prince*, abused and falsified perhaps even more than his *Discourses*. Yet, when we read his moral and political judgments on some of the crucial issues discussed in both works, we find the similarities striking. Thus, to take the literally vital example of him talking about the sustainable order that must be created in his country, which was in grave crisis and disunion that affects inevitably the whole people, we should remember the following passage quoted from a few pages before the very end of Machiavelli's book *The Prince* and written in the same spirit as his words in the last chapter of his *Discourses*. This is how the passage in question reads:

> Having carefully considered the subject of the above discourses, and wondering within myself whether the present times were propitious to a new prince, and whether there were the elements that would give an opportunity to a wise and virtuous one to introduce a new order of things which would do honour to him and good to the people of this country, it appears to me that so many things concur to favour a new prince, that I never knew a time more fit than the present. And if, as I said, it was necessary that the people of Israel should be captive so as to make manifest the ability of Moses; that the Persians should be oppressed by the Medes so as to discover the greatness of the soul of Cyrus; and that the Athenians should be dispersed to illustrate the capabilities of Theseus; then at the present time, in order to discover the virtue of an Italian spirit, it was necessary that Italy should be reduced to the extremity she is now in, that she should be more enslaved than the Hebrews, more oppressed than the Persians, more scattered than the Athenians; without head, without order, beaten, despoiled, torn, overrun; and to have endured every kind of desolation.[13]

Machiavelli is perfectly consistent also in saying, as we have seen before, that "where the *fear of God* is wanting, it comes about either that a kingdom is ruined, or that it is kept going by the *fear of a prince*, which makes up for the *lack of religion*."[14]

In this way, by assigning religion and politics to their right setting and proper use, Machiavelli opens up a radically new way of evaluating moral and political matters in a truly emancipatory spirit. It is thus fitting to conclude this section by quoting from *The Modern Prince*, written by another great Italian thinker and political actor, Antonio Gramsci, under conditions of great hardship in Mussolini's prison. These are his words:

The fundamental characteristic of *The Prince* is that it is not a systematic treatment, but a "living" book, in which political ideology and political science are fused in the dramatic form of a myth ... as a creation of concrete fantasy which works on a *dispersed and pulverised people* in order to arouse and organise *their collective will*. The *utopian* characteristic of *The Prince* lies in the fact that the Prince did not exist in historical reality, did not present himself to the Italian people in a directly objective way, but was a purely doctrinaire abstraction, the symbol of a leader, the ideal *condottiere* ... and the argument is conducted with rigorous logic, with *scientific detachment;* in the conclusion Machiavelli makes himself the people, merges himself with the people, not with the people in a "general" sense, but with the people whom Machiavelli has convinced with the preceding tract, whose conscious expression he becomes and feels himself to be, with whom he feels himself identified: it seems that the whole of the "logical" work is only a reflection of the people, an internal reasoning which takes place inside the popular consciousness and has its conclusion in an impassioned, urgent cry.[15]

These words put in their proper perspective the great significance of the work of Niccolò Machiavelli even for our own times.

CAMPANELLA'S *CITY OF THE SUN*

As clearly indicated by the twenty-seven years that had to be spent in prison, Tommaso Campanella also had a painfully troubled life. He lived fourteen years longer than Thomas More and thirteen years longer than Machiavelli, but most of his adult life he had to suffer strictest detention, repeatedly enduring torture.

Campanella was born in 1568 in Stilo, in the Calabria region of Italy, where he entered the Dominican Order at the age of fifteen, and died in 1639 in a Dominican Convent of Paris, at the age of seventy-one. He could work untroubled in the last five years of his life in Paris, thanks to being respected and welcomed by that time there by Cardinal Richelieu. However, his prison years started four decades before he died, which means that after the long years of his studies—first he was studying theology in Cosenza and then philosophy in the Morgentia Convent in Abruzzo—only thirteen years could be used by him for his chosen purpose of contributing to the cause of anti-scholastic moral and political enlightenment, inspired by the renaissance philosophical spirit of Nicolas of Cusa and Bernardino Telesio.

Our direct interest, his utopian work on the *City of the Sun (Civitas solis)*, was completed by Campanella in 1602 but published only in 1623. He wrote also a number of more complex philosophical works, among them *Philosofia sensibus demonstrata*, which he wrote as a very young man in 1691, as a defense of Bernardino Telesio's philosophy of nature, in sharp rejection of scholasticism. Ironically, in Campanella's age, due to the major contradictions among the rival nations, the direct political causes and the material interests corresponding to them greatly complicated the ideological differences for which the philosophical representatives of the accused side had to suffer. Thus, during Campanella's imprisonment by the Spanish Inquisition, even the plea of the Pope for the Spanish king's intervention in favor of Campanella's release could not produce the hoped-for positive result. For the triumphant unfolding of capitalism carried with it also the intensification of national antagonisms.

Campanella's *City of the Sun* has for its subtitle: "A Political Dialogue between a Grandmaster of the Knights Hospitallers and a Genoese Sea-Captain, His Guest." But it could hardly be called a proper dialogue. Nearly all the time the Sea-Captain tells his story, obviously in the tradition of More's *Utopia,* with a few admiring questions and words of approval added in by the Grandmaster Knight from time to time. The main points of Campanella's work can be summed up quite briefly. To quote the general characterization of the *City of the Sun* and its people by the Sea-Captain:

> This race of men came from India, flying from the sword of the Magi, a race of plunderers and tyrants who laid waste their country, and they determined to *lead a philosophic life in fellowship with one another*.... All things are common with them, and their dispensation

is by the *authority of the magistrates*. Arts and honors and pleasures are common, and are held in such a manner that *no one can appropriate anything to himself*. They say that all *private property* is acquired and improved for the reason that each one of us by himself has his own home and wife and children. From this *self-love springs*.... But when we have *taken away self-love,* there remains only *love for the State*.... Whatever is *necessary* they have, they receive it *from the community*, and the magistrate takes care that no one receives more than he deserves.... Moreover, the magistrates govern well, so that no one in the fraternity can do injury to another.[16]

In this way we are offered the main defining characteristics of life in the *City of the Sun,* with the elimination of private property and its self-love, enabling thereby the people to live in a philosophically praiseworthy fellowship among themselves, under the strictly disciplined rules of the ideal—well-governing—magistrates. As in More's *Utopia,* a regimented life under strict authority is considered the happy way of living. Punishments to offenders are severe, but unquestioningly endured because they are accepted by them as *correctives* and not *punishments*.[17] Thus we find in this City not only ideal magistrates but also ideal people who not only accept their severe sentences as welcome correctives but in their daily work they consider the heaviest and the most demanding occupations to be the most highly regarded.[18] Even in terms of love, there is a sharp contrast in their life in comparison to other places. For "the love born from eager desire is not known among them; only that born of friendship."[19]

The Chief Priest, Hoh, is the absolute authority, whose name is also "Metaphysicus," that is, some kind of a Platonic "Philosopher King" without that formal title. His primary concern is the preservation of the *State* and its *absolution* from its sins. "He offers sacrifice to God, that he should *pardon the State* and *absolve* it of its sins, and to teach and defend it. Once in every year, the chief priests of each separate subordinate State confess their sins in the presence of Hoh. Thus, he is not ignorant of the wrongdoings of the provinces, and forthwith he removes them with all human and heavenly remedies."[20] Accordingly, the problems of the State and its provincial "subordinate States" in his troubled historical times are in a way acknowledged by Campanella, but they are readily resolved in the form of the Christian confession of sins, and immediately absolved through (unspecified) "human and heavenly remedies."

In More's *Utopia,* as we have seen, there is slavery, but not in the *City of the Sun.* In *Utopia* people work few hours, compared to the general rule even in our own time. In *Utopia* they work for *six hours* a day and in the *City of the Sun* even less, only *four hours.* But they are said to be able to produce what they need. However, Campanella also talks of "what is *necessary,*" which may well mean not more than the distribution of misery shared in common, although called *"abundance"* in another passage,[21] and justified by the ideal people's *acceptance* of what the magistrates *assign* to them as "deserved" or, rather, as "not more than deserved."

So much in these utopian philosophies and state conceptions can only be spelled out in the form of *negative* determinations of their wishful thinking, contrary to the illusions of their authors of offering the vision of a positively cohesive order. For they are unable to assess the social metabolic ground on which the actually existing societies, including their own, reproduce themselves. Unreal gesture-like counter-images must therefore be invented by them as the alternative to the way in which the criticized order is perceived. Naturally, in this sense, in Campanella's *City of the Sun* "gold and silver are reckoned of little value among them except as material for their vessels and ornaments, which are common to all.... Moreover, the race is managed for the *good of the commonwealth,* and not of *private individuals*, and the magistrates must be obeyed."[22]

This is the basis on which universal harmony is projected by Tommaso Campanella in his nobly intended anti-scholastic tract. In the end the metaphysical philosophy at the roots of his state conception is summed up by him in this way: "We are born and live by chance; but in respect to God, whose instruments we are, we are formed by prescience and design, and for a high end.... Nonentity is incompatible with the infinite entity of God. They [the believers in the *City of the Sun*] lay down two principles of metaphysics, entity which is the highest God, and nothingness which is the defect of entity. Evil and sin come of the propensity to nothingness; the sin having its cause not efficient, but in deficiency.... We know not what we do, but God knows, whose instruments we are."[23]

That is really the final message of Campanella's *City of the Sun*. What an age, in which the man who had such deeply held beliefs about God had to be imprisoned and tortured in the name of God's Inquisition!

VICO'S *NEW SCIENCE*

Giambattista Vico had put at the center of his theory the pathbreaking idea that human beings are the makers of their history. Underlining at the same time the contradictions involved in the particularistic aims set by the human subjects and their effective realizations, this is how he put it, thus unmistakably anticipating the Hegelian historical conception of the "*Cunning of Reason*":

The world of civil society has certainly been made by men.... Whoever reflects on this cannot but marvel that the philosophers should have bent all their energies to the study of the *world of nature*, which, since *God made it*, He alone knows; and that they should have neglected the study of the *world of nations*, or *civil world*, which, *since men had made it, men could come to know*.... This world without doubt has issued from a mind often diverse, at times *quite contrary*, and always *superior* to the *particular ends* that men had proposed to themselves; which narrow ends, made means to serve wider ends, it has always employed to preserve the human race upon this earth. Men mean to gratify their bestial lust and abandon their offspring, and they inaugurate the chastity from which the *families* arise. The fathers mean to exercise without restraint their paternal power over their clients, and they subject them to the *civil powers* from which the *cities* arise. The reigning orders of nobles mean to abuse their *lordly freedom* over the *plebeians*, and they are obliged to submit to the laws which establish *popular liberty*. The free peoples mean to shake off the *yoke of their laws*, and they become *subject to monarchs*.[24]

Thus we see a radical switch from the religiously inspired view of world history, expressed at its peak in the great work of St. Augustine's *City of God*, to a fundamentally *secular conception* in which explanations for the identifiable changes can no longer be provided in terms of *by definition eternalized* "good" and "evil" or "sinfulness," unlike in St. Augustine's assertion according to which "in the torrential stream of human history, two currents meet and mix: the current of evil which flows from Adam and that of good which comes from God."[25] As we have seen, as late as Campanella's *City of the Sun*, the contradictions of the state are still indicated as "sins" and naively "resolved" by being *confessed* to the Chief Priest Hoh/Metaphysicus, who offers sacrifices to God in order to *pardon* and *absolve* the state of its sins. Vico's conception moves in a very different way. He draws attention to the "world of nations" and the "civil world" in terms of which the unfolding social and historical transformations must be explained and altered. And that remains in these matters the vital orienting principle after Vico.

The seventeenth as well as the eighteenth centuries bring their own ever-intensifying economic, social, and political contradictions and the corresponding state theories designed to overcome them. However, despite the solutions offered by all such state theories, the crises continue to deepen and indeed explode in the form of massive social upheavals, reaching their climax in the American and the French revolutions in the last third of the eighteenth century, with their reverberations and major armed confrontations well into the nineteenth all over the greater part of Europe.

Naturally, these crises carry with them also some fundamental utopian conceptions of the new secular type, which begin to focus attention not only on political and cultural but also on materially based class antagonisms. Understandably, the new secular utopian theories at first try to accommodate their vision within the anti-feudal perspective, but in due course, inevitably, due to the sharpening of the class antagonisms, they begin to focus also on the plight of the *working class* in its confrontation with the *bourgeois* domination of economy and society. These problems, as reflected in the qualitatively different secular approaches, are the subject of the remaining chapters here on modern utopianism.*

---

* Mészáros refers here to four projected chapters on modern utopias of what was to be volume 1 of *Beyond Leviathan*, titled "From Bacon and Harrington to Thomas Paine and Robert Owen (the present chapter 19), plus three other chapters that were never completed: (1) "Search for Truth Under the Scottish Enlightenment," (2) "From Kant and Lessing to Thomasius and Bloch's *Principle of Hope*" (part of which was drafted and has been included below as chapter 20 under the title "Thomasius and Bloch's *Principle of Hope*"), and (3) "Pessimistic Utopias of Capital's Inescapable Order."—Ed.

CHAPTER NINETEEN

From Bacon and Harrington to Thomas Paine and Robert Owen

Francis Bacon and James Harrington belonged to the high nobility and offered their utopian conceptions in tune with the limitations of that perspective. Bacon was Baron Verulam of Verulam and Viscount St. Albans, the younger son of Sir Nicholas Bacon who, as a prominent anti-Catholic, was made by Queen Elizabeth Lord Keeper of the Great Seal and in charge of church affairs. The philosopher and statesman Francis Bacon lived in the last four decades of the sixteenth century and the first three of the seventeenth, between 1561 and 1626. The other English utopian thinker from the high nobility, James Harrington, lived entirely in the seventeenth century, between 1611 and 1677. He was the eldest son of Sir Sapcotes Harrington of Exton, in Rutlandshire. Astonishingly, the Harrington family in its time "produced no less than eight dukes, three marquises, seventy earls, twenty-seven viscounts, and thirty-six barons, sixteen of them all being Knight of the Garter."[1]

With reference to Bacon and Harrington, we are talking about an age of increasingly dramatic developments, marked even by the prolonged armed confrontations of the English Civil War in the case of James Harrington. And that was by no means the climax of the then unfolding historical transformations. For the eighteenth century had brought with it the American and French revolutions and the sharpening of the class antagonism between the constituent parts of the Third Estate in France, as well as their socioeconomic and political parallels elsewhere, namely the antagonism between the bourgeoisie and the working class. Understandably, the social background of the intellectual representatives of the new trends subsequent to the age of Bacon and Harrington had to change with these developments, moving increasingly from the critically quite limited horizon of anti-scholastic and anti-feudal nobility toward the advocacy of the strategic alternative vision of the working class through the various conceptions of utopian socialism.

BACON'S *NEW ATLANTIS*

Francis Bacon's best-known philosophical works are *The Advancement of Learning*, published in 1605; *Novum Organum*, published in 1620; and an extended version of *The Advancement of Learning* in Latin, titled *De Augmentis Scientiarum*, published in 1623. After he died, his works in the field of legal theory and practice were published: *Maxims of the Law*, in 1630; *Elements of the Common Laws of England*, also in 1630; and *Readings on the Statute of Uses*, in 1642. His unfinished utopian work, *The New Atlantis*, was also published posthumously, in 1629, three years after his death.

It is most relevant to mention here that Francis Bacon had a prominent political career. After his studies in Cambridge and at Gray's Inn, he became an MP in 1584. He was knighted in 1603, in recognition of his subservience to the Crown; in 1607 he was promoted to the position of Solicitor-General, in 1613 Attorney-General, in 1616 Privy Councillor, in 1617 Lord Keeper, and in 1618 Lord Chancellor.

Thus, in political terms Sir Francis Bacon was a thoroughly uncritical figure, to put it mildly. It is thus utterly surprising to find socially and politically progressive criticism in his utopian *New Atlantis*. In fact, apart from a few rather generic remarks, like his words in defense of the institution of marriage,[2] significant social criticism is totally absent from this work. It can be characterized perhaps best as a form of *technological utopianism*, in line with Bacon's general philosophical approach in favor of *experimental knowledge* to be pursued by the method of eliminative induction, in contrast to scholasticism and deductive logic. Bacon's claim in *The New Atlantis* is that such an ideal—for which the original inspiration came from the early Renaissance representatives of natural philosophy—had already been accomplished in that faraway land.

This claim is presented by Bacon by quoting the words of the most authoritative figure of the newly discovered vast territory of *"New Atlantis."* He describes that place not as a relatively small island, like Thomas More's *Utopia,* but as an immense land in the South Seas, southwest of Peru, whose circumference was said by him to be 9,000 miles. These are the words of that summary of claimed achievements quoted by Sir Francis Bacon: "The end of our foundation is *the knowledge of causes*, and secret motions of things; and the *enlarging of the bounds of human empire*, to the effecting of all things possible."[3]

After that general statement, Bacon offers in *The New Atlantis* a long list of feats and deeds that supposedly were accomplished in that faraway world, corresponding to what in his view could be provided by the application of experimental science on the five human senses. An enumeration of their achievements is always combined by Bacon with the repeated assertion by a quoted high authority that "we have this or that which you have not."

To take an example: "We have also sound-houses, where we practise and demonstrate all sounds and their generation. We have harmony which you have not, of quarter sounds and lesser slides of sounds. Divers instruments of music likewise to you unknown, some sweeter than any you have; with bells and rings that are dainty and sweet. We represent small sounds as great and deep, likewise great sounds extenuate and sharp. . . . We have also perfume-houses, wherewith we join also practices of taste. We multiply smells which may seem strange: we imitate smells, making all smells to breathe out of other mixtures than those that give them. We make divers imitations of taste likewise, so that they will deceive any man's taste. . . . We have also engine-houses, where are prepared engines and instruments for all sorts of motions. There we imitate and practise to make swifter motions than any you have either out of your muskets or any engine that you have ... to make them stronger and more violent than yours are, exceeding your greatest cannons and basilisks."[4]

Naturally, this kind of enumeration could go on and on endlessly, since we receive from Bacon in this work a very odd mixture of practicable suggestions overwhelmed by completely idle fantasy-fragments. No wonder that Lord Verulam of Verulam could not bring them together coherently into something scientifically instructive and productive, as he would have liked, let alone could he make them add up into its promised usefulness toward "enlarging of the bounds of human empire." The technological utopianism of Sir Francis Bacon's *New Atlantis* had to remain fancifully unfinished on account of its missing progressive social dimension.

HARRINGTON'S *OCEANA*

In contrast to Sir Francis Bacon, James Harrington was a socially concerned man of the highest integrity. His utopian world was neither a small imaginary island, nor a Baconian immense, faraway, territory, but a place in Europe transfigured into an ideal commonwealth. To be precise, "The Commonwealth of *Oceana* was England. Harrington called Scotland Marpesia; and Ireland, Panopea. London he called Emporium; the Thames, Halcionia; Westminster, Hiera; Westminster Hall, Pantheon; the Palace of St. James was Alma; Hampton Court, Convallum; Windsor, Mount Celia. By Hemisua, Harrington meant the river Trent. Past Sovereigns of England he renamed for Oceana; William the Conqueror became Turbo; King John, Adoxus; Richard II, Dicotome; Henry VII, Panurgus; Henry VIII, Coraunus; Elizabeth, Parthenia; and James I, Morpheus. He referred to Hobbes as Leviathan; and to Francis Bacon as Verulamius. Oliver Cromwell he renamed as Olpheus Megaletor."[5]

Among the actually existing states, James Harrington had the greatest sympathy for Venice, with a major qualification regarding the future.

That qualification was clearly expressed on the last page of his utopian work, where he wrote: "The sea gives law to the growth of Venice, but the growth of Oceana gives law to the sea."[6] And that was meant by Harrington to indicate that the truly viable form of government in the future can only be the Oceana type of commonwealth.

James Harrington lived through, and also had to suffer from, the civil war in the British Isles. Through his high-nobility family connections he already knew King Charles I, and in 1646 he was appointed to be one of the fallen king's attendants. Soon, however, he was dismissed from that role by Parliament on the basis of some groundless suspicion. Yet, while he was still in the king's service, as a man of principle he did not try to hide from the king his own preference for the commonwealth form of government. The king "loved Harrington's company, and, finding him to be an ingenious man, chose rather to converse with him than with others of his chamber: they had often discourses concerning government; but when they happened to talk of a commonwealth the King seemed not to endure it."[7] Fully in his own character, however, James Harrington always retained his great respect for Charles I, and he was one of the people who accompanied him to the scaffold to comfort him.

Naturally, Oceana, as a qualitatively different form of government, in Harrington's view had particular relevance against the grave crisis of the English Civil War. In 1656, when it was being prepared for publication, with the intention of its author to dedicate it to Oliver Cromwell, the man who could practically implement the positive message of Harrington's long book, the manuscript was confiscated, and reprieved only through the intervention of Cromwell's daughter, Mrs. Claypole, with her father. As a result, it became possible to publish *Oceana* in 1656, as originally intended. However, in 1661, under the order of King Charles II, James Harrington was arrested, with the absurd pretense that he tried to overthrow the Constitution—single-handedly, without any organization—and jailed without any trial for a very long time. He was released only after his health had been destroyed, and died in September 1677, at the age of sixty-six.

One of James Harrington's great concerns was that "a people, when they are reduced to *misery and despair*, become *their own politicians*, as certain beasts, when they are sick, become their own physicians, and are carried by a *natural instinct* to the desire of such herbs as are their proper cure."[8] He wanted to provide a lasting solution to this problem through his own vision of the ideal commonwealth, by both preventing the *misery and despair* of the people and the necessity to resort to the—in his view unworkable—remedy by the people themselves to become *their own politicians*. For he was convinced that *natural instinct* and *passion* cannot provide the enduring ground for a viable government, needing, in its stead, a well-designed constitution for the state's stability, based on *"liberty of conscience"* and *reason*.[9]

Obviously, those in charge of the *established* state institutions were inimical both to his characterization of the possibility of the "misery and despair of the people" and to his vision of how to prevent them from entering the political stage thanks to the rational Constitution of the Commonwealth based on the principles of "civil liberty" and the "Liberty of Conscience." Having had the temerity to exercise his own Liberty of Conscience in *Oceana* was enough for them to condemn James Harrington to permanent incarceration, without even allowing him to defend himself in a trial.

PAINE'S *THE RIGHTS OF MAN*

With the American and the French revolutions, the eighteenth century moved in a socially more radical direction than what could be contained within the framework of an anti-feudal perspective. In the case of the American Revolution, this matter was greatly complicated by the circumstance that the armed struggle between the adversaries inevitably had to mean the end of political/military domination by the English Crown in North America and, in due course, the redefinition of interstate relations on a much broader international scale, both in the direction of the east, directly involving several countries of Europe, and toward the countries situated on the South American Continent. At the same time, since such huge masses of people had become more or less directly involved in military clashes, the social and historical

FROM BACON AND HARRINGTON TO PAINE AND OWEN   355

transformations in the last decades of the eighteenth century presented the hope to find sustainable solutions to the conflicting social interests without armed confrontations exploding among the participants. Thus, the inherently social and political/military dimensions in that way had become not only intertwined but also rather confused.

One of the most representative and for a long time very influential intellectual who offered his solution to this challenge was the Englishman Thomas Paine, who sided with the cause of the American Revolution from the beginning, and also with the French Revolution, which was fiercely denounced in his own country. He firmly advocated the thoroughly illusory belief that it was possible to eliminate war altogether by a *rational agreement* among the conflicting bourgeois nations to sort out their disagreements through arbitration and mediation in the framework of an international institution designed for the purpose. This proved to be impossible even in the heroic phase of the bourgeois revolutions, when Thomas Paine's first works appeared, nor was it possible with the later variants of international mediating institutions, from Metternich's "Holy Alliance" and the "Three Emperors' League" set up by Bismarck all the way to the "League of Nations" inspired by the Kantian dream of the coming "Eternal Peace."

Thomas Paine appealed to the historical memory of the French King Henry IV, who in 1610 "proposed a plan for abolishing war in Europe. This plan consisted in constituting a European Congress, or as the French authors style it, a Pacific Republic, by appointing delegates from the several nations who were to act as a Court of Arbitration in any disputes that might arise between nation and nation."[10] In this sense Paine tended to mythologize in a positive way the nations and in an opposite sense the governments of the same nations. He wrote:

> As war is the system of Government of the old construction, this animosity which Nations reciprocally entertain is nothing more than what the policy of their Governments excites to keep up the spirit of the system. Each Government accuses the other of perfidy, intrigue, and ambition, as a means of heating the imagination of their respective Nations, and incensing them to hostilities. Man is

not the enemy of Man, but through the medium of a false system of Government. Instead, therefore, of exclaiming against the ambition of Kings, the exclamation should be directed against the principle of such Governments; and instead of seeking to reform the individual, the wisdom of a nation should apply itself to reform the system."[11]

The trouble is that from the standpoint of the bourgeoisie even in the system's *ascending phase* of development, there cannot be a real understanding of the system's *objective inner antagonisms* as *class antagonisms*. They must be transformed in their ideological conceptualizations into *morally reprehensible individual characteristics*, like corruption, intrigue, ambition, perfidy, etc., and then quasi-mythically projected as all-round defining characteristics of the criticized system. And in that way the problems can all be rather conveniently confined to the strictly *political* dimension, without raising the difficult question of materially dominant property relations. All this is quite prominent in Thomas Paine's diagnoses. Accordingly, he writes: "The moving power of this species of Government is of necessity corruption."[12]

It is hard to even imagine a more *optimistic* response to the two bourgeois revolutions of the late eighteenth century—the American and the French—than what we find in Paine's *Rights of Man*. His utopian anticipations of the future are boundlessly *positive* and totally *illusory*. He writes at the end of Part I of his book: "From what we now see, nothing of reform in the *political world* ought to be held improbable. It is an age of Revolutions, in which everything may be looked for. The intrigue of Courts, by which the system of war is kept up, may provoke a Confederation of Nations to abolish it; and an European Congress to patronize the progress of free Government, and promote the civilization of Nations with each other, is an event nearer in probability than once were the revolutions and Alliance of France and America."[13]

Thomas Paine's view of the enthusiastically commended Constitution could not be more naive. He wrote: "A Constitution is not the act of a Government, but of a people constituting a Government; and Government without a Constitution is power without a right."[14]

He simply—and wishfully—contrasted the "hereditary principle" as *"slavery,"* with a totally idealized view of *representation,* and categorically asserted that *"representative government is freedom."*[15] Behind these naive illusions we find the correspondingly wishful definition of the *"nature of man"* by Paine, who decrees—in tune with the aprioristically postulated "conclusion"—that *"man,* were he not *corrupted by Government,* is *naturally* the *friend of man."*[16] But at that point Thomas Paine also postulated that what in the past was "subservient to the purposes of taxation, is now yielding to the dictates of reason, interest [that is, bourgeois self-interest], and humanity."[17] Accordingly, "For what we can foresee, all Europe may form but one great Republic, and man be free of the whole."[18] Indeed, in this way *all dimensions* of an ideal condition of the social and political order were supposed to be fully realized. For the imaginary optimistic transformation "takes ground on every character and condition that appertains to man, and blends the individual, the Nation, and the world."[19]

In this conception of *The Rights of Man* by Thomas Paine, the circularly assumed identity of "Reason and Common Interest" is the guarantee of success. Paine can even offer—in minute detail—a relatively enlightened form of budgeting sympathetic about the condition of "the poor," as well as the successful elimination of war through *universally beneficial* commerce. There could be no question of painful inequalities asserting themselves through the actually existent social/structural *power relations*. The projected happy *Alliance* between America, Britain, and France is Thomas Paine's model for the "general commerce of the world,"[20] combined with opening up for such process the South American Continent. Naturally, Simon Bolívar was much more realistic in the same historical period when he feared from this kind of development the domination of North American imperialism over the entire region, including his own country.

THE UTOPIAN SOCIALISTS: OWEN AND FOURIER

As it happened, reality refused to conform to Thomas Paine's wishful thinking of universal happiness through the vaguely defined adjustment of the *political domain*, without any *substantive change* in the *structurally entrenched* domination and exploitation of the social order. In the course of the Napoleonic Wars and in their aftermath, the emergent bourgeois socioeconomic system succeeded in stabilizing itself, retaining the exploitation of the subordinate part of the Third Estate—its overwhelming majority—while "changing the personnel" of the dominant class from the feudal to the bourgeois. However, the class antagonisms could not disappear in that way. On the contrary, they tended to intensify and to find before long their expression in the form of projecting the radically different alternative vision of a sustainable social order in the writings of utopian socialists. Three names are particularly important in this respect for the early phase of such developments: Charles Fourier (1737–1809), Henry Saint-Simon (1760–1825), and Robert Owen (1771–1858).

Charles Fourier exposed with merciless satire the absurd contradictions and hypocrisy of "civilized" society in which the overproduced abundance of commodities was inseparable from the misery of the masses. He also insisted that "the extension of the priviliges of women is the basic principle of all social progress."[21] For his own part, Saint-Simon was stressing the necessity of a socialist order in which *everybody worked*, and the parasitic existence of the *idlers* who lived on their revenue was permanently confined to the past. And the third of these early utopian socialists, Robert Owen, was directly involved at New Lanark in Scotland in managing a less exploitative form of production, also attempting the organization of the workers in a "Grand National Consolidated Trades Union" in 1834 to defend their interests.[22] In 1825, Owen and his supporters established a utopian community called New Harmony in Indiana, and others in England, including one in Hampshire called Harmony Hall, beginning in 1839, which survived until 1845.

With this kind of intellectual development social criticism shifted from the wishful remedy of envisaging the required changes by vaguely defined notions of the "rights of man," confined to the political domain, to the necessity of transforming the *social order itself* in a structurally meaningful way. Fourier was devastatingly sarcastic in this respect in exposing the vacuity of talk merely in terms of wishfully projected rights that ignored the tangibly identifiable issues. "He would not debate, as he put it, on those *'renewed reveries of the Greeks, these Rights of Man* that have become so ridiculous.' Political controversies would only engender bloody upheavals like the French Revolution, if civilized men persisted in neglecting the *'first right, the only useful right, the right to work.'"*[23]

Indeed, Thomas Paine's discourse on *The Rights of Man* was coupled with his deification of the American Constitution as the model of the ideal resolution of the painful social and political problems. He declared that the enlightened American Constitution represented the triumph over *slavery* manifested in the past modes of governing, decreeing at the same time, as we have seen above, that "representative government is Freedom." In reality, some "Founding Fathers" of the American Revolution, and outstanding figures of its representative government, were perfectly happy to carry on with their privileged existence, disregarding the fundamental tenets of their own Constitution on freedom and equality, as *slave-owners* in their structurally entrenched hierarchical social order. They could see nothing wrong with that.

All these problems remained major challenges for the future. The absolutely fundamental question was *decision-making* by everybody, including all those who continued to be *excluded from it* even in the *"representative"* form of government. Robert Owen had put it honestly and beautifully when talking about his own workers, when he said that *"they are at my mercy."* The vacuous promise of "representative government," even if it could be made real, instead of a systemically violated promise, as it happens to be the case in actuality, would make no difference at all to that. No one should be "at the mercy of capital"—or even of its most enlightened decision-making personifications, as controllers of a structurally alienated mode of societal decision-making, not only in politics but also in material and cultural production.

The utopian socialists started to raise these problems, in conjunction with an increasingly organized working-class movement, from the Chartists in England to the various militant forces of later revolutionary upheavals in many different countries. The historical chronicles speak of victories and defeats in the centuries following the critical diagnoses of early utopian thinkers. What is most relevant in this regard is that even despite the worst defeats the vital issue of social emancipation, on the basis of substantive equality, which already appeared and was defeated during the French Revolution with François Babeuf and his "Society of Equals," could never be eliminated from the social agenda of our time.

CHAPTER TWENTY

Thomasius and Bloch's Principle of Hope

The appendix in Ernst Bloch's book on *Natural Law and Human Dignity* on the work of Christian Thomasius (1655–1728), is the finest piece of that volume, written with real devotion and passion.[1] The title itself is already revealing, indicating a programmatic and hopeful intention on Bloch's part to carry on work in his new surroundings, after his return to East Germany from his exile in the United States. The title is "Christian Thomasius, a German Scholar Without Misery."*

Written in 1949, more or less at the same time as Theodor Adorno and Max Horkheimer went to West Germany, where they collaborated

---

* The last three chapters referred to in Mészáros's "Original General Plan for *Beyond Leviathan*" were never finished (see Appendix I). The first and third of these final chapters were apparently not drafted at all. However, this was not the case with respect to the second to last chapter (listed as "section 3.7" in the planned volume), originally titled, "From Kant and Lessing to Thomasius and Bloch's Principle of Hope." Although there were no discernible traces of the first section of this chapter, on Kant and Lessing, the second section, on "Thomasius and Bloch's Principle of Hope," has been excavated from Mészáros's "second version" draft (*Critique of Leviathan: Reflections on the* State) and is being published here as the final chapter of the present volume and as an appropriate conclusion. See the Editor's Introduction.—Ed.

with the American Occupation Authorities (serving their propaganda), Bloch stressed in this fine analysis of Thomasius's trajectory, the significance of Thomasius's strand for the German Enlightenment, and the hints of this "German Scholar Without Misery" with regard to a "social utopia without property," and at the same time his (Bloch's) belief in and advocacy of a *socialist future* for humanity.

Bloch sharply criticized Horkheimer's absurd views on the Enlightenment, contrasting them with Lukács's position.[2] In the essay, richly documented with quotations from the works by Thomasius, Bloch did not *name* Adorno and Horkheimer but their sterile (and culturally prodigal) views are implicitly criticized.[3] We know that Adorno considered Bloch's writing and thought "outdated." Even the Bloch volume's translator, Dennis J. Schmidt, rejected this judgment as wrong.[4] In truth, there is no comparison between the relevance of Bloch's work and the spineless self-promoting "culture industry" of "critical theory" exemplified by Adorno.

Bloch wrote about Thomasius that "he *never bent a knee* . . . he put himself in the middle of all *German misery* and took a *stand against it*."[5] This is in sharp contrast to Adorno (and some other Frankfurters) who were "bending knees" all their lives, with nauseating opportunism and accommodation.

The Adorno/Horkheimer kind of irresponsible dismissal of the Enlightenment is forcefully condemned by Bloch, even if he does not explicitly name them, by stressing that "the imperialist age only treats the entire Enlightenment *disparagingly*, and with categories such as *superficial, flat, trivial, banal*, and so on—so that there can be no doubt about *the denigration of the social task*."*

Thomasius is characterized by Bloch as the diametrical opposite and "opponent of the *bloated platitude sitting on its high horse* with a 'view' of everything except *Thomasius's principle*: 'That there is only one truth. That this truth consists in the living knowledge of the true good.'" And again, in the next sentence we find a fitting characterization

---

* Bloch does refer critically to Horkheimer elsewhere in *Natural Law and Human Dignity*. See Bloch, *Natural Law and Human Dignity*, 169-70.—Ed.

of the Adorno type of pretentious philosophizing as "a *shrewd obscurantism* and, with it, the dogmatic clericalism that *unquestionably knows everything*."[6]

Both Bloch and Lukács were passionate believers that it is necessary to "*take a stand against German misery*," as Marx advocated in his time. The capitulatory and accommodatory "critical theory," with its pretentiously propagandized but socially evasive "bloated platitudes sitting on its high horse," represented the polar opposite to their stand.*

These are the first lines of Bloch's moving essay on Thomasius: "It is time to commemorate *an upright* man. He was justly uncomfortable in his sleepy and servile surroundings. If they had had their way, then they would have destroyed this annoying innovator. But this did not happen; instead once again an honorable spirit, one who is both *honorable and spirited*, and who speaks of progress, makes himself unavoidable in the long run."[7]

Given that it was written shortly after his return to East Germany in 1949, this meticulous study of Thomasius could also have been Bloch's inaugural lecture at the University of Leipzig, where he had the Chair of Philosophy. This was the same city from which Thomasius had been chased away by the obscurantists, because of his progressive, and in many ways most radical, Enlightenment views.

Bloch does not try to idealize Thomasius. He does not hide his limitations both in historical and in intellectual terms. But he puts into relief the often-astonishing innovatory aspects of Thomasius's work, showing the deep-seated connections with the German Enlightenment tradition in its specificity, and highlighting the organic development of his theory of natural law in terms of the intellectual and social movements of his time. Precise quotations from Thomasius's main works are given, making very clear the terms of Bloch's analysis. At the same time, it is also very clear why Bloch considers the work of this intellectual ancestor highly relevant to the concerns of the contemporary world in which *social emancipation* and "*uprightness*" *of human rights* go together.

---

* Two words within parentheses in the sentence excluded as indecipherable. —Ed.

The main reason for Bloch's advocacy of Thomasius's relevance—his anticipation of the need for a *communal* social order *without property*—is stressed in the quotations given in the adjoining notes on "*Bloch in praise of Thomasius.*" In this respect a few additional points need to be made. Some of the important aspects of Thomasius are stressed by Bloch in this way:

> Grotius had said that the law of reason was valid even when—though this is impossible—there was no God; Thomasius intensified this principle by saying that one could not speak of natural law at all if there was a God above men.... Among the traditional obligations to God only those that are *valid according to reason* remain valid, namely those that manifest themselves in the *fulfillment of obligations toward one's self and others*. In this way the philosophy of right is removed from the vicinity of theology.[8]

According to Bloch, "Thomasius even radicalizes Grotius himself. In place of a proximity to religion there is only a *proximity to morality*, whose content is *earthly* in the best sense of the word.... He [Thomasius] characterized the 'ought' of the social ensemble as *happiness and peace*.... Peace is founded on the pure *positivum* of intention. ... The commandment of the *honestum* of ethicality dwells in the *positivum* of intention, in the *forum internum*, and it runs [in Thomasius's words]: 'Do not be a hypocrite, apply to yourself the perfection that you demand of others.... No one is a good *politicus* who is not in fact a good *ethicus.*'"[9] Bloch stresses that this is an anticipation of Kant's principle spelled out in *Perpetual Peace*.

Bloch's critique of natural law—including Thomasius's stand—is summed up like this: "The general limits that Thomasius's natural law shares with every modern bourgeois natural law are evident: the assumption of a static human nature, an unmediated human ideal, whose 'universal good' is impossible in antagonistic class society."[10]

But Thomasius's *Introduction to the Science of Ethics* offers something else considered by Bloch "the socialist consequences of human rights."[11] According to Thomasius:

> Now there follows the indissoluble community of all goods, and similarly all reasonable conduct and behavior, as the complete testimony, that henceforth reasonable love has arrived at its perfection. ... And therefore all property must disappear and *everything must be held in common*, because all forms of property are born of a lack of love and of disunion. We have detailed this elsewhere and shown from the beginning of the world there has been a *community of goods* ... and that even at the beginning of Christianity, when Christian love still retained the ardor that belongs to it, *all goods were held in common among the first Christians*. ... God wanted that *no person be poor or rich*.[12]

Bloch continues after quoting Thomasius:

> Thomasius is referring to the social utopian book by Vairasse, *The History of Severambes* (1672), but in the content of this and many other passages he goes *beyond the bourgeois natural* law by means of *the natural law of the revolutionary sect*s, with which Thomasius was well acquainted, and by means of the *primitive communist goal* they contained. And Thomasius does not describe the *society of communal property* in a utopian novel, but in his *doctrine of ethics, a scholarly work* that demonstrated the seriousness of the deduction current at the time. This was *an act of great audacity*, especially in Germany, the land where the *peasant wars* had hardly been forgotten; it was an audacity even if one recognized that it was Christian love that opened the way, and not revolt as in Müntzer. "Bring love to the people first, and then the questions of property or of the *community of goods will resolve themse*lves"* (*On the Art of Loving Reasonably or Virtuously*, p. 310)—that is naive, but is it not true that this naiveté reaches up to Ludwig Feuerbach?"[13]

---

* Mészáros placed a double exclamation mark in the left margin here (a device he sometimes used to indicate dissent on a particular point in a quote in his handwritten draft), clearly directed in this case at the words "resolve themselves," seen as representing an idealistic view.—Ed.

Bloch further comments,

> Today the same type of person as Thomasius . . . would have an answer in the *real attempts* at the *socialism of communal property*; he would have *half the world as a model** and as an answer to the question that refers to the public world—"what sort of shape would it have if there were no property?" Besides, for the man who drew *the conclusion of real humanity* from natural law this would not be a question; this is only a question, what Thomasius called a scruple, for those who "have been entangled in property" until their will and intellect have been *enchained*. For Thomasius, the innate fundamental right is the right to happiness; a true community should bring with it the whole of happiness without hindrance, and the basic means to this end is the *abolition of property*.[14]

Here it is relevant to return to a quote from Bloch's book on *Natural Law and Human Dignity* on Thomasius: "For Thomasius the commandment of the *honestum*, of ethicality, dwells in the *positivum* of intention, in the *forum internum*, and it runs: 'Do to yourself that which you want the other to do to himself.' Or, according to the commentary that Thomasius appends to it: 'Do not be a hypocrite, apply to yourself the perfection you demand of others.'"[15] † Viewed in terms of

---

* Here Mészáros put a triple exclamation mark in the left margin of his draft, indicating his dissent regarding Bloch's characterization of post-revolutionary societies at the time Bloch was writing, which, by the time Mészáros was writing, no longer existed. Nevertheless, the principles represented by Thomasius and Bloch remained necessary in present and future struggles for a substantive society.—Ed.

† In his introduction to Thomasius's *Institutes of Divine Jurisprudence*, Thomas Ahnert writes: "The third level of obedience to natural law was the *honestum* (the honest), which demanded that humans rid themselves of corrupt passions and be guided by reasonable love, for the sake of their own happiness and well-being. Thomasius summarized the main command of the *honestum* as 'Do unto yourself what you would like others to do to themselves.' The *honestum* represented the highest degree of conformity of natural law. Thomas Ahnert, Introduction, in Christian Thomasius, *Institutes of Divine Jurisprudence* (Indianapolis: Liberty Fund, 2011), xxiii.—Ed.

its historical development, from the *ascending* phase of the bourgeoisie, we can identify here the *completion* of the *full circle*.

The relationship between law and ethicality was always problematical in bourgeois theories of Right (law/*Recht*). The idea of bringing into harmony the *externum* (with its system of *obligations* and *sanctions*) and the *internum* was never achieved, or even coherently *articulated*. But in the ascending phase it was *indicated* as a *postulate* and even a *challenge*. Bloch makes the connection (though in exaggerated form) between Thomasius's quoted principle and Kant.[16] (There is no sign in Kant of Thomasisus's *communal* advocacy and dismissal of property. But at least he *postulates* the ideal of the *moral politician*.) Still, there is not the least sign (in Kant) of condemnation of those who fail to live up to Thomasius's principle of *honestum* arising from (or conforming to the requirements of) *internal form* as hypocritical.

This stands as a fateful contrast to the *moral depravity*—in full conformity with the role of "*liberal democratic*" law—both in Thomasisus's time and in our own time of the consummation of the *descending phase* of capital's historical development. Hypocrisy and cynicism are the salient features of the fateful contradiction between *ethicality and law* in our time. No room even for the most abstract *postulate* of the "*moral politician*." On the contrary, a kind of "counter-selection" is in evidence, rewarding the diametrical opposite. Tony Blair is a blatant example.

Appendices

Notes

Index

APPENDIX 1

Original Plan for *Beyond Leviathan**

VOLUME 1: THE HISTORIC CHALLENGE
Chapter 1: From Relative to Absolute Limits: Historical Anachronism of the State
1.1 Historical Constitution and Antagonistic Reality of the State
1.2 Freedom Is Parasitic on Equality: Common Denominator of Antagonistic Political Formations and the Qualitative Determination of Disposable Time
1.3 From Primitive Equality to Substantive Equality—via Slavery
1.4 Capital's Deepening Structural Crisis and the State
1.5 The Historic Circle Is Closing—The Challenge to Secure Exit

Chapter 2: The Mountain We Must Conquer
2.1 The End of Liberal-Democratic Politics
2.2 The "Withering Away" of the State?
2.3 The Wishful Limitations of State Power
2.4 The Assertion of Might-as-Right
2.5 Eternalizing Assumptions of Liberal State Theory
2.6 Hegel's Unintended Swan Song and the Nation-State
2.7 Capital's Social Metabolic Order and the State
2.8 Conclusion

Chapter 3: Ancient and Modern Utopias: From Plato and Aristotle to Kant and Beyond
3.1 From Plato's Cave to the Sombre Light of *The Laws*

---

* Mészáros's intention was to publish *Beyond Leviathan* as a three-volume work, one which, however, remained incomplete at the time of his death (see the Editor's Introduction to this volume). This was his draft outline of the general plan for the entire work.—Ed.

3.2 Equality in the Broken Mirror of Justice: The Meaning of
 Aristotelian *Politeia*
3.3 Primitive Accumulation and the Nightmare World of More's *Utopia*
3.4 Machiavelli and Campanella on the Road to Giambattista Vico
3.5 From Bacon and Harrington to Thomas Paine and Robert Owen
3.6 Search for Truth Under the Scottish Enlightenment
3.7 From Kant and Lessing to Thomasius and Bloch's *Principle of Hope*
3.8 Pessimistic Utopias of Capital's Inescapable Order
3.9 Looking Ahead

Addenda
I   Customs, Tradition and Explicit Law: Historical Boundaries of the Legal and Political Superstructure
II Substantive Equality and Substantive Democrarcy

VOLUME 2: THE HARSH REALITY
Chapter 4: Hobbes Haunting Humanity
Chapter 5: Religion, Morality and Politics: Forms of Advocating Legitimate Decision-Making
Chapter 6: Revolution and Restoration: Promises of the Enlightenment Derailed
Chapter 7: Hegel's State Theory: The Reverse View of Equality and Freedom
Chapter 8: Projections and Reality of Liberalism and Utilitarianism

VOLUME 3: THE NECESSARY ALTERNATIVE
Chapter 9: "Dixi et salvavi animam meam": Marx's Critique of the State and the Global Wars of Monopolistic Imperialism
Chapter 10: Lenin's State and Revolution in Its Historic Setting —and in Ours
Chapter 11: The Moment of Truth: The Structural Crisis of Politics and Its State-Oriented Denial
Chapter 12: The Critical Alternative: Radical Restructuring of the Social Metabolism on the Ground of Substantive Equality
Conclusion: Paths of Transition
1. Pensioning-Off Hydra Altogether: The Role of Critical Jurisprudence
2. Articulating Global Extra-Parliamentary Mass Action
3. Contestable Values and Viable Decision-Making: The Constituton of Solidarity in the Planetary Household

APPENDIX 2

Historical Boundaries of the Legal and Political Superstructure

Talking about the emergence of rent, Marx stresses the vital importance of 1) a sufficiently large surplus of labor-power; and 2) the natural productivity of the land, as the necessary conditions for introducing rent. At the same time, he adds: "It is not this possibility which creates the rent, but rather *compulsion* which turns this possibility into reality.* But the possibility itself is conditioned by subjective and objective natural circumstances."[1]

From such considerations he moves on to assess the role of *tradition* and the emergence of *law* in terms of the requirements of the fundamental social metabolism, saying:

> It is evident that *tradition* must play a dominant role in the primitive and undeveloped circumstances on which these social production relations and the corresponding mode of production are based. It is furthermore clear that here as always it is in the interest of the *ruling* section of society to *sanction the existing order as law* and to legally establish its limits given through *usage and tradition*. Apart from all else, this, by the way, comes about of itself as soon as the *constant reproduction* of the basis of the existing order

---

* This appendix is taken from the third section (3.3) of Chapter 3, "Key Concepts of the Dialectic of Base and Superstructure," in István Mészáros, *The Dialectic of Structure and History*, vol. 2 of *Social Structure and Forms of Consciousness* (New York: Monthly Review Press, 2011), 115–29. The original title/subtitle for this section was "Customs, Tradition, and Explicit Law: Historical Boundaries of the Political and Legal Superstructure." Here it is shortened to the subtitle alone. Mészáros stipulated in his plan for *Beyond Leviathan* that this section of *The Dialectic of Structure and History* should be incorporated as an appendix to the work. —Ed.

and its fundamental relations assumes a *regulated and orderly form* in the course of time. And such *regulation and order* are themselves indispensable elements of *any* mode of production, if it is to assume *social stability* and independence from mere chance and arbitrariness. These are precisely the form of its social stability and therefore its relative freedom from mere arbitrariness and mere chance. Under backward conditions of the production process as well as the corresponding social relations, it achieves this form by mere *repetition* of their very reproduction. If this has continued on for some time, it *entrenches* itself as *custom and tradition* and is finally *sanctioned* as an *explicit law*.[2]

As we can see, though the truly extra-economic category of *naked compulsion* needs no historical explanation (the spontaneous exercise of brute force on the basis of differential natural strength is sufficient to set it into motion), the appearance of *legalized* compulsion, that is, legally sanctioned and institutionally enforced compulsion, is an entirely different matter.

To explain the genesis of law, it is necessary to bring into play a number of very different factors, from the elementary requirements of the social metabolism as such to more mediated superstructural mechanisms. "Continued reproduction," "regulation and order," "social stability," and "independence from mere chance and arbitrariness" are all vital requirements of any mode of production, irrespective of its relative degree of historical development. Thus "regulation" and "orderly reproduction" arise as the elemental material imperatives of social stability as such, prior to any conceivable legal regulation. Law itself must be first established on the same material basis before it can determine the specific form in which subsequent social interaction may legitimately take place. As the point of departure for a theoretically viable account, it is not possible to assume more than the mere fact of *repetition* as the necessary condition of any successful societal reproduction. This much, of course, one may rightfully assume, since it is simply inconceivable to envisage any mode of socioeconomic reproduction, no matter how "innovative," in which "repetition"—or "continuity"—does not play a significant part.

The social practice (and the corresponding category) of "repetition" represents the necessary point of departure toward the establishment of law, through the mediation of "usages," "customs," and "tradition." Once reproduction is reinforced and stabilized through continued repetition of its fundamental processes to the point of becoming well established "usages and customs" of the given society—thereby securing and safeguarding the "regulated and orderly form" of reproduction in the interest of social stability—the transition from *direct material determinations* (subject to the rule of "mere chance and arbitrariness") to the active intervention of *superstructural* constituents is successfully accomplished. For inasmuch as usages and customs *entrench themselves* and acquire the power of *tradition*, the door to formally codifying the more or less generally accepted (and at any rate effectively working) normativity of tradition by explicit law is wide open, together with the possibility of manipulating the beliefs associated with all forms of customs and tradition. By the same token, those who happen to be in some key position with respect to the implementation of customs and tradition (as guardians of the associated ritual practices, for instance) do not *ipso fqcto* merely have a vested *interest* in reinforcing their own relatively privileged position but also the *ability* to do so.

Another point of great importance is that the existence of a regulatory system of customs and traditions makes it not only possible (and relatively easy) to establish "explicit law" as the watchdog of the ruling order, but also facilitates the task of the latter by exercising many of its controlling functions, thereby reducing to a minimum the need for a direct repressive (legal) intervention in areas over which customs and traditions can maintain effective control. Hence there is always a dialectical relationship between tradition and law in that

1. no society can regulate itself on an enduring basis by the power of "explicit law" alone;
2. there is "two-way traffic" between law and tradition inasmuch as one can reinforce the other; or take over some functions of the other when the latter fails effectively to exercise them; or initiate some new functions and later assign them to the other, etc.;
3. the more customs and traditions successfully embrace, the less explicit or codified law needs regulating;
4. the broad framework of the law itself is powerfully conditioned by the existing system of customs and traditions, that is, no legal system can diametrically oppose the established system of customs and traditions without losing its own credibility and efficacy;
5. major socioeconomic changes initiate corresponding transformations in tradition and law alike, but the effective unfolding and implementation of such changes may be retarded for a considerable time by the power of inertia of the latter;
6. law, by definition, can respond more quickly than tradition to basic socioeconomic determinations (and in general to the need for significant social change); however, due to the interdeterminations referred to in point 4, the pace at which law can effectively respond to the requirements of major

social change cannot ignore the limitations (and potentialities) of tradition itself as an integral part of the overall transformation;

7. *In the last* analysis, in the dialectical relationship between *law* and *tradition* the latter is structurally more important, even though, as a matter of brute fact, law assumed the dominant position in the course of history. What this vital consideration with regard to the alienating historical reversal of the objective structural primacy of tradition over the legal and political superstructure amounts to is that the progressive transcendence of explicit law (envisaged by Marx in order to do away with its negative, repressive dimension) is inseparable from independently articulated law and "*Staatswesen*"[3] as such—and thus is conceivable only if society can transfer all the regulative functions of explicit law to the "self-activity," that is, the conscious or spontaneous "customs and tradition" of the social body itself.

It is also clear from the Marxian account that the superstructure must be constituted and articulated within the framework of customs and traditions *well before* it can assume the form of "legal and political superstructure." The prominence of legal and political determinations in exercising the essential functions of the social metabolism is characteristic of *class societies*, including the long historical period of transition from the capitalist social formation to the "higher phase of socialism" (or communism). According to Marx, only the latter can bring a radical change in this respect, when—beyond the earlier regulatory constraints—the self-determined interaction of social individuals is governed by the principle "to everyone according to their need," rather than by the institutionalized rule of a separate legal system and its corresponding "state form," be that of the most enlightened kind.

Once the superstructure takes on the characteristic form of "legal and political superstructure" in the course of historical development—a form appropriate to various modes of "orderly" reproduction within the confines of the hierarchical-structural division of labor—the whole of the superstructure, even its most mediated dimensions (religious beliefs, artistic practices, philosophical conceptions, etc.), must be brought under its determinations, though, of course, in the earlier dialectical sense of the term. For the legal and political superstructure is by its very nature a "totalizing" all-comprehensive structure. It reaches down to the most fundamental levels of social interchange, regulating the social metabolism itself by imposing and safeguarding the property relations of the given mode of production.

We must recall in this context Marx's characterization of the completed capitalist order as a historically constituted totality and, as such, an "organic system."[4] Within the framework of this "organic system," everything must be in tune with the necessary *practical presuppositions* of the dominant mode of production, based on a perverted form of *"universality."* This is, in reality, a pseudo-universality in that it is determined negatively, by way of *exclusion*, so that citizenship, for instance, is circumscribed with reference to barriers and various disqualification clauses; and, likewise, the pseudo-positive concept of "conformity to the law" is defined in terms of the conditions of its violation, together with a set of more or less arbitrarily stipulated sanctions. All of this is in perfect agreement with the dictates of *exclusivistic* (rather than simply private) *property relations* that assign control over the vital reproductive functions of society to a small minority, in sharp contrast to genuinely all-inclusive *communal* property relations that embrace all members of society.

Since the development of such social formations takes place on the material foundations (and regulatory premises) of a structurally divided class society, those parts of the "organic system" in question possess the greatest strategic relevance—and a corresponding ability to extend their power over every sphere—which are the most directly involved in reproducing the iniquitous *structural parameters* and operating conditions of the overall social complex. This is the principal reason why the *legal and political* superstructure acquires its paramount importance in the course of historical development.

Parallel to the consolidation of exclusivistic property ownership and the emergence of the ruling order's need for a radical redefinition of universality, the legal and political superstructure becomes the *"uebergreifendes Moment,"* and in the end a one-sidedly dominant constituent, of the superstructure as a whole. For no other part of the superstructure can satisfy this need—absolutely vital from the perspective of the ruling order—with a comparable practical effectiveness.

Religion and art, for instance, must maintain their claims to potentially all-inclusive and communally shared universality (from which in principle not even the members of the most hostile foreign state can be excluded, however illusory and "other-worldly" their terms of reference might be) so as not to contradict their self-definition and thereby lose their authenticity and credibility. Accordingly, the practical role they are allowed to play must be a subsidiary one with regard to the structural parameters and operating conditions of established society. All the more so, in fact, the greater the complexity of the reproductive interconnections within an increasingly more integrated, and in the end globally intertwined, socioeconomic framework.

In this sense, one can truly say that several dimensions of the superstructure become "marginalized" and condemned to an essentially supportive role in the course of historical development, in direct proportion to the rise of the legal and political superstructure. At the same time, "practical reason" under all its aspects must remain subjected to the materially determined normative requirements directly manifest in the coordinating and "totalizing" function of the legal and political *uebergreifendes Moment*. It is by no means accidental in this respect that precisely those dimensions of the non-legal/political superstructure that happen to be the most sensitive from the point of view of the societal reproduction process are brought under the direct control of the ever more powerful legal and political superstructure (in contrast to the pre-capitalist past when they were much more directly influential). This is evidenced not only in the relationship between the modern state and the churches (notwithstanding all talk about their separation) but also in the way in which the artistic and educational institutions of society are being controlled.

As we have seen, the normative dominance of law and politics becomes possible only at a relatively recent stage of historical development. The original constitution and long drawn-out transformation of the regulatory principles necessary for sustained social reproduction can be identified in the following terms:

1. The exposure of "primitive communities" to the rule of chance and arbitrariness; *naked compulsion* as the only feasible regulatory force, with all its *wastefulness* and *instability*; total absence of normativity;
2. The emergence of stabilizing factors through *repetition*, on the basis of "trial and error," representing the first—*spontaneous*—steps in the direction of emancipation from chance and arbitrariness;
3. The consolidation of the positive achievements of repetition in the form of—instrumentally oriented—*specific usages*;
4. The coordination of a multiplicity of recurrent usages into a fairly coherent body of *customs*; normativity is still primarily concerned with the objective requirements of production and reproduction, that is, with the enforcement of predominantly instrumental necessities; this remains the case for a long time, even though the imperatives associated with the reproduction of the operating conditions of production (articulated as a set of well-marked customs) introduce a strong element of social normativity, preparing the ground for a much more problematical social division of labor;
5. The integration of the most varied and long-established customs into the *universally respected tradition* of the given community, representing a mode of regulation that lays great stress on *values* transmitted from generation to generation, coupled with ritual reinforcement that involves the active participation of all; societies regulated by the normativity of tradition may remain for an indefinite period of time

thoroughly egalitarian in character, as historical records show, although the entrenchment of the new regulatory modalities opens the door to the development of separate forms of institutional enforcement and to the structural hierarchies that go with them;

6. The emergence of *explicit law*; tradition *selectively* elevated to the status of law, with its *sanctions* and separate organs of law enforcement at the service of the *ruling order*; the exploitative minority interests of the established social formation codified as "the law," self-interestedly redrawing the boundaries of legitimate social intercourse and redefining the meaning of "society," "communality," and "universality" in accordance with the aprioristic requirements of *structural domination*, so that the concept of "social organism" acquires a profoundly conservative and apologetic meaning. At the same time, the potentially dissenting social forces are strictly (and punitively) subordinated to the new, rather abstract and instrumentally enforced system of overall coordination and normativity, hence the inescapably *negative* articulation of the legal and political regulatory framework.

Thus, though it is undoubtedly true that the various "moments" referred to here become not only practically but also formally *subsumed* under the fully articulated legal and political superstructure, they nevertheless remain directly or indirectly *operative* within the totalizing framework of the latter, however unpalatable this may sound to those who continue to idealize and "eternalize" the triumph of "Leviathan" as equivalent to civilized human existence, from the earliest theorists of the "social contract" to present-day apologists of the capitalist state. For the historically recent legal and political regulatory machinery simply could not fulfill its vital metabolic functions without effectively bringing into play all the other—structurally more fundamental—moments as well, redefined as subordinate parts of its own "orderly" self-constitution. Even *naked compulsion* remains an integral part of the (no matter how "refined") legal and political superstructure, convenient though it might be to ignore this fact as far as the established socioeconomic order is concerned, since it happens to clash with the self-mythology of the dominant interests. As Marx rightly observed:

> All the bourgeois economists are aware of is that production can be carried on better under the modern police than e.g. on the principle of might makes right. They forget only that this principle is also a legal relation, and that the right of the stronger prevails in their "constitutional republics" as well, only in another form.[5]

Indeed, the right of the stronger—that is, the necessary dominance of those who own and/or control the means of production—must prevail, ultimately at all costs, since the stability of the *relations* of production (the material underpinning of the legal and political superstructure) is crucial to the successful reproduction of the operating conditions of production. Law and the institutions of its enforcement are eminently suitable to such a role under the conditions of social antagonism, that is, when the management of the essential reproductive structures of society remains irreconcilably contested. Consequently, only the radical supersession of social antagonisms could do away with naked compulsion and institutionalized violence, however "civilized" and liberally "sophisticated," which must be at least "implicit"—and at times of major crises openly reactivated—in all forms of "explicit law."[6]

All this does not alter the fact that the historically primary and ontologically fundamental—and in that sense "absolute"—moment is the necessity of *orderly regulation*, in the interest of socioeconomic advancement and the expansion and satisfaction of historically produced needs on the ground of such advancement, and not the *specific form* [in which this presently occurs through second-order mediations]. All the less since the form in question can only secure the required reproduction at the devastating social cost of reproducing at the same time the structural hierarchies and antagonisms of the established order both on an expanding scale and with a growing intensity, which carry grave implications for the future.

The most problematic aspect of the historically evolved and, up until the present time, dominant mode of social regulation (from which many others follow) is that *appropriation* falls under the rule of minority-controlled property and alienated legality that sustains such property in the form of separately constituted political power. Indeed, one of the vicious circles we can identify in this sphere concerns the separately articulated legal and political superstructure that necessarily implies the material dominance of exclusivistic/minority-controlled property (and the corresponding modality of iniquitous appropriation at all planes) and vice versa. Thus, in class societies the legal and political form is both a regulator of social intercourse and a usurper in the service of the usurpers of social wealth. And even after the intended postrevolutionary break with the past, it represents one of the greatest challenges to extricate the new society of "associated producers" from the clutches of these determinations, which tend to resist or subvert precisely their practical self-definition as associated producers.

It is by no means surprising that so long as the legal form remains dominant, the structural iniquities of discriminatory appropriation are reproduced with it. This is particularly revealing in the light of some major reversals to which modern history bears witness. For in the course of revolutionary upheavals, conscious efforts are made, at times, to introduce some truly egalitarian principles for the regulation of production and appropriation—as for instance during the initial phase of the Russian Revolution—which are later reversed, parallel to the reconstitution of the state that emerges more powerful than ever from the crisis. Such reversals, rooted in the vicious circle between separate legality and iniquitous appropriation, underline the hopeless inadequacy of explaining these problems in terms of "post-revolutionary bureaucratization"—and associated categories—which at best only beg the question. One cannot reduce a whole range of objective structural determinations to subjective defects.[7]

Historically the emergence and consolidation of the legal and political superstructure runs parallel to the conversion of communal appropriation into exclusivistic property. The more extensive the practical impact of the latter on the prevailing modality of social reproduction (especially in the form of fragmented private property), the more pronounced and institutionally articulated the totalizing role of the legal and political superstructure must be. It is therefore by no means accidental that the centralizing and bureaucratically all-invading *capitalist* state—and not a state defined by vague geographic terms as "the modern Occidental state"—acquires its preponderance in the course of the development of generalized commodity production and the practical institution of the property relations in tune with it, notwithstanding the "free market" and "laissez-faire" mythology of its beneficiaries. Once this connection is omitted, as indeed for ideological reasons it must be in the case of all those who conceptualize these problems from the standpoint of the ruling order, we end up with a mystery as to why the state assumes the character it happens to have under the conditions of generalized commodity production. The mystery becomes a complete mystification when Max Weber tries to unravel it by suggesting that "it has been the work of jurists to give birth to the modern Occidental state."[8] Hegel's idealism at least offered us the good services of the "World Spirit" in explanation of such monumental miracles, not the misty *Kopfarbeit* of drunken judges.

The more fully articulated the legal and political superstructure is, the more closely it embraces and dominates not only the material practices but simultaneously the most varied "ideal forms" of social consciousness. As a result, the theoretical, philosophical, artistic, etc., forms of activity cannot directly reflect, or respond to, the needs and demands of the social base. They must do so via the necessarily *biased mediation* of the legal and political superstructure.

Two sets of questions are particularly important in this respect. The first concerns the nature of practical mediations within the capitalistic framework of social reproduction, and the second the perverse configuration of this formation as an "organic system."

Since these problems are discussed in considerable detail in *Beyond Capital*, let it suffice to say here briefly, with regard to the first set, that the mediations in question—which negatively affect the production of all forms and modalities of social consciousness—are the structurally vitiated and reified *second-order mediations* of WAGE LABOR, PRIVATE PROPERTY, and EXCHANGE, asserting themselves through the controlling power of capital (which arises from its monopoly over the means of production) and the corresponding hierarchical social division of labor. Naturally, given the way in which class society is constituted on the ground of objective contradictions (held together by a multiplicity of interlocking determinations), the legal and political superstructure formally regulates and reinforces this network of alienated second-order mediations, enlisting in its task the contribution of all the other parts of the superstructure as well, and thereby it plays a vital role in the successful reproduction of the entire system.

As to the second set of problems, what is relevant in the present context is that the practically crucial role of the legal and political superstructure in the overall reproduction process—which turns it into the *uebergreifendes Moment* of the entire superstructure—confers upon the legal and political superstructure a highly privileged status in the "organic system" of the established social order. As a result, the other parts of the superstructure cannot gain access to the necessary means of their own activity without the (explicit or implicit) stamp of approval by the legal and political superstructure. In this sense, the "organic system" of capital articulates itself also at the plane of the superstructure as a complex network of subordinations and superordinations, even if intellectuals tend to forget about the paradoxical relationships of superstructural dependency into which they are, as individuals, inescapably inserted.

On both counts, therefore, the "full emancipation" of art, philosophy, etc., from the rule of capital is inseparable from the "withering away" of the legal and political superstructure as such. Since under the prevailing system the non-legal/political parts of the superstructure can only gain access to the conditions of their effective functioning through the necessarily biased mediation of the legal and political superstructure, there is a *prima facie* tension between the two. Under favorable circumstances this tension can assume the form of critical emancipatory contestation. Indeed, one may rightfully assert that there is a genuine emancipatory interest on the side of art, critical social theory, etc., opposed to the legal and political superstructure for as long as the latter retains its normative preponderance in the overall reproduction process. Such emancipatory interest, though, must be located in an empirically identifiable social agency as its carrier, rather than hypostatized on a fictitiously self-supporting ideal/intellectual terrain, as often happens with the representatives of the Frankfurt School, including Marcuse's desperate yet mysteriously emancipatory "Aesthetic Dimension."[9] Moreover, since by its very nature "explicit law" can never acquire the character of *self-activity*, in that it must set itself up above all members of society in its spurious claims to universal validity, the practical realization of socialist emancipation envisaged by Marx is in principle unthinkable within the structural constraints of the legal and political superstructure as such. In other words, according to the Marxian conception the legal and political superstructure not only in its capitalist form but *in all conceivable forms* must be considered the necessary target of emancipatory social practice.

In relation to these considerations, it becomes clear why the historical boundaries of the legal and political superstructure must be drawn with great care, both with regard to the past and in the direction of the future. For, as no one could seriously dispute it, no society can adequately reproduce itself and advance in its capacity to satisfy an expanding range of human needs without creating reliable normative structures and institutions, in accordance with the cumulative regulatory requirements of an increasingly more complex and intertwined social metabolism. In this sense, once the phase regulated by the crudest material determinations is left behind, social intercourse is inconceivable without the growing intervention of superstructural factors, with their corresponding forms of normativity. Nor is it conceivable to do away with normativity as such in a socialist society. If anything, its role, on the contrary, is bound to increase with the mastery of material necessities and the successful removal of external constraints. For the fully acknowledged *reciprocity* of the interacting social individuals as "associated producers" necessarily implies as its precondition the *internal normativity* of a new mode of action, oriented within, and envisaging the reproduction of, a consciously adopted overall societal framework from which the aprioristic (materially prejudged and vitiated) predominance of partial interests has been removed in the course of historical development.

Thus, although the "new historic form"—Marx's code name for a truly socialist society—is totally unthinkable without its properly articulated superstructure, it is quite another matter as far as the legal and political superstructure is concerned. For the normativity of the latter, very far from being *internal* and thus suitable to the exercise of consciously pursued and fully equitable reciprocity, is in fact *external* and alienated normativity par excellence.

With respect to the past, the historical boundary of the legal and political superstructure is marked by the radical displacement and domination (though, for reasons already indicated, by no means the liquidation) of the earlier forms of normativity—in their inception spontaneously all-embracing and participatory. Furthermore, throughout its long history the legal and political superstructure is characterized by the practical reproduction of yet another, somewhat paradoxical, vicious circle. Through this circle it *sustains* the dominance of minority-controlled property, and at the same time—in regard to its ultimate *sanction* that materially grounds, in principle at least, its own power of domination over all particular individuals. *It is itself sustained by property*, in the form of its selectively exercised negation of the right of determinate individuals to enjoy their property and the freedoms associated with their possessions, without disrupting its own subservience to the dominant class or classes at the level of collective relations.

As for the future, the historical boundary of the legal and political superstructure can only be drawn in practical terms by the structural crisis of the mode of social interchange that must rely on minority-controlled property as the principal motivating force of its system of productive reproduction. For so long as the operating conditions of social production remain tied to the structural hierarchies of the established social division of labor, the vicious circle is bound to be reproduced with them, even if in an altered form.

This means that under such conditions the dominance of the alienating normativity of the law—deeply rooted in the reproductive processes themselves—cannot be superseded. At the same time, it is also clear that the retention of the alienating normativity of the legal and political superstructure is totally incompatible with the idea of socialist emancipation. It is not surprising, therefore, that the Marxian project had to be spelled out from the very beginning as a revolutionary critique of the state. A critique that envisaged the state's complete transcendence in Marx's very early writings (such as the *Critique of the Hegelian Philosophy of Right*, among others), reiterating the same point with great emphasis in the assessment of the Paris Commune's historical significance and in some passages of the *Critique of the Gotha Programme* that envisage the necessary historical supersession of the state form and the radical transcendence of the law (or "explicit law") as such. Thus, there can be no compromise as far as the "withering away of the state" and the progressive "*Aufhebung*" of the legal and political superstructure—in favor of a qualitatively redefined and correspondingly restructured superstructure—are concerned. In terms of the Marxian vision, any accommodation on this point amounts to abandoning the idea of a socialist transformation of society altogether.

This is why concern with the relationship between the material base and the superstructure of the various sociohistorical formations occupies such an important place in the Marxian conception.

As we have seen, according to Marx the "superstructure" in its primary sense is *radically* different from the superstructure articulated as "legal and political superstructure." The emergence and consolidation of a separate legal and political framework to which all the other parts of the superstructure must be subjected is due to much more recent sociohistorical factors and determinations than the original constitution of the *superstructure as customs and tradition*. Appropriately, the latter thus assumes a particular significance in the assessment of the issues at stake. For it remains the structurally and ontologically fundamental constituent, notwithstanding the dominant position of law and politics throughout the history of class societies.

Ultimately, it is the Marxian way of drawing the line of demarcation between the ontologically untranscendable *superstructure* and the historically limited *legal and political* superstructure that makes it possible to anticipate the "withering away" of the state and the end of the domination of social life by separate legality and abstract normativity, with all the emancipatory potential inherent in such "withering away" with regard to both the primary material and the corresponding regulatory superstructural practices of the "freely associated producers."

APPENDIX 3

Substantive Equality and Substantive Democracy

The problem of substantive determinations concerns a fundamental change of a future society in which, in order that such society should be historically sustainable, the vital orienting principle of the social metabolism must be substantive equality.* It goes without saying that likewise some other regulatory concepts, for instance, substantive democracy, are inseparable from the same requirement, in the sense that they all must be conceived and implemented in the spirit of substantive equality.

For me it is a matter of the greatest theoretical and practical political importance that we should contrast our conception of the radically different social metabolism of the future, without which humanity could not possibly survive, with the existing forms. This is why I use the expression "substantively democratic"—and of course "substantive democracy," in its fundamental defining characteristics inseparable from "substantive equality"—in contrast to the once genuine liberal conception of democracy, which could not possibly be under any condition substantive, even when it managed to be more or less substantial in a limited political sense. In that limited sense, politics can be more or less "substantially democratic" under a liberal regime, but never substantively democratic. In the case of my contrast, there can be no "more or less substantively democratic" or "more or less substantively equal." It is either

---

* "Substantive Equality and Substantive Democracy" was first drafted by Mészáros on April 20, 2015, in correspondence with Professor Eduardo Gasca, the Venezuelan translator of *Beyond Capital*, whom Mészáros referred to as "my great friend and wonderful Spanish translator" (István Mészáros, "Substantive vs. Substantial" [document] sent to John Bellamy Foster, May 11, 2015). On July 1, 2017, Mészáros sent a shortened version (with personal aspects of the correspondence removed), then entitled "Substantive Equality amd Substantive Democracy." In his original three-volume plan for *Beyond Leviathan*, it was to be included as an appendix at the end of the first volume.—Ed.

substantively democratic and substantively equal, or it is not. In other words, in the latter case it is not substantive at all. By contrast it is perfectly legitimate to talk about "more or less substantially democratic" or "more or less substantially equal" political/social relations under certain historical conditions. This is the sense in which I used the expression "substantive" in *Beyond Capital* and continue to use it here in *Beyond Leviathan*. In fact, I discussed these problems in the same sense in my book, *Marx's Theory of Alienation*, which I started to write in 1959 in London. And indeed, my deep concern with the crucial substance of this matter goes back in a quite explicit form all the way to the autumn of 1951, to a conversation that I had with Georg Lukács, at the time when the Hungarian government increased the price of the vital food and clothing items by 300 percent, and the salaries/wages by only 18 to 21 percent.

At that time, we had a discussion of this measure in the Hungarian Writers' Association with Márton Horváth (who strongly attacked Lukács in the 1949–51 "Lukács debate"), who was the Member of the Party's Politburo responsible for Cultural/Ideological Matters. Some of my writer friends and colleagues recited the answer Horváth wanted to hear, saying that the people enthusiastically approved the declared change. I stayed in total silence, but he turned to me and asked: "And you, Comrade Mészáros, what have you heard?" My answer was: "I don't know which part of the country my friends have visited, but where I live, in a working-class district, people are swearing and cursing the Party and Government."

Characteristically, he retorted: "Comrade Mészáros, you are supposed to lead them, not to tail them!" This showed that he knew very well what the people at large thought, but he wanted to know how the writers would propagandize the Party's decision. Given the big difference in income between the workers and the leading writers, the vital food and clothing price increases did not significantly affect the writers, but they did the workers, painfully. The 18 to 21 percent increase in their salary reasonably compensated the writers, whereas the workers suffered a major reduction in their need primarily for essential food and clothing supplies as a result of their inadequate wages.

Next day I told Lukács about this bewildering experience in the Writers Association and he laughed with me with irony and even sarcasm, signaling his disapproval of Horváth's behavior. And then he explained to me that a more equitable solution would be impossible, requiring massive sums that the economy could not afford. At that time the only thing I could say was: "I understand that, but there must be another way." At that stage in my life I had no proper idea what that "other way" could and should be, and how a real alternative to the existing huge inequities could be brought to practical realization. I only knew that "there must be another way." And, of course, I also knew that the masses of the people were swearing and cursing and that they were my class comrades and childhood companions.

It took me several decades of hard work, in a period of great historical storms and reversals, to understand the complex historical and social ramifications of the vital difference between what is called "greater equality" (which means no real equality at all) and the historically irrepressible requirement of substantive equality.

Liberal democratic societies often assert their claim to insuperable political legitimacy by their proclaimed intent to institute political reforms for "representative democracy," "greater equality" (coupled with "progressive taxation," etc.), and promising to guard society from "excessive state interference." In reality, very few of all these claims and intents stand up to serious examination. But Soviet type post-revolutionary societies also failed to live up to their proclaimed tenets and in the end reverted to the most iniquitous capitalist mold (see Gorbachev, etc.). By temporarily overthrowing the capitalist state, they were able to introduce for a while some limited social reforms but not the necessary structural change that entered the historical horizon through the objective challenge for the realization of substantive equality.

In truth, the question of *substantive equality* is linked to a number of vital issues that I can only summarily mention here. It concerns capital as such, that is, the capital system in its entirety, and not just capitalism.

Likewise, it concerns the state of the capital system as such, that is, the capital state in any one of its known and feasible varieties, and not just the capitalist state. In other words, it is a question of the redefinition and historically viable ongoing reproduction of the social metabolism in its entirety, and not just the overthrow of the established political domain.

The illusions attached to the notion of "direct democracy," etc., must be evaluated in this sense, within the framework of the radically redefined mode of societal reproduction. For the unrealizable projections of "direct democracy" remain unrealizable precisely because they are trapped by the structural limitations of the given political domain, when the unavoidable historical challenge is the radical transformation of all levels of the social metabolism in a non-hierarchical way. Politics can initiate major, indeed fundamental, social metabolic changes, but by itself it cannot constitute them. It can affect in a significant way the conditions of material reproduction, but it is itself dependent—even for the way in which it can articulate its demands for major change—on the nature of the given or envisaged material (as well as, of course, corresponding cultural/ideological) reproductive framework.

Strategic political changes are always formulated in terms of such a material-structural framework, no matter how inexplicit or even cynically camouflaged, as can be seen in relation to those conditions of past history marked by the objective premises of class determination and class exploitation. And when in our time a socialist political decision-making process is envisaged for the future, it must spell out its own practical terms of reference in accordance with the envisaged material reproductive framework of the new society. In this respect, "direct political" action means very little, if anything at all, whereas materially substantive action (as Babeuf was demanding it—in his words, "under the roofs of our houses") makes all the difference.

For its historical viability, this kind of redefinition of politics and society requires the total eradication of capital from the social metabolism. There can be no substantive equality (or substantive democracy) without that. Naturally, this requirement carries with it also the total eradication, the "withering away," of the state as we know it. Capital's reproductive metabolism cannot be eradicated without it. For the state is by its innermost nature necessarily hierarchical. It has been historically constituted as the expropriator and usurper of overall decision-making from the societal reproduction process. Moreover, the material reproductive framework of capital's social metabolic order could not function without the structurally entrenched hierarchical decision-making processes of the corresponding capital state.

One more consideration must be firmly emphasized here: capital's powers of restoration. For by its nature capital cannot be other than inexorably all-dominating, since it cannot acknowledge any limit. Hence we can see the complete absurdity of the Gorbachevian (and any similar) fantasy postulating the "controlled market society." As we know only too well, this fantasy can have many wishful varieties, especially under conditions of severe economic crises.

In view of all these considerations, the only historically sustainable solution for the future is the radical reconstitution of the social metabolism in the spirit of the orienting principle of substantive equality. This can only be envisaged well beyond the unrealizable "substantially more equitable" never-nowhere-land of pious hope. It is by no means surprising that in the course of historical development, advertised in terms of the wishful postulates of liberal-democratic "more equitable redistribution of wealth" in the name of the "welfare state," or whatever else, the promises came to absolutely nothing. Not only were these not "substantially more equitable" social relations but they were not even a little more so. On the contrary, we have witnessed the obscenely ever greater concentration of wealth. So much so that even some decent neoclassical political economists, like Thomas Piketty, expose it in their writing, even if without any solution.

Reorganizing society by transferring the power of decision-making to the freely associated producers is the only feasible way of introducing meaningful planning. This happens to be an absolute condition, totally incompatible with the inherent nature of capital because of its structurally insuperable centrifugality. This dimension of the fundamental social metabolism of our established order—namely its incompatibility with comprehensive planning, rather than partial/antagonism-generating big corporation "planning"—is further aggravated by the systemic requirement of capital's material reproductive metabolism that inexorably tends toward materially invasive globalization, without any feasible corresponding overall decision-making process on the state-legitimated political plane. For it is nothing short of complete absurdity if (or when) the apologists of capital's established social metabolic order envisage a global system of their liking without a globally viable and historically sustainable planning process.

Naturally, a non-antagonistic rational planning process on a comprehensive global plane is inconceivable without its appropriate modality of interchange among the constitutive cells—or "microcosms"—of the all-embracing social order. In this sense, globally viable planning is feasible only on the basis of a laterally coordinated (truly non-hierarchical) societal reproduction process. This is a paradigm question of social reciprocity at the core of which we find the historic requirement of substantive equality. Without planning, the unavoidable global interchange in our present and future societal reproduction cannot be considered historically sustainable. At the same time, planning on a global scale is inconceivable without the removal of structural-hierarchical iniquities so evident in our present world.

In this respect, again, the advocacy of "substantial" in terms of some postulated—but unrealizable—change means nothing at all, because within its orienting framework and corresponding measure remain the existing, structurally entrenched hierarchical order. The "more equitable" claim may be "relatively more substantial" in a partial sense than its earlier variety, but it inevitably fails—as historical development amply proves—in the sense that it represents no real challenge to the existing social order with regard to its self-sustaining and self-justifying structural parameters, well illustrated by the proclaimed liberal "more equitable" claim. (See the original projections by the liberal Lord Beveridge and others on "the welfare state" and its pathetic historical realization and ultimate liquidation even in the handful of privileged capitalist countries.) To get out of that structurally iniquitous social order we need qualitatively different substantive equality as the orienting principle and also the appropriate measure of achievement.

This is also the only way in which the question of transition toward a socialist transformation of the social metabolic order can acquire its proper meaning: by providing the criteria as well as the measure in terms of which particular achievements toward a substantively equitable society as a whole can be ascertained.

To be sure, for historically understandable reasons, the particular political movements that try to assert their policies must promise tangible results to their potential followers. This is a very difficult problem because it tends to impose the demands arising from the short-term hopes of political movements on the historically sustainable perspective of the long term. In truth, however, strategically viable transformation is not feasible without the full observance of the objective and subjective requirements of the long term. Yet unfortunately, often the distinction between "strategy and tactics" is used to justify the neglect of the long term, by saying that "so-and-so" was meant "only tactically," although it directly contradicted the strategically viable long term.

The truth of the matter is that the pursuit of such tactics can painfully derail the necessary long-term strategy. Moreover, there can be no viable strategy without an orienting framework appropriate to the overall determinations of the historically ascertainable long-term tendencies and potentialities. This is why our concern with the contrast between substantive and substantial is a matter of vital importance. In envisaging a historically sustainable socialist transformation there can be no departure from the radical orienting principle and measure of substantive equality, in terms of which the period of transition to a fundamentally different social metabolic order can be constantly evaluated.

All this is perfectly compatible with Marx's views. But in our given historical time the conceptual framework must be articulated in the above sense, reflecting the aggravated and ever worsening conditions of capital's irreversible descending phase of development, with its tendency toward humanity's global destruction, preventable only through the constitution of a substantively equitable social metabolic order. Our critique of the state must be conceived from this perspective.

APPENDIX 4

How Could the State "Wither Away"?

The history of post-capitalist states, in sharp contrast to original expectations, confronts us with some weighty problems.* They may be summed up as follows:

1. To acknowledge that there has been no sign of the state's "withering away" would amount to an evasive understatement. For actual developments not merely did not live up to expectations; they moved in the opposite direction, massively strengthening the power of the political over the social body. The anticipated short historical phase of proletarian dictatorship, to be followed by a sustained *process* of "withering away" to the point of the retention of purely administrative functions—did not materialize. Instead, the state assumed control over all facets of social life, and the dictatorship of the proletariat was promoted to the status of being the permanent political form of the *entire* historical period of transition.
2. To add insult to injury, the capitalist state itself—again, contrary to expectations—did not become an extreme authoritarian state: fascist-type state formations remained episodic in the history of capitalism up to the present time. Though no one should underestimate the danger of right-wing dictatorial solutions at times of acute crises, such solutions, nevertheless, seem to be very much at odds with the objective requirements of the capitalist process of production and circulation at its relatively undisturbed phases of development. The long established "civil society," articulated around the structurally

---

* This appendix is from chapter 13 of István Mészáros, *Beyond Capital* (New York: Monthly Review Press, 1995), 460–95. Mészáros stipulated in his second edition draft notes for *Beyond Leviathan* that it should be incorporated as an appendix to that work.—Ed.

entrenched economic power of competing private capitals, both secures and safeguards the capitalist domination of the political state and, through it, society as a whole. Any reversal of such power relations in favor of the authoritarian political state at times of acute crises is a double-edged sword indeed, threatening the established order as much as defending it: by disrupting the *normal* mechanism of structural domination and by bringing into play the frontal collision of antagonistic forces, in place of the overpowering inertia of the formerly accepted state of affairs. The customarily prevailing relationship between "civil society" and the political state greatly enhances the ideological power of mystification of the bourgeois political state—by advertising itself as the insuperable model of non-interference and individual freedom—and, through its inertia, constitutes a paralyzing material obstacle to any strategy of transition. For it imposes on its socialist adversary the imperative of promising "freedom from state domination" in the near future, while, in fact, the sustained socialist power of the post-capitalist state (the modalities of which are very far from being even touched upon, let alone fully exhausted, by summary references to the "proletarian dictatorship") over against the inherited, capitalistically structured "civil society," is a condition sine qua non of the necessary structural change.

3. To state that "acting within political forms belongs to the old society" (in view of the continued existence of a separate political sphere) is as true in its ultimate perspectives as it is inadequate as far as the problems of transition are concerned. Since the *act* of liberation cannot be separated from the process of liberation, and since the political state, while being conditioned, is simultaneously a vital conditioning factor, the socialist emancipation of society from the oppressive rule of the political sphere necessarily presupposes the radical transformation of politics as such. This means that the advocated transcendence of the state can only be accomplished through the heavily conditioning instrumentality of the state itself. If this is the case, as undoubtedly it happens to be, how can we escape from the vicious circle? For even if we all agree that the political state in its essential characteristics belongs to the old society, the question remains: how to turn the inherited state into a genuinely *transitional* formation from the all-embracing and necessarily *self-perpetuating* structure that it has become in the course of capitalist development. Without a realistic identification of the necessary theoretical mediations and the corresponding social/material forces involved in such transitional change, the program

of abolishing politics through a socialist reorientation of politics is bound to sound problematical.

4. To question the validity of Marxism on account of its conception of the state is a matter of far-reaching implications. Indeed, it is in no way comparable to the tendentiously belabored but peripheral disputes over the fact that socialist revolutions erupted in underdeveloped rather than in advanced capitalist countries. As I have argued, Marx's idea of "uneven development" could account for discrepancies in that respect.[1] And in any case his theory was primarily concerned with the plain necessity of socialist revolutions, and not with the inevitably changing circumstances and modalities of their practical unfolding. By contrast, should the Marxian theory of the state be invalidated, that would render Marxism as a whole thoroughly untenable, in view of the centrality of its belief in the dialectical reciprocity between base and superstructure, the material foundations of society and its political sphere. (To be sure, it is precisely in this sense that the so-called crisis of Marxism has been repeatedly interpreted in the recent past, jumping in panicky haste to aprioristic conclusions from the mere assertion of that crisis, instead of tackling its constituents from a positive perspective.) What makes the matter particularly acute at this critical time in history is that it has *direct* political implications for the strategies of all existing socialist movements, in the East and West alike. In this sense, it is not simply the heuristic value of a social theory that is called into question but something incomparably more tangible and immediate. This is why a searching examination of the Marxian theory of the state, in the light of post-revolutionary developments, is unavoidable today.

1. The Limits of Political Action

Marx's earliest conception of politics was articulated in the form of a threefold negation, aimed at putting in perspective the potentialities and limitations of the political mode of action. Understandably, given the circumstances of what he called the "German misery," the accent had to be put on the severity of these limitations. Whatever changes appeared in this respect in Marx's later writings, the prevalently negative definition of politics remained a central theme of his work to the very end of his life.

Marx's negation was directed at three clearly identifiable objects, and the conclusions derived from their assessment fused into an imperative to identify the constituents of a radically different mode of social action.[2]

1. The first object of his criticism was German underdevelopment itself, and the hopelessness of political action under the constraints of a semi-feudal capitalism, a world situated in terms of the French political calendar well before 1789, as he put it.
2. His second object of negation was Hegel's political philosophy, which elevated to the level of a claimed "science" the illusions of producing the much-needed change, while remaining within the confines of the anachronistic political mold.
3. And, finally, the third prong of Marx's attack was directed at the limitations of even the most advanced French politics. For though the latter was "contemporary" to the present in strictly political terms, it was, nevertheless, hopelessly inadequate as far as the imperative of a radical social transformation was concerned, under the conditions of the growing social antagonism.

Thus, the inner logic of Marx's critical assessment of *German* political limitations pushed him from the first critical stance of simply rejecting the local political constraints toward a radical questioning of the nature and inherent limits of *political action as such*. This is why there had to be a break with his first political comrades at a very early stage in his development. For the latter the critique of Hegel could only mean rendering German politics a little more "contemporary to the present." By contrast, for Marx it was just a preamble to advocating a very different mode of social action: one that started from the premise of consciously rejecting the crippling determination of social action by the necessary one-dimensionality of *all politics* "properly so called." The task of understanding the "anatomy of bourgeois society"—through a critical evaluation of political economy—was the next logical step, in that the positive counterpart to his threefold negation had to be situated on a material plane, if it was to avoid the illusions of not only Hegel and his epigones but also of the contemporary French socialists who tried to impose their politically constrained view on the orientation of the emerging working-class movement.

Talking about the political bias in the outlook of his socialist comrades, Marx complained that "even radical and revolutionary politicians seek the root of the evil not in the *essential nature* of the state, but in a definite *state form*, which they wish to replace by a *different* state form. From the political point of view the *state* and the *system of society* are not *two* different things. The state is the system of society."[3] For Marx it was imperative to get *outside* the "political point of view" in order to be truly critical of the state. He insisted:

The mightier the state, and the *more political* therefore a country is, the less is it inclined to grasp the *general* principle of *social* maladies and to seek their basis in the *principle of the state*, hence in the *present structure* of society, the active, conscious and official expression of which is the state. The *political* mind is a *political* mind precisely because it thinks *within* the framework of politics. The keener and more lively it is, the *more incapable* is it of understanding *social* ills. The classic period of political intellect is the *French Revolution*. Far from seeing the source of social shortcomings in the principle of the state, the heroes of the French Revolution instead saw in social defects the source of political evils. Thus, *Robespierre* saw in great poverty and great wealth only an *obstacle* to pure democracy. Therefore, he wished to establish a universal Spartan frugality. The principle of politics is the *will*. The more one-sided and, therefore, the more perfected the political mind is, the more does it believe in the omnipotence of the *will*, the more is it blind to the *natural* and spiritual *limits* of the will, and the more incapable is it therefore of discovering the source of social ills.[4]

Politics and *voluntarism* are thus wedded, and the unreality of wishful political remedies emanates from the inherent "substitutionism" of politics as such: its necessary *modus operandi* that consists in substituting itself for the *social* and thus denying to the latter any remedial action that cannot be contained within its own—self-oriented and self-perpetuating—framework. To oppose within the confines of politics Stalin's "substitutionism," advocating the replacement of the "bureaucrat" by the "enlightened political leader," is, therefore, another form of political voluntarism, however well intentioned. For the question is, according to Marx, which one is the truly comprehensive category: the political or the social. Politics, the way it is constituted, cannot help substituting its own partiality for the authentic universality of society, superimposing its own interests on those of the social individuals, and appropriating to itself the power to arbitrate over conflicting partial interests in the name of its own usurped universality.

Non-substitutionist politics, therefore, would imply a whole range of social mediations—and, of course, the existence of the corresponding social/material forces—which represent an acute problem for us but were absent from the historical horizon within which Marx was situated all his life. Hence the retention of the prevalently negative definition of politics even in his latest writings, notwithstanding his sober appreciation of a necessary involvement in politics (as opposed to abstentionism[5] and indifference to politics[6]), be that for the purposes of negation or for acting, even after the conquest of power, "within the old forms."

The way Marx perceived it, the contradiction between the social and the political was irreconcilable. Given the antagonistic character of the social base itself, perpetuated as such by the political framework, the state was irredeemable and therefore had to go. For

> confronted by the consequences which arise from the unsocial nature of this civil life, this private ownership, this trade, this industry, this mutual plundering of the various circles of citizens, confronted by all these consequences, *impotence* is the *law of nature* of the administration. For this fragmentation, this baseness, this *slavery of civil society* is the natural foundation on which the *modern state* rests, just as the *civil society of slavery* was the natural foundation on which the ancient state rested. The existence of the state and the existence of *slavery* are inseparable.... If the modern state wanted to abolish *private life*, it would have to abolish itself, for it exists only in the contradiction to private life.[7]

Thus, stressing the need to abolish the state in order to resolve the contradictions of civil society was coupled with the realization that the state—and politics in general, as we know it—are by their very nature incapable of abolishing themselves.

The imperative to abolish the state was emphatically put into relief, but not in voluntaristic terms. On the contrary, Marx never missed an opportunity for reiterating the utter futility of voluntaristic efforts. It was clear to him from the very beginning that no material factor can be "abolished" by *decree*, let alone the state itself, one of the most overpowering of all material factors. Talking about the French Revolution's attempt to abolish pauperism by decree, he focused on the inescapable limitations of politics as such: "What was the result of the Convention's decree? That one more decree came into the world, and one year later starving women besieged the Convention. Yet the Convention represented the maximum of political energy, political power, and political understanding."[8]

If the state was as powerless as this in the face of tangible social problems the claimed mastery of which constituted its tenuous legitimation, how could it conceivably confront the full burden of its own contradictions, for the sake of abolishing itself in the interest of general social advancement? And if the state itself was incapable of undertaking such task, what force of society could do so? These were the questions that had to be answered in that they were put on the historical agenda by the growing socialist movement. The widely differing answers that we can find in the annals of the epoch speak of qualitatively different strategies of men engaged in the struggle.

2. Main Tenets of Marx's Political Theory

As far as Marx himself was concerned, the answer was forcefully and clearly formulated in the early 1840s, with repeated warnings against voluntarism and adventurism as "Leitmotifs" of his political vision. The main points of Marx's answer may be summed up as follows:

1. The state (and politics in general, as a separate domain) must be *transcended* through a radical transformation of the whole of society, but it cannot be *abolished* by decree or, for that matter, even by a whole series of political/administrative measures.
2. The coming revolution cannot be simply a political one; it must be a *social* revolution if it is not to be trapped within the confines of the self-perpetuating system of social/economic exploitation.
3. Social revolutions aim at removing the contradiction between partiality and universality that political revolutions of the past always reproduced, subjecting society as a whole to the rule of political partiality,[9] in the interest of the dominant sections of "civil society."
4. The social agency of emancipation is the proletariat because it is forced by the maturation of the capital system's antagonistic contradictions to overthrow the prevailing social order, while it is incapable of superimposing itself as a new dominant partiality—a ruling class kept by the work of others—on the whole of society.
5. Political and socioeconomic struggles constitute a dialectical unity and consequently the neglect of the social/economic dimension deprives the political of its reality.
6. The absence of objective conditions for implementing socialist measures, ironically, can only result in carrying out the adversary's policies in the event of a premature conquest of power.[10]
7. The successful social revolution cannot be local or national—only political revolutions can confine themselves to a limited setting, in keeping with their own partiality—it must be global/universal, which implies the necessary transcendence of the state on a global scale.

Clearly, the elements of this theory constitute an organic whole from which they cannot be separated one by one. For each of them refers to all the others, and they acquire their full meaning through their reciprocal interconnections. This is fairly obvious in considering 1, 2, 5, 6 and 7 together, since they are all concerned with the inescapable objective conditions of social transformation, conceived as a complex social totality with an inner dynamism of its own.

Numbers 3 and 4 seem to be the "odd ones out," in that advocating the resolution of the contradiction between partiality and universality appears to be an unwarranted intrusion of Hegelian logic into Marx's system, and number 4 looks like an imperatival translation of this abstract logical category into a pseudo-empirical entity.

To be sure, Marx's adversaries interpreted his theory precisely in such terms, denying objective reality to the concept of the proletariat and "invalidating" his theory as a whole on account of its "unverifiability," etc. In truth, Marx's procedure is perfectly legitimate, even if the connection with Hegel cannot—nor should it—be denied. For the similarity between Hegel's "universal class" (the idealized bureaucracy) and Marx's proletariat is superficial, since their discourses belong to quite different universes. Hegel wants to preserve (indeed glorify) the state and invents the bureaucratic "universal" class as a quintessential Sollen. an "ought to be." The latter fulfills its function of reconciling the contradictions of warring interests by preserving them, thus safeguarding and securing the permanence of the established structure of society in its antagonistic form. Marx, in complete contrast, is concerned with the transcendence of the state and politics as such, and he identifies the proletariat's paradoxical universality (a not yet given, still to be realized universality) as a necessarily *self-abolishing partiality*.

Thus, while Hegel's fictitious "universal class" is a *classless* entity (and as such a contradiction in terms), Marx's proletariat is thoroughly class-like (and in that sense inevitably partial) and real. In its "historic task" it has an objectively grounded universalizing *function* to fulfill. At the same time, its partiality is also unique, since it cannot be turned into an *exclusive ruling* condition of society. Consequently, in order to "rule," the proletariat must generalize its own condition of existence: namely the inability to rule as a partiality, at the expense of other social groups and classes. (Obviously, this is in total contrast to the bourgeoisie and other ruling classes of past history that ruled precisely by excluding and subjugating other classes.) It is in this sense that classlessness (the establishment of a classless society) is linked to the peculiar class rule of "self-abolishing partiality" whose measure of success is the generalization of a mode of existence totally incompatible with (exclusively self-favoring) class rule.

The rule of partiality over society as a whole is always sustained by politics as the necessary complement to the iniquitousness of the established material power relations. This is why the emancipation of society from the rule of partiality is impossible without radically transcending politics and the state. In other words, so long as the proletariat acts *politically,* it remains in the orbit of partiality (with serious implications as to how the proletariat is necessarily affected by the rule of its own partiality), whereas the realization of the *social* revolution advocated by Marx involves many other factors too, well beyond the political level, together with the maturation of the relevant objective conditions. Naturally, the proletariat, so long as it exists, is situated at a greater or lesser distance from the realization of its "historic task" at any particular point in history, and the assessment of the class's changing sociological composition and relationship to other forces, together with its relative achievements and failures, etc., requires detailed investigations in accordance with the specific circumstances. In the present context, the point is simply to stress the unbreakable links between points 3 and 4 above and the rest of Marx's political theory. On the one hand, it is precisely his category of objectively grounded *universality* that puts politics in perspective: by getting "outside" politics, which means beyond the constraints imposed by "thinking within the framework of polities," as Marx puts it. This must be done in order to be able to *negate* the chronic partiality of politics; and to do this not from an abstract metaphysical-logical level, but from the basis of the one and only non-fictitious (not *Sollen-like*) universality, that is, the fundamental *metabolism* of society, the *social*. (Such grasp of universality is both historical and transhistorical, in that it highlights the changing conditions of the social metabolism while indicating the ultimate limits beyond which even the most powerful means and mode of this metabolism—capital, for instance—lose their vitality and historical justification.) On the other hand, the *proletariat* as an actual socioeconomic reality was a leading actor on the historical stage well before Marx. It demonstrated its ability to gravitate toward a "revolution within the revolution" in the immediate aftermath of 1789, attempting to acquire an independent role, in its own interest, in contrast to its subordinate position up until then within the Third Estate. In this way, negating the newly won political framework the moment it came into being, as Pierre Barnave shrewdly observed from the standpoint of the emerging bourgeois order as far back as 1792. Thus, to deny the actuality of the proletariat is a curious twentieth-century pastime.

The fact that Marx theoretically linked the proletariat to the necessity of the *social* revolution and to the condition of universality, was not a dubious functional requirement of a system still dependent on Hegel, but a profound insight into the world-historical novel character of the social antagonism between capital and labor. The progression from local tribal interchanges to world history, from action confined to an extremely limited sphere to one reverberating across the world, is not a matter of conceptual transformations but concerns the actual development and reciprocal integration of increasingly more comprehensive and complex structures. This is why solutions of a partial kind—which are perfectly feasible, indeed unavoidable, at an earlier stage—must be displaced by more and more all-embracing ones in the course of world-historical development, with an ultimate tendency toward "hegemonic" solutions and toward universality. Marx's characterization of the proletariat thus reflects and articulates the highest intensity of hegemonic confrontations and the historical impossibility of partial solutions at a determinate stage of global/capitalistic developments.

Significantly, in its own way Hegel's theory incorporated this problematic, even if in a mystified form. He fully acknowledged the imperative of a "universal" solution that should supersede the collisions of warring partialities. However, thanks to the standpoint of political economy (that is, the standpoint of capital) that Hegel shared with his great English and Scottish ancestors, he was forced to transubstantiate the perceived elements of an inherently contradictory reality into the pseudo-empirical, "universalistically" reconciliatory fantasy figure of the selfless state bureaucrat. But even such mystifications cannot obliterate Hegel's achievements on account of which he stands at a qualitatively higher level of political theorizing than anyone else before Marx, including Rousseau. Those who tried to censure (and heavily censor) Marx for his alleged "Hegelianism" while glorifying Rousseau, forgot that in comparison to the paradigm *categorical imperative* of the latter's "General Will," Hegel's attempt to embody his category of political universality in an actual social force, despite its class biased subjectivism, is objectivity itself. However halfhearted and contradictory this Hegelian attempt at sociologically circumscribing the political will was, it was a sign of the times and as such it reflected an objective historical challenge, representing a giant step in the right direction.

Thus, returning to the main points of Marx's political theory taken as a whole, it becomes clear that none of the other points make sense if the social agency of revolutionary transformation is abandoned. For what could it mean to say that the state can only be "transcended" but not "abolished" (whether in a limited national setting or on a global scale) if there is no social force willing and able to undertake the task? Similarly, with all the other points. The distinction between social and political revolution has a content only if some existing social agency or agencies can *actually* make sense of it, through the precise aims and strategies of their action and through the new social order arising from that action. In the same way, it is impossible to predicate an all-embracing reciprocity between politics and economics before a fairly advanced stage of socioeconomic development, which in its turn presupposes that the major forces of society be actually engaged in an inextricably political as much as economic confrontation with one another. Likewise, revolutions are "premature" or "belated" only in terms of the specific dynamics of the agencies in question, defined with reference to both the relevant range of objective circumstances and the greatly varying requirements of conscious action. Peasant revolutions of the past, for instance, were defined as "premature" not so much on account of some voluntaristic engagement in violent confrontations but rather, in view of a hauntingly *chronic* insufficiency of this agency with respect to its own aims, some sort of a "historical conspiracy of circumstances" that imposed on the peasant masses the burden of fighting for someone else's causes—and even winning them on occasions—while suffering heavy defeats for themselves. On the other hand, several colonial revolutions of the postwar years seem to be "belated" even when they are "premature," and defeated even when they appear to be successful. For under the historically constituted and still prevailing relation of forces, the "underdeveloped" revolutionary agency is defined by its massive dependency on the inherited structures of "neocolonialism" and "neocapitalism."

Naturally, these interconnections are no less in evidence the other way around. This is because the proletariat as a vital concept of Marx's theory derives its meaning precisely from those objective conditions and determinations that are articulated, on the basis of the dynamic social reality they reflect, briefly surveyed a few pages back. Without the latter, references to the proletariat amount to no more than empty catchwords so scornfully condemned by Marx in his polemics against Schapper and others.*

Thus, the transcendence of the state and its initiator, the proletariat—or, to use a theoretically more precise term, labor, the structural antagonist of capital—inseparably belong together and constitute the pivotal point of Marx's political theory. There is no romanticism involved in stressing their importance in this way, just a note of caution. For all those who want to expurgate them from Marx's conceptual framework should realize how much more—in fact nearly everything else—would have to be thrown overboard with them.

---

* In *Beyond Capital* (518) Mészáros observes the following with respect to the premature conquest of power: "This point is well illustrated by the confrontation between Marx and Schapper: 'I have always defied the momentary opinions of the proletariat. We are devoted to a party which, most *fortunately* for it, cannot yet come to power. If the proletariat were to come to power the measures it would introduce would be petty-bourgeois and not directly proletarian. Our party can come to *power* only when the conditions allow it to put *its own* view into practice. Louis Blanc is the best instance of what happens when you come to power prematurely. In France, moreover, it isn't the proletariat alone that gains power but the peasants and the petty-bourgeois as well, and it will have to carry out not its, but *their* measures.'" Marx at the "Meeting of the Central Authority," September 15, 1850, Marx and Engels, *Collected Works*, vol. 10, 628–29.—Ed.

3. Social Revolution and Political Voluntarism

There can be no question about the fundamental validity of Marx's approach to politics insofar as he is concerned with the *absolute parameters*—the *ultimate* criteria—that define and strictly circumscribe its role among the totality of human activities. The difficulties lie elsewhere, as we shall see later on. The core of Marx's political conception—the assertion that politics (with particular gravity in its version as tied to the modern state) *usurps* the powers of overall social decision-making for which it *substitutes* itself—is and remains completely unassailable. For abandoning the idea that socialist politics must concern itself in all its steps, even the minor ones, with the task of *restituting* to the social body the usurped powers, inevitably deprives the politics of transition of its strategic orientation and legitimation, thus *reproducing* in another form the inherited "bureaucratic substitutionism," rather than creating it anew on the basis of some mythical "personality cult." Consequently, socialist politics either follows the path set to it by Marx—*from substitutionism to restitution*—or ceases to be socialist politics and, instead of abolishing itself in due course, turns into authoritarian self-perpetuation.

To be sure, there are many unanswered questions and dilemmas that must be examined in their proper context. What will be particularly important to assess is this: to what extent and in which way the changing historical conditions and acute pressures of the unfolding social antagonism may significantly modify the Marxist political strategy without destroying its core. But before we can turn to these questions, it is necessary to have a closer look at Marx's relationship to his political adversaries inasmuch as it affected the formulation of his theory of the state.

In sharp contrast to Hegel's "false positivism," Marx never ceased to stress the essentially *negative* character of politics. As such, politics was suitable to fulfill the *destructive* functions of social transformation—like the "abolition of wage slavery," the expropriation of the capitalists, the dissolution of bourgeois parliaments, etc., all achievable by decree—but not the *positive* ones that arise from the restructuring of the social metabolism itself. Because of its inherent *partiality* (another way of saying "negative"), politics could only be a most inadequate *means* to serve the desired end. At the same time, the measure of approaching the latter was to be precisely the degree to which such constraining means could be discarded altogether, so that ultimately the social individuals should be able to function in a direct relationship with one another, without the mystifying and restrictive intermediary of the "cloak of politics."

Since the negating subjectivity of the will that runs riot in politics says "yes" only by saying "no," the usefulness of politics was considered extremely limited even after the conquest of power. It is not surprising, therefore, that the *Critique of the Gotha Programme* expected of it in the society of transition no more than a negative intervention, asking it to act "unequally" on the side of the weak, so that the worst inequalities inherited from the past should be faster removed. For whereas socialism required the greatest *positive* transformation in history, the negative modality of politics ("class *against* class," etc.,) made it, on its own, completely inadequate to the task.

Marx conceptualized the way of overcoming the problematical relationship between politics and society by consciously superimposing on the political revolution its hidden social dimension. He insisted:

> Whereas a *social revolution* with a *political* soul is a *paraphrase* or nonsense, a *political revolution* with a *social* soul has a rational meaning. *Revolution* in general—the *overthrow* of the existing power and dissolution of the old relationship—is a *political act*. But socialism cannot be realized without revolution. It needs this political act insofar as it needs *destruction and dissolution*. But where its *organising* activity begins, where its *proper object*, its *soul* comes to the fore, there socialism throws off the *political* cloak.[11]

From such vantage point—in his critical assessments of Proudhon and Stirner, Schapper and Willich, Lassalle and Liebknecht, Bakunin and his associates, as well as the authors of the Gotha Programme—Marx succeeded in laying down the broad outlines of a strategy free from voluntaristic constituents.

For Marx, the necessity of the revolution was neither an economic determinism (of which he is frequently accused) nor a sovereign act of the arbitrary political will (of which he is, curiously, also accused). Those who judge him in these terms only prove that they themselves are unable to think without the prefabricated schematism of such false alternatives. For Marx, the social revolution stood for a number of determinate functions. It had to arise on the ground of some objective conditions (which constituted its necessary prerequisites) so as to go far beyond them in the course of its development, radically transforming both the circumstances and the people involved in the action. It was precisely this dialectical objectivity and complexity of the social revolution that disappeared through its Procrustean reduction into the one-dimensional political act—whether we think of the pre-revolutionary theories of anarchist voluntarism or of the equally arbitrary, and far more damaging, reductionist and substitutionist political practices of post-revolutionary "bureaucratism."

The first question, therefore, concerned the grasp of the nature of both the social revolution and its agency. Bakunin conceived the latter as a "revolutionary General Staff composed of devoted, energetic and intelligent individuals. . . . The number of these individuals should not be too large. For the international organisation throughout Europe *one hundred* serious and firmly united revolutionaries would be sufficient."[12] This self-myth of the "revolutionary General Staff" corresponded, naturally enough, with a mythical conception of the revolution itself as well as its masses. The revolution was said to be "slowly maturing in the *instinctive conscience* of the popular masses" (not in the objective conditions of the social reality), and the role of the "instinctive masses" was confined to that of being the "army of the revolution"—the "cannon fodder," as Marx rightly exclaimed.[13]

Marx's condemnation of such views could not have been more scathing. Speaking of Bakunin he wrote, "He understands absolutely nothing of social revolution, only its political rhetoric; its *economic* conditions simply do not exist for him. . . . Willpower, not economic conditions, is the basis of his social revolution."[14]

Marx called Bakunin's views "schoolboyish rot" and reiterated that "a radical social revolution is bound up with definite historical conditions of economic development; these are its premises. It is only possible, therefore, where alongside capitalist production the industrial proletariat accounts for at least a significant portion of the mass of the people. And for it to have any chance of victory, it must be able, *mutatis mutandis*, at the very least to do as much directly for the peasants as the French bourgeoisie did in its revolution for the French peasantry at that time. A fine idea to imagine that the rule of the workers implies the oppression of rural labour!"[15]

The multidimensional, objective determinations of the social revolution which foreshadowed an extended time-scale—"15, 20, 50 years," as Marx put it against Schapper's romantic fantasies—also implied the necessity of renewed upheavals and the unworkability of accommodations. For

1. Given the historically attained stage of social antagonism between capital and labor, there was no possibility of "partial emancipation" and "gradual liberation."[16]
2. The ruling class had too much to lose; it would not yield on its own accord; it must be overthrown in a revolution.[17]
3. The revolution cannot succeed on a narrow basis; it requires "the production on a *mass scale*" of a revolutionary consciousness, so that the revolutionary class as a whole can "succeed in ridding itself of all the muck of ages and become fitted to found society anew"— which is possible only through the *practice* of actual revolutionary transformations.[18]

4. Learning how to master the difficulties, burden, pressures and contradictions of the exercise of power requires active involvement in the revolutionary process itself, on a painfully long time-scale.[19]

As we can see, social necessity in the Marxian conception is not some mechanical determinism. Quite the contrary, it is a dialectical grasp of what needs to be and can be accomplished on the ground of the objectively unfolding tendencies of reality. As such, it is inseparable from a consciousness that adjusts itself to the changing conditions and sobering lessons of the world it tries to transform. The varieties of anarchistic voluntarism, from Proudhon to Bakunin,[20] stand diametrically opposed to such a view, since they fail to understand the weighty economic dimension of the task. They substitute their subjective images of agitational fervor for the objective conditions even when they talk about "the force of circumstances." Marx, on the other hand, articulates his conception in terms of a completely different time scale, envisaging for a long time to come the role of *opposition* for the working-class movement before the question of *government* would ultimately arise.[21]

The inherent limits of the political forms (even the most advanced ones), in contrast to the fundamental metabolic dimension of the social revolution, are summed up in a key passage of Marx's analysis of the Paris Commune. It reads as follows:

As the state machinery and parliamentarism are not the *real life* of the ruling classes, but only the organised general organs of their dominion, the political guarantees and forms of expression of the old order of things, so the Commune is not the *social movement* of the working class and therefore of a general regeneration of mankind, but the organised means of action. The Commune does not do away with the class struggles, through which the working classes strive to the abolition of all classes and, therefore, of class rule (because it does not represent a peculiar interest. It represents the liberation of "labour," that is, the *fundamental and natural* condition of individual and social life which only by *usurpation,* fraud and artificial contrivances can be shifted from the few upon the many), but it affords the rational medium in which that class struggle can run through its different phases in the most rational and humane way.... The working class know that they have to pass through different phases of class struggle. They know that the *superseding* of the *economic* conditions of the slavery of labour by the conditions of free and associated labour can only be *the progressive work of time* ... that they require not only a change of *distribution,* but a new organisation of *production,* or rather the delivery (setting free) of the social forms of production in present organised labour, (engendered by present industry), of the trammels of slavery, of their present class character, and their harmonious national and *international* coordination. They know that this work of *regeneration* will be again and again relented and impeded by the resistance of vested interests and class egotism. They know that the present "spontaneous action of the natural laws of capital and landed property" can only be *superseded* by "the *spontaneous* action of the laws of the social economy of free and associated labour" by a *long process* of development of new conditions.[22]

Thus, the real task, with all its immense complications, only *begins* where political subjectivism imagines to have solved it for good.

The issue at stake is the creation of the "new conditions": the transcendence/supersession of the "spontaneous action of capital's natural law"—that is, not its simple political "abolition," which is inconceivable—and the long-drawn-out development of a *new spontaneity*, "the spontaneous action of the laws of the social economy" as the radically restructured mode of the new social metabolism. The expressions "general regeneration of mankind" and "work of regeneration," linked to a repeated emphasis on the necessity of "different phases" of development through a "progressive work of time," clearly indicate that the power of politics must be very limited in this respect. Hence, to expect the generation of the new spontaneity (a form of social intercourse and mode of life-activity that becomes "second nature" to the associated producers) by some political decree, be it the most enlightened one, would be a contradiction in terms. For whereas *distribution* is immediately amenable to change by decree (and even that only to an extent strictly limited by the socially attained level of productivity), the material conditions of *production* as well as its hierarchical organization remain exactly the same the day after the political revolution as before. This is what makes it practically impossible for the workers to become the anticipated "free associated producers" for a long time to come even under the politically most favorable circumstances.

Furthermore, the qualification that the socialist "regeneration of mankind" necessarily calls for a "harmonious national and international coordination" puts politics in perspective again. For it is in the nature of political voluntarism to misrepresent also this dimension of the problem. It treats the failure of realizing the Marxian requirement as a simple political deficiency for which its own policies cannot be held responsible—the famous "encirclement," with its automatic self-justification—while, in truth, the "harmonious national and international coordination" concerns the vital conditions of labor: the profound interrelatedness of objective economic structures on a global scale.

Such is, then, the true nature of the "work of regeneration," the true magnitude of its multidimensional objectivity. The rule of capital over labor is fundamentally *economic*, not political in character. All that politics can do is to provide the "political guarantees" for the continuation of a materially already established and structurally entrenched rule. Consequently, the rule of capital cannot be broken at the political level, only the guarantee of its *formal* organization. This is why Marx, even in his most positive references to the political framework of the Paris Commune, defines it *negatively* as a "lever for *uprooting* the economical foundations upon which rests the existence of classses," indicating the positive task in the economic emancipation of labor.[23] And further on in the same work, Marx compares the "organised public force, the state power" of bourgeois society to a political *engine* that "forcibly perpetuates the *social* enslavement of the producers of wealth by its appropriators, of the *economic rule of capital* over labor,"[24] again making it amply clear what has to be the fundamental objective of the socialist transformation.

It must be underlined here that Marx's adversaries completely failed to understand the interconnection between *the state, capital and labor,* and the existence of quite different levels and dimensions of possible change. Due to their reciprocally self-sustaining interrelationship, the state, capital, and labor could only be done away with simultaneously, as a result of the radical structural transformation of the entire social metabolism. In this sense, all three could not be "overthrown/abolished" but only "transcended/superseded." This constraint, in its turn, carried with it both the extreme complexity and the long-term temporality of such transformations.

At the same time, all three had a dimension immediately accessible to change, without which the very idea of a socialist transformation would have been a romantic pipe dream. It consisted in the social specificity of their historically prevalent form of existence. That is to say, in the attained level of concentration and centralization of capital—"monopoly/imperialist," "semi-feudal," "colonially dependent," "underdeveloped," "military-industrial-complex orientated," or whatever else; in the corresponding variety of specific capitalist state formations, from the Bonapartist state to tsarist Russia just before the revolution, and from the "liberal" states running the British and French empires to fascism and to the present-day varieties of military dictatorship engaged in neo-capitalist "development," under the tutelage of our great democracies; and finally, in all those specific forms and configurations through which "wage labor," in close conjunction with the dominant form of capital, reshaped the productive practices of each country, making it possible for capital to function as a truly interconnected global system.

It was at this level of sociohistorical specificity that direct intervention in the form of "overthrow/abolition" could and had to be envisaged as a first step. But success depended on understanding the dialectic of the historically specific and the transhistorical, linking the necessary first step of what could be immediately overthrown to the *strategic* task of a long sustained "transcendence/supersession" of capital itself (and not just capitalism), of the state in all its forms (and not merely the capitalist state), and of the *division of labor* (and not simply the abolition of wage labor). And while the *political* revolution could score successes at the level of the immediate tasks, only the *social* revolution as conceived by Marx—with its positive "work of regeneration"—could promise lasting achievements and truly irreversible structural transformations.

4. Critique of Hegel's Political Philosophy

Bakunin's ultimate argument in favor of the immediate abolition of the state was a reference to *human nature* which, he claimed, is tempted by the very existence of the state into perpetuating the rule of a privileged minority over the majority. In this curious way, "libertarian anarchism" displayed its liberal-bourgeois ancestry, with all its contradictions. For the liberal theory of the state was founded on the self-proclaimed contradiction between the assumed total *harmony of ends* (the ends necessarily desired by all individuals, in virtue of their "human nature"), and the total *anarchy of means*—the *scarcity* of goods and resources, which makes them fight and ultimately destroy one another by *bellum omnium contra omnes*, unless they somehow succeed in establishing over above themselves a *permanent* restraining force, the bourgeois state. Thus, *deus ex machina*, the state was invented in order to turn "anarchy into harmony" (to harmonize the anarchy of means with the wishfully postulated harmony of ends), by reconciling the violent antagonism of two powerful *natural factors*—human nature and material scarcity—thanks to the absolute permanence of its own "artificial contrivance," to use Marx's expression. The fact that the stipulated human nature was merely a self-serving assumption and that scarcity was an inherently *historical* category, had to remain concealed in liberal theory beneath its multiple layers of *circularity*. It was the latter that enabled the representatives of liberalism to freely move backwards and forwards from arbitrary premises to the desired conclusions, establishing on the a priori foundations of such ideological circularity the "eternal legitimacy" of the liberal state.

Bakunin, in his own version of the stipulated relationship between the state and an arbitrarily assumed "human nature," simply reversed the equation, claiming that the *natural* tendency for *class* domination (what an absurd notion!) will, somewhat mysteriously, disappear with the revolutionary state's immediate self-abolition by decree. And since the sovereign frame of reference of Bakunin's wishful act of self-abolition remained the elitistically conceived politics of the "General Staff," references to "human nature" again, could only serve the purpose of legitimating the circularity of self-perpetuating politics.

Marx, by contrast, insisted that the political act of decreed self-abolition is nothing but self-contradiction, since only the radical restructuring of the *totality* of social practice can assign to politics an ever-diminishing role. At the same time he stressed that critically challenging the predominant, arbitrary conceptions of "human nature"—for human nature in reality was nothing but the "community of men,"[25] the "ensemble of social relations"[26]—was an elementary condition for escaping from the straitjacket of inherited political circularity.

NATURALLY, THE CIRCULARITY IN QUESTION was not simply a philosophical construct but, as we shall see in a moment, a theoretical reflection of the practical perversity of class society's political self-reproduction across the ages. This is why Marx kept it at the forefront of his attention in his *Critique of Hegel's Philosophy of Law*.

Commenting on Hegel's definition of the monarchy: "Taken without its monarch and the articulation of the whole which is the indispensable and direct concomitant of monarchy, the people is a formless mass and no longer a state,"[27] Marx wrote: "This whole thing is a *tautology*. If a people has a monarch and an articulation which is its indispensable and direct concomitant, i.e., if it is articulated as a monarchy, then extracted from this articulation it is certainly a formless mass and a quite general notion."[28]

If a great philosopher, like Hegel, indulges in such violations of logic, there must be more to it than mere "conceptual confusion," this pseudo-explanatory *trouvaille* of "analytical philosophy," that "explains" what it terms "conceptual confusion" by circularly asserting the presence of conceptual confusion.

Indeed, the Hegelian leapfrogging from tautology to tautology—from the just seen definition of the monarchy to the circular determination of the political sphere, and from the tautological characterization of the "universal class" to proving the "rationality of the state" by its mere assertion—is a striking feature of this political philosophy, but by no means unique to it. Underneath it all we find the ideological determinations that induced liberal theory as a whole to argue from unsustained premises to the desired conclusions (and *vice versa*), so as to be able to "eternalize" the bourgeois relations of production, together with their corresponding state formations.

What was specific to Hegel was that, living at a juncture of history that displayed in an acute form the explosion of social antagonisms—from the French Revolution to the Napoleonic Wars and to the appearance of the working-class movement as a hegemonic force, envisaging its own mode of social metabolic control as a radical alternative to the existent—he had to face openly many a contradiction that remained hidden from his predecessors. If he was more contrived in his philosophy than such predecessors, that was largely because he had to be far less "innocent" than they, attempting to embrace and integrate within his system a far greater range of objective problems and contradictions than they could even dream about. If in the end he could only achieve this in an abstract/logical, often definitional/circular, and cerebralized fashion, that was primarily due to the insuperable taboos of his bourgeois "political-economist standpoint." The penalty he had to pay for sharing that standpoint was the mystifying conflation of the categories of *logic* with the objective characteristics of *being* while he was attempting to conjure up the impossible, namely, the final "reconciliation" of the antagonistic contradictions of the perceived sociohistorical reality.

THE HEGELIAN CHARACTERIZATION OF the "universal class" is a graphic example of such ideological circularity and conflation. We are told that "the universal class, or, more precisely, the class of civil servants, *must* purely in virtue of its character as *universal,* have the *universal* as the end of its *essential* activity."[29]

By the same token, the "unofficial class" displays its suitability to fit into the Hegelian scheme of things by "renouncing itself" so as to acquire a true political significance. But, as Marx rightly comments, the claimed political act of the "unofficial class" is a "complete transubstantiation." For "in this political act civil society *must* completely renounce itself as such, as unofficial class, and assert a part of its essence which not only has nothing in common with the *actual* civil existence of its essence, but *directly opposes* it."[30] Thus the fictitious universality (by stipulated essence) of the "universal class" carries with it the equally dubious redefinition of the actual forces of "civil society," so that the contradictions of the social world should be reconciled, in accordance with the "Idea," in the idealized domain of the Hegelian state.

As Marx exclaims, "the bureaucracy is a *circle* from which no one can escape."[31] This is because it constitutes the operative center of a circular construct that reproduces, even if in a bewildering fashion, the actual perversity of the bourgeois world. For the political state as an abstraction from "civil society" is not Hegel's invention but the result of capitalistic developments. Nor are "fragmentation," "atomism," "partiality," "alienation," etc., figments of Hegel's imagination, no matter how idealistically he treats them, but objective characteristics of the dominant social universe, as is the challenge of "universality" mentioned above. Indeed, Marx does not simply turn his back to this problematic. He reorients it toward its objective ground, by insisting: "The abolition/supersession [*Aufhebung*] of the bureaucracy can only consist in the *universal* interest becoming *really*—and not, as with Hegel, becoming purely in thought, in abstraction—*a particular* interest; and this is possible only through the particular interest *really* becoming *universal*."[32]

In other words, the circle of bureaucracy (and of modern politics in general) is a very real circle from which one must organize a correspondingly real escape.

Marx also acknowledges that "Hegel's keenest insight lies in his sensing the *separation* of civil and political society to be a *contradiction*. But his error is that he contents himself with the appearance of its dissolution, and passes it off as the real thing."[33] The fact that Hegel cannot find a way out of the perceived contradiction is, again, not his personal limitation. For the practice of simply assuming a necessary relationship between a "civil society" (torn apart by its contradictions) and the political state (which resolves or at least keeps in balance these contradictions) was, as we have seen, a characteristic feature of liberal theory in general, fulfilling, thanks to its ahistorical circularity, a much needed social/apologetic function. When Hegel "presupposed the separation of civil society and the political state (which is a modern situation), and developed it as a necessary moment of the Idea, as an absolute truth of Reason,"[34] he merely adapted the general practice of liberal theory to the specific requirements of his own philosophical discourse.

The greatest deficiency of Hegel's approach is the way in which he deals with the need for "mediation," though it cannot be stressed enough, the difficulty of mediation exists for him as a constantly recurring problem, while in liberal theory in general it tends to be narrowly reduced to a question of a more or less ready-made "balancing" instrumentality, if it is not ignored altogether. Hegel realizes that, if the state is to fulfill the vital functions of totalization and reconciliation assigned to it in his system, it must be constituted as an *organic* entity; one adequately fused with society, and not mechanically superimposed upon the latter. In this spirit he goes on to say:

> It is a prime concern of the state that a *middle class* should be developed, but this can be done only if the state is an organic unity like the one described here, i.e., it can be done only by *giving authority to spheres of particular interests*, which are relatively independent, and by appointing an army of officials whose personal arbitrariness is broken against such authorised bodies.

The problem is, however, that the picture we are presented with here is nothing but a stipulated/idealized version of the political state-formation of divided "civil society," one that preserves all the existing divisions and contradictions while conveniently conjuring away their ultimate destructiveness. As Marx put it in his comments appended to these lines: "To be sure the people can appear as one class, the middle class, only in such an organic unity; but is something that keeps itself going by means of the *counterbalancing of privileges* an organic unity?"[35]

Thus, the envisaged solution is even self-contradictory (defining "organicity" in terms of a perilously unstable "counterbalancing" of hostile centrifugal forces), not to mention its fictitious character, which predicates a *permanent* remedy on the basis of an ever-intensifying real conflictuality. In this wishful "*Aufhebung*" of the growing social contradictions through the magic circle of an omniscient bureaucracy and the heaven-sent expansion of the "middle class," we are provided with a veritable model of all twentieth-century theories of social accommodation, from Max Weber to the "managerial revolution," from Max Scheler and Mannheim to the "end of ideology," and from Talcott Parsons to the "knowledge-oriented post-industrial society" of "modernity" and "post-modernity" as the ultimate solution. (But mark, Hegel only says that this middle class "*should be* developed," while twentieth-century apologists claim that it has *actually* arrived already, bringing with it the end of all major social contradictions.)[36]

The modern political state in reality was not constituted as an "organic unity" but, on the contrary, was imposed upon the *subordinate* classes of the *materially* already prevailing power relations of "civil society," in the preponderant (and not carefully "counterbalanced") interest of capital. Thus, the Hegelian idea of "mediation" could only be a false mediation, motivated by the ideological needs of "reconciliation," "legitimation," and "rationalization" (the latter in the sense of accepting and idealizing the prevailing social relations).

Hegel's "logical inconsistencies" arise from the soil of such motivations. The established facticity and separateness of "civil society" and its political state are simply assumed as given, and as such they are kept apart; hence the crude circularity of Hegelian "tautologies" and self-referential definitions. At the same time, the need for producing an "organic unity" generates the more subtle "dialectical circularity" of mediations (which, in the end, turns out to be anything but dialectical). The crisscrossing of reciprocal references arranged around a middle term creates the semblance of a movement and genuine progression, though in fact it reflects and reproduces the brutally self-sustaining dual facticity of the given social order ("civil society" and its political state-formation), only now in a deductively transubstantiated abstract philosophical form.

As Marx observes, "If civil classes as such are political classes, then the mediation is not needed; and if this mediation is needed, then the civil class is not political, and thus also not this mediation.... Here, then, we find one of Hegel's inconsistencies within his own way of reviewing things: and such *inconsistency* is an *accommodation.*"[37] Thus, ultimately, what gives the game away is the apologetic character of its "mediation." It reveals itself as a sophisticated reconstruction of the ahistorically assumed dualistic reality—and eternalized as such—within the Hegelian discourse, and no real mediation at all. As Marx puts it: "In general, Hegel conceives of the syllogism as middle term, a *mixtum compositum.* We can say that in his development of the rational syllogism all of the transcendence and mystical dualism of his system becomes apparent. The middle term is the wooden sword, the concealed opposition between universality and singularity."[38]

The logical deficiency referred to here is thus not a matter of conceptually not knowing the difference between "universality" and "singularity," but that of a perverse necessity to *conceal* the irreconcilable opposition between them as they actually confront one another in social reality. Worse still, the need for preserving the given in its dominant facticity produces an overturning of the actual sets of relations inasmuch as it disregards the new hegemonic/universal potential of labor and misrepresents a *subservient partiality*—the idealized state bureaucracy—as "true universality." This is why the lofty enterprise of the Hegelian "rational syllogism" culminates in the prosaic modality of apologetic rationalization. Understandably, therefore, the "wooden sword" of false mediation only manages to carve out of the sand dunes of this conceptual universe a spitting image of the dualistic bourgeois world. This is all the more telling in view of Hegel's explicit rejection—could it be through the voice of "bad conscience"?—of all forms of philosophical dualism.

All this is by no means surprising. For once the reciprocal circularity of "civil society" and its political state is assumed as the absolute premise of political theory, the rules of the game enforce themselves with iron determination. It is painful to witness the way in which a thinker of Hegel's stature is reduced in size, almost to the point of writing "schoolboy nonsense," under the impact of such determinations. This is how Marx characterizes Hegel's self-imposed straitjacket:

> The sovereign, then, had to be the middle term in the legislature between the executive and the Estates, and the Estates between him and civil society. How is he to mediate between what he himself needs as a mean lest his own

existence becomes a one-sided extreme? Now the complete absurdity of these extremes, which interchangeably play now the part of the extreme and now the part of the mean, becomes apparent.... This is a kind of *mutual reconciliation society*.... It is like the lion in *A Midsummer Night's Dream* who exclaims: "I am the lion, and I am not the lion, but Snug." So here each extreme is sometimes the lion of opposition and sometimes the Snug of mediation.... Hegel, who reduces this absurdity of mediation to its abstract logical, and hence pure and irreducible, expression, calls it at the same time the speculative mystery of logic, the rational relationship, the rational syllogism. *Actual extremes cannot be mediated* with each other precisely because they are actual extremes. But neither are they in need of mediation, because they are opposed in essence. They have nothing in common with one another; they neither need nor complement one another.[39]

Seeing Hegel shipwrecked on the rocks of his false mediation, Marx realized that it was the very premises of politics itself that needed drastic revision in order to break its vicious circle. For so long as "mediation" remained tied to the political state and its supporting anchorage, the established "civil society," the critical aspirations of political theory had to be systematically frustrated, allowing for only an institutionally constrained margin of easily integrated protest. Envisaging *structural* change in terms of the accepted premises was a priori out of the question. For the prevailing order helped to reproduce itself by riveting philosophy to the dead weight of dualistic immobility, and by restricting "mediation" to the self-serving circularity of traditional political discourse.

THERE ARE TIMES IN HISTORY—as a rule its periods of transition—when the inner contradictions of particular social formations come to the fore with much greater clarity than under normal circumstances. This is because at such times the principal forces of the ongoing social confrontation put forward their rival claims more openly as hegemonic alternatives to one another. This gives not only a greater fluidity but also a greater transparency to the social processes. By the time the contesting forces settle down to a more firmly regulated (indeed, to a large extent institutionalized/routinized) mode of interaction, under the predominance of one of them—and for what appears to the participants an indeterminate period of time—the lines of social demarcation become increasingly blurred. The formerly acute conflict loses its cutting edge and its animators appear to be assimilated or "integrated," at least for the time being.

Hegel's philosophy is the product of such a historical period of dramatic fluidity and relative transparency. Fittingly, he completed the monumental synthesis of *The Phenomenology of Mind* in Jena at the time when Napoleon—the subject of his greatest hope for a radical transformation of the anachronistic social structures of the *ancien régime* all over Europe—was marshalling his forces for a decisive battle on the surrounding hills. And even though by the time of writing his *Philosophy of Right* Hegel had settled into a more conservative mold, his philosophy as a whole confronted and embodied—notwithstanding its mystifications—the dynamic contradictions of the not-yet-consolidated world of capital, together with the somber recognition of the menacing world-historical potential of its antagonist.

Given the vastness of the Hegelian vision, and the way in which it articulated the incommensurable complexities of this restless age, with its apparently unending cycles of revolutions and counterrevolutionary upheavals, Marx could not have had a more fertile point of departure in his "critical settling of accounts" with the standpoint of capital. For the Hegelian system clearly demonstrated—consciously, through its genuine insights, and unconsciously, through its class-imposed contradictions and mystifications—what an immense role politics plays in the extended self-reproduction of the world dominated by capital; and vice versa: in what an elemental way the "civil society" of the capital system shapes and reproduces the political formation in its own image. The ultimate secret of the astonishing, naked circularity of Hegel's sophisticated political philosophy was this: the real circle of capital's self-expanding reproduction from which there seemed to be no escape, thanks to the interlocking *dual circles* of "civil society/political state" and "political state/civil society," with their reciprocal *assumption* of and *derivation* from each other, and with capital at the core of both.

The abstract dualism of Hegelian political philosophy thus revealed itself as the sublimated expression of the suffocatingly real world of a "dual-concentric" circularity through which capital politically reproduces itself: by a priori defining the very terms and framework of "reform" that promises to supersede (by means of some fictitious "mediation") its deep-seated structural deficiencies, without questioning in the slightest the fatal immobilizing power of the political circle itself. This is why the task of emancipation had to be radically redefined in terms of breaking the vicious circle of politics as such. This had to be done, according to Marx, so as to be able to pursue the struggle against the power of capital at the level where it really hurts: well beyond the false mediations of politics itself, on capital's own material ground.

5. *The Displacement of Capital's Contradictions*

Marx worked out his conception of the socialist alternative at the closing stage of this dramatic period of transition, just before capital succeeded in firmly consolidating its newly won position on a global scale: first by resolving its national rivalries for the next historical phase through the Napoleonic Wars; and later by ruthlessly extending its sphere of domination to the farthest corners of the planet through its various empires. His formative years coincided with the defiant appearance of the working class as an independent political force all over Europe, culminating in the achievements of the Chartist movement in England and in revolutionary uprisings of growing intensity in France and Germany in the 1840s.

Under these circumstances, the relative transparency of the social relations and their antagonistic contradictions greatly favored the formulation of Marx's comprehensive synthesis that consciously traced the dynamics of the fundamental tendencies of development. He was always looking for the *classical*[40] configuration of forces and events, highlighting their ultimate structural significance even when starting out from the raw everydayness of their phenomenal manifestations.[41] It was, undoubtedly, this ability to situate the minutest detail within the broadest perspectives that made Engels write in 1886: "Marx stood higher, saw further and took a wider and quicker view than all the rest of us."[42]

But, of course, such ability, in order to realize itself, had to find its objective complement in the given sociohistorical reality. For it would have been futile to see further and wider, from the vantage point of an individual talent no matter how great, if all that one could perceive amounted only to vague outlines and confounding complexities, on the soil of inconsistent social movements, bent on blurring the real lines of demarcation and—preoccupied with the narrow practicalities of accommodation and compromise—avoiding like the plague the open articulation of their latent antagonisms. The intellectual desert of the age of reformist social democracy bears eloquent witness to this depressing truth.

It was the historical coincidence of the type and intensity of Marx's personal qualities with the dynamic transparency of the age of his formative years that enabled him to work out the fundamental outlines—the veritable "Grundrisse"—of the socialist alternative. By defining the meaning of socialist politics as the total restitution of the usurped powers of decision-making to the community of associated producers, Marx laid down the synthesizing core of all radical strategies that may arise under the changing conditions of development. The validity of these outlines extends over the whole historic period that goes from capital's worldwide domination to its structural crisis and ultimate dissolution, and to the positive establishment of a truly socialist society on a global scale.

However, to stress the epochal validity of Marx's overall vision, emphasizing its organic links to the relative transparency of the age that made it possible, is not meant to suggest that such ages are nothing but pure blessing for theory, in the sense that they do not impose any limitation on the worldviews that originate on their soil. Precisely because they put sharply into relief the basic polarities and alternatives, they tend to push into the background tendencies and modalities of action that point toward the continued reproduction of the prevailing social order, just as extended periods of compromise and accommodation create a general climate of opinion that strongly discourages the articulation of radical criticism, dismissively labeling it as "Messianic" and "Apocalyptic."

Marx was in his element at times when the manifestations of crisis were at their most intense. By the same token, he experienced great difficulties from the 1870s, which represented a period of major success in capital's global expansion. Such difficulties presented themselves not only politically, in relation to some important organizations of the working class, but also theoretically, in assessing the new turn of developments. Reflecting this, the intellectual production of his last fifteen years bears no comparison to the previous decade and a half, nor with the fifteen years just before that.

Not that he changed his approach as "old Marx." On the contrary, his work retained its most remarkable unity even under the *internally* most difficult circumstances. Throughout his life he was looking for tendencies and signs of development that would provide cumulative evidence for the validity of the "fundamental outlines." They were streaming forward, in great abundance, during the historic phase of the more open and transparent sharp alternatives, so much so, in fact, that they could hardly be contained even within the massive works of creative explosion of the first twenty-five years. Given the then prevailing relation of forces and the great fluidity of the overall sociohistorical situation, the possibility of capital's structural collapse was an *objective* one. It was the latter that found its forceful articulation in Marx's correspondingly dramatic writings. For these were times when even the London *Economist* had to admit—as Marx enthusiastically quoted it in a letter to Engels—that capital all over Europe "escaped only by a hair's-breadth from the impending crash."[43]

The difficulties started to multiply for him at the time when those immediate possibilities receded, opening new outlets for stabilization and expansion that capital did not fail to exploit in its subsequent global development. It was under such conditions, with contradictory objective alternatives *within* the major classes on both sides of the great divide—and not only *between* them—that the internal divisions in the practical strategies of the working-class movement strongly surfaced, inducing Marx to write at the end of his comments on the Gotha Programme, with a tone of militant resignation: *Dixi et salvavi animam meam* (I have spoken and saved my soul), as we have seen above.

Two points must be firmly made in this context. First, that the passing away of some objective, historically specific possibilities of change does not eliminate the fundamental contradictions of capital as a mode of social metabolic control, and hence it does not invalidate Marx's overall theory, concerned with the latter. And second, that an attempt to identify the difficulties and dilemmas inherent in some of Marx's conclusions is not the projection of hindsight upon his work (which would be totally ahistorical, thus inadmissible), but rests on explicit or implicit elements of his own discourse.

To be sure, the apologists of the established order greet every escape from the crisis as their final victory as well as the ultimate refutation of Marxism. Since they cannot and will not think in historical terms, they fail to grasp that the *boundaries of the capital system* may indeed historically expand—through opening up new territories, protected by colonial empires, or by the more up-to-date ways of "neo-capitalism" and "neo-colonialism." Equally, they may expand through "internal colonization," that is, the ruthless establishment of new productive outlets at home, safeguarding the conditions of their sustained expansion by a more intensive exploitation of both the producer and the consumer, etc.—without doing away with the *structural limits* and contradictions of capital as such.

Marx's theoretical framework can easily weather all these wishful refutations. For it is oriented toward the central contradictions of capital, pursuing their unfolding from the early developments to the global domination and to the ultimate disintegration of this controlling force of social production. Specific historical evidence is relevant in this framework of analysis to the extent to which it affects the basic structural relations, on the broadest historical time-scale, which happens to be the appropriate temporality of the basic categories scrutinized by Marx. To judge such a theoretical system—which is primarily concerned with the *ultimate* limits of capital and with the conditions/necessities of reaching them—on the short-term temporality of alleged predictions as to what exactly the day after tomorrow might or might not bring, is utter futility, if not blatant hostility, dressed up as a "scientific" quest for "verification or "falsification."

Marx would indeed be refuted if it was proved that the limits of capital are *indefinitely* expandable: namely, that the power of capital is itself limitless. Since, however, to prove such a thing is quite impossible, his adversaries prefer to *assume* it as the circular axiom of their own world of "piecemeal social engineering." The latter thus becomes the self-evident measure of all criticism and, as such, by definition, cannot possibly be itself the subject of scrutiny and criticism. At the same time, Marxism may be freely denounced and dismissed as "unverifiable ideology," "holism," "metaphysical deductionism," and who knows what else.

But even beyond such hostile views, there persists a serious misconception of the nature of Marx's project. On the one side, there is the expectation/accusation of immediate predictive implications, together with disputes over their realization or non-realization, as the case might be. On the other, in complete contrast, we find the characterization of Marx's conception as a self-articulating, quasi-deductive system, without empirical connections, following its own rules of theoretical production, thanks to the somewhat mysterious "discoveries" of its "scientific discourse" concerning the "continent of history."*

Against the first misconception, it cannot be stressed enough that, inasmuch as Marx's aim is the identification of capital's fundamental contradictions and ultimate limits, the characterization of the given sociohistorical setting (from which predictions may follow about the near future) is always subject to manifold qualifications in view of the virtually endless number of variables at work and therefore must be treated with extreme care. This is by no means a conveniently prefabricated escape clause, nor an attempt to take refuge from the difficulties of facing reality in the clouds of a self-referential discourse. The point is that contradictions may be *displaced* as a result of the specific interplay of determinate forces and circumstances, and there can be no a priori way of prefiguring the concrete forms and particular historical boundaries of displacement when, in fact, the dynamic configurations of the interplay itself are impossible to freeze into an arbitrary, schematic mold.

Saying this in no way implies a defensive denial of the predictive aspirations and value of Marxist theory. The question of displacement refers to the *specificity* of these contradictions, and not to the determination of the *ultimate limits* of the capital system. In other words, the contradictions of capital are displaced only *within* such limits, and the process of displacement may continue only to the point of the ultimate *saturation* of the system itself and the blocking of the expansionary outlets (the conditions of which can be defined

---

* Mészáros is referring here to the views of Louis Althusser. See Louis Althusser, *Lenin and Philosophy* (New York: Monthly Review Press, 2001), 4. —Ed.

with precision), but not endlessly or indefinitely. Margins of displacement are created by a multiplicity of contradictions given in a specific configuration and by the unevenness of development, and decidedly not by the *disappearance* of the contradictions themselves. Thus, the concepts of "displacement," "saturation," and "structural crisis" acquire their meaning in terms of the ultimate limits of capital as a global system, and not in terms of any one of its transient forms. Displacement means *postponing* (not liquidating) the saturation of the available outlets and the maturation of the fundamental contradictions. It also means *extending* capital's given historical boundaries but not eliminating its ultimately explosive objective structural constraints. In both cases we are talking about inherently temporal processes that foreshadow a necessary closure of the cycles involved, though of course on their own time-scale. And while all this certainly puts the predictive anticipations of Marxist theory in perspective, it also reasserts their legitimacy and validity with the greatest emphasis in terms of the appropriate time-scale.

As to the claimed deductive character of Marx's discourse, some say it's a most unhappy mixture of Hegelian deductivism and scientism/positivism/empiricism, the question concerns the relationship between reality and the theoretical framework. No doubt Marx's method of presentation (and his positive references to Hegel) may at times create the impression of a strictly deductive procedure. Besides, things are further complicated by the fact that Marx apodeictically concentrates on the fundamental conditions and determinations; on the necessities at work in all social relations; on the objective dynamism of the unfolding contradictions; and on the explanation of men and ideas—as situated within the parameters of a strictly defined material foundation—in terms of a subtle but no less objective necessity of dialectical reciprocity.

However, this forceful articulation of the necessary connections, centered on a few vital categories—e.g., capital, labor, surplus-value, modern state, world market, etc.—does not mean the replacement of social reality by the deductive matrix of a self-referential discourse. Nor, indeed, the superimposition of a set of abstract categories of the "Science of Logic" on actual relations, as happens to be the case with Hegel; categories whose connections and reciprocal derivations are formally/deductively/circularly established on the mystifying ground of complex ideological determinations, as we have seen.

The apodeictic rigor of Marxian analysis as arising from the necessary connections of his system of categories is not the *formal* characteristic of a "theoretical practice," but his way of conveying the *objectively* structured architecture of the social totality. For categories, according to Marx, are not timeless philosophical constructs but DASEINSFORMEN: forms of being, condensed reflections of the essential relations and determinations of their society. What defines with precision the theorizable character of any given society is the *specific configuration* of its dominant objective categories. In this sense, while several categories of modern bourgeois society originated on a very different soil, and some of them are indeed bound to extend over post-capitalist formations as well, it is the unique combination of CAPITAL, WAGE-LABOR, WORLD MARKET, and the MODERN STATE that *together* identify the *capitalist formation* in its historical specificity.

The way in which some categories cross the frontiers of different social formations, shows the objective dialectic of the *historical* and the *transhistorical* at work. This must be grasped in theory both in terms of the objectively different levels and scales of *temporality* and as a vital characteristic of the given social *structures*. (The latter exhibit the correlation between the historical and the transhistorical in the form of *continuity* in discontinuity, and *discontinuity* in even the apparently most stable continuity.) In Marx's view, stressing these links and determinations serves to articulate in theory the historical dynamism of the social processes and the objective structural characteristics of all the relevant factors that together constitute the real ground of all categorial condensations and reflections. Thus, the contrast with deductivism and with all past conceptions of the nature and importance of categories could not be greater.

MARX'S REAL DILEMMAS, WHICH affected his theory in significant ways, concerned the question of capitalist crisis and the possibilities of its displacement inasmuch as they were visible in his age. As already mentioned, raising this issue is not the projection of hindsight on a work articulated from a very different vantage point, but rather an attempt to understand the theoretical consequences of his conscious decision to assign a subordinate position to certain—discernible in his lifetime—tendencies that to us appear to possess in their own historical context a much greater relative weight. This is a problem of great complexity, since a number of very different factors come together in it to produce the result in question, and none of them could yield an acceptable answer if taken separately.[44] The main factors referred to here are:

1. The dramatic polarities and alternatives of Marx's formative years (making the collapse of capitalism, in view of its far more limited developmental/ expansionary outlets at the time, historically quite feasible);
2. Marx's method of analysis, as arising from the soil of such dramatic alternatives and greatly favored by them in their call for sharply drawn

outlines and for the articulation of the central antagonisms (and by the same token not favoring, of course, a method of manifold qualifications that would not dare to go beyond the amassed details of "overwhelming evidence");
3. The principal political confrontations in which Marx happened to be involved (especially his struggle against anarchist political voluntarism);
4. The main intellectual targets of his critique, above all Hegel and the "standpoint of political economy."

All these determinations and motivations combined produced that negative definition of politics we have seen above, carrying with it not only the radical rejection of the liberal problematic, but also an extreme skepticism with regard to the possibilities of displacing the structural crisis of capital for much longer. It must be stressed this applies to Marx's work as a whole, including his last few years when he crossed out some excessively optimistic remarks from his letters.[45] At the same time, and it cannot be repeated enough since it is generally ignored, this problem existed for Marx as a serious *dilemma*. And even though he resolved it the way he did, he was nevertheless fully aware of the fact that the advocated solution was not without its great difficulties.

TO APPRECIATE HOW INVOLVED and delicate a matter this is, we have to set side by side two of his letters: one well known, the other strangely forgotten. Various critics and refiners of Marx are fond of quoting the first in which he tells Engels that he is "working frantically, well into the night" to complete his economic studies, so as to have "clearly worked out at least the fundamental outlines [the *Grundrisse*] before the deluge."[46] In the light of the apparently chronic crisis of the middle 1850s—which could not be ignored or readily dismissed even by *The Economist,* as we have seen above—Marx's expectation of "deluge" and the excited tone of his letters are well understandable.

However, his reflections do not stop there. For he sizes up with great realism the full burden of the socialist undertaking, as it transpires through the other, much neglected, letter:

There is no denying that bourgeois society has for the second time experienced its 16th century which, *I hope,* will sound its death knell just as the first ushered it into the world. The proper task of bourgeois society is the creation of the world market, at least in outline, and of the production based on that market. Since the world is round, the colonisation of California and Australia and the opening up of China and Japan would seem to have completed this process. For us, the difficult *question* is this: on the Continent revolution is imminent and will, moreover, instantly assume a socialist character. Will it not necessarily be *crushed* in this little corner of the earth, since the *movement* of bourgeois society is still in the *ascendant* over a far greater area.[47]

One could not sum up more clearly even today the problems at stake, though from our own historical vantage point the various trends of development surveyed by Marx assume a rather different significance. For, indeed, the viability of capital is inseparable from its full expansion into an all-embracing world system. Only when that process is accomplished can the *structural* limits of capital come into play with their devastating intensity. Until that stage, however, capital maintains the dynamism inherent in its historical ascendancy. And together with this dynamism capital retains, of course, also its power to bend, subdue, and crush the forces that oppose it in many "little corners" of the world, inasmuch as its socialist opponents do not produce adequate strategies to counter the growing power of capital on its own terrain.

Thus, the crucial question is this: Under what conditions can the process of capital expansion come to a close on a truly global scale, bringing with it the end of crushed and perverted revolutions, opening thereby the new historic phase of an irrepressible socialist offensive. Or, to put it in another way: what are the feasible—though by no means inexhaustible—modalities of capital's revitalization, both with respect to its direct outlets and its power to acquire new forms that significantly extend its boundaries within the framework of its ultimate structural determinations and overall historical limits.

The real magnitude of the problem becomes clearer when we remind ourselves that even today—well over 150 years after Marx first articulated his vision—the world of capital still cannot be considered a fully extended and integrated global system, even if by now it is not far from being that. This is where we can also see that we are not imposing this problematic on Marx in hindsight, since the objective trends of capital's actual and potential development were unhesitatingly acknowledged by him with reference to its historical "ascendancy" all over the world, in contrast to what was likely to happen in the "little corner" of Europe. The differences concern the *relative weight* of the trends identified and the temporalities involved. For while the world is certainly round, it is equally true that capital has the power of discovering new continents for exploitation that were formerly hidden beneath the crust of its own relative inefficiency and underdevelopment. Only when there are no more "hidden continents" to be discovered, only then may one consider the process of capital's global expansion fully accomplished and its latent structural antagonisms—the central object of Marx's analysis—dramatically activated.

The difficulty is that capital can restructure its outlets according to the requirements of an *intensive totality* when the limits of its *extensive totality* are reached. Until that point, capital too pursues the line of least resistance, whether we are thinking of the historical changes in the mode of exploiting the metropolitan working classes or of its different ways of ruling the colonized and underdeveloped world. For only when the flow of *absolute surplus-value* is no longer adequate to its need for self-expansion, only then is the incomparably vaster territory of *relative surplus-value* fully explored, removing the obstacles from the road of capital's unhindered development due to the original inefficiency of its natural greed. In this sense, the size of the "round world" may well be doubled, or even multiplied tenfold, depending on a number of other—including political—conditions and circumstances. Similarly, under the pressure of its own inner dynamic as well as of various other factors beyond its control, capital can assume a multiplicity of "mixed" or "hybrid" forms—all of which help to extend its life span.

In this perspective, it matters very little that the expected "deluge" of the 1850s and 1860s did not materialize. First, because capital's collapse does not have to take the form of a deluge at all (though, of course, at some stage even the latter cannot be excluded). And second, because what really does matter— the structural disintegration of capital in *all* its historically viable forms—is a question of the time-scale that adequately matches the inherent nature of the social determinants and processes involved. If a particular thinker's "revolutionary impatience"—his subjective temporality—conflicts with the objective historical time-scale of his own vision, this by itself does not invalidate his theory in the slightest. For the validity of his views hinges on whether or not his overall historical perspective objectively grasps the fundamental trends of development as they unfold on no matter how long a time-scale. Subjective temporality should not be confused with *subjectivism*. The former—like Gramsci's optimistic *will*, contrasted by him to the "pessimism of the *intellect*"—is an essential motivating force that sustains the individual under difficult circumstances, within the horizons of a worldview that must be judged on its own merits. Subjectivism, by contrast, is an arbitrary image that substitutes itself for the required comprehensive view of the world and runs diametrically counter to the actual trends of development.

While undoubtedly in Marx's work too, one can detect a conflict of varying intensity between the subjective and the objective scales of temporality (a much sharper one in the 1850s and 1860s than after the defeat of the Paris Commune), he never allowed even his most optimistic hope to undermine the monumental architecture of his "fundamental outlines." He warned with great realism that the "doctrinaire and fantastic anticipations of the programme of action for a revolution of the future diverts us from the struggle of the present."[48] Marx was able to put the present in its proper perspective because he assessed it from the temporally not hurried, global point of view of capital's social formation in its entirety—from its "ascendancy" to its pregnancy with the "new historic form"—which alone can assign their true significance to all partial events and developments. And since we continue to live in the orbit of the same broad historical determinations, Marx's overall conception is—and remains for a long time to come—the inescapable horizon of our own predicament.

6. *Temporal Ambiguities and Missing Mediations*

Within such horizons, however, the relative weight of the forces and tendencies that confront us requires a significant redefinition. To put the key issue in one sentence: The *mediations* so stubbornly resisted by Marx are no longer anticipations of a more or less imaginary future but ubiquitous realities of the present. We have seen that the way in which the Marxian system was constituted brought with it both the radically negative definition of politics and the abhorrence of mediations as the miserable practice of reconciliation and complicity with the established order. The break had to be envisaged as the most radical possible, allowing even socialist politics an extremely limited, strictly transient role. This is clearly expressed in the following passage:

> Since the proletariat, during the period of struggle to overthrow the old society, still acts on the basis of the old society and consequently within political forms which more or less belong to that society, it has, during this period of struggle, not yet attained its *ultimate structure,* and to achieve its *liberation* it employs means which will be *discarded after the liberation.*[49]

In this uncompromising negativity toward politics, a number of determinations came together and reinforced one another. They were: the contempt for the political constraints of "the German misery"; the critique of Hegel's conception of politics, on account of the "false positivity" of its reconciliations and mediations; the rejection of Proudhon and the anarchists; extreme doubts about the way the German working class's political movement was developing; and so on. Understandably, therefore, Marx's negative attitude could only harden, if anything, as time went by, instead of positivistically maturing, as the legend would have it.

The most important factor in Marx's radical rejection of mediations was the global historical character of the theory itself and the relatively premature conditions of its articulation. Far from the time of any actual "deluge," his conception was spelled out well before one could see what alternative ways capital could pursue to displace its internal contradictions when they erupted on a massive scale. Thus, Marx was looking—to the very end of his life—for strategies that could prevent capital from penetrating into those territories it had not fully conquered, so as to secure its earliest possible demise. For, with regard to the maturation of capital's structural contradictions, it was not a matter of indifference how far the sphere of domination of this mode of production would extend. So long as new countries could be added to capital's existing domain, the corresponding increase in material and human resources would help the development of new productive potentialities and, therefore, postpone the crisis. In this sense, the eruption and consummation of a structural crisis within the constraints of capitalistic developments in the 1850s and 1860s—that is, without an effective economic integration of the rest of the world within the dynamics of global capital expansion—would have meant something radically different from facing the same problem in the context of the incomparably more flexible resources of a successfully completed world system. If, therefore, important territories could have been prevented from being engulfed by capital, in principle that should have accelerated the maturation of its structural crisis.

It is highly significant precisely for this reason that Marx's last important project concerned the nature of developments in Russia, as evidenced by the immense care with which he tried to define his position in relation to "archaic modes of production" in the draft letters to Vera Zasulich. In his spirited defense of the future potentialities of the archaic modes—containing also the tempting polemical remark that capitalism itself "has reached its withering stage and soon will become nothing but an 'archaic formation,'" which he later rightly cut from his letter,[50] he was eager to explore the viability of a direct move from the existing form of "archaic collectivism" to its historically superior, namely socialist form, bypassing altogether the capitalist phase. At the same time, he was also trying to find political inspiration and ammunition for the *social* revolution in the postulated need to defend the existing archaic collectivist form, with all its positive potentialities, from being destroyed by the capitalistic processes. By contrast, as a result of the developments that had actually taken place in the intervening decades, Lenin's approach could not have been more different. He started out from the firm premise that the capitalist penetration into Russia had been irretrievably accomplished, and therefore the task was to break the "weakest link" of the global chain so as to precipitate a chain reaction for the *political* revolution of the world capitalist system.

MARX'S FRAME OF REFERENCE was the *whole historical phase* of capital's social formation, from its original accumulation to its ultimate dissolution. One of his principal concerns was to demonstrate the inherently *transitional character* (*Ubergangscharakter*) of the capitalist system *as such,* in constant polemics against the eternalization of this mode of production by bourgeois theoreticians. Inevitably, such concentration on the broad historical framework brought with it a shift in perspective that sharply emphasized the fundamental outlines and basic determinants and treated the partial transformations and mediations as of secondary importance, and indeed often directly responsible for the detested mystifications and mediatory reconciliations.

In any case, when one's frame of reference is a whole historical phase, *it* is very difficult to keep constantly in view—while addressing oneself to the immediate present—that the conclusions are valid on a long-term scale of temporality; and it is particularly difficult to do so at the level of political discourse, which aims at direct mobilization. If, however, this ambiguity of temporalities is left unresolved, its necessary consequences are ambiguities at the core of the theory itself. To illustrate this, let us concentrate on a few directly relevant examples.

The first of them can be found in the penultimate quotation above in which Marx assigns politics to the old society. He speaks of an *"ultimate* structure" that must be reached, insisting at the same time that politics "will be *discarded* after the *liberation."* Just how it is possible to "discard" politics after the liberation is far from clear. But beyond this, the real ambiguity concerns *liberation* itself. What is its precise temporality? It cannot be the conquest of power only (though in the primary sense of the term it could be), since Marx links it to the *"ultimate* structure" (*schliessliche Konstitution*) of the proletariat. This means, in fact, that the act of liberation (the political revolution) falls well short of liberation as such. And the difficulties do not stop there. For the "ultimate structure" of the proletariat is, according to Marx, its necessary self-abolition. Consequently, we are asked to accept simultaneously that politics can be unproblematical—in the sense that the proletariat can simply *use* it as a *means* to its own sovereign end, whereafter it is discarded—and that it is extremely problematical, in view of its belonging to the "old society" (and therefore inescapably conditions and fetters all emancipatory efforts), for which reason it must be radically transcended.

All this sounds somewhat bewildering. And yet, there is absolutely nothing wrong with this conception if it is assigned to its appropriate, *long-term* scale of temporal reference. The difficulties start to multiply when one tries to make it operational in the context of immediate temporality. In that case it becomes suddenly clear that the translation of the long-term perspectives into the modality of immediately practicable strategies cannot be done without first elaborating the necessary *political mediations*. It is the structural gap of such missing mediations that is being filled by the theoretical ambiguities, matching the unresolved ambiguity of the two—fundamentally different—time-scales involved.

An equally serious theoretical ambiguity surfaces in *Wages, Price and Profit*, a work in which—in contrast to narrow trade unionist strategies—Marx recommends to the working class: "Instead of the conservative motto, '*A fair day's wage for a fair day's work!*' they ought to inscribe on their banner the *revolutionary* watchword, '*Abolition of the Wages System!*'" [51]

Undoubtedly, Marx's advocacy of attacking the *causes* of social evils, instead of fighting necessarily lost battles against the mere *effects* of capital's ongoing self-expansion, is the only correct strategy to adopt. However, the moment we try to understand the practical/operational meaning of "abolition of the wages system," we are struck by a major ambiguity. For the scale of immediate temporality—the necessary frame of reference of all tangible political action—defines it as the abolition of private property and thus as the "expropriation of the expropriators," which can be achieved by decree in the aftermath of the socialist revolution. Not surprisingly, this is how Marx's "revolutionary watchword" concerning the abolition of the wages system has been interpreted as a rule.

The trouble is, though, that there is a great deal in the "wages system" that cannot be abolished by any revolutionary decree and consequently must be transcended on the long-term time-scale of the new historic form. For immediately after the "expropriation of the expropriators," not only the inherited means, materials, and technology of production remain the same, together with their links to the given system of exchange, distribution, and consumption, but the very organization of the labor process itself stays deeply embedded in that *hierarchical social division of labor*, which happens to be the heaviest burden of the inherited past. Thus, on the necessary scale of long-term temporality—the only one fit to achieve *irreversible* socialist transformations—the Marxian call for the "abolition of the wages system" not only does not mean abolition of the *wages system:* it does not mean *abolition* at all.

The real target of the strategy advocated by Marx is the hierarchical social division of labor, which simply cannot be *abolished*. Just like the state, it can only be *transcended* through the *radical restructuring* of all those social structures and processes through which it necessarily articulates itself. Again, as we can see, there is nothing wrong with Marx's overall conception and its long-term historical temporality. The problem arises from its direct translation into what he calls a "revolutionary watchword" to be inscribed on the banner of the given movement. For it is simply *impossible* to translate the *ultimate* perspectives *directly* into practicable political strategies.

As a result, the gap of *missing mediations* is filled by the profound ambiguity of Marx's terms of reference as linked to their temporal dimensions. And though he is absolutely right in insisting that "the working class ought not to exaggerate to themselves the *ultimate* working of these *everyday* struggles,"[52] the passionate reassertion of the validity of the broad historical perspectives does not solve the problem.

The conflict in temporality reveals an inherent difficulty in the realization of the strategy itself, one that cannot be eliminated by metaphors and ambiguities but only by the historically feasible material and institutional mediations. For the dilemma, in its stark reality, is this: the revolutionary act of liberation is not quite liberation (or emancipation) itself, and the "abolition of the wages system" is far from being its real transcendence.

It is the historical unavailability of the necessary practical mediations that makes Marx settle for a solution that simply reiterates the ultimate aim as the general rule to guide the immediate action, bridging the gap between the far-distant horizon and what is practically feasible in the proximate future by saying that the working class *ought to* use "their organised forces as a *lever* for the *final* emancipation of the working class, that is to say, the *ultimate* abolition of the wages system."[53]

Thus, the crucial issue for socialist politics is: how to gain a firm hold on the *necessary mediations* while avoiding the trap *of false mediations* constantly produced by the established order so as to integrate the forces of opposition. For the actuality of a given set of "bad mediations"—with all their "false positivity" rightly condemned by Marx—can only be countered by another set of specific mediations, in accordance with the changing circumstances. In other words, the accommodating pressures of *immediate* temporality cannot be effectively transcended by simply reasserting the validity of the overall historical horizons. And whereas the social formation of capital is, as Marx says, undoubtedly *transitory* in character (if considered on its proper historical scale, embracing the whole epoch), from the point of view of the forces *immediately* engaged in fighting its deadening domination, it could not be further from being transitory. Thus, to turn the socialist project into an *irreversible reality*, we have to accomplish many *"transitions within the transition,"* just as under another aspect socialism defines itself as constantly self-renewing *"revolutions within the revolution."*

In this sense, the radical transcendence of the state is one side of the coin, representing the *ultimate* horizons of all socialist strategy. As such it must be complemented by the other side, namely the project of concrete *mediations* through which the ultimate strategy can be progressively translated into reality. The question is, therefore, how to acknowledge, on the one hand, the demands of *immediate temporality* without being trapped by it; and on the other, how to remain firmly oriented toward the ultimate *historical* perspectives of the Marxian project without becoming remote from the burning determinations of the immediate present.

Since for the foreseeable future the horizons of politics as such cannot be transcended, this means simultaneously negating the state and operating on its terrain. As the general organ of the established social order, the state is inevitably biased in favor of the immediate present and resists the actualization of the broad historical perspectives of a socialist transformation that postulates the state's "withering away." Thus, the task defines itself as a dual challenge for

1. instituting non-state-organs of social control and growing self-management that can increasingly take over the most important areas of social activity in the course of our "transition within the transition"; and, as conditions permit, for
2. producing a conscious shift in the state organs themselves—in conjunction with point 1 and by means of the necessary internal and global mediations, so as to make feasible the realization of the ultimate historical perspectives of the socialist project.

TO BE SURE, ALL SUCH developments are tied to the maturation of some objective conditions. Confronting the problematic of the state in its entirety involves a multiplicity of internal and external determinations in their close interconnectedness, in that the state is both the general organ of a given society and represents the links of the latter with the social totality of its historical epoch. Consequently, the state is, in a sense, *mediation par excellence,* since it combines around a common political focus the totality of internal relations—from the economic interchanges to the strictly cultural ties—and integrates them to varying degrees also into the global framework of the dominant social formation. Since capital, in Marx's lifetime, was very far from its present-day articulation as a truly global system, its overall political command structure as a system of globally interconnected states was far less visible. It is therefore by no means surprising that Marx never succeeded in sketching even the bare outlines of his theory of the state, although the latter was assigned a very precise and important place in his projected system as a whole. Today the situation is quite different, in that the global system of capital, under a variety of very different (indeed contradictory) forms, finds its political equivalent in the totality of interdependent state and interstate relations. This is why the elaboration of a Marxist theory of the state is both possible and necessary today. Indeed, it is vitally important for the future of viable socialist strategies.

THE MARXIAN PROPOSITION, *"Men must change from top to bottom the conditions of their industrial and political existence, and consequently their whole manner of being,"* remains more than ever valid as the necessary strategic direction of the socialist project. For the defeats suffered in the twentieth century were to a large extent due to the abandonment of the real target of socialist transformation. That is, the necessity to win the epochal war by going irreversibly beyond capital (this is what is meant by reaching the "new historic form"), instead of being satisfied with ephemeral victories in a few battles against the weaker divisions of capitalism (e.g. the economically backward and militarily defeated tsarist system in Russia), remaining at the same time hopelessly trapped by the alienating imperatives of the capital system itself. Indeed, what makes matters worse in this respect is that a socialist revolution even in the most advanced capitalist country would in no way alter the need for, and the difficulties involved in, going beyond capital.

Economic backwardness is only one of the many obstacles that must be overcome on the road to the "new historic form," and by no means the greatest of them. The temptation to relapse into the formerly settled ways of running the social metabolism in a formerly dominant advanced capitalist country, once the worst conditions of the crisis that precipitated the revolutionary explosion had been left behind—so as to be able to follow again "the line of least resistance" at the expense of others who find themselves in dependency to the metropolitan developed country in question—cannot be underrated. The successful realization of the task of radically restructuring the global capital system—with its multifaceted and unavoidably conflicting internal and international dimensions—is feasible only as an immense historic enterprise, sustained over many decades. It would be reassuring to think, as some people had actually suggested, that once the capitalistically advanced countries embark on the road of socialist transformation, the journey will be an easy one. However, it is usually forgotten in such sanguine projections that what is at stake is a monumental leap from the rule of capital to a *qualitatively* different mode of social metabolic control. And in that respect the fact of being tied by a more perfected network of structural determinations to the reproductive and distributive practices of advanced capitalism represents a rather dubious asset.

The imperative to go beyond capital as a social metabolic control, with its almost forbidding difficulties, is the shared predicament of humanity as a whole. For the capital system by its very nature is a global/universalistic mode of control that cannot be historically superseded except by a likewise all-embracing social metabolic alternative. Thus, every attempt to overcome the constraints of a historically determinate stage of capitalism—within the structural parameters of the expansion-oriented and crisis-prone capital system—is bound to fail sooner or later, irrespective of how advanced or underdeveloped the countries that attempt to do so might be. The idea that once the relation of forces between capitalist and post-capitalist countries changes in favor of the latter, humanity's journey to socialism will be plain sailing, is naive at best. It was conceived in the orbit of the "encircled revolution," attributing the failures of the Soviet-type system to external factors (also when talking about the "internal sabotage of the enemy"), ignoring or willfully disregarding the material and political antagonisms necessarily generated by the forcibly surplus-labor extracting post-capitalist order both under and after Stalin. It is the *internal* dynamics of development that ultimately decides the issue, potentially deciding it for the worse even under the best external relation of forces.

Thus, the concept of *irreversibility* of socialist transformation is meaningful only if it refers to the point of no return in the internal dynamics of development, beyond the structural determinations of capital as a mode of social metabolic control, fully embracing all three dimensions of the inherited system: capital, labor, and the state. The *qualitative leap* in Marxian discourse—the well-known aphorism in *The Eighteenth Brumaire of Louis Bonaparte* about "Hic Rhodus, hic salta!"—anticipates the time when the long-sustained struggle to move beyond capital becomes *globally irreversible* because it is fully in tune with the *internal* development of the countries concerned. And in Marx's view, that becomes possible only as a result of the cumulative corrective impact of radical self-criticism exercised by the social agency of emancipation, labor, which must be not nominally (as seen so far, under the authority of the post-capitalist "personifications of capital") but genuinely and effectively in charge of the social metabolic process.

Clearly, the process of socialist transformation—precisely because it must embrace all aspects of the interrelationship between *capital, labor,* and the *state*—is conceivable only as a form of transitional restructuring based on the inherited and progressively alterable leverage of material mediations. As in the case of Goethe's father (even if for very different reasons), it is not possible to pull down the existing building and erect a wholly new edifice in its place on totally new foundations. Life must go on in the shored-up house during the entire course of rebuilding, "taking away one storey after another from the bottom upwards, slipping in the new structure, so that in the end none of the old house should be left." Indeed, the task is even more difficult than that. For the decaying timber frame of the building must also be replaced in the course of extricating humankind from the perilous structural framework of the capital system.

Disconcertingly, the "expropriation of the expropriators" leaves the edifice of the capital system standing. All it can achieve on its own is to change the *type* of personification of capital, but not the need for such personification. Often even the personnel can remain the same (as not only the significant continuity in the commanding economic and state personnel in post-revolutionary societies demonstrated but even more so the post-Soviet restoratory moves all over Eastern Europe), changing, so to speak, the Party membership card only. This is because the three fundamental dimensions of the system—capital, labor, and the state—are *materially* constituted and linked to one another, and not simply on a legal/political basis.

Accordingly, neither capital, nor labor, nor indeed the state can be simply *abolished* by even the most radical juridical intervention. It is, therefore, by no means accidental that historical experience had produced plentiful examples of the *strengthening* of the post-revolutionary state, but not even the smallest step in the direction of its "withering away." For post-revolutionary labor in its immediately feasible mode of existence, whether in formerly advanced capitalist or in underdeveloped countries, remains directly tied to the substance of capital, that is, the latter's material existence as the ongoing structural determination of the laborr process, and not to its historically contingent form of juridical personification. The substance of capital as the materially embedded, incorrigibly hierarchical, expansion-oriented and accumulation-driven determining power of the social metabolic process remains the same for as long as this system—whether in its capitalist or in its post-capitalist forms—can successfully exercise the historically alienated controlling functions of labor. By contrast the political/juridical forms of personification through which the objective reproductive imperatives of the capital system—"the rule of wealth over society" in Marx's words—continue to be imposed on labor *can and must* vary in tune with the changing historical circumstances, in that such variations arise as necessary attempts to remedy some major disturbance or crisis of the system within its own structural parameters. This is true not only in the historically rather rare cases of dramatic shift from a capitalist to a post-capitalist form of social metabolic reproduction but also in the much more frequent and in its character on the whole temporary changes from liberal-democratic to military-dictatorial varieties of capitalism, and back again to the economically more viable liberal-capitalist form. The only thing that must remain constant regarding the personifications of capital in all such metamorphoses of the controlling personnel, across centuries, is that their functional identity must be always defined in *contra-position* to labor.

Given the inseparability of the three dimensions of the fully articulated capital system—capital, labor, and the state—it is inconceivable to emancipate labor without simultaneously also superseding capital and the state as well. For, paradoxically, the fundamental material supporting pillar of capital is not the state but labor in its continued structural dependency from capital. Lenin and others spoke of the unavoidable necessity "to smash the bourgeois state" as the immediate task of the proletarian dictatorship in the aftermath of the conquest of political power. At the same time, as a warning, Lukács projected the picture of the proletariat "turning its dictatorship against itself," as we have seen above. The difficulty is, though, that the conquest of state power is very far from equaling the control of social metabolic reproduction. It is indeed possible to smash the bourgeois state through the conquest of political power, at least to a significant extent. However, it is quite impossible to smash labor's inherited structural dependency from capital. For that dependency is materially secured by the established hierarchical structural division of labor. It can be altered for the better only through the radical restructuring of the totality of social reproductive processes, that is, through the progressive rebuilding of the inherited edifice in its entirety. Preaching the necessity—and the ethical rightfulness—of high labor discipline, as Lukács tried to do, avoids (at best) the question of who is actually in charge of the productive and distributive determinations of the post-revolutionary labor process. So long as the vital controlling functions of the social metabolism are not effectively taken over and autonomously exercised by the associated producers, but left under the authority of a separate controlling personnel (the new type of personification of capital), labor self-defeatingly continues to reproduce the power of capital over against itself, materially maintaining and extending thereby the rule of alienated wealth over society.

This is what makes all talk about the "withering away of the state" totally unrealistic under such circumstances. For in the aftermath of the "expropriation of the expropriators" and the institution of a new, but equally separate and superimposed, controlling personnel, the authority of the latter [that is, the party, bureaucracy, etc.] must be politically established and enforced in the absence of the old juridical entitlement to control the productive and distributive practices on the basis of private property ownership. Thus the *strengthening* of the post-revolutionary state not simply in relation to the *outside* world—which, after the defeat of the interventionist forces in Russia was unable to exercise a major impact on the course of *internal* developments—but against the *labor force*, for the sake of the politically regulated maximal extraction of surplus-labor, becomes a perverse structural necessity, and not a more or less easily corrigible "bureaucratic degeneration" to be rectified on the political plane thanks to a new "political revolution." As the implosion of the Soviet capital system demonstrated, given the enormously strengthened state power in the country it was much easier to engineer a *political counter-revolution from above* than to realistically envisage a *political revolution from below* as the corrective to the contradictions of the established order. For even if a new political revolution of the masses could prevail for a while, the real task of fundamental restructuring of the post-capitalist capital system would still remain. By contrast, Gorbachev's pretended "perestroika" did not have to restructure anything at all in the domain of the given hierarchical/structural social metabolic control. For its proclamation of the "equality of all types of property"—that is, the *juridical restoration of the rights of capitalist private property* for the benefit of the few—operated in the sphere of the personifications of capital, making only "justifiably" hereditary (in the name of the promised economic rationality and market efficiency) what they already controlled de facto. Instituting legal/political changes on the plane of entitlement to property is child's play compared to the burdensome and prolonged task of superseding capital's mode of controlling the social reproductive order.

The "withering away of the state"—without which the idea of realizing socialism cannot be seriously entertained for a moment—is inconceivable without the withering away of capital as the regulator of the social metabolic process. The vicious circle of labor being locked into its structural dependency from capital, on the one hand, and into a subordinate position at the level of political decision-making by an alien state power on the other, can only be broken if the producers progressively cease to reproduce the material supremacy of capital. This they can only do by radically challenging the hierarchical structural division of labor. It is therefore most important to bear in mind that the perverse strengthening of the post-capitalist state is not a self-sustaining cause but inseparable from the structural dependency of labor from capital. This contradictory determination of labor under the continued rule of capital (even if in a new form) asserts itself despite the fact that capital always was—and can only be—reproduced as the embodiment of labor in an alienated and self-perpetuating form. Since the antagonistic determination in question is inherent in the *material command structure of capital,* which is only *complemented by* but not *grounded in* the state as the system's comprehensive political command structure, the problem of labor's self-emancipation cannot be addressed at the level of politics only (or even primarily). The countless "revolutions betrayed" across modern history provide painfully abundant evidence in this respect.

The necessary critique of state power, with the aim of radically curtailing and ultimately superseding it, acquires its sense only if it is practically implemented in its social-metabolic/material-reproductive setting. For the "withering away" of the state implies not only the withering away of capital (as the objectified and reified controller of the social reproductive order) but also the self-transcendence of labor as subordinate to capital's material imperatives enforced by the prevailing system of structural/hierarchical division of labor and state power. This is possible only if all controlling functions of the social metabolism—which must be under all forms of the rule of capital vested in the material and political command structure of an alienated decision-making power—are progressively appropriated and positively exercised by the associated producers. In this sense, the objective structural (in contrast to by itself unsustainable political/juridical) displacement of the personifications of capital through a system of genuine *self-management* is the key to a successful rebuilding of the inherited structures.

Undoubtedly, recent developments in Eastern Europe can open up some new possibilities for profitable capital accumulation in the dominant Western capitalist countries, above all in the Federal Republic of Germany. However, given the relatively limited scale of such economic openings, as well as the political complications inseparable from them, it would be naive to expect the solution of the structural defects of the Western capital system as a whole from the new market opportunities emerging in the East.

Notes

Introduction

1. István Mészáros to John Bellamy Foster, September 19, 2012, personal correspondence
2. István Mészáros to John Bellamy Foster, October 10, 2015, personal correspondence.
3. Mészáros commonly referred to his handwritten drafts as the "second version" of his work on the state (no first version has survived) while the final book was to be the "third version." As he wrote to me on July 9, 2017, "If all goes well, I should be able to finish the last chapter of Volume 1 towards the end of the current year. Then I 'take a deep breath' and dive into volume 2. I have already the second version of volumes 2 and 3. But that is still very chaotic. I consider always only the third version acceptable. Again, if all goes well, volumes 2 and 3 should be completed in 2 or 3 years, i.e. by the middle of 2020." István Mészáros to John Bellamy Foster, July 9, 2017, personal correspondence.
4. Mészáros to Foster, October 10, 2015.
5. István Mészáros to John Bellamy Foster, December 8, 2015, personal correspondence
6. István Mészáros, *Marx's Theory of Alienation* (London: Merlin Press, 1975), 10; István Mészáros, *The Necessity of Social Control* (Isaac Deutscher Memorial Lecture) (London: Merlin Press, 1971), reprinted in István Mészáros, *The Necessity of Social Control* (New York: Monthly Review Press, 2015), 23–51. All subsequent references to *The Necessity of Social Control* refer to his 2015 book of which the 1971 lecture was a part.

7. István Mészáros, *Lukács's Concept of Dialectic* (London: Merlin, 1972); István Mészáros, *The Power of Ideology* (New York: New York University Press, 1989); István Mészáros, *The Work of Sartre: The Search for Freedom*: (Brighton: Harvester, 1979, first edition); István Mészáros, *Social Structures and Forms of Consciousness*, vol. 1, *The Social Determination of Method* (New York: Monthly Review Press, 2010), vol. 2, *The Dialectic of Structure and History* (New York: Monthly Review Press, 2011).
8. István Mészáros, *Beyond Capital: Towards a Theory of Transition* (New York: Monthly Review Press, 1995).
9. Mészáros, *Beyond Capital*, 460–95, 673–770.
10. Chávez dedicated a volume of Símon Rodríguez's writings to Mészáros in Caracas on September 10, 2001, inscribing "István, Senalador de caminos" (pathfinder).
11. István Mészáros, *Social Structures and Forms of Consciousness*, vol. 2, *The Dialectic of Structure and History*, 85–141. "How Can the State Wither Away," from *Beyond Capital,* and "Customs, Traditions, and Explicit Law: Historical Boundaries of the Legal and Political Superstructure, from *The Dialectic of Structure and History* from Appendices IV and II, respectively, in the present volume. The original title of "Customs, Traditions, and Explicit Law" was dropped in his plan for inclusion of it as an appendix in *Beyond Leviathan* and only the subtitle was used.
12. István Mészáros, *Socialism or Barbarism* (New York: Monthly Review Press, 2001); István Mészáros, *The Challenge and Burden of Historical Time* (New York: Monthly Review Press, 2008); István Mészáros, *The Structural Crisis of Capital* (New York: Monthly Review Press, 2010).
13. István Mészáros, *The Work of Sartre* (New York: Monthly Review Press, 2012, expanded second edition).
14. All in-text page-number citations in this introduction refer to the present volume.
15. Norberto Bobbio, "Is There a Marxist Theory of the State?," *Telos* 35, no. 4 (1978): 5–16. Parts of Mészáros's second-version draft treatment of Bobbio were incorporated into Part Two of *Beyond Leviathan* [9:1–3] . Moreover, some aspects of this drew on passages that had appeared earlier in *Beyond Capital* dealing with Bobbio's ideas in *The Future of Democracy* on the extension of rights and Mészáros's criticisms of this from the standpoint of the uncontrollability of capital. See Mészáros, *Beyond Capital*, 712–13; Norberto Bobbio, *The Future of Democracy* (London: Polity, 1991).
16. Bobbio, "Is There a Marxist Theory of the State?," 8.
17. Bobbio, "Is There a Marxist Theory of the State?," 5, 11.
18. The importance of Bobbio and Ernest Barker, whose ideas are discussed in the following paragraphs, was strongly emphasized by Mészáros in a number of discussions I had with him, in which he depicted these thinkers

as representing in somewhat different ways the modern liberal conception of the state. Mészáros frequently mentioned his great respect and affection for Bobbio. He wrote: "I last visited Bobbio in Torino a few months before he died, and we talked for hours at that unforgettable meeting." István Mészáros to John Bellamy Foster, January 13, 2015, personal correspondence. On another occasion he observed: "Bobbio was a very close and dear friend of mine over many years. I visited a few weeks before he died. We were very conscious of our differences, but there was an ample common ground for our critique of the established order. Leo Valiani (the head of the Italian guerilla movement in the North, who captured and tried Mussolini), was also a very close and dear Friend. I was with him in Milan not long before he died.... These were most remarkable people. They were both 'Senator for Life' in the Italian Upper House." István Mészáros to John Bellamy Foster, June 24, 2017, personal correspondence.
19. Norberto Bobbio, *The Future of Democracy: A Defence of the Rules of the Game* (Cambridge: Polity, 1987), 24–25. The exclusive liberal association of the state with the rule of law means that the analysis is completely unable to comprehend the fascist state (10:5).
20. Max Weber, *From Max Weber* (Oxford: Oxford University Press, 1946), 78. In his notes, Mészáros referred to the "Weberian apologetics of (declamatorily) internalized *violence* (i.e. too be internalized, in the service of the apologetics of the *ruling* order." István Mészáros, Uncatalogued Archival Notes, Mészáros Family Papers, George Mészáros Collection, block 5:8–9.
21. Bobbio argued that "the term 'state' is too abstract" thus avoiding the larger question. Bobbio, *The Future of Democracy*, 114.
22. Ernest Barker, translator's introduction in Otto Gierke, *Natural Law and the Theory of Society, 1500 to 1880* (Cambridge: Cambridge University Press, 1934), ix–xci.
23. Barker, translator's introduction in Gierke, *Natural Law and the Theory of Society*, xxviii.
24. Barker, translator's introduction in Gierke, *Natural Law and the Theory of Society*, xxiii, emphasis added.
25. István Mészáros to John Bellamy Foster, December 23, 2015, personal correspondence.
26. Mészáros, *Beyond Capital*, 712–13.
27. Ibid., 713.
28. István Mészáros to John Bellamy Foster, January 13, 2015, personal correspondence.
29. Extract from Book Proposal for *Beyond Capital* presented to New Left Books, quoted in Mészáros to Foster, January 13, 2015.
30. Mészáros, *The Dialectic of Structure and History*, 130; Raymond Williams, *Problems in Materialism and Culture* (London: Verso, 1980), 31–49.

31. Mészáros planned to address these two works in volume 3 of *Beyond Leviathan*. See Appendix I in this volume. On Mészáros's view of Marx's *Critique of the Gotha Programme*, see Mészáros, *The Challenge and Burden of Historical Time*.
32. Mészáros, *The Challenge and Burden of Historical Time*, 327–28.
33. Some of these thinkers are addressed only or mainly in those portions of Mészáros's second-version draft intended for volumes 2 and 3 of his work, which will later be published as *Critique of Leviathan: Reflections on the State*. Perhaps the most notable absence among the political theorists addressed in *Beyond Leviathan* was John Locke, who, in Mészáros's view, was overshadowed by his predecessor, Hobbes.
34. Karl Marx and Frederick Engels, *Ireland and the Irish Question* (Moscow: Progress Publishers, 1971), 142. In 2013 Mészáros stated: "If I had to modify today Rosa Luxemburg's famous words about 'socialism or barbarism' I would have to add: 'Barbarism if we are lucky.' Because the extermination of humanity is the unfolding menace. For as long as we fail to solve our grave problems which extend over all dimensions of our existence and relationship to nature, that danger will remain on our horizon." István Mészáros interviewed by Elenora de Lucena, "Barbarism on the Horizon," MR Online, December 31, 2013, https://mronline.org/2013/12/31/meszaros311213-html/.
35. These biographical notes on Mészáros draw directly on John Bellamy Foster, "István Mészáros (1930–2017)," *Notes from the Editors*, *Monthly Review* 69, no. 7 (December 2017). See also Terry Brotherstone, "A Tribute to István Mészáros (1930–2017)," *Critique* 46, no. 2 (2018): 327–37; Terry Brotherstone, "Obituary: István Mészáros, Hungarian Marxist Political Philosopher Who Taught at St. Andrews," *The Scotsman*, November 18, 2017; István Mészáros (interviewed by Joseph McCarney and Chris Arthur), "Marxism Today," *Radical Philosophy* 62 (Autumn 1992): 27–34.
36. Mihály Vörösmarty, *Csonger és Tünde*, translated by P. Zollman (Budapest: Merlin International Theatre Budapest, 1996).
37. The volume on aesthetics, which he said he took with him in leaving Hungary, was most likely his dissertation, *Satire and Reality*.
38. In 1964 he wrote his work on Attila József, also published in Italian: István Mészáros, *Attila József e l'arte moderna* (Milan: Lerici, 1964).
39. Donald C. Savage, "Keeping Professors Out," *Dalhousie Review* 69, no. 4 (1990): 511–12; "Profs Might Help Mészáros," *The Ubyssey* 54, no. 8 (October 6 1972), https://open.library.ubc.ca/collections/ubcpublications/ubysseynews/items/1.0126452#p2z-3r0f:meszaros.
40. Daniel Singer, "After Alienation," *The Nation*, June 10, 1996, https://www.thenation.com/article/archive/after-alienation/.
41. President Hugo Chávez's Remarks on Presenting the Liberatador Award

for Critical Thinking (the Bolívar Prize) to István Mészáros, September 14, 2009.
42. István Mészáros to John Bellamy Foster, July 28, 2007, May 12, 2008, personal correspondence. Beyond cancer there was the question of his heart. In the letter in 2012 in which he said he was turning full time to writing what was to be *Beyond Leviathan* he stated: "I had a great deal of trouble with my health [recently]. This time mainly with my heart, because the blood vessels, which were replaced by a big operation in 1998 (4 of them) are getting clogged up again, and of course there can be no question of another heart surgery at my age. Fortunately, the cancer is still under control, and I carry on as long as I can." Mészáros to Foster, September 19, 2012.
43. István Mészáros, Uncatalogued Archival Notes, Mészáros Family Papers, George Mészáros Collection, block 5:6; Dylan Thomas, "Do Not Go Gentle into that Good Night," https://poets.org/poem/do-not-go-gentle-good-night.
44. István Mészáros to John Bellamy Foster, July 25, 2017.
45. Mészáros, "Barbarism on the Horizon."
46. See Renato Constantino, *Neo-Colonial Identity and Counter-Consciousness*, edited by István Mészáros (London: Merlin Press, 1978), reprinted as István Mészáros, "Neo-Colonial Identity and Counter-Consciousness," *Journal of Contemporary Asia* 30, no. 3 (2000): 308–21.
47. Hugo Chávez, *Pueblo, Sufragio y Democracia* (Yara: Ediciones MBR-200, 1993), 5–6; Mészáros, *Beyond Capital*, 710–11.
48. Mészáros, *Beyond Capital*, 711.
49. István Mészáros, *Más allá del capital*, translated by Eduardo Gasca (Caracas: Vadell Hermanos, 2001).
50. This introduction to the Latin American Spanish edition has since been translated into English (the original English version was lost) by Brian M. Napoletano and Pedro Urquijo and published on MR Online as: István Mészáros, "The Historical Challenges Facing the Socialist Movement," Monthly Review Essays, March 26, 2021, https://mronline.org/2021/03/26/the-historical-challenges-facing-the-socialist-movement/.
51. István Mészáros to John Bellamy Foster, February 16, 2015, personal correspondence.
52. The following three paragraphs are adapted from John Bellamy Foster, "Chávez and the Communal State: On the Transition to Socialism in Venezuela," *Monthly Review* 66, no. 11 (April 2015): 9–10.
53. For a summary of this aspect of Mészáros's thought see John Bellamy Foster, "Foreword," in Mészáros, *The Necessity of Social Control* (2015), 1–21.
54. Mészáros, *Beyond Capital*, 758–68; Mészáros, *The Challenge and Burden of Historical Time*, 251–53. It was this understanding that the population would defend the revolution that allowed Chávez to arm the

people, creating a widespread system of armed militias encompassing a very large portion of the population. See Misión Verdad, "Civic-Military Union," *Internationalist 360°*, May 7, 2020, https://libya360.wordpress.com/2020/05/07/civic-military-union-the-chavista-paradigm-that-defined-the-latest-events-in-the-war-against-venezuela/.
55. Marta Harnecker, *A World to Build* (New York: Monthly Review Press, 2015), 74–77; *Leyes del Poder Popular*, 57 (Ley Orgánica De Las Comunas, Articulo 35, https://mronline.org/wp-content/uploads/2018/07/Ley_Organica_de_las_Comunas.pdf).
56. Chávez quoted in Michael A. Lebowitz, *The Socialist Alternative* (New York: Monthly Review Press, 2010), 80–81; Mészáros, *Marx's Theory of Alienation*, 76–77.
57. Mészáros, *The Structural Crisis of Capital*, 124.
58. Mészáros, *Beyond Capital*, 187–223.
59. Lebowitz, *The Socialist Alternative*, 24–25, 85. Lebowitz played a crucial role in interpreting this aspect of Mészáros analysis for Chávez at the latter's request. This story is told in Michael Lebowitz, *The Socialist Imperative* (New York: Monthly Review Press, 2015), 111–33 (a book dedicated to Chávez).
60. See Mészáros, *Beyond Capital*, 710; Mészáros, *The Structural Crisis of Capital*, 126–30.
61. Hugo Chávez, "Onwards Toward a Communal State," February 21, 2010 (posted February 25, 2010), http://venezuelanalysis.com; Mészáros, *Beyond Capital*, 709.
62. Hugo Chávez, "Strike at the Helm," October 20, 2012, https://monthlyreview.org/commentary/strike-at-the-helm/.
63. Mészáros, *The Necessity of Social Control* (2015), 199, 215, 314. The discussion here is partly based on conversations that I had with Mészáros on the subject.
64. Mészáros, *The Necessity of Social Control*, 215–17. On vernacular evolutionary traditions see Teodor Shanin, ed., *Late Marx and the Russian Road* (New York: Monthly Review Press, 1983), 243–75.
65. On these concepts see Foster, Foreword, in Mészáros, *The Necessity of Social Control* (2015), 9–21; Foster, Foreword, in Mészáros, *The Challenge and Burden of Historical Time*, 11–16. Mészáros indicated at one point that in his view capital, understood as a command structure geared to accumulation of wealth, "precedes capitalism by thousands of years." In this perspective, "capitalism is a relatively easy object in this enterprise because you can in a sense abolish capitalism through revolutionary upheaval and intervention at the level of politics, the expropriation of the capitalism. You have put an end to capitalism, but you have not even touched the power of capital when you have done it." Mészáros, "Marxism Today." See also Brotherstone, "A Tribute to István Mészáros," 335–36.

66. Mészáros, *Beyond Capital*, 187–210.
67. Mészáros to Foster, December 23, 2015; Mészáros, *Beyond Capital*, 109–10.
68. Mészáros to Foster, December 23, 2015; Karl Marx, *A Contribution to a Critique of Political Economy* (Moscow: Progress Publishers, 1970), 20.
69. Mészáros's argument on *correctiveness* or *corrective adjustment* is systematically developed in his "second version" draft (*Critique of Leviathan: Reflections on the State*) though crucial to his entire perspective. In his notes, he indicates that "correctability" is closely related to planning. It is associated with the "the interrelation (dialectical) between metabolic-material development and corrective state determination." István Mészáros, Uncatalogued Archival Notes, Mészáros Family Papers, George Mészáros Collection, block 2:10. (Note: In organizing the photos of ninety-two pages of mostly handwritten archival notes for *Beyond Leviathan*, George Mészáros divided them into eight blocks for sending. This is used as the basis of the reference system here, which will be used to distinguish the various sections of this part of the collection of Mészáros's papers. The numbers after the colon indicate the position of particular pages/photos within a given block.)
70. István Mészáros to John Bellamy Foster, June 11, 2017, personal correspondence.
71. István Mészáros, Uncatalogued Archival Notes, Mészáros Family Papers, George Mészáros Collection, block 2:7.
72. István Mészáros, Uncatalogued Archival Notes, Mészáros Family Papers, George Mészáros Collection, block 1:6.
73. In line with Mészáros's analysis, Chávez sought to make the Bolivarian Revolution irreversible by shifting the power to the people through the promotion of communes. See Foster, "Hugo Chávez and the Communal State," 2–3.
74. Mészáros, *The Challenge and Burden of Historical Time*, 366–80.
75. István Mészáros, Uncatalogued Archival Notes, Mészáros Family Papers, George Mészáros Collection, block 1:10, 2:9.
76. Karl Marx and Frederick Engels, *Collected Works* (New York: International Publishers, 1975), vol. 6, 127; Mészáros, *The Challenge and Burden of Historical Time*, 43.
77. István Mészáros, Uncatalogued Archival Notes, Mészáros Family Papers, George Mészáros Collection, block 2:9.
78. Mészáros, *The Challenge and Burden of Historical Time*, 269.
79. Mészáros, *The Necessity of Social Control* (2015), 180; see Appendix IV in this volume.
80. István Mészáros, Uncatalogued Archival Notes, Mészáros Family Papers, George Mészáros Collection, block 7:2.

81. The question of Adam Ferguson did come up briefly in our discussions in passing in relation to Ferguson's impact on Hegel, as indicated in Lukács's *The Young Hegel*. Georg Lukács, *The Young Hegel* (Cambridge, Massachusetts: MIT Press, 1975), 402–05; see also Adam Ferguson, *An Essay on the History of Civil Society* (Edinburgh: T. Caddel, 1773). For Mészáros, Smith's emphasis was to "keep *politics* (proletarians) out of his idealist *natural* system." István Mészáros, Uncatalogued Archival Notes (blocks 2 and 3), Mészáros Family Papers, George Mészáros Collection, block 2:12, 3:9.
82. Thomas Ahnert, introduction in Christian Thomasius, *Institutes of Divine Jurisprudence* (Indianapolis: Liberty Fund, 2011), xx–xxiii; Ernst Bloch, *Natural Law and Human Dignity* (Cambridge, Massachusetts: Harvard University Press, 1986), 293–314.
83. Bloch, *Natural Law and Human Dignity*, 302–09. On Thomasius's courageous opposition to witch trials, which proved so important, see Christian Thomasius, *Essays on Church, State, and Politics* (Indianapolis: Liberty Fund, 2007), 207–54. Mészáros of course recognized the contradictions in the natural law tradition, particularly in its later more apologetic uses. As he observed in his notes: "Equally, we should not forget in the field of social and political theory those approaches which postulated an original '*state of nature*' for humanity's development, and in the conceptions on the state of the advocates of 'Natural Law.' All of this can lead to very problematic conclusions; sometimes even to the assertion of the diametrical opposite of the real state of affairs even in the case of very great thinkers. Thus Hegel and Kant." István Mészáros, Uncatalogued Archival Notes, Mészáros Family Papers, George Mészáros Collection, block 8:11.
84. István Mészáros, Uncatalogued Archival Notes, Mészáros Family Papers, George Mészáros Collection, block 6:9.
85. Bloch, *Natural Law and Human Dignity*, 10–16, 288–89, 308. Mészáros did not explore the Epicurean roots of Thomasius's philosophy directly. But at the time he was working on the "preface" to *Beyond Leviathan* in his last year he had included in his notes a directive to himself to study various works related to Epicurus on my recommendation, including Bloch's section on Epicurus in his *On Karl Marx*, Benjamin Farrington's *The Faith of Epicurus* (New York: Herder and Herder, 1971), John Bellamy Foster, *Marx's Ecology* (New York: Monthly Review Press, 2000), and the chapter on Epicurus in John Bellamy Foster, Brett Clark York, *The Critique of* Intelligent Design (New York: Monthly Review Press, 2008). István Mészáros, Uncatalogued Archival Notes, Mészáros Family Papers, George Mészáros Collection, block 3:4.
86. Mészáros's reference to the "Principle of Hope" in the title of his chapter on "Thomasius and Bloch's Principle of Hope" was a clear reference to Bloch's

magnum opus, his *The Principle of Hope* (Cambridge, Massachusetts: MIT Press, 1986, three volumes). Mészáros was particularly influenced by *Natural Law and Human Dignity* but also drew on *The Principle of Hope*. He writes on Bloch himself and his relation to Hegel in the "second version" draft of *Critique of Leviathan: Reflections on the State*.
87. Bloch, *The Principle of Hope*, vol. 1, 445–46; Brotherstone, "A Tribute to István Mészáros," 337.
88. Mészáros to Foster, December 23, 2015. Mészáros had in mind, for example, Bloch's (and Lukács's) rejection of Horkheimer's notorious attempt to create a continuum between bourgeois revolution in its most radical phase and Hitler's burning of the Reichstag. Ernst Bloch, *Natural Law and Human Dignity*, 170–73; István Mészáros, "Bloch on Horkheimer and Lukács," in *Critique of Leviathan* ("second version" draft of *Beyond Leviathan*, unpublished manuscript).
89. Rodney Livingstone, Perry Anderson, and Francis Mulhern, "Presentation IV" in Ernst Bloch, Georg Lukács, Bertolt Brecht, Walter Benjamin, and Theodor Adorno, et al., *Aesthetics and Politics* (London: Verso, 1977), 142–43. Martin Jay, *Adorno* (Cambridge, Massachusetts: Harvard University Press, 1984), 44–47; Martin Jay, *The Dialectical Imagination* (Boston: Little, Brown and Company, 1973), 201–02.
90. See Paul Baran and Herbert Marcuse, "The Baran Marcuse Correspondence," MR Online (March 2014), https://monthlyreview.org/commentary/baran-marcuse-correspondence/.
91. Livingstone, et al., "Presentation IV," 143; Theodor Adorno, "Reconciliation Under Duress," in Bloch, et al., *Aesthetics and Politics*, 151–76; Mészáros, *The Power of Ideology*, 91–130.
92. Georg Lukács, *The Theory of the Novel* (London: Merlin Press, 1971), 22. Mészáros, *The Power of Ideology*, 91–130. Horkheimer as well as Adorno were part of this Grand Hotel Abyss for Lukács. As Martin Jay noted, the later "Horkheimer froze the conditions of the present into an endless repetitive pattern with no apparent way out.... Religion rather than social action was seen as the major repository of hopes in what Horkheimer called 'the entirely other.'" Martin Jay, *Marxism and Totality* (Berkeley: University of California Press, 1984), 219.
93. Mészáros to Foster, December 23, 2015.

Preface
1. Karl Marx, *The Poverty of Philosophy* (London: Lawrence and Wishart, n.d.), 123.
2. Thomas Hobbes, *Leviathan* (London: Penguin, 1985), 186. All further quotations from this work will be given from this most easily accessible edition.

3. Hobbes, *Leviathan*, 187.
4. Hobbes, *Leviathan*, 187–88.
5. Hobbes, *Leviathan*, 215.
6. Hobbes, *Leviathan*, 216.
7. Naturally, blind reactionary state apologetic theories, characteristically dominant in the descending phase of the social metabolic order, rule themselves out in this context.
8. Plato, *The Laws* (London: Penguin, 1970), 517.
9. See Niccolò Machiavelli's *Prince* and *Discourses* on the subject. Niccolò Machiavelli, *The Prince* (New York: Alfred A. Knopf, 1992); *The Discourses* (Lonson: Penguin Books, 2003).
10. Plato, *The Laws*, 523.
11. Many centuries later, in Johann Gottlieb Fichte's *Ephorate*, the ultimate decision-making "Ephors" of his constitution-safeguarding institution are meant to fulfill a very similar task. Plato, *The Laws*, 530.
12. Plato, *The Laws*, 524.
13. Plato, *The Republic*, iv, 425–26, in Francis Cornford, ed., *The Republic of Plato* (Oxford: Oxford University Press, 1945), 117–18.

1. The Historic Anachronism and Necessary Supersession of the State

1. Karl Marx, *Capital*, vol. 1 (New York: International Publishers, 1967), 235.
2. Marx, *Capital*, vol. 1, 269.
3. For instance, the Liberal State, or the Fascist State, or for that matter the post-revolutionary Soviet-type State.
4. Associated with Giovanni Giolitti's Liberal government in Italy in 1922.
5. See, for instance, Hegel's far-reaching arguments on the nation-state.
6. For an outstanding pioneering work on the socialist left published on this subject, see John Bellamy Foster, *Marx's Ecology: Materialism and Nature* (New York: Monthly Review Press, 2000); see also John Bellamy Foster, Brett Clark, and Richard York, *The Ecological Rift: Capitalism's War on the Earth* (New York: Monthly Review Press, 2010). On the latest phase, see the powerfully argued and richly documented book by Ian Angus, *Facing the Anthropocene: Fossil Capitalism and the Crisis of the Earth System* (New York: Monthly Review Press, 2016).
7. This lecture was written in 1970 and delivered at the London School of Economics on January 26, 1971.
8. Karl Marx and Frederick Engels, *Collected Works*, vol. 5 (New York: International Publishers, 1975), 52.
9. Marx and Engels, *Collected Works*, vol. 5, 73.
10. Marx and Engels, *Marx and Engels Collected Works*, vol. 5, 87.
11. Naturally, Marx and Engels were avid readers of *The Economist*.
12. Karl Marx to Frederick Engels, October 8, 1858, in Marx and Engels,

Collected Works, vol. 40 (London: Lawrence & Wishart, 1983), 347. Emphasis in boldface added.
13. Engels made it clear in the preface of *Anti-Dühring* that he wrote the book because "people were preparing to spread Dühring's doctrine in a popularized form among the workers."
14. Marx to L. Kugelman, January 27, 1870, Marx and Engels, *Collected Works*, vol. 43, 528.
15. Eduard Bernstein, *Evolutionary Socialism* (New York: Schocken Books, 1961), 209–13.
16. This is the danger anxiously stressed in the increasing threat to the Earth System itself, under the current conditions of the *Anthropocene*.
17. Martin Wolf, *Why Globalization Works: The Case for the Global Market Economy* (New Haven: Yale University Press, 2004), 320.
18. G. C. A. Gaskin, introduction to Thomas Hobbes, *Leviathan* (Oxford: Oxford University Press, 1991), xlii–xliii.
19. See C. B. Macpherson, *The Political Theory of Possessive Individualism* (Oxford: Oxford University Press, 1962).
20. The Third Estate and the Estates General.
21. Adam Smith, *The Wealth of Nations* (New York: Random House, 1965), 423.
22. Smith, *The Wealth of Nations*, 423.
23. Jean-Jacques Rousseau, *Social Contract and Discourses* (London: J. M. Dent, 1913), 281.
24. Rousseau, *The Social Contract and Discourses*, 45, emphasis added.
25. Rousseau, *The Social Contract and Discourses*, 40.
26. Rousseau, *Social Contract and Discourses*, 271, emphasis added.
27. Rousseau, *The Social Contract and Discourses*, 22, emphasis added.
28. Immanuel Kant, "Eternal Peace," in Kant, *The Philosophy of Kant: Moral and Political Writings* (New York: Random House, 1949), 448–49.
29. Kant, "Eternal Peace," 452–53.
30. Kant, *The Philosophy of Kant*, 418, emphasis added.
31. Rousseau, *The Social Contract*, 22.
32. Kant, *The Philosophy of Kant*, 417, emphasis added.
33. "*eine verschwindende Notwendigkeit*" (a vanishing one), in sense of necessity. Marx, *Grundrisse* (London: Penguin, 1973), 832, italics added.

2. Freedom Is Parasitic on Equality

1. Xenophon, *Cyropaedia* II, i, 14 (Cambridge, Massachusetts: Harvard University Press, 1960), 143.
2. Karl Marx, *Grundrisse* (London: Penguin, 1973), 88, 103.
3. See the discussion of these problems in István Mészáros, *Marx's Theory of Alienation* (London: Merlin Press, 1970).

3. From Primitive to Substantive Equality—via Slavery

1. See Leo Valiani, *Memorie di un patriota: Mihály Károlyi* (Milan: Feltrinelli, 1958) on the president of the Hungarian Republic after the collapse of the Austro-Hungarian Empire in 1918. See also Valiani's seminal book *The End of Austria-Hungary* (New York: Knopf, 1973).
2. See on this subject Christopher Hitchens, *The Trial of Henry Kissinger* (London: Verso, 2002).
3. See István Mészáros, *Social Structure and Forms of Consciousness*, vol. 2, *The Dialectic of Structure and History* (New York: Monthly Review Press, 2011), 241–95.
4. See G. W. F. Hegel, *The Philosophy of Right* (Oxford: Oxford University Press, 1952), 130.
5. G. W. F. Hegel, *The Philosophy of History* (New York: Dover, 1956), 457.
6. Hegel, *The Philosophy of Right*, § 324, 210.
7. See the discussion of this problem in G. W. F. Hegel, *The Philosophy of Mind* (Oxford: Oxford University Press, 1971).
8. G. W. F. Hegel, *The Encyclopaedia Logic* (Indianapolis: Hackett, 1991), 284; *The Science of Logic* (New York: Humanity Press, 1969), 746.
9. Thomas Hobbes, *Leviathan* (London: Oxford University Press, 1909), 303. Italics in original.
10. Hegel, *The Encyclopaedia Logic*, 284.
11. Hegel, *The Philosophy of History*, 104. Author's translation.
12. Georg Lukács, *The Young Hegel* (Cambridge, MA: MIT, 1975).
13. Karl Marx, *Capital*, vol. 1 (New York: International Publishers, 1967), 741.
14. Adam Smith, *The Wealth of Nations* (Edinburgh: Adam and Charles Black, 1863), 273.
15. Hegel, *The Philosophy of History*, 39.
16. Hegel, *The Philosophy of History*, 103.
17. Hegel, *The Philosophy of History*, 142–43.
18. Hegel, *The Philosophy of History*, 78–79.
19. See István Mészáros, "The Activation of Capital's Absolute Limit," chap. 5 in *Beyond Capital*.
20. Hegel, *The Philosophy of History*, 456.
21. Hegel, *The Philosophy of Right*, 210.
22. Immanuel Kant, *Moral and Political Writings* (New York: Random House, 1949), 418.
23. Adam Smith, *Moral and Political Philosophy* (New York: Hafner, 1948), 291.

4. Capital's Deepening Structural Crisis and the State

1. "Breaking the US Budget Impasse," *Financial Times*, June 1, 2011.

2. See my 2009 *Denate Socialista* interview, republished as "The Tasks Ahead," in *The Structural Crisis of Capital* (New York: Monthly Review Press, 2010), 173–202.
3. This quotation is taken from section 18.2.1 of *Beyond Capital* (New York: Monthly Review Press, 1995), 680–82.
4. Sartre's interview given to the Italian Manifesto group was published as "Masses, Spontaneity, Party," in *The Socialist Register 1970*, ed. Ralph Miliband and John Saville (London: Merlin Press, 1970), 245.
5. Sartre, "Masses, Spontaneity, Party," 242.
6. Sartre, "Masses, Spontaneity, Party," 238–39.
7. The gravity of this problem can no longer be ignored. To realize its magnitude it is enough to quote a passage from an excellent book that offers a comprehensive account of the unfolding process of planetary destructiveness as a result of crossing some prohibitive thresholds and boundaries put into relief by environmental science: "These thresholds have in some cases already been crossed and in other cases will soon be crossed with the continuation of business as usual. Moreover, this can be attributed in each and every case to a primary cause: the current pattern of global socioeconomic development, that is, the capitalist mode of production and its expansionary tendencies. The whole problem can be called 'the global ecological rift,' referring to the overall break in the human relation to nature arising from an alienated system of capital accumulation without end. All of this suggests that the use of the term Anthropocene to describe a new geological epoch, displacing the Holocene, is both a description of a new burden falling on humanity and a recognition of an immense crisis—a potential terminal event in geological evolution that could destroy the world as we know it. On the one hand, there has been a great acceleration of the human impact on the planetary system since the Industrial Revolution, and particularly since 1945—to the point that biogeochemical cycles, the atmosphere, the ocean, and the Earth System as a whole can no longer be seen as largely impervious to the human economy. On the other hand, the current course on which the world is headed could be described not so much as the appearance of a stable new geological epoch (the Anthropocene), as an end-Holocene, or more ominously, end-Quarternary terminal event, which is a way of referring to the mass extinctions that often separate geological eras. Planetary boundaries and tipping points, leading to the irreversible degradation of the conditions of life on Earth, may soon be reached, science tells us, with a continuation of today's business as usual. The Anthropocene may be the shortest flicker in geological time, soon snuffed out." John Bellamy Foster, Brett Clark, and Richard York, *The Ecological Rift: Capitalism's War on the Earth* (New York: Monthly Review Press, 2010), 18–19.

8. See my Isaac Deutscher Memorial lecture, "The Necessity of Social Control," delivered at the London School of Economics on January 26, 1971. Italics in the original. Reprinted in *Beyond Capital*, 872–97.
9. Sartre, "Masses, Spontaneity, Party," 239.
10. Rosa Luxemburg, *The Accumulation of Capital* (London: Routledge, 1963), 466.

5. Capital's Historic Circle Is Closing

1. All quotations of Franklin D. Roosevelt's speeches are taken from B. D. Zevin, ed., *Nothing to Fear: The Selected Addresses of Franklin Delano Roosevelt, 1932–1945* (London: Hodder and Stoughton, 1947).
2. Ibid., "Annual Message to Congress," Washington, D.C., January 11, 1944.
3. Ibid. See Franklin D. Roosevelt's letter to Cordell Hull, January 24, 1944, *Nothing to Fear*.
4. Ibid., Franklin D. Roosevelt, "Address on the Fiftieth Anniversary of the Statue of Liberty," New York City, October 28, 1936.
5. Renato Constantino, *Neo-Colonial Identity and Counter-Consciousness* (London: Merlin, 1978), 234. Naturally, this kind of absurdly high differential rate of exploitation—of twenty-five to one in the Philippines in the late 1960s and early '70s—could not last forever. With the unfolding of the capital system's structural crisis, since the early 1970s, the original differential rate had to be modified in the sense of becoming the downward equalization of the differential rate of exploitation, negatively affecting the working classes in the capitalistically most advanced countries, including the United States.
6. In this respect, see in particular my Isaac Deutscher Memorial lecture, "The Necessity of Social Control," delivered at the London School of Economics and Political Science on January 26, 1971; my article "Political Power and Dissent in Postrevolutionary Societies," *New Left Review* 108 (1978): 3–21; my long study on "Il rinnovamento del Marxismo e l'attualità storica dell'offensiva socialista," *Problemi del Socialismo* 23 (1982): 5–141; and my book *Beyond Capital: Toward a Theory of Transition* (New York: Monthly Review Press, 1995), on which I worked for twenty-five years, first published in English in 1995. Naturally, *Beyond Leviathan* was conceived in the same period. However, its material foundation had to be spelled out first in *Beyond Capital*, in contrast to idealist theories that would concentrate one-sidedly on politics and the state. Nevertheless, the problems of the state in their materiality are clearly indicated in the works just mentioned, as well as in *The Power of Ideology*, first published in English in 1989. They also clarify the difference between the materiality of the state as such and the state's "legal and political superstructure." For it is a total misinterpretation of the Marxian position to consider the state itself only as a superstructure. Marx never had any doubt about the materiality—indeed the massive

repressive materiality—of the state as such. The state has, of course, its superstructural dimension, legitimately characterized as the "legal and political superstructure." But the state as such cannot be reduced simply to a superstructure.
7. G. W. F. Hegel, *The Philosophy of History* (New York: Dover, 1956), 31.
8. Ibid., 39.
9. Winston Churchill, *A History of the English Speaking Peoples*, vol. 3 (London: Cassell, 1956), ix.
10. Elizabeth Longford, *Wellington: Pillar of State* (New York: Harper and Row, 1972), 413, quoted in Andrew Roberts, *Napoleon the Great* (London: Penguin, 2014), 809.
11. Robin Lane Fox, *Alexander the Great* (London: Penguin, 1975), 398–99.
12. Roosevelt, "Address on the Fiftieth Anniversary of the Statue of Liberty," New York City, October 28, 1936, *Nothing to Fear*.
13. See in this respect Paul Baran's outstanding book *The Political Economy of Growth* (New York: Monthly Review Press, 1957), in which he rightly points out that "the assertion of American supremacy in the 'free' world implies the reduction of Britain and France (not to speak of Belgium, Holland and Portugal) to the status of junior partners of American imperialism" (vii).
14. See in this respect the opening epigraphs on page 281, Part Two, of my book *Beyond Capital*.
15. G. W. F. Hegel, *The Philosophy of Right* (New York: Oxford University Press, 1952), 130.
16. Hobbes, *Leviathan* (Oxford: Oxford University Press, 1909; reprint of 1651 edition), 94. (Actual page number, although facing page 95, says 92, due to an error in the original edition.)
17. From the final scene of *No Exit*.
18. See in this respect my book *The Work of Sartre* (New York: Monthly Review Press, 2012).
19. Goethe, *Faust*, part II, lines 11559–86, trans. Louis MacNeice and E. L. Stahl (Oxford: Oxford University Press, 1956), 287.

6. The Mountainous State

1. See Fred Magdoff and John Bellamy Foster, "The Plight of U.S. Workers," *Monthly Review* (January 2014): 1–22.
2. See the discussion of this problem in my 1971 Isaac Deutscher Memorial Lecture, "The Necessity of Social Control," in István Mészáros, *The Necessity of Social Control* (New York: Monthly Review Press, 2015), 23–51. To quote here a relevant passage from section 7 (47): "The reality of the different rates of exploitation and profit does not alter in the least the fundamental law itself; i.e., the growing *equalization* of the differential

rates of exploitation as the *global trend* of development of world capital. . . . Let it now suffice to stress that 'total social capital' should not be confused with 'total national capital.' When the latter is being affected by a relative weakening of its position within the global system, it will inevitably try to compensate for its losses by increasing its specific rate of exploitation over against the labor force under its direct control—or else its competitive position is further weakened within the global framework of 'total social capital.' Under the system of capitalist social control there can be no way out from such 'short-term disturbances and dysfunctions' other than the intensification of the specific rates of exploitation, which can only lead, both locally and in global terms, to an explosive intensification of the fundamental social antagonism in the long run. Those who have been talking about the 'integration' of the working class—depicting 'organized capitalism' as a system which succeeded in radically mastering its social contradictions— have hopelessly misidentified the manipulative success of the differential rates of exploitation (which prevailed in the relatively 'disturbance-free' historic phase of postwar reconstruction and expansion) as a basic *structural remedy*. As a matter of fact, it was nothing of the kind. The ever-increasing frequency with which 'temporary disturbances and dysfunctions' appear in all spheres of our social existence, and the utter failure of manipulative measures and instruments devised to cope with them, are clear evidence that the *structural crisis* of the capitalist mode of social control has assumed all-embracing proportions."

7. The End of Liberal-Democratic Politics

1. Edward Heath, *The Course of My Life: My Autobiography* (London: Hodder and Stoughton, 1989), 29. Harold Macmillan also scathingly referred to Margaret Thatcher's privatization policies as "selling the family silver."
2. Even in its nineteenth-century origin this notion goes back to Prime Minister Benjamin Disraeli, the promoter of "One Nation Conservatism," who was created Earl of Beaconsfield by Queen Victoria in 1876.
3. Heath, *The Course of My Life*, 169.
4. Ibid.
5. Paul A. Baran, *The Political Economy of Growth* (New York: Monthly Review Press, 1957), vii. See my discussion of these matters—including Roosevelt's ironical dismissal of Churchill's British Empire-retaining fantasies—in my *Socialism or Barbarism: From the "American Century" to the Crossroads* (New York: Monthly Review Press. 2001), 23–56.
6. István Mészáros, *Marx's Theory of Alienation* (London: Merlin Press, 1970), 310.
7. See in this respect Hegel's sharp critique of English constitutionality and his *Lectures on the Philosophy of History* in numerous places, in ibid.

8. The "Withering Away" of the State?

1. Marx to Engels, October 8, 1858, Karl Marx and Frederick Engels, *Selected Correspondence* (Moscow: Progress Publishers, 1975), 103–4.
2. See my discussions of these problems, with specific reference to Bismarck's role in defeating the Paris Commune, in Mészáros, *The Necessity of Social Control* (New York: Monthly Review Press, 2015), 208–10.
3. Marx to Engels, February 18, 1865, Marx and Engels, *Selected Correspondence*, 153–55.
4. Engels to Bebel, March 18–28, 1875, Marx and Engels, *Selected Correspondence*, 272–77.
5. See István Mészáros, "How Could the State Wither Away?," in *Beyond Capital* (New York: Monthly Review Press, 1995), 460–95. Reprinted as Appendix IV in this volume.

9. The Wishful Limitations of State Power

1. Norberto Bobbio, "Is There a Marxist Theory of the State?," *Telos* 35/4 (Spring 1978): 11.
2. Norberto Bobbio, *Quale Socialismo* (Torino: Einaudi, 1976).
3. At times he even admits, "I have no precise answer at all to this question." Bobbio, *Quale Socialismo?*, 106.
4. See Norberto Bobbio, *Da Hobbes a Marx* (Napoli: Morano Editore, 1965). In another important article on "Studi Hegeliani" contained in the same volume of essays (165–238), first published in *Belfagor* in 1950, Bobbio's attitude is more negative in relation to a dialectical conception of history, suggesting that in Marx's "philosophy of history" we find a Hegelian eschatological *closure* of history (211), when in fact Marx contrasts "humanity's *prehistory*" with the beginning of *"real history"* as a result of the radical emancipatory transformation of society at present dominated by alienation.
5. Bobbio, *Da Hobbes a Marx*, 251.
6. Ibid., 263.
7. "Anyone who has read the writers in the liberal tradition from Locke to Spencer, or the great Italian liberals from Cattaneo to Einaudi, knows that their main preoccupation has always been to restrain the state, to save civil society (in the Marxian sense) from excessive interference." Bobbio, "Is There a Marxist Theory of the State?," 10–11.
8. Philippe Sands, *The Lawless World: America and the Making and Breaking of Global Rules* (London: Penguin, 2005).
9. Ibid., 230–31.
10. Ibid., xix.

10. The Assertion of Might-as-Right

1. See in this respect Lukács's analysis of Weber's own acceptance of

dictatorial repression, even to the point of his full agreement with proto-fascist General Ludendorff's views on "the leader." General Ludendorff, Marshal Hindenburg's chief of staff in the First World War, was one of Hitler's earliest supporters in the German military hierarchy. See István Mészáros, *The Social Determination of Method*, vol. 1: *Social Structure and Forms of Consciousness* (New York: Monthly Review Press, 2010). 433–34.
2. G. W. F. Hegel, *The Philosophy of Right* (Oxford: Oxford University Press, 1952), 222. Emphasis added.
3. Ernst Barker, Introduction to Otto Gierke, *Natural Law and the Theory of Society, 1500 to 1800* (Boston: Beacon Press, 1957), xxiii.
4. Ibid., xxviii.
5. Ibid., lxxxvii.
6. Margaret Thatcher, "Speech to the 1922 Committee," https://www.margaretthatcher.org/document/105563; "Thatcher Was to Call Labour and Miners 'Enemy Within' in an Abandoned Speech," *The Guardian*, October 2, 2014.

11. Eternalizing Assumptions of Liberal State Theory

1. Nothing could be more *Sollen*-like than that, although Hegel sharply objected to the Kantian "ought-to-be," just as he censured Kant for using his "faculty-bag" (Hegel's depreciative expression) to find solutions in it when he needed them. This Hegel did even if on occasion he committed the same sin himself, as for instance when he dismissed the demands for *equality* as "the *folly of the understanding*," in tune with his own "faculty-bag," contrasting the "higher faculty of reason" to the lower faculty of understanding. See Hegel's discussion of equality, nature, and "ought-to-be" in *The Philosophy of Right*, 130.
2. G. W. F. Hegel, *The Philosophy of History* (New York: Dover, 1956), 15.
3. Ibid., 17.
4. John Austin, *The Province of Jurisprudence Determined and the Uses of the Study of Jurisprudence* (London: Weidenfeld and Nicolson, 1965), 287–88.
5. Ibid., 288.
6. Ibid.
7. Ibid., 285.
8. Ibid., 390. It is very doubtful that the less progressive Austin had the same concern about "sinister interest" when he spoke about it in the plural, as did Jeremy Bentham, the term's originator. Bentham used it in 1822 in scathing condemnation of Alexander Wedderburn who, in addition to his manifold social privileges, was also rewarded with the near astronomic sum of £15,000 a year as attorney general and, more than that, received later the annual remuneration of £25,000 as lord chancellor, with the power of veto on all justice matters in the latter capacity. See Jeremy Bentham, *An*

Introduction to the Principles of Morality and Legislation (London: Athlone Press, 1970), 15. This fundamental work was first printed in 1780, amended in 1789, and complimented by Bentham with the "greatest happiness or greatest felicity principle" in 1822.

9. Bentham, *An Introduction to the Principles of Morality and Legislation*, 307. The words "powers" and "duties" are italicized by Jeremy Bentham.
10. Ibid., 294-95.
11. Ibid., 296.
12. Austin, *The Province of Jurisprudence*, 366-67. Austin's emphasis.
13. Ibid., 269.
14. Ibid., 273.
15. Ibid., 194-95. Austin's emphasis.
16. Bentham, *An Introduction to the Principles of Morality and Legislation*, 74.
17. Ibid.
18. Ibid., 12.
19. Ibid., 13.

12. Hegel's Unintended Swan Song and the Nation-State

1. G. W. F. Hegel, *The Philosophy of Right* (Oxford: Oxford University Press, 1952), 12-13.
2. "The rational, the divine, posesses the absolute power to actualize itself, and has, *right from the beginning*, fulfilled itself: it is not so impotent that it would have to wait for the beginning to its actualization." Hegel, *The Philosophy of Mind* (Oxford: Oxford University Press, 1971), 62. Emphasis added.
3. See in this respect Lukács's great book, *The Young Hegel*, written in Moscow in the late 1930s as a forceful refutation of the dogmatic Stalinist line which, turning the truth upside down, condemned Hegel as a "conservative reaction against the French Revolution." It was first published in German in 1948 in Austria, and in English in 1973, in London. In Austria it was published with the help and active contribution by Wilhelm Szilasi, who was designated by Husserl as the successor to his University Chair of Philosophy, and later sacked by the Nazi Heidegger.
4. Hegel, *The Philosophy of Right*, 212.
5. Ibid., 214. Emphasis added.
6. Ibid., 209-10.
7. See the discussion of Bentham and Austin in chapter 11.
8. On the deeply interrelated socioeconomic and political/military grounds of these developments, see Harry Magdoff's seminal book, *The Age of Imperialism: The Economics of US Foreign Policy* (New York: Monthly Review Press, 1966). See also a fine collection of Harry Magdoff's essays: *Imperialism without Colonies*, edited by John Bellamy Foster, published by

Monthly Review Press on the occasion of his ninetieth birthday. The best way to honor this great thinker is to make the teaching of his most essential writings on modern imperialism our own.
9. As we have seen in this chapter, Hegel forcefully stressed that "the *rational, the divine*, possesses the absolute power to actualize itself and has, *right from the beginning*, fulfilled itself." Emphasis added.
10. Hegel, *The Philosophy of Right*, 217.
11. Ibid., 218.
12. G. W. F. Hegel, *The Philosophy of History* (New York: Dover, 1956), 103. Emphasis added.
13. Hegel, *The Philosophy of Right*, 222-23.
14. Friedrich Schlegel, *The Philosophy of Life, and Philosophy of Language, in a Course of Lectures* (London: Henry G. Bohn, 1847), 116.
15. Ibid., 114, 140, 163, 186, 328-29.

13. Capital's Social Metabolic Order and the Failing State

1. See Phillipe Buonarroti, *Buonarroti's History of Babeuf's Conspiracy for Equality* (London: H. Hettherington, 1836), 220. Translation by author from Philippe Buonarroti, *Conspiration pour légalité dite de Babeuf* (1828), 297.
2. Buonarotti, *Buonarroti's History of Babeuf's Conspiracy for Equality*, 82, 111, 345-47. Translation by author from original French edition.

   Under the name of politics, chaos has reigned for too many centuries . . . equality was nothing but a beautiful and sterile legal fiction. . . . From time immemorial they hypocritically repeat, *all men are equal;* and from time immemorial the most degrading and monstrous inequality insolently weighs upon the human race. . . . We need not only that equality of rights written into the Declaration of the Rights of Man and Citizen; we want it in our midst, under the roofs of our houses. . . . We declare that we can no longer put up with the fact that the great majority work and sweat for the smallest of minorities. . . . Let it at last end, this great scandal that our descendants will never believe existed! Disappear at last, revolting distinctions between rich and poor, great and small, masters and servants, *rulers* and *ruled*. . . . The aristocratic charters of 1791 and 1795 tightened your chains instead of breaking them. That of 1793 was a great step toward true equality, and we had never before approached it so closely. But it did not yet touch the goal, nor reach common happiness, which it nevertheless solemnly consecrated as its great principle.
3. Simón Bolívar, *Selected Works* (New York: Colonial Press, 1951), vol. 2, 603.
4. Anonymous pamphlet of 1821: *The Source and Remedy of the National*

Difficulties, deduced from principles of political economy in a letter to Lord John Russell, quoted in Marx's *Grundrisse,* 397.
5. Hegel, *The Philosophy of History* (New York: Dover, 1956), 15. Emphasis added.
6. Ibid., 17.
7. Ibid., 212.
8. Marx, *Grundrisse,* 105.
9. Ibid., 106.
10. See István Mészáros, *Social Structure and Forms of Consciousness,* vol. 2, *The Dilaectic of Structure and History* (New York: Monthly Review Press, 2011), 166–234.
11. See my discusssion of Robert Cooper's views on "liberal imperialism" and the "failed states"—describing the former colonial territories to be conquered again—in István Mészáros, *The Challenge and Burden of Historical Time* (New York: Monthly Review Press, 2008), 418–22; originally published in Brazil in 2007. Cooper was called by the *Observer Magazine,* which promoted his ideas, "Tony Blair's Guru."

15. From Plato's Cave to the Sombre Light of *The Laws*

1. Paradoxically, Sir Thomas More was for many years a most faithful servant and a high-ranking official of King Henry VIII. But in the end, he refused to conform to the king's grave violation of Christian religion pursued in the interest of his marriages and the expropriation of Church property. For such unforgivable opposition to royal convenience, Sir Thomas More was executed on King Henry's orders in 1535. On the same account he was declared four centuries later a saint by the Roman Catholic Church, in 1935.
2. Karl Marx, *Early Writings* (London: Penguin, 1974), 421–23. *Theses on Feuerbach,* written in 1846.
3. One mina was equivalent to 100 drachmas. Thus, Anniceris is said to have paid for Plato's release 2,000 drachmas.
4. Diogenes Laertius, *Lives and Opinions of Eminent Philosophers* (London: Henry G. Bohn, 1853), Book 3 (Plato), 120.
5. Plato, *The Dialogues of Plato,* trans. B. Jowett (Oxford: Oxford University Press, 1892), vol. 3, 437, emphasis added. Timaeus is presented in the dialogue named after him as "the most of an astronomer amongst us, and has made the nature of the universe his special study" (447). In fact, by far the greatest part of the dialogue *Timaeus* is dedicated to his account of the origin and "nature of the universe" (448), representing Plato's conception of the cosmos.
6. Ibid., 447, emphasis added.
7. Ibid., 446, emphasis added. These were the words of Critias, "I have told

you briefly, Socrates, what the aged Critias [his grandfather] heard from Solon and related to us. And when you were speaking yesterday about your city and citizens, the tale which I have just been repeating to you came into my mind, and I remarked with astonishment how, by some *mysterious coincidence*, you agreed in almost every particular with the *narrative of Solon*."

8. Ibid., 445–46, emphasis added. As an Egyptian priest in Grandfather Critias's account tells Solon: "Many great and wonderful deeds are recorded of your state in our histories. But one of them exceeds all the rest in greatness and valour. For these histories tell of a mighty power which unprovoked made an expedition against the whole of Europe and Asia and to which your city put an end. . . . This vast power, endeavoured to subdue at a blow our country and yours and the whole of the region; and then, Solon, your country shone forth, in the excellence of her virtue and strength, among all mankind. She was preeminent in courage and military skill, and was the leader of the Hellenes. And when the rest fell off from her, being compelled to stand alone, after having undergone the very extremity of danger, she defeated and triumphed over the invaders, and *preserved from slavery* those who were not yet subjugated, and generously *liberated all the rest of us* who dwell within the pillars."

9. Kant, *The Philosophy of Kant: Kant's Moral and Political Writings* (New York: Random House, 1949), 448 ("Eternal Peace"), emphasis in original text.

10. Adam Smith, *The Wealth of Nations* (New York: Random House, 1937), 572, emphasis added.

11. G. W. F. Hegel, *The Philosophy of Right* (Oxford: Oxford University Press, 1952), 130, emphasis added.

12. Thomas Hobbes, *Leviathan* (Oxford: Oxford University Press, 1909; reprint of 1651 edition), 94, emphasis added.

13. Kant, *The Philosophy of Kant*, 418.

14. Ibid., 120–21, emphasis added. In this sense Kant declares: "Without these essentially unlovely qualities of asociability, from which springs the resistance which everyone must encounter in his egotistic pretensions, all talents would have remained hidden germs. If man lived an Arcadian shepherd's existence of harmony, modesty and mutuality, man, good-natured like the sheep he is herding, would not invest his existence with greater value than that his animals have. Man would not fill the vacuum of creation as regards his end, rational nature. Thanks are due to *nature* for his *quarrelsomeness*, his *enviously competitive vanity*, and for his *insatiable desire to possess* or to *rule*, for without them all the excellent faculties of mankind would forever remain undeveloped" (emphasis added).

15. Ibid., 123, emphasis added. Kant uses a graphic image to convey this view

of human nature by insisting that "one cannot fashion something absolutely straight from *wood which is as crooked as that of which man is made*. Nature has imposed upon us the task of approximating this idea" (emphasis added).

16. Ibid., 452–53, emphasis added.
17. Herodotus, *The Histories* (London: Penguin, 2013), 45, emphasis added. In the account of Herodotus these words have been uttered by Croesus, who attacked, and was defeated by, Cyrus the Great. Thus, the lines quoted on war overturning the original order of nature expressed in a way the repentance of Croesus, who had brought the calamity of humiliating defeat upon himself. And Cyrus—who was not the guilty party of the war which the two armies had to fight—duly forgave him after hearing those words, fully in tune with the spirit of generosity historically attributed to him.
18. It was in "woeful plight" because it disobeyed the original laws of Poseidon whose island the legendary *Atlantis* was supposed to be.
19. Plato, *Dialogues of Plato*, vol. 3, 543.
20. Ibid., vol. 2, 156, emphasis added.
21. Ibid., vol. 2, 151–54, emphasis added.
22. Liberal theory of the "democratic state" fails to acknowledge that many of the authoritarian requirements of the capital system are abundantly provided, even if in a different form, by the *tyranny of the market itself*, which happens to be as a rule idealized by liberalism.
23. Plato, *Dialogues of Plato*, vol. 2, 153, emphasis added.
24. Hegel, *The Philosophy of History*, 449.
25. "You are our child and slave, as your fathers were before you." Plato, *Dialogues of Plato*, vol. 2, 152.
26. When Plato sings the praises of heroically triumphant Athens over Atlantis by asserting that his legendary hero "defeated and triumphed over the invaders, and *preserved from slavery* those who were not yet *subjugated*, and generously *liberated all the rest of us* who dwell within the pillars." Plato, *Dialogues of Plato*, vol. 3, 446.
27. See Hegel, *The Philosophy of Right*, 212, emphasis added.
28. Socrates accepts the Law's judgment which decrees that he is "*thrice wrong;* first because in disobeying us he is disobeying his parents; secondly, because we are the authors of his education; thirdly, because he has made an agreement with us that he will duly obey our commands; and he *neither obeys them nor convinces us* that our commands are *unjust.*" Plato, *Dialogues of Plato*, vol. 2, 153, emphasis added. Yet, in such a picture of the Law and the State, as well as their "Justice," the Law and the State are not only the authoritarian Legislator and Administrator of self-proclaiming and self-justifying "Justice" but also the *executioners*, enforcing in their own way the social metabolic imperatives of the Leviathan state. Thus the state and its Law cannot be other than the arbitrarily commanding organ of

hierarchically entrenched decision-making alienated from the social body even when it fulfills its repressive determinations, as the Liberal Democratic state "with a smiling face."
29. Plato, *Dialogues of Plato*, volume 3, 214-18, emphasis added.
30. Ibid., 212-13, emphasis added.
31. Georg Lukács, *History and Class Consciousnes* (London: Merlin Press, 1971), 140.
32. Hegel, *The Philosophy of Right*, 130.
33. As Plato asserted on the last page of *The Laws*, if the legal framework commended in it by the three interlocutors—the Athenian, standing for Plato himself, Cleinias, the Cretan, and the Spartan Megillus—were adopted in a state, then *"no modern legislator will want to oppose us."* Plato, *The Laws* (London: Penguin, 1970), 530, emphasis added.
34. Ibid., 229, emphasis added.
35. Ibid., 230, emphasis added.
36. Ibid., 230-31, emphasis added.
37. Ibid., 229, emphasis added.
38. Ibid., 230, emphasis added.
39. Ibid., 174, emphasis added.
40. Ibid., 359-60, emphasis added.
41. Ibid., 447, emphasis added.
42. Ibid., 526-28, emphasis added.
43. See the general first section of Hegel's *Philosophy of Art*, as recorded in P. von der Pforden's manuscript of 1826. G. W. F. Hegel, *The Introduction to Hegel's Philosophy of Fine Art* (London: Kegan, Paul, Trench, Co., 1886).
44. Hegel, *The Philosophy of History*, 15, emphasis added.

16. Equality in the Broken Mirror of Justice: The Meaning of Aristotelian *Politea*

1. Plato, *The Laws* (London: Penguin, 1970), 229, emphasis added.
2. Aristotle, *The Politics* (London: Penguin Books, 1981), 64-65, emphasis added.
3. Ibid., 57, emphasis added.
4. Plato does not hesitate to say, about the difficulties involved in assessing the problems of real equality and inequality—in sharp contrast in his view to the easily accomplished task of distributing awards by lot on the ground of weights, measures and numbers—that "it needs the wisdom and judgement of Zeus." Plato, *The Laws*, 229. And a few lines further he offers his own painfully circular definition of inequality and justice in the context of advocating for his ideal state the exercise of *"strict justice"* (emphasis added)
5. Ibid., emphasis in the original text.

6. The reference is to Aristotle's *Nichomachean Ethics*, V iii, where he says that it is *just* to give more property and privileges to the more deserving, and less to the less deserving persons. Aristotle, *Nicomachean Ethics* (London: Penguin, 2004), 118–20.
7. Aristotle, *Politics*, 195, emphasis added.
8. In Aristotle's discussion of the nature of human association the concept of antagonistic social classes is totally absent. He defines the state as "an *aggregate* of citizens." Ibid., 168. This is well in tune with his way of dealing with the question of proper equality/inequality when he adds the clause "*for whom*" as the necessary *personal* qualifier.
9. Ibid., 188, emphases added.
10. Ibid., 187, emphasis added.
11. Ibid., 188. In truth what Aristotle is talking about at this point is the distressing fact that if the slave *perishes* (another translation renders this as "deteriorates"), the master is left empty-handed.
12. Ibid., 187, emphasis added.
13. Ibid., 207, emphasis added.
14. Plato, *Laws*, 230, emphasis added.
15. Kant, *The Philosophy of Kant: Moral and Political Writings* (New York: Random House, 1949), 418, emphasis added.
16. As Plato, impersonated in *The Laws* as "The Athenian," says about the idealized Statesman: "I think he should make every effort to get an *overall understanding of his aim*, as well as see it in its *various contexts*." Plato, *The Laws*, 521, emphasis added. This is no doubt a good guiding principle for the Platonic statesman's conduct. But it cannot provide support for the underlying assumption of using "nature" as the justification of class slavery.
17. Aristotle, *Politics*, 208–9, emphasis added.
18. The socially determined irresponsible treatment of *ecology*, under the imperatives of *wasteful capital-expansion*, offers a potentially most destructive example of that kind of relationship to nature and the state for our future.
19. Plato, *The Laws*, 523, emphasis added.
20. Aristotle, *Politics*, 209.
21. Ibid., 59, emphases added except for the word "good," which is italicized in the original text.
22. Ibid., emphasis added.
23. Ibid., 60, emphases added.
24. Ibid., emphases added.
25. Indeed, we should recall here that even the interest confined to the *mere survival* of the slave, as Aristotle himself concedes it, is "*primarily* for the benefit of the master and only *incidentally* for the benefit of the slave." Aristotle, *Politics*, 188.
26. Ibid., 61.

27. Ibid., 68. This approach produces a rather grotesque judgment by asserting: "It is *nature's purpose* to make the *bodies of free men* to differ from those of *slaves*, the latter strong enough to be used for necessary tasks, the former *erect* and useless for that kind of work, but *well suited for the life of a citizen of a state*, a life which is in turn divided between the requirements of *war and peace*" (69).
28. St. Augustine, *City of God* (Garden City, NY: Doubleday, 1958), 460, emphasis added.
29. Kant, *The Philosophy of Kant*, 418, emphasis added.
30. Ibid., 420.
31. No less a historic figure than his former pupil, Alexander the Great, helped Aristotle to fulfill that interest. "It is said that when Alexander became king, he used his power to help his old tutor get specimens: Orders were given to some thousands of people throughout the whole of Asia Minor and Greece … to see that Aristotle was informed about any creature born in any region." Pliny the Elder, *Natural History: A Selection* (London: Penguin, 1991), 114,VII, 44, quoted in Anthony Gottlieb, *The Dream of Reason: A History of Philosophy from the Greeks to the Renaissance* (London: Penguin Books, 2016), 237.
32. Ibid., 226
33. Ibid., 60–61, emphasis added.
34. The relevant passages from Aristotle's *Ethics* in this context are: I x, II ii, vi, VII xiii, and X vii. See Aristotle, *Nicomachean Ethics*, 22–25, 33–34, 39–43, 185–87, 273–76.
35. Aristotle, *Politics,* 266, emphasis added.
36. Ibid., 267, emphasis added.
37. Ibid., 268, emphasis added.
38. Ibid., 272, emphasis added.
39. Ibid.
40. Ibid., 299.
41. Ibid., 326, emphasis added.
42. Ibid., 330, emphasis added.
43. Ibid., 410, emphasis added.
44. Rousseau, *The Social Contract* (London: J. M. Dent, 1913), 19, emphasis added.

17. Primitive Accumulation of Capital and the World of More's *Utopia*

1. Ironically, Sir Thomas More was sent to Brussels by Cardinal Wolsey, who would eventually become More's ultimate rival. However, at the time of his posting to Brussels no one could imagine the critical outcome of that event, resulting in Thomas More writing *Utopia* during his stay in that city. Moreover, in 1523 Cardinal Wolsey wanted to send Sir Thomas More to Spain as permanent ambassador, so as to have him out of the way. But More

appealed to the King against that mission, pretending that the Spanish climate would be fatal to his health. At that time Sir Thomas More was fully in Henry VIII's favor. Thus, the king granted More's appeal, and kept him in London as someone to rely upon for his own authoritarian royal purposes. In effect, in 1529 King Henry appointed Sir Thomas More as Lord Chancellor, replacing Cardinal Wolsey.
2. The young Thomas More first met Erasmus in 1499 when Erasmus visited England.
3. Denis Diderot's entry on *Journalier* in the French *Encyclopédie*.
4. Denis Diderot, *Supplément au Voyage de Bougainville*, in *Oeuvres Philosophiques*, ed. Paul Vernière (Paris: Garnier, 1956), 482.
5. Karl Marx, *Capital*, vol. 1 (London: Penguin, 1976), 871.
6. Thomas More's *Utopia* in *Ideal Commonwealths*, introduced by Henry Morley (New York: Colonial Press, 1901), 8. This volume includes More's *Utopia*, Francis Bacon's *New Atlantis*, Tommaso Campanella's *City of the Sun*, and James Harrington's *The Commonwealth of Oceana*. Henceforth this volume will be referred to simply as *Ideal Commonwealths*.
7. *Ideal Commonwealths*, 10, emphasis added.
8. Ibid., 12–13, emphasis added.
9. Ibid., 14, emphasis added.
10. Ibid., 99, emphasis added.
11. Ibid., 16, emphasis added.
12. Indeed, one of the versions of the Hydra mythology claimed that Hydra could grow as many as *one thousand* heads when one of them had been cut off. But even that pales to insignificance when compared to the endless proliferation of laws invented by actually existing states.
13. As we read on page 72 of *Ideal Commonwealths*: "They have but *few laws*, and such is their constitution that they *need not many*. They very much condemn other nations, whose laws, together with the commentaries on them, swell up to so many volumes; for they think it an unreasonable thing to oblige men to obey a body of laws that are both of *such a bulk and so dark* as not to be read and understood by every one of the subjects. They have *no lawyers* among them, for they consider them as a sort of people whose profession it is to disguise matters and to wrest the laws; and therefore they think it is much better that every man should *plead his own cause*, and trust it to the judge, as in other places the client trusts it to a counsellor. By this means they both cut off many *delays*, and find out *truth more certainly*" (emphasis added).
14. For the discussion of religious matters see esp. *Ideal Commonwealths*, 83–88.
15. During his stay in Oxford Thomas More was particularly devoted to the study of Greek language and culture. This is tellingly reflected in his *Utopia* at a point where Hythloday claims to have given some books—including

many works by Plato and *some* by Aristotle—to the Utopians and he comments by saying: "They are unwearied pursuers of knowledge; for when we had given them some hints of the learning and discipline of the Greeks, concerning whom we only instructed them (for we know that there was *nothing among the Romans*, except their historians and their poets, that they would value much), it was strange to see how eagerly they were set on learning that language. . . . I am indeed apt to think that they learned that language the more easily, from its having some relation to their own. I believe that they were *a colony of the Greeks*" (ibid., 65, emphasis added). In this way Thomas More even tries to establish some kind of family relationship between the utopian way of life and the highly appreciated values of Greek antiquity.
16. *Ideal Commonwealths*, 95, emphasis added.
17. Ibid., 12.
18. Ibid., 96, emphasis added.
19. Ibid.
20. Liberal political theorists of the state, even the best of them, who idealize "representative democracy," could learn a great deal from these passionately uttered words of Raphael Hythloday about the far from representative nature of their Leviathan state.
21. *Ideal Commonwealths*, 96–97, emphasis added.
22. Ibid., 96.
23. Ibid., 51.
24. Ibid., 53. Ironically, in our society the parasitic "filthy rich" from "oil money" or other forms of exploitative business can afford to have not only their chamber pots but also their bathtubs made from gold, and have them decorated with precious stones despised by Thomas More's Utopians.
25. *Ideal Commonwealths*, 41.
26. Ibid., 44, emphasis added.
27. Ibid., 97–98.
28. Ibid., 50.
29. Ibid., 45, emphasis added.
30. Ibid., 70, emphasis added.
31. Ibid., 71, emphasis added.
32. Frederick Engels, *Anti-Dühring* (London: Lawrence & Wishart), 1975, 314–15. Some chapters of *Anti-Dühring* were also published by Engels as a popular pamphlet, with the title *Socialism: Utopian and Scientific*.

18. Machiavelli and Campanella on the Road to Giambattista Vico

1. Machiavelli, *The Discourses*, trans. Leslie J. Walker, S.J., with revisions by Brian Richardson, edited with an Introduction by Bernard Crick (London: Penguin Books, 1970), 139.
2. Ibid., 140, emphasis added.

3. Ibid., 141, emphasis added.
4. Ibid., 142, emphasis added.
5. Ibid, emphasis added.
6. Ibid., emphasis added.
7. That is, "the moment of overriding importance."
8. It is worth remembering that in More's assertion, on the legendary island of *Utopia* the people reject the superstitions but accept, like in Christianity in general, the *miracles* in tune with their faith. Even today in Christianity, when someone is recommended for *sainthood*—like Thomas More himself, who was both recommended and elevated to it—one of the qualifying requirements is the claimed proof that he or she performed some miracles. More qualified for sainthood in 1935 also on that ground. And the views he expressed in *Utopia* about miracles could not be held against him.
9. Machiavelli, *The Discourses*, 142–46, emphasis added.
10. Ibid., 144–45.
11. See Machiavelli, *The Discourses*, 513–16.
12. Hegel uses this term quite often as a high accolade worthy of Divinity, by talking about the *"Cunning of Reason,"* associated in his conception with the *"World Spirit."*
13. Machiavelli, *The Prince* (London: Dent, Everyman Library Edition, 1992), 119.
14. Machiavelli, *The Discourses*, 141, emphasis added.
15. Antonio Gramsci, *The Modern Prince and Other Writings*, trans. Louis Marks (London: Lawrence and Wishart, 1967), 135–36, emphasis added.
16. *Ideal Commonwealths*, introduced by Henry Morley (New York: Colonial Press, 1901), 147–48, emphasis added.
17. Ibid., 74.
18. Ibid., 165.
19. Ibid., 157.
20. Ibid., 174, emphasis added.
21. Ibid., 167, emphasis added.
22. Ibid., 156, emphasis added.
23. Ibid., 179.
24. Giambattista Vico, *The New Science* (Ithaca, NY: Cornell University Press, 1970), 52–53 and 382–83, emphasis added.
25. St. Augustine, *City of God* (New York: Doubleday & Co., 1958), 523.

19. From Bacon and Harrington to Thomas Paine and Robert Owen

1. Henry Morley, Introduction to *Ideal Commonwealths* (New York: Colonial Press, 1901), vii. This volume includes More's *Utopia*, Francis Bacon's *New Atlantis*, Tommaso Campanella's *City of the Sun*, and James Harrington's *The Commonwealth of Oceana*. This volume will subsequently be referred to as simply *Ideal Commonwealths*.

2. Here is an example: "with them [the people of the New Atlantis] there are no stews, no dissolute houses, no courtesans, nor anything of that kind. Nay, they wonder, with detestation, at you in Europe, which permit such things. They say ye have put marriage out of office; for marriage is ordained a remedy for unlawful concupiscence; and natural concupiscence seemeth as a spur to marriage. But when men have at hand a remedy, more agreeable to their corrupt will, marriage is almost expulsed." Bacon, *The New Atlantis*, in *Ideal Commonwealths*, 125.
3. Ibid., 129.
4. Ibid., 134–35.
5. Harrington, *Oceana*, in *Ideal Commonwealths*, xi.
6. Ibid., 416.
7. Antony à Wood's account, quoted in *Ideal Commonwealth*, six–x.
8. Harrington, *Oceana*. in *Ideal Commonwealths*, 321, emphasis added.
9. Toward the end of his work, Harrington insisted that it was most appropriate to propagate the spirit of the exemplary commonwealth in the rest of the world, and he wrote that "if you add to this propagation of *civil liberty* (so natural to this commonwealth that it cannot be omitted) the propagation of the *liberty of conscience,* this empire, this patronage of the world, is the kingdom of Christ." Ibid., 382, emphasis added.
10. Thomas Paine, *The Rights of Man* (New York: Everyman, 1979), 136.
11. Ibid., 137.
12. Ibid., 131.
13. Ibid., 138, emphasis added.
14. Ibid., 182.
15. Ibid., 202, emphasis added.
16. Ibid., 210, emphasis added.
17. Ibid., 211.
18. Ibid.
19. Ibid., emphasis added.
20. Ibid., 277.
21. Charles Fourier, *The Theory of Four Movements* (Cambridge: Cambridge University Press, 1996), 132. Also Frederick Engels, *Anti-Dühring* (Moscow: Foreign Languages Publishing House, 1959), 357.
22. As Engels pointed out about Robert Owen, "Whilst his competitors worked their people thirteen or fourteen hours a day, in New Lanark the working-day was only ten and a half hours. When a crisis in cotton stopped work for four months, his workers received their full wages all the time. And with all this the business more than doubled in value, and to the last yielded large profits to its proprietors. In spite of all this, Owen was not content. The existence which he secured for his workers was, in his eyes, still far from being worthy of human beings. *'The people were slaves at my mercy'*" Ibid., 360, emphasis added.

23. Charles Fourier, *The Utopian Vision of Charles Fourier: Selected Texts on Work, Love and Passionate Attraction*, edited and with an introduction by Jonathan Becher and Richard Bienvenu (Boston: Beacon Press, 1972), 30, emphasis added.

20. Thomasius and Bloch's Principle of Hope

1. Ernst Bloch, *Natural Law and Human Dignity* (Cambridge, MA: MIT Press, 1986), 281–316.
2. Ibid., 170–73.
3. Dennis J. Schmidt, Introduction in Bloch, *Natural Law and Human Dignity*, xxiii.
4. Bloch, *Natural Law and Human Dignity*, 311, emphasis added.
5. Ibid., 312, emphasis added.
6. Ibid., emphasis added.
7. Bloch, *Natural Law and Human Dignity*, 281, emphasis added.
8. Ibid., 296–98, emphasis added.
9. Ibid., 298.
10. Ibid., 313.
11. Ibid.
12. Ibid., emphasis added.
13. Ibid., 314, emphasis added.
14. Ibid., emphasis added.
15. Ibid., 298.
16. Ibid., 298.

Appendix 2. Historical Boundaries of the Legal and Political Superstructure

1. Karl Marx, *Capital* (Moscow: Foreign Languages Publishing House, 1967), vol. 3, 792.
2. Ibid., 793, emphasis added.
3. The term often used by Marx, *Staatswesen*—rather than simply "*Staat*," or "state"—approximately translated as "state-matter," refers to a number of specific functions exercised by the state institutions that articulate the material relations of sovereignty and dependence in a political form. Many of these functions are absolutely vital to the process of social reproduction, but by no means in the form they assume in class societies. Thus, the project of socialist transformation is defined by Marx in this respect as the *restitution* of the vital metabolic functions of separate *Staatswesen* to the social body itself, thereby superseding their alienated character.
4. See Marx's *Grundrisse* (London: Penguin, 1973), 86–87.
5. Ibid., 88.
6. The emergence of Fascism out of the crisis of liberal-democratic capitalism in Italy and Germany speaks for itself in this respect, just as in 1973 the violent

destruction of Allende's democratic regime in Chile, or the conspiratorial attempt by none other than the president of the Italian Republic, Pietro Segni—supposedly the custodian of the constitution—to overthrow the "constitutional republic," or indeed a little later yet another attempt, with the same objective in mind, by Prime Minister Tambroni, failed not for want of trying hard but by the successful mobilization of the popular forces. Less well known but equally serious in its overall impact was the destruction of militant trade unionism in the United States with the help of armed violence, supported by state institutions not only by closing both eyes to the lawless acts of private armies but also in the direct intervention of law-enforcing agencies—all in the struggle to suppress all radical opposition to the rule of capital.

Anti-trade union legislation in Britain under Margaret Thatcher followed well-established tradition for creating an up-to-date framework in which the "full might of the law" can be "legitimately" exercised against labor in the event of crisis and confrontation, as the weapons used against the miners in their one-year-long strike clearly demonstrated. A more recent case, that of press magnate Rupert Murdoch and his self-metamorphosing companies against the printers' unions, highlighted the oppressive character of the law devised to facilitate the performance of the *"vanishing capitalist"* trick. Thanks to the law in question capitalists engaged in a trade union dispute can now "disappear" through the convenient device of a legal fiction, and reappear at once in a suitably transubstantiated form—under a different business name; the *same* capitalists, confronting the *same workers*—whereupon the formerly legitimate trade union dispute of the workers suddenly becomes *unlawful*, so that the full might of the law can be turned against them. Thus, institutionalized and legally enforced violence is only the other side of the coin of "explicit law" as such.

We must also notice here that the *vanishing capitalist* trick, performed with the active complicity of the law, is only the "legal" adaptation of the long-established and widespread *material* practice of capitalist fraudulence—the normality of capitalist "civil society"—to the regulatory requirements of changing class relations in the sphere of politics. For there is an obvious *structural homology* between the legal fiction that allows capitalist enterprises to "go out of existence" in order to reappear almost instantly—under a new name, with the same "actors" pulling the strings of continued exploitation, sometimes openly, sometimes only from the background and then, thanks to their fictitious reconstitution, be conveniently freed in the eyes of the law from their former material liabilities and legal obligations. Thus, the primacy of the material base also asserts itself on this terrain, producing legislative devices for political domination on the model of ubiquitous capitalist material structures.

7. Lenin's legendary sense of realism would never allow him to offer explanations on the model of "the revolution betrayed." Yet even he had to face some insurmountable dilemmas with regard to the relationship between post-revolutionary state power and the associated producers in his recommendations concerning what he called "the central distribution of labor power." For a discussion of these problems see my essay on "Political Power and Dissent in Postrevolutionary Societies," *New Left Review* 108 (March–April 1978): esp. 4–17 (repr. in Part 4 of *Beyond Capital*).

8. H. H. Gerth and C. Wright Mills, eds., *From Weber: Essays in Sociology* (London: Routledge & Kegan Paul, 1948), 299. As usual, Weber turns everything upside down. For it would be much more correct to say that the objective needs of the modern capitalist state give birth to its class-conscious army of jurists, rather than the other way around, as Weber claims, with mechanical one-sidedness. Besides, Weber's curious followers—some of them former "vulgar Marxists"—fail to notice that their newfound idol uses the idealist version of the selfsame "obstetric metaphor" for which they castigate Marx.

   Of course, in reality we must speak in this respect of a dialectical reciprocity, and not of a one-sided determination. But we must also recall that it is not possible to make more than tautological sense of such reciprocity unless we recognize—something Weber cannot do, because of his far from neutral ideological allegiances—that the "*uebergreifendes Moment*" in this relationship between the ever more powerful capitalist state (with all its material needs and determinations) and the "jurists" happens to be the former, [that is, the capitalist state itself] notwithstanding the Weberian-type rationalizations that hypostatize the heroic birth pangs and "fiercely independent" deliveries of "legal brains."

9. See Marcuse, *Die Permanenz der Kunst* (Munich: Carl Hanser Verlag, 1977); in English: *The Aesthetic Dimension* (London: Macmillan, 1979).

Appendix 4. How Could the State "Wither Away"?

1. See István Mészáros, *Beyond Capital* (New York: Monthly Review Press, 1995), 447–50.

2. He even spoke about a "categorical imperative," in the context of discussing the social agency—the proletariat—which he considered both necessary and adequate to the task of structural change. See Karl Marx, "Contribution to Critique of Hegel's Philosophy of Law," Introduction, in Karl Marx and Frederick Engels, *Collected Works* (New York: International Publishers, 1975), vol. 3, 175–87.

3. Karl Marx, "Critical Marginal Notes on an Article by a Prussian," in Marx and Engels, *Collected Works*, vol. 3, 197 (emphases in the original).

4. Ibid., 199 (emphases in the original). We can see here how strongly Marx is opposed to any mechanical and reductionist position.
5. See Karl Marx and Frederick Engels, "Fictitious Splits in the International: Circular from the International Working Men's Association," written in January–March 1872, in Marx and Engels, *Collected Works*, vol. 23, 79–123.
6. See Karl Marx, "Indifference to Politics," written in January 1873, in Marx and Engels, *Collected Works*, vol. 23, 392–97.
7. Marx, "Critical Marginal Notes on the Article by a Prussian," 198 (emphases in the original).
8. Ibid., 197.
9. "Germany, as the deficiency of the political present constituted as a particular world, will not be able to throw down the specific German limitations without throwing down the *general* limitations of the *political* present. It is not the radical revolution, not the *general* human emancipation which is a Utopian dream for Germany, but rather the *partial,* the merely political revolution, the revolution which leaves the pillars of the house standing." Marx, "Contribution to Critique of Hegel's Philosophy of Law," 184 (emphasis added).
10. This point is well illustrated by the confrontation between Marx and Schapper: "I have always defied the momentary opinions of the proletariat. We are devoted to a party which, most fortunately for it, cannot yet come to power. If the proletariat were to come to power the measures it would introduce would be petty-bourgeois and not directly proletarian. Our party can come to *power* only when the conditions allow it to put *its own* views into practice. Louis Blanc is the best instance of what happens when you come to power prematurely. In France, moreover, it isn't the proletariat alone that gains power but the peasants and the petty-bourgeois as well, and it will have to carry out not its, but *their* measures." Marx and Engels, *Collected Works*, vol. 10, 628–29 (emphases in original).

This sober realism could not contrast more with Schapper's bombastic voluntarism at the same meeting: "The question at issue is whether we ourselves chop off a few heads right at the start or whether it is our own heads that will fall. In France the workers will come to power and thereby we in Germany too. Were this not the case I would indeed take to my bed; in that event I would be able to enjoy a different material position. If we come to power we can take such measures as are necessary to ensure the rule of the proletariat. I am a fanatical supporter of this view. . . . I shall certainly be guillotined in the next revolution, nevertheless I shall go to Germany. . . . I do not share the view that the bourgeoisie in Germany will come to power and on this point I am a fanatical enthusiast—if I weren't I wouldn't give a brass farthing for the whole affair" (ibid., 628). As we can see, Schapper (who died in ripe old age in his bed) supports the soundness of his voluntaristic conception of politics by nothing else than twice repeating that he fanatically believes in it.

Marx is right in stressing in opposition to Schapper and others like him that "the revolution is seen not as the product of realities of the situation but as the result of an effort of *will*. Whereas we say to the workers: you have 15, 20, 50 years of civil war to go through in order to alter the situation and to train yourselves for the exercise of power it is said: we must take power *at once,* or else we may as well take to our beds. Just as the democrats abused the word 'people' so now the word 'proletariat' has been used as a mere phrase. To make this phrase effective it would be necessary to describe all the petty-bourgeois as proletarians and consequently in practice represent the petty-bourgeois and not the proletarians. The actual revolutionary process would have to be replaced by revolutionary catchwords. This debate has finally laid bare the differences in principle which lay behind the clash of personalities." Ibid., 626–27 (emphases in original).

11. Marx, "Critical Marginal Notes on the Article by a Prussian," Marx and Engels, *Collected Works*, 206 (emphases in original).
12. Quoted in Karl Marx and Frederick Engels, "The Alliance of Socialist Democracy and the International Working Men's Association" (written in 1873), Marx and Engels, *Collected Works*, vol. 23, 470.
13. Ibid.
14. Marx, "Notes on Bakunin's *Statehood and Anarchy*," written in December 1874–January 1875, Marx and Engels, *Collected Works*, vol. 24, 518.
15. Ibid.
16. See Marx, "Contribution to Critique of Hegel's Philosophy of Law: Introduction," Marx and Engels, *Collected Works,* vol. 3, 186.
17. See *The German Ideology,* Marx and Engels, *Collected Works*, vol. 5, 53.
18. Ibid., 52–53.
19. See in this respect not only Marx's polemics against Schapper, but also his analyses of the Paris Commune of 1871.
20. Mr. Bakunin has only translated Proudhon's and Stirner's anarchy into the barbaric idiom of the Tartars." Karl Marx, "Notes on Bakunin's *Statehood and Anarchy*," in Marx and Engels, *Collected Works*, vol. 24, 521.
21. "It is self-evident that a secret society of this kind which aims at forming not the *government* party of the future but the *opposition party of the future* could have but few attractions for individuals who on the one hand concealed their personal insignificance by strutting round in the theatrical cloak of the conspirator and on the other wished to satisfy their narrow-minded ambition on the day of the next revolution, and who wished above all to seem important at the moment, to snatch their share of the proceeds of demagogy and to find a welcome among the quacks and charlatans of democracy." Karl Marx, "Revelations Concerning the Communist Trial in

Cologne" (written in December 1852), Marx and Engels, *Collected Works*, vol. 11, 449 (emphases in original).
22. Karl Marx, *The Civil War in France*, in Marx and Engels, *Collected Works*, vol. 22, 490–91 (emphases added).
23. Ibid., 334–35.
24. Ibid., 535 (emphases added).
25. "But the *community* from which the worker is *isolated* is a community the real character and scope of which is quite different from that of the *political* community. The community from which the worker is isolated by his *own labour* is *life* itself, physical and mental life, human morality, human activity, human enjoyment, human nature. *Human nat*ure is the *true community* of men. The disastrous isolation from this essential nature is incomparably more universal, more intolerable, more dreadful, and more contradictory, than isolation from the political community." Marx, "Critical Marginal Notes on the Article by a Prussian," 204–5 (emphases in original).
26. Karl Marx, "Theses on Feuerbach," in Marx, *Early Writings* (London: Penguin, 1974), 423.
27. Hegel quoted in Karl Marx, *Critique of Hegel's Philosophy of Right* (Cambridge: Cambridge University Press, 1970), 29.
28. Ibid., 76.
29. Ibid., 76 (emphasis added).
30. Ibid., 77 (emphases added).
31. Ibid., 77.
32. Ibid., 48 (emphasis added).
33. Ibid., 76 (emphasis added).
34. Ibid., 73.
35. Ibid., 54 (emphases added).
36. Mannheim, for instance, who enthusiastically approves Scheler's grotesque idea that ours is "the epoch of equalization" (*Zeitalter des Ausgleichs*), claims at the same time that formerly antagonistic classes "are now, in one form or another, *merging into one another.*" See *Ideology and Utopia* (New York: Harcourt Brace Jovanovich, 1936), 279 (emphasis added). He adds to this fiction another bit of fantasy about the "free-floating intelligentsia" (*freischwebende Intelligenz*)—a first cousin of Hegel's "universal" bureaucrat—which is supposed to "subsume in itself *all* those interests with which social life is permeated" (ibid., 140). I discussed these problems in "Ideology and Social Science" in István Mészáros, *Philosophy, Ideology and Social Science* (New York: St. Martin's Press, 1986), 1–56.
37. Marx, *Critique of Hegel's Philosophy of Right*, 96 (emphases added).
38. Ibid., 85.
39. Ibid., 88–89 (emphasis added).

40. A long time before analyzing the "classical" conditions of capitalist development in England and in the writings of "English political economy, i.e., the scientific reflection of English economic conditions" ("Critical Marginal Notes on the Article by a Prussian," 192), Marx discussed the social turmoil of Germany in the same terms, insisting that "Germany is just as much *classically* destined for a *social* revolution as it is incapable of a *political one.*" Ibid., 202 (emphases in original).
41. *The Eighteenth Brumaire of Louis Bonaparte* and *Civil War in France* are masterful examples of this Marxian achievement. In both works Marx sets out from the "red-hot immediateness" of current events—which frightens away traditional historians—and, by integrating them within the sharply defined outlines of the prevalent historical tendencies, derives from them some major theoretical insights. The latter illuminate not only the scrutinized events themselves, but simultaneously the epoch as a whole, becoming thus new building blocks and further supporting evidence of Marx's constantly developing vision. The ability to treat facts and events as classically significant manifestations of major social trends and forces is inseparable from the stark vision that guides it (determining, by the way, the methodology of its "classical" orientation in the conception and presentation of the fundamental theoretical propositions). The conditions of possibility of this vision were precisely the fluidity and transparency of an age of transition—with the relative openness and clarity of purpose of the contesting alternatives—which characterized the social confrontations of Marx's formative years.
42. Frederick Engels, "Ludwig Feuerbach and the End of Classical German Philosophy," in Marx and Engels, *Selected Works,* Moscow, 1951, vol. 2, 349.
43. Letter dated December 8, 1857, in Marx and Engels, *Collected Works*, vol. 40, 217.
44. See in this respect Mészáros, *Beyond Capital*, 486–89.
45. Compare his draft letters to Vera Zasulich with the final version, written end of February/beginning of March, 1881, in Karl Marx, "Marx-Zasulich Correspondence: Letters and Drafts," in *Late Marx and the Russian Road*, ed. Teodor Shanin (New York: Monthly Review Press, 1983), 97–133.
46. Marx to Engels, December 8, 1857, in Marx and Engels, *Collected Works*, vol. 40, 217.
47. Marx to Engels, October 8, 1858, in Marx and Engels, *Collected Works,* vol. 40, 347 (emphasis in original).
48. Marx to Ferdinand Domela Nieuwenhuis, February 22, 1881, in Marx and Engels, *Collected Works*, vol. 46, 65–67. Author's translation.
49. Karl Marx, "Conspectus of Bakunin's Book *State and Anarchy,*" in Marx and Engels, *Collected Works*, vol. 24, 521. Author's translation (emphasis added).
50. Marx, "Marx-Zasulich Correspondence," 103, 123–24.

51. Marx, "Lohn, Preis und Profit" (Wages, Price and Profit), published in English as "Value, Price and Profit," in Marx and Engels, *Collected Works*, vol. 20, 149 (emphases in the original).
52. Marx and Engels, *Collected Works*, vol. 20, 148 (emphasis added).
53. Ibid., p. 149 (emphases added).

Index

Adam (Biblical), 347
Adorno, Theodor, 34–35, 361–62, 444n89, 444n92
Ahnert, Thomas, 366n, 444n82
Alexander the Great, 101, 102, 150, 151, 152, 463n30
Allende, Salvador, 98, 468n6
Althusser, Louis, 11, 195–96, 421n
Anderson, Perry, 444n89
Angus, Ian, 447n6
Aristotle, 7, 10, 28, 99, 100, 101–2, 175, 264, 294, 298–316, 322, 332, 371, 372, 462n6, 462n7, 462n8, 462n11, 462n25, 463n34, 464n15
Arthur, Chris, 441n35
Augustine, St., 10, 309, 347, 463n28, 466n25
Austin, John, 214–18, 455n4

Babeuf, François-Noël, 16, 28, 100, 226, 239–40, 246, 389
Bacon, Francis, 16, 322, 349–52, 372, 464n6, 466n1

Bakunin, Mikhail Alexandrovich, 72n20, 404–5, 406, 409–10, 472n144
Baran, Paul A., 35, 184, 444n90, 452n13, 453n5
Barker, Ernest, 12–13, 16, 204–7, 439n18, 440n22, 455n3
Beaconsfield, Earl of, 453n2
Bebel, August, 192, 454n4
Becher, Jonathan, 468n23
Benjamin, Walter, 444n89
Bentham, Jeremy, 121, 124, 178, 215–17, 219, 220–21, 455n8
Bernstein, Eduard, 68–69, 448n15
Bevan, Aneurin, 160
Beveridge, Lord, 390
Bienvenu, Richard, 468n23
Bismarck, Otto von, 65, 120, 191, 230, 355, 454n2
Blackstone, William, 215
Blair, Tony, 14, 199, 367, 458n11
Blanc, Louis, 402n, 471n10
Bloch, Ernst, 16, 31, 33–34, 35, 348n, 361–67, 361n, 362n, 366n,

372, 444n82, 444n83, 444n85,
  444n86, 444n88, 444n89, 468n1,
  468n3, 468n4
Bobbio, Norberto, 10–11, 13,
  16, 195–98, 439n15, 439n18,
  440n19, 440n21, 454n1, 454n4,
  454n7
Bohn, Henry G., 458n4
Bolívar, Simón, 25, 48, 77, 240–41,
  242, 357, 457n3
Bougainville, Louis Antoine de, 321
Brecht, Bertolt, 35, 444n89
Brotherstone, Terry, 441n35
Bruno, Giordano, 335
Büchner, 68
Buonarroti, Phillipe, 457n1, 457n2
Bush, George W., 199

Campanella, Tommaso, 16, 334–36,
  342–46, 372, 464n6, 466n1
Cardenal, Ernesto, 16
Castro, Raul, 23
Cattaneo, 454n7
Cerroni, Umberto, 196
Charles I, King, 353
Charles II, King, 353
Charondas, 313
Chávez, Hugo, 9, 16, 19, 20–27, 48,
  240, 439n10, 441n41, 442n47,
  442n55, 443n56, 443n59,
  443n61, 444n73
Churchill, Winston, 73, 151, 182,
  452n9, 453n5
Clark, Brett, 447n6, 450n7
Clausewitz, Carl Marie von, 230,
  256
Claypole, Elizabeth, 353
Colet, John, 319
Colletti, Lucio, 11
Columbus, Christopher, 320–21

Constantino, Renato, 143, 442n46,
  451n5
Cooper, Robert, 458n11
Craxi, Bettino, 195
Crick, Bernard, 338–39, 464n1
Critias, 267–69, 458n7, 459n8
Croesus, 460n17
Cromwell, Oliver, 352, 353
Cyrus the Great, 88, 122, 341,
  460n17

Diderot, Denis, 321, 464n3, 464n4
Diogenes Laertius, 267, 458n4
Disraeli, Benjamin, 453n2
Dühring, Eugen, 67–68, 448n13

Eden, Anthony, 182, 183–84, 187
Einaudi, Luigi, 198, 454n7
Eisenhower, Dwight, 73, 146, 183
Elizabeth, Queen, 352
Engels, Frederick, 16, 66, 190,
  192, 333, 418, 441n34, 444n76,
  447n8, 447n12, 448n13, 454n1,
  454n3, 454n4, 464n32, 467n21,
  467n22, 470n2, 470n3, 471n5,
  471n6, 471n10, 472n11, 472n12,
  472n14, 472n16, 472n20,
  472n21, 472n22, 474n42,
  474n43, 474n46, 474n47,
  474n49, 474n51, 475n52
Epicurus, 33–34, 444n85
Erasmus, 318, 328, 464n2
Espinoza, Manuel, 22

Farrington, Benjamin, 444n85
Fechner, Gustav, 68
Ferguson, Adam, 32, 444n81
Feuerbach, Ludwig, 65, 296, 365,
  472n26, 474n42
Fichte, Johann Gottlieb, 16, 447n11

Foster, John Bellamy, 37, 386n, 438n3, 439n18, 440n25, 440n28, 441n35, 442n42, 442n52, 444n85, 444n88, 447n6, 450n7, 452n1, 456n3
Fourier, Charles, 333, 357–60, 467n21, 468n23
Fox, Robin Lane, 452n11
Frias, Hugo Chávez: *see* Chávez, Hugo

Gasca, Eduardo, 21–22, 386n, 442n49
Gaskin, G. C. A., 72–73, 448n18
Gerth, Hans Heinrich, 470n8
Gierke, Otto, 12, 16, 455n3
Giolitti, Giovanni, 447n4
Glaucon, 287–90
Goethe, Johann Wolfgang von, 18, 160–62, 433–34, 452n19
Gomulka, Władysław, 200
Gorbachev, Mikhail, 145, 154, 174, 200, 388, 389, 436
Gottlieb, Anthony, 463n30
Gramsci, Antonio, 10, 11, 16, 44, 341–42, 425, 466n15
Grotius, 364

Hale, Matthew, 215
Harnecker, Marta, 443n55
Harrington, James, 16, 349–50, 352–54, 372, 464n6, 466n1, 467n5, 467n8
Harrington, Sapcotes, 349
Hart, H. L. A., 214–15
Heath, Edward, 182, 183, 453n1
Hegel, Georg Wilhelm Friedrich, 10, 12, 16, 29, 30, 44, 68, 87, 100–113, 116, 122, 150, 151, 156, 157, 176, 187–88, 196, 197, 198–99, 202, 203, 213–14, 223–37, 239, 241, 247–49, 255, 269, 270–72, 274, 284, 286, 293, 296, 311, 345, 372, 399, 400, 401, 403, 410–15, 416, 421, 423, 426, 444n81, 444n86, 449n4, 452n7, 452n15, 453n7, 455n1, 455n2, 456n1, 456n2, 456n3, 457n12, 459n11, 460n24, 460n27, 461n32, 461n43, 466n12, 470n2, 472n16, 472n27, 473n37
Heidegger, Martin, 456n3
Henry IV, King, 355
Henry VII, King, 319, 352
Henry VIII, King, 317, 319, 327, 352, 458n1, 463n1
Hermanos, Vadell, 22
Herodotus of Halicarnassus, 278–79, 460n17
Hettherington, H., 457n1
Hindenburg, Marshal, 454n1
Hitchens, Christopher, 449n2
Hitler, Adolf, 98, 114, 182, 444n88, 454n1
Hobbes, Thomas, 10, 12, 16, 28, 29, 42–44, 73, 102, 103–4, 117, 157, 187–88, 202–3, 213, 270, 271, 282, 304, 339, 352, 372, 441n33, 446n2, 448n18, 449n9, 452n16, 459n12
Horkheimer, Max, 16, 34–35, 361–62, 362n, 444n88, 444n92
Horthy, Miklós, 17, 98
Horváth, Márton, 387
Husserl, Edmund, 456n3
Hythloday, Raphael, 320, 322–25, 328, 329–30, 331, 464n15, 464n20

Jay, Martin, 444n89, 444n92

INDEX 479

John, King, 352
József, Attila, 441n38
Julius Caesar, 101, 150, 151

Kádár, János, 200
Kant, Immanuel, 16, 28, 29, 31, 33, 78–82, 83, 85, 105, 106, 111, 176, 203, 230, 232, 269, 270, 272–78, 283, 286, 293, 303, 309, 348n, 355, 361n, 364, 367, 372, 448n28, 449n22, 455n1, 459n9, 459n14, 459n15, 462n15, 463n29
Khrushchev, Nikita, 153, 200
Kissinger, Henry, 98
Klemperer, Otto, 17
Kodály, Zoltán, 18
Kugelman, L., 448n14

Lange, Friedrich, 67–68
Lassalle, Ferdinand von, 65, 191, 404
Lebowitz, Michael A., 25, 443n56, 443n59
Lenin, V. I., 10, 11, 15, 16, 44, 120, 193, 372, 470n7
Lessing, 31, 33, 348n, 361n, 372
Lewis, John, 195–96
Liebknecht, 404
Linacre, 319, 328
Livingstone, Rodney, 444n89
Locke, John, 282, 441n33, 454n7
Longford, Elizabeth, 452n10
Lucena, Elenora de, 441n34
Ludendorff (General), 208, 454n1
Lukács, Georg, 17, 35, 106, 293, 362, 363, 387, 435, 444n81, 444n88, 444n89, 444n92, 449n12, 454n1, 456n3, 461n31

Luther, Martin, 101, 150
Luxemburg, Rosa, 10, 11, 16, 44, 136, 441n34, 451n10
Lycurgus, 313, 338

Machiavelli, Niccoló, 10, 16, 29, 45, 334–42, 372, 447n9, 464n1, 466n9, 466n11, 466n13, 466n14
Macmillan, Harold, 182, 453n1
Macpherson, C. B., 448n19
Magdoff, Fred, 452n1
Magdoff, Harry, 456n3
Maine, Henry, 16
Mannheim, 413, 472n36
Mao Zedong, 200
Marcuse, Herbert, 35, 130, 383, 444n90, 470n9
Marie-Antoinette, 178
Marks, Louis, 466n15
Martí, José, 48
Marx, Karl, 9, 10, 11, 14, 16, 25, 28, 30–31, 42, 44, 49, 57, 58, 59, 63–64, 65, 66, 68–69, 89, 97, 107, 120, 126, 137–38, 139, 144, 155, 180, 186–87, 189–94, 196–97, 201, 227, 238, 239, 240, 241, 243, 244, 249–51, 265, 277, 372, 373–74, 376–77, 379, 383–85, 387, 391, 394–433, 402n, 438n6, 441n31, 441n34, 444n76, 446n1, 447n8, 447n12, 448n2, 448n3, 448n14, 448n33, 449n13, 451n6, 453n6, 454n1, 454n3, 454n4, 458n2, 464n5, 468n1, 468n3, 468n4, 470n2, 470n3, 470n8, 471n4, 471n5, 471n6, 471n7, 471n9, 471n10, 472n11, 472n12, 472n14, 472n16, 472n20, 472n21, 472n22, 472n26, 472n27, 473n37, 474n41,

474n42, 474n43, 474n45,
  474n46, 474n47, 474n48,
  474n49, 474n50, 474n51,
  475n52
May, Theresa, 53
McCarney, Joseph, 441n35
Merton, Cardinal, 318–19, 323
Mészáros, Donatella Morisi, 18, 19, 23
Mészáros, Giorgio (George), 18, 442n43, 444n69, 444n81, 444n85
Mészáros, István, 7–9, 10–17, 20–27, 54, 348n, 361n, 365n, 366n, 371n, 373n, 386n, 387, 392n, 402n, 421n, 438n3, 438n6, 439n15, 439n18, 440n25, 440n28, 440n30, 441n31, 441n33, 441n34, 441n35, 441n38, 442n42, 442n46, 442n49, 442n55, 443n59, 443n63, 443n65, 444n69, 444n73, 444n83, 444n85, 444n86, 444n88, 444n92, 448n3, 449n3, 452n2, 453n6, 454n1, 454n5, 458n11, 470n1
Mészáros, Laura, 18
Mészáros, Susie, 18
Metternich, Klemens von, 355
Miliband, Ralph, 14, 450n4
Mill, John Stuart, 121, 137
Mills, C. Wright, 470n8
Mitterrand, François, 14
More, Thomas, 16, 263–64, 317–33, 335, 336, 342, 343, 344, 345, 351, 458n1, 463n1, 464n2, 464n6, 464n15, 464n24, 466n1, 466n8
Morley, Henry, 466n1, 466n16

Morpheus, James I., 352
Morris, William, 318
Moses, 341
Mulhern, Francis, 444n89
Mussolini, Benito, 61, 98

Napoleon, 101, 111, 121, 150, 151–52, 416
Napoletano, Brian M., 442n50
Nenni, Pietro, 195
Newton, Isaac, 104
Nicolas of Cusa, 343
Nieuwenhuis, Ferdinand Domela, 474n48
Nozick, Robert, 16
Numa Pompilius, 337–38

Owen, Robert, 16, 124, 333, 348n, 357–60, 372, 467n22

Paine, Thomas, 16, 348n, 354–57, 359, 372, 467n10
Parsons, Talcott, 413
Paul, St., 309
Pertini, Sandro, 195
Pforden, P. von der, 461n43
Piketty, Thomas, 389
Pinochet, Augusto, 98
Plato, 7, 10, 29, 45–46, 48–49, 264, 267–69, 279–300, 302–6, 310, 311, 316, 320, 322, 327, 332, 344, 371, 447n10, 458n5, 460n23, 460n26, 460n28, 461n4, 461n29, 461n33, 462n16, 464n15
Pliny the Elder, 463n30
Poulantzas, Nicos, 14
Proudhon, 404, 406, 426
Puskás, Ferenc, 17
Putin, Vladimir, 200

INDEX

Rákosi, Mátyás, 17
Reagan, Ronald, 14
Richard II, King, 352
Richardson, Brian, 464n1
Richelieu, Cardinal, 342
Roberts, Andrew, 452n10
Rodríguez, Simón, 23, 26, 241
Romulus, 337
Roosevelt, Franklin Delano, 141–42, 153, 451n1, 452n12, 453n5
Rousseau, Jean-Jacques, 10, 16, 21, 26, 44, 76–78, 79, 82, 83, 107, 198, 218–19, 312, 315, 401, 448n21, 463n44
Russell, John, 245

Saint-Simon, Henry, 333, 358
Sands, Philippe, 199, 201, 454n8
Sartre, Jean-Paul, 16, 129–35, 158–59, 450n4, 451n9
Savage, Donald C., 441n39
Saville, John, 450n4
Savonarola, Girolamo, 335, 338
Schapper, 402, 402n, 404, 405–6, 471n10
Scheler, Max, 413, 472n36
Schlegel, Friedrich, 234, 457n14
Schmidt, Dennis J., 468n3
Schopenhauer, Arthur, 35
Segni, Pietro, 468n6
Shanin, Teodor, 474n45
Singer, Daniel, 19, 441n40
Smith, Adam, 16, 32, 75, 101, 111–12, 119, 198, 232, 236, 269, 444n81, 448n21, 449n14, 449n23, 459n10
Socrates, 267–69, 280–85, 287–90, 458n7, 460n28
Solon, 313, 338, 458n7, 459n8
Spencer, 454n7

Stalin, Joseph, 120, 138, 200, 396, 433
Stirner, Max, 404
Szilasi, Wilhelm, 456n3

Tambroni, Fernando, 468n6
Telesio, Bernardino, 343
Thatcher, Margaret, 14, 154, 174, 182, 209–10, 453n1, 455n6, 468n6
Theseus, 341
Thomas, Dylan, 19, 442n43
Thomasius, Christian, 16, 31, 33–34, 348n, 361–67, 361n, 366n, 372, 444n82, 444n83, 444n85
Timaeus, 267, 458n5
Tito (Josip Brozl), 200
Troeltsch, Ernst, 16
Truman, Harry, 153, 159

Urquijo, Pedro, 442n50

Vairasse, Denis, 365
Valiani, Leo, 449n1
Verlag, Carl Hanser, 470n9
Vespucci, Amerigo, 320, 321
Vico, Giambattista, 16, 232, 346–48, 372, 466n24
Victoria, Queen, 453n2
Vörösmarty, Mihály, 17–18, 441n36

Walker, Leslie J., 340, 465n1
Warrender, Howard, 73
Weber, Max, 12, 16, 96, 116, 201, 203, 207–8, 381, 413, 440n20, 470n8
Wedderburn, Alexander, 455n8
Wellington, Duke of, 121, 151–52
William the Conqueror, 352

Williams, Raymond, 14, 440n30
Willich, August, 404
Wolf, Martin, 72, 448n17
Wolsey, Cardinal, 319, 320, 463n1
Wood, Antony à, 467n7

Xenophon, 88, 448n1

Yeltsin, Boris, 200
York, Richard, 447n6, 450n7

Zasulich, Vera, 427, 474n45
Zeus (god), 279–80
Zevin, B. D., 451n1
Zollman, P., 441n36